JOAN NATHAN'S JEWISH HOLIDAY COOKBOOK

JOAN NATHAN'S JEWISH HOLIDAY COOKBOOK

REVISED AND UPDATED ON THE OCCASION
OF THE 25TH ANNIVERSARY OF THE PUBLICATION
OF *THE JEWISH HOLIDAY KITCHEN*

JOAN NATHAN

SCHOCKEN BOOKS, NEW YORK

This work includes all text, recipes, and drawings from *The Jewish Holiday Kitchen,*
published by Schocken Books, a division of Random House, Inc., New York, in 1988.
Copyright © 1988 by Joan Nathan. It also includes much of the text and recipes from
The Jewish Holiday Baker, published by Schocken Books, a division of
Random House, Inc., New York, in 1997. Copyright © 1997 by Joan Nathan.

Grateful acknowledgment is made to the following for permission to reprint previously
published material: Crown Publishers: Excerpt from "Two Shalachmones" from *Tevye's
Daughters* by Sholem Aleichem. Copyright © 1949 by the Children of Sholem Aleichem
and Crown Publishers, a division of Random House Inc. Reprinted by permission of Crown
Publishers, a division of Random House Inc. • Jonathan David Publishers, Inc.: Excerpt from
The Sephardic Kosher Kitchen by Suzy David. Copyright © 1984. Reprinted by permission of
Jonathan David Publishers, Inc., Middle Village, N.Y. 11379. www.jdbooks.com. • Curt
Leviant: Excerpt from "Dreydl," "The Passover Eve Vagabonds," and "Geese" by Sholem
Aleichem, translated by Curt Leviant. Copyright © 1968, 2002 by Curt Leviant. Reprinted by
permission of Curt Leviant, author of *Ladies and Gentlemen, the Original Music of the Hebrew
Alphabet and Weekend in Mustara.* • Edda Servi Machlin: Recipes for "Italian Matzah,"
"Il Bollo," and "Ceciarchiata Taiglach" adapted from *The Classic Cuisine of the Italian Jews,*
volume 1 by Edda Servi Machlin (Giro Press, Croton-on-Hudson, N.Y., 1981). Adapted by
permission of the author. • The University of Chicago Press: Excerpt from "The Baklava Story"
from *Folktales from Israel* by D. Noy. Copyright © 1963 by The University of Chicago.
Reprinted by permission of The University of Chicago Press.

Library of Congress Cataloging-in-Publication Data
Nathan, Joan.
Joan Nathan's Jewish holiday cookbook: revised and updated on the occasion of
the twenty-fifth anniversary of the publication of the Jewish holiday kitchen /
Joan Nathan.—Rev. and updated.
p.   cm.
". . . a cookbook that combines the Jewish holiday kitchen and the
Jewish holiday baker . . ."—Pref.
Includes bibliographical references and index.
ISBN 0-8052-4217-1
1. Cookery, Jewish.   2. Holiday cookery.   I. Title: Jewish holiday cookbook.
II. Nathan, Joan. Jewish holiday kitchen.   III. Nathan, Joan. Jewish holiday baker.
IV. Title.
TX724.N37 2004   641.5'676—dc22   2003060640

www.schocken.com

Book design by M. Kristen Bearse

Printed in the United States of America
First Edition
2   4   6   8   9   7   5   3   1

TO ALL THE WOMEN AND MEN OF VALOR
WHO HAVE PASSED DOWN THESE RECIPES

AND TO MY CHILDREN,
DANIELA, MERISSA, AND DAVID,
WHO WILL INHERIT THEM

CONTENTS

PREFACE

It hardly seems possible that twenty-five years have gone by since the publication of *The Jewish Holiday Kitchen*. But this year does not mark a milestone just for me. This year we celebrate the three hundred and fifty years that have passed since the first Jews arrived in America. It is, therefore, a special honor that Schocken Books chose to publish my comprehensive new cookbook as *Joan Nathan's Jewish Holiday Cookbook* to mark this momentous occasion, a cookbook that combines both *The Jewish Holiday Kitchen* and *The Jewish Holiday Baker,* as well as a selection of the articles I have written for the *New York Times* over the last twenty-five years.

The Jewish Holiday Kitchen has brought me great joy through the years, due in no small part to the wonderful feedback I have received from readers and people I have met in my travels on the lecture circuit. Hundreds of others have written me letters—though now most send e-mail—with their own family recipes, many of which have been included in subsequent editions of this book. Recipes come from so many countries: Mexico, Yemen, Algeria, Bulgaria, Poland, Russia, Egypt, and Israel, just to name a few. Some of them, such as the Yemenite High Holiday Soup Stew, may date back to the time of the Queen of Sheba. Some are the last vestige of families of Holocaust survivors, who brought to this country recipes that became a testament to those family members who were destroyed, recipes that now, as then, serve as a reminder of what we have lost. How many times people have come up to me and told me that they wished they had taken the time to watch a parent or grandparent cook! They are thrilled to find their lost family recipes in my cookbook.

To write *The Jewish Holiday Kitchen,* which first appeared in 1979, I tracked down the best Jewish cooks I could find. The men and women cooks were often already in their seventies or eighties. Measuring cups and spoons in hand, I spent hours, sometimes days, watching them cook and learning their techniques. And I listened to their stories, trying as best I could to record their oral histories with their recipes. Even though we have so many "updated" recipes these days, I am thrilled that the dishes in this book have stood the test of time and will always, I hope, be with us—to help us celebrate our holidays and to comfort us throughout the year. Sadly, many of the men and women who contributed to *The Jewish Holiday Kitchen* have now passed away, but their wonderful dishes remain as tasty memories of the Jewish past. This is their legacy to us.

The last quarter century has been an extraordinarily productive time in the Jewish cookbook world. In 1979, the Library of Congress, which houses the world's largest collection of books, listed no more than one hundred Jewish cookbooks, from here or anywhere else in the world, in their entire catalogue. Since then, more than three hundred new Jewish cookbooks have been added to the Library's collection. This does not include most of the cookbooks published by sisterhood and other organizations. Titles cover nearly every ethnic cuisine: Kurdish, Italian, Moroccan, Turkish, South African, Bulgarian, and more. Cookbooks for Jewish vegetarians are now available, as are cookbooks in Hebrew devoted to kugels and *pashtidot*. Claudia Roden's comprehensive *The Book of Jewish Food*, Elizabeth Ehrlich's *Miriam's Kitchen*, and Cara DaSilva's *In Memory's Kitchen*, which captures the spirit of women who perished in Theresienstadt, are among the greatest contributions to our understanding of the importance of food.

In the Jewish cooking of Borscht Belt boardinghouses and Lower East Side delis, it was usually "Mama" who cooked home-style stuffed cabbage and brisket in the back room. Gradually, as business improved, outside cooks began to take over the kitchen, but they served the same family-style food. Today there is a new breed of young American superstar chefs—many of whom just happen to be Jewish—men and women with college educations who have chosen the profession as their creative outlet. Sometimes these chefs draw upon their Jewish roots when crafting their menus. And at their own holiday tables, traditional recipes, with regional variations, invariably find a place. These are among the recipes I have included. As Julia Child told me recently, in the old days the cookbook writers set the pace. Now it is the chefs.

Kosher caterers are lightening their foods, seeking to please the ever more sophisticated palates of their customers. It is no longer unusual for food manufacturers to have kosher products. With over 150,000 kosher products in the grocery stores, the Ⓤ and other kosher symbols are a good housekeeping stamp of approval and mean better business, not just from Jewish consumers but from the growing number of vegetarian, lactose intolerant, and Muslim customers. I first learned this many years ago in New Iberia, Louisiana, when a rice cake producer told me how important it was to him that his products be certified kosher. When I was a child, kosher wine was Manischewitz sweet or Israeli Carmel. Now California wineries and vineyards in France, Chile, Australia, Canada, Hungary, Italy, South Africa, Argentina, and Spain, are producing award-winning kosher wines for year-round enjoyment.

After twenty-five years I am more convinced than ever that good traditional recipes are the dishes that make a culture. Although this is a holiday book, these nearly four hundred recipes do not have to be restricted to the Jewish holiday table. Use them for your dinner parties every day: My Mother's Brisket, the Algerian Swiss Chard Bestels, the Cabbage Strudel, the vegetable kugels, and some of my dessert favorites: the *Zwetschgenkuchen*, the Chocolate Soufflé Roll, the Moroccan Coconut-Sabra Torte, the *babka*, and the Matzah Almond Torte, glazed with lemon. And try making challah just once. By doing so, you will not only be performing a mitzvah, you will be communicating with your culture—an experience as sublime as the taste of the bread itself. And believe me, the taste will be far superior to any bakery product available. As you meet and cook with the many wonderful people throughout this book, I hope that your copy of *Joan Nathan's Jewish Holiday Cookbook* will become a kitchen staple in your home.

JOAN NATHAN'S
JEWISH HOLIDAY
COOKBOOK

INTRODUCTION

Better is a dinner of herbs where love is,
Than a stalled ox and hatred therewith.

Better is a dry morsel and quietness therewith,
Than a house full of feasting with strife.

Proverbs 15:17; 17:1

Miriam Steinberg of Highland Park, Illinois, would never think of making her weekly challah without first separating some dough, reciting a blessing over it, and then burning it in the oven, in accordance with the biblical commandment. Cyrel Deitsch of Crown Heights, Brooklyn, breaks each egg into a separate bowl to check that there is no drop of blood, which would make the food *tref*. To Miriam Steinberg and Cyrel Deitsch and all observant Jewish women of any age, these acts are as automatic as setting the table before a meal. But for second- and third-generation assimilated Americans like myself, they are fast becoming relics of the past. Yet these seemingly benign and ostensibly eccentric rituals carry within them the legends and traditions of the Jews. With the help of women and men throughout the country, I have tried to piece together some of the folklore and foods of our people.

Like many Jews in America, I have become passionately involved in discovering my roots. As a food writer, my explorations have not been confined to assembling family genealogies; rather, whenever I have tested a recipe, I have attempted to discover the origin of the dish and of the ingredients. These recipes often unfold the backgrounds of the people who have passed them down.

When I lived in Israel from 1970 to 1972, I often daydreamed about the early Israelites, my ancestors. Driving through the sand dunes of Beersheba and the hills surrounding Jerusalem, I tried to visualize the lives the nomadic Israelites led. Ancient olive trees still abound there. The other foods mentioned in Deuteronomy—wheat and barley, grapes, figs, pomegranates, honey made from bee nectar, date jam—are still produced in abundance. In the marketplace of Jerusalem's Old City, they have altered only slightly in form over the past two thousand years.

As I traveled from Mount Sinai back to Jerusalem, layers of civilizations and thousands of years unwound like a newsreel before me at each fork in the road. In Jerusalem the modernity is most startling. The Bedouins' tented existence, where everyone shared the same pot, has gradually been replaced. Jerusalem's fast-food restaurants are light-years away from the nomadic feasts in the desert.

My quest for culinary roots began in Jerusalem in 1970. It spurred me to write, together with Judy Stacey Goldman, *The Flavor of Jerusalem* (Boston: Little, Brown, 1975), in which we tried to portray the ethnic groups and foods of the Holy City. My search continued in my other books, in the PBS television series *Jewish Cooking in America,* and in the food articles I have written throughout the years for *Hadassah* magazine, *Cooking Light, Bon Appetit,* the *Boston Globe, Washington Post,* and now the *New York Times.* More often than not my stories have centered around octogenarian immigrants whose culinary knowledge and folk history have been passed on by word of mouth from generation to generation.

ANCIENT FOOD TRADITIONS

Before delving into the holiday recipes we use now, let us go back to ancient Palestine to see where some of these festival dishes may have originated and to examine the dietary laws that have always differentiated Jewish foods from those of other peoples. Despite the wanderings of the Jews throughout millennia, their foods still have the ring of that ancient authenticity. Holidays and festive occasions may not originally have come with gefilte fish, latkes, hamantashen, baklava, or blintzes. Yet these modern dishes are the offspring of ancient symbols, combined with ingredients available during the great Diaspora.

Nomadic societies of the ancient Middle East subsisted on berries, grains, insects, and other foods found in the woods, fields, and desert. The everyday diet of these nomads was rather sparse: birds' eggs, yogurt, sheep or goat milk, wild bee honey, wine, olive oil, lentils, fresh or dried dates and figs, pomegranates, wild melons, cucumbers, sesame seeds, garlic, onions, and grain from barley and wheat. They ate most of these foods as they found them. Some, such as oil, were pressed, and others, such as yogurt, were fermented. Only occasionally did they kill a wild animal as a dietary supplement. Naturally, the seasons greatly influenced the foods they ate.

In ancient Palestine, the first grain planted and harvested or the felling of an animal large enough to feed many people provided an occasion for jubilation and festivity among Jews. They offered sacrifices to God—sometimes in gratitude, sometimes in fear, and sometimes as an expression of regret for sin. The laws of sacrifice in Judaism, however, were strictly governed, both as to the manner of sacrifice and the disposition of the food afterward.

Ceremonial foods thus performed two major functions for the ancient Israelites. They served as a means of expression of the relationship between nature and God, and between the tribe of Levi (priests) and the rest of the Israelite people.

For Jews, then, foods have deep symbolic value. Each act of dining, from the preparation of food to the grace after meals, is carefully prescribed by Jewish law.

THE JEWISH HOLIDAYS

For many people of all ethnic groups, holidays are the last ties binding them to their family and their traditions. Whether or not they have adopted standard American daily fare, they turn to traditional, ethnic food for the holidays. This is even more true for the Jews, given the importance of our dietary laws and the table-centered rituals involved in the Sabbath and holidays. Judaism is a religion based on the combination of belief, practice, and piety. Many of the commandments require some sort of accompanying physical action for fulfillment. The symbolic foods are just one of the means by which the lofty ideals of Judaism are transmitted to everyday living. One can see that even where some of the more stringent commandments have been forgotten, the festive holiday get-togethers are scrupulously and lovingly perpetuated.

The three major seasonal festivals are Passover, marking the beginning of the barley harvest, in the springtime; Shavuot (the Feast of Weeks), marking the end of it, seven weeks later; and Sukkot (the Feast of Booths), celebrating the harvesting of the grain at the commencement of autumn. Historically, all three festivals have become associated with the Exodus from Egypt—Passover representing the release from bondage; Shavuot, the giving of the Torah at Mount Sinai and the completion of the Covenant between God and His people; and Sukkot, the sojourn of the Israelites in the wilderness on their way to the promised land. The three festivals thus represent a covenant between God and the Jews. In ancient times, they were marked by pilgrimages to the Temple in Jerusalem and special offerings of food to God in thanksgiving.

If we look at each Jewish holiday, we can see how closely connected feasting and fasting are to jubilation and penitence. Moreover, the times of the year in which these occasions occur show that account has been taken of the seasonal abundance of certain foods.

The celebration of Rosh Hashanah, the New Year, always includes honey and a new fruit for a sweet year ahead. At Sukkot, the fall harvest festival, families eat their meals for one week in a specially constructed booth, covered with branches or bamboo sticks and decorated with small jars of wine, flour, and oil, among other things. At Hanukkah, fruits or potatoes, abundant in winter, are cooked in oil. Many pastries are eaten at Purim, the last festival before Passover, when the yearly store of flour must be used up. At Passover, for eight days dishes prepared with unleavened bread and with eggs, abundant in the spring, are eaten. The historian Josephus describes the event in ancient Israel whereby hundreds of thousands of newborn lambs were sacrificed at the Temple in Jerusalem at Passover. On Shavuot, the feast of the first fruits and the time of the receiving of the Torah, milk products are traditionally eaten, probably accounted for by the small amount of meat available at the time of newborn animals. The Sabbath is usually marked by two symbolic loaves of bread with wine, fish, meat, and other special foods for a special day. Cooking is not allowed on this day, and thus all may share in the Sabbath rest.

THE LIFE CYCLE

In addition to the seasonal cycle of festivals, there are meaningful events in the individual Jewish life. Days of rejoicing for births, bar and bat mitzvahs, and weddings have particular twists in the symbolic foods used. Foods can be used to symbolize fertility, prosperity, good luck, and immortality—all the good things that one wishes another. Birth and death have their special foods, such as eggs and bagels—symbolizing the circle of life—and lentils. Fatty foods augur a rich and good life; thus, golden chicken soup is served at weddings. Fish symbolizes fertility and prosperity; it is eaten on Friday night and served at weddings and at Rosh Hashanah.

KASHRUT

Many religions have special days devoted to feasting or fasting. Judaism, however, has a complete written code of religious dietary laws governing every single act of eating. The Torah includes no rationale for the laws, and today some dismiss them as merely ancient sanitary precautions. Throughout the centuries, various hygienic and theological reasons have been suggested. But there has always been a core of the faithful who followed this proscription because it is a commandment of God. No reason is necessary.

A number of principles of kashrut are mentioned in the Bible. These have been codified and elaborated upon throughout the centuries. The rules and the rabbis' commentaries are codified in the *Shulhan Arukh*, the standard code of Jewish law. The following are some of the major regulations governing food.

"Whatsoever parteth the hoof, and is wholly cloven-footed, and cheweth the cud . . . that may ye eat" (Leviticus 11:3). Both these conditions limit the kinds of animals Jews may eat. Permissible species include ox, sheep, goat, hart, gazelle, roebuck, antelope, and mountain sheep. Prohibited are, in addition to pork, such foods as horsemeat, camel, rabbit or hare, and whale steaks.

No signs to identify permissible fowl are given in the Torah. Rather, the Bible enumerates twenty-four species of impermissible fowl, and some general rules can be deduced from them: birds of prey may not be eaten; edible fowl have in common a projecting claw, a crop, and a gizzard or stomach that can be peeled readily of its inner lining. Local tradition determines which are kosher; for example, some Yemenite Jews will not eat geese, but geese were eaten by Eastern European Jews.

"These may ye eat of all that are in the waters: whatsoever hath fins and scales in the waters, in the seas, and in the rivers, them may ye eat" (Leviticus 11:9). A kosher fish must have both fins and scales, and the scales must be detachable from the skin. For this reason, sturgeon, whose scales are not removable unless the skin is also removed and swordfish, which in its adult stage lacks scales, are not considered kosher by some authorities. Shellfish, such as shrimp and oysters, lack fins and scales and are scavengers. They are not kosher.

Much anthropological discussion has ensued on the arbitrariness of Jewish dietary laws, especially concerning the exclusion of shellfish and pork. British anthropologist Mary Douglas thinks that the exclusion of some animals was arbitrary and reinforced the concept of exclusiveness of the Jews: "Moses forbade most delicious meats. The lawgiver sternly forbade all animals of land, sea or air whose flesh is the finest and fattiest, like that of pigs and scaleless fish, knowing that they set a trap for the most slavish of senses, the taste, and that they produced gluttony." Douglas feels that the dietary laws in general and the avoidance of eating pig—the pagan delicacy—in particular made of the Jews an exclusive people, one set apart from its neighbors. Columbia University anthropologist Marvin Harris offers an economic reason for the exclusion of pigs to the Jews. In the ancient Middle East, the Jews wandered in the hot desert where pigs, although delicious, would have been difficult if not impossible to maintain. Thus, the Torah cleverly forbade them, as they did not fit into the economic system. Though there may be some truth in both Douglas's and Harris's interpretations of the prohibition of pork, probably no one will ever know the real reason.

Before permissible meat is eaten, the animal must first be slaughtered. A limb torn or cut from a living animal is forbidden. An animal that is not slaughtered but that dies of itself is prohibited. Only select animals, thoroughly tested, are used.

Another Jewish distinction is the way in which animals are slaughtered. The rules for slaughtering spring from ethical principles and are also designed to reject the sacrificial practices of paganism. "Thou shalt kill of thy herd and of thy flock, which the Lord hath given thee, as I have commanded thee, and thou shalt eat within thy gates, after all the desire of thy soul" (Deuteronomy 12:21). All animals and birds require *shehitah,* ritual slaughter. The method of slaughter is prescribed by tradition. Each knife must be twice as long as the width of the animal's throat and extremely sharp and smooth. The *shohet* (the slaughterer) must sever the major portions of the animal's trachea and esophagus without grazing its spine. Further, the knife must be drawn gently across the throat without hesitation or pressure. Even a fraction of a second's delay makes the killing invalid.

Before and after each kill, the *shohet* must check the condition of the blade and, when necessary, sharpen it on a fine, smooth stone. He is required to view the incision to make certain that the throat has been cut sufficiently. If the blade is nicked, or if any hair clings to it, the animal is ruled ritually unfit. After the carcasses are removed from the slaughtering ramp, the lungs are cut open and checked for abnormalities. Later, the lungs are removed and examined for discolored areas and other symptoms of disease. If they show no irregularity, the *shohet* assumes that the animal is healthy and pronounces the meat fit to eat. If he suspects some disorder but cannot spot it, he blows air into the lungs. If the lungs hold air, the animal is kosher; if they don't, it's *tref,* unfit.

The *shohet* follows a tradition dating back three thousand years to the meat sacrificed at the Tabernacle in Jerusalem when he says, "Blessed art Thou, O Lord our God, King of the Universe, who has commanded us in koshering."

After slaughtering, the *shohet* rejects cattle with certain types of adhesions, cuts, and bruises. Generally, only the forequarters of the approved cattle are used because of the cost of butchering the hindquarters, which requires the labor-intensive removal of the sciatic nerve.

In the Bible there is an absolute prohibition against the consumption of blood. "Therefore I said unto the children of Israel: No soul of you shall eat blood. . . . Ye shall eat the blood of no manner of flesh; . . . whosoever eateth it shall be cut off" (Leviticus 17:12, 14). Thus, the blood must be extracted from the meat through salting or broiling. This prohibition against the eating of blood was the result of a deliberate, reasoned enactment of the early Israelites against the pagan practice of drinking blood. To the Jew, blood is sacred, a gift of God. "I have given it [the blood] to you upon the altar to make an atonement for your souls" (Leviticus 17:11). Blood is thus also a means of atonement. In the Exodus, paschal blood is smeared upon doorposts and lintels to ward off future harm. It expiates sin when dashed upon the side of the altar. This superstition might even be behind the original circumcision rite.

After all the blood is removed by soaking in cold water for half an hour, the meat is then salted for one hour with coarse kosher rather than fine-grained salt (which would dissolve instead of drawing out the blood). Then the salt is shaken off and the meat washed three times so that no blood remains.

The excessive use of salt in Judaism recalls the salting of sacrifices in the Tabernacle. Salt, a pure preservative, was always used, whereas honey and leaven—both in a state of fermentation—were not. With the destruction of the Temple, the home table is now as much God's table as the altar was. On the one hand, the salt recalls the purity of God and the Temple. On the other, this white condiment could ward off evil spirits. Salt is a symbol of permanence, purity, and a good omen; it is understandable that newborn babies were once sprinkled with salt. Bread and salt are the traditional offerings to new homeowners, securing the household against evil spirits.

Before a meal is begun, salt must be set on the table. After the blessing, salt is always sprinkled on bread. However, some people feel that salt is not needed on the Sabbath because no harm will come to a family if it celebrates the day of rest.

Fish does not need to be made kosher by salting, but some people, probably out of superstition, even salt fish.

Another dietary law prohibits cooking or eating meat and milk together. "Thou shalt not seethe a kid in its mother's milk" (Deuteronomy 14:21), the basis of the prohibition, prevented the ancient Hebrews from participating in pagan customs of animal sacrifice. It was also a way of helping digestion. Two separate sets of utensils must be provided for the preparation, serving, and storing of milk and meat dishes. The utensils must be washed separately. Traditional Jews may have two sinks, and two sets of sponges, mixing bowls, and dishes, or two sets of blades and bowls for mixers and food processors. Between eating a milk and a meat meal, one must merely rinse out the mouth or eat a morsel of bread. For this there is no waiting requirement. Between a meat and a milk meal, however, where digestion is more difficult, observant Jews wait between one and six hours, depending on their tradition.

Neutral or pareve foods, such as fish, eggs, and vegetables, may be used with either milk or meat. Originally, all Jews used olive oil as the main cooking oil, causing no problems at dairy (*milchig*) and meat (*fleishig*) meals. Later, Northern and Eastern European Jews had little access to olive oil or even vegetable oils. They depended on butter or meat fats for cooking. Since butter, a dairy product, cannot be eaten with meat, and since lard, a pork fat, is forbidden to Jews, chicken and other poultry fats figured importantly in a number of European-Jewish cuisines. Jews could not even eat pareve foods outside the home for fear that they were cooked in a forbidden fat. Thus, cooking agents became one way of separating the Jews from the Gentiles. Today in America, observant Jews can use olive oil and pareve margarine.

Hundreds of thousands of prepared products, marked with symbols such as Ⓤ or Ⓚ to indicate that a Jewish organization has approved them as kosher, prevail in supermarkets throughout the United States and Canada.

As we can see from this brief introduction to Jewish holidays and the dietary laws, much of Jewish communal life centers around the dinner table. By scrutinizing each act in the kitchen, the Jew is forever aware of his separateness and his oneness with God.

Having to do without certain ingredients has given the Jewish people the opportunity to experiment with the properties of foods. The world's greatest long-simmering stews might have all originated in the Sabbath *cholent* cooking in overnight ashes. And how many festive dishes have been created out of meager ingredients! Take gefilte fish, for example. The Talmud suggests that Jews eat fish on Friday night. Eastern European Jews created this delicacy when they removed the bones (so that the Jew would not pick, or *borer*) and stretched precious fish, so expensive for these poor people, with bread crumbs, onions, and eggs, and poached it in broth. The leftover broth could then be used during the week as a soup, with potatoes. The Jews, unlike the French and the Chinese—who created masterful cuisines based on cream sauces and last-minute stir-frying—had to create a holiday-oriented cuisine prepared in advance.

During the nineteenth century, German Jews were the leaders in most Jewish communities throughout the United States. The earlier Sephardic families had already integrated into American life and had never constituted the numbers the Germans did.

German cuisine was the first to influence the mainstream of American-Jewish life. The earliest cookbooks in English in which Jewish recipes were included stemmed from the tradition of the German forebears, most of whom were adherents of Reform Judaism, which by the mid-nineteenth century had pronounced kashrut incompatible with the enlightened spirit of the age. Side by side with recipes for Passover or Friday night were dishes for oysters, crab, and the like. The first American kosher cookbook was Esther Levy's *Jewish Cookery Book,* published in Philadelphia in 1871. In *Aunt Babette*'s nonkosher cookbook of 1889, however, appeared Easter dishes for Passover—almond tortes, krimsel, schalet—but no gefilte fish. A third well-known cookbook, especially in the South, was the *Twentieth Century Cookbook,* published in 1897 in Montgomery, Alabama, by C. F. Moritz and Adelle Kahn. It did not even boast a Passover section but included an occasional Jewish recipe such as Purim puffs, basically a doughnut cooked in chicken fat rather than the lard prescribed for doughnuts in the same book. The most important cookbook for Jews was *The "Settlement" Cook Book,* which to this day has influenced American-Jewish women who want the recipes their parents used to make. Published in 1901 by Mrs. Simon Kander to raise funds for the Settlement House in Milwaukee, it offered basic German recipes but also included those of the poor Russian immigrants helped by the Settlement House. Thus, matzah balls, potato pancakes, and "filled fish" (gefilte fish) finally worked their way into a major American cookbook. In all three cookbooks, however, the Jewish and general recipes are of distinctly German flavor. Many latter-day synagogue cookbooks are considerably more universally Jewish, and more American.

At the time these books were published, Jewish immigrants from Russia did not yet need cookbooks. Neither did they think of abandoning kashrut for distinctly American foods. Recipes were usually handed down by word of mouth and by watching. As late as 1931, *Tempting Kosher Dishes, Prepared by World-Famous Manischewitz Matzo Products* did not include a recipe for gefilte fish. The Russian influence was felt later in the mass marketing of such items as gefilte fish, matzah balls, rye bread, and borscht.

About the time of World War I, mass marketing of food came into existence. Italian, German, and Jewish foods, eaten usually by ethnic groups only, slowly became available to all Americans. Today, "You don't have to be Jewish to love Levy's rye bread" or the Hebrew National advertisements are reminders of how times have changed. Gefilte fish, borscht, matzah, and of course bagels are all marketed for both Jews and non-Jews. Indeed, Manischewitz wine is sold to a primarily non-Jewish clientele. This coming of age of Jewish and all ethnic foods makes Jewish holiday cooking a different phenomenon from what it was a hundred years ago. Ethnic food is a matter of public pride rather than something hidden in the home. Major publishers have Jewish cookbooks on their lists, and almost every sisterhood has published a cookbook. Since the late 1950s, people have been desperately trying to record their culinary roots. Cookbooks and mass production of food are a far cry from the biblical foods of the desert, but somehow there are unifying threads—the holidays and kashrut.

I have read hundreds of folktales and scanned popular cookbooks in three of the great Judaica collections in the United States—Harvard University, the New York Public Library, and the Library of Congress—for clues to the customs and backgrounds of foods and recipes used by Jews in this country. Some of the most interesting revelations have come from nineteenth-century Christian cookbooks. (At the back of this book is a list of the major works consulted.) I have also tried to visit some of the centers of American Jewry and have interviewed people to see which recipes have regional popularity and from which area they come.

Fortunately for me, too, my late aunt Lisl Regensteiner, who was an excellent cook, found a well-worn book of favorite recipes my grandmother compiled as a young bride almost a hundred years ago in Augsburg, Germany. While German fare seems to have been eaten during the week, Jewish recipes were used for the holidays. My mother, Pearl Gluck Nathan, who is now in her nineties, is also a whiz in the kitchen and a splendid hostess. Born in Manhattan of immigrant parents from Cracow and Hungary, she learned to cook via The "Settlement" Cook Book and by watching her maternal grandmother prepare holiday recipes, which she has passed on to me. More faithful to the world depicted by Sholom Aleichem and American immigrant food, post-1900, was my mother-in-law, Paula (Peshka) Gerson. She cooked like her mother did in Zamosc, Poland, a small city near the Russian border.

This is an American-Jewish holiday cookbook. Its more than four hundred recipes come from Central and Eastern European Jews, as well as those Sephardic Jews from Spain and Portugal who came here either via Holland and Latin America or after sojourns in the countries of the Ottoman Empire. Where appropriate, I include the native name of the dish; many of the Sephardic foods have Ladino names.

Seasonal recipes such as a Lebanese stuffed zucchini with apricot sauce at Rosh Hashanah or a Russian stuffed cabbage at Sukkot have stories behind them. The vignette preceding each recipe might be a description of a challah baker, the origin of pomegranates, or an interview with a cook who provides us with a link to our culinary roots. We live in such an international environment today that a Russian-Jewish family living in Chicago should feel no qualms at including a Hungarian cabbage strudel from Staten Island at Sukkot or, at Passover, an Austrian chocolate soufflé roll whose creator escaped the Holocaust and set up what many consider to be Boston's finest pastry shop. The recipes—all of which I have personally tested and tasted—are sensational, and no dish is included that I would not be proud to serve in my own home. The ingredients are all natural, and often meats, fruits, vegetables, and grains are healthily combined in one holiday dish.

Since the Sabbath is the basis of holiday cuisine in general, recipes can often be used for several holidays, for example, the six different challah recipes. Don't be afraid to try a prune and meat tsimmes for Purim, although it is listed for Sukkot. Moroccan couscous is traditionally served at Rosh Hashanah; try it for Friday night sometime—or for your next dinner party. And try, as some have done, to have an Italian Shabbat dinner and then an Iranian one. You can learn culture while eating.

Many of the dishes I give are suitable at different times of the year. In modern America—with our ability to grow, transport, and store food almost without regard to season or distance—procuring the ingredients will generally cause no problem. However, if you attempt to accord your holiday menus more closely with those of our ancestors—choosing, for instance, lamb and egg dishes in spring, fresh fruits and milk products in summer, grains and squashes in fall, and fried foods in winter—you may find yourself adding an extra ingredient to your feasts: a heightened awareness of the order of the world and of our place in nature.

All recipes are labeled as (P) = pareve; (D) = *milchig* (dairy); or (M) = *fleishig* (meat). Variations on recipes are also indicated where applicable, often telling of the twist of lemon or sprinkle of pepper one cook prefers to another. In some instances the original recipes called for hours of painstaking cutting and slicing, not to mention simmering and sautéing. Wherever possible, I have shown how hurried modern cooks can reduce the time—without affecting the authenticity—by using a food processor, blender, or mixer.

Since American-Jewish brunch fare has become popular for Jews and non-Jews alike, I have included, for Shavuot and the Sabbath, recipes worthy of the finest brunch. There are also menu suggestions for every holiday and the Sabbath. I have tried to confine myself to using recipes most suitable to our holiday cooking in present-day Jewish America.

In sum, in this book I have attempted to answer the many questions Jewish and non-Jewish friends and readers have posed to me and which I have often asked myself: "Why do Jews eat fish on Friday night?" "Why potato latkes?" "Why can't we make our own matzahs for Passover?" The recipes and their stories will provide all our families with a wealth of delicious holiday foods.

THE
SABBATH

THE SABBATH

It is a sign between Me and the children of Israel for ever; for in six days the Lord made heaven and earth, and on the seventh day He ceased from work and rested.

Exodus 31:17

More than Israel has kept the Sabbath, the Sabbath has kept Israel.

Ahad Ha-am

On Friday night, every observant Jewish family the world over recites three blessings before dinner. The first is over the candles, thanking God for sanctifying the Sabbath, the second is over wine in thanks for the fruit of the vine, and the third is over two covered loaves of challah. This last prayer gives thanks to God as *hamotzi lechem min ha'aretz*—"the one who brings forth bread from the earth." Then a morsel of bread for each person at the meal is broken off before the words *Shabbat shalom* (Sabbath peace) are spoken. The blessing over the bread at the beginning of every meal connects Jews continuously to the food that grows in the earth and to God. On the Sabbath, the bread becomes a symbol of holiness.

Every European language has a word for the Sabbath, the day of rest. Although no one knows its real origin, the concept of one day of the week different from all the others has been part and parcel of religions since earliest times. Many primitive Sabbaths were market days, when normal village routines were suspended while everyone was away selling wares at a central depot. Some groups determined their Sabbath days by the phases of the moon. Not every Sabbath occurred every seven days; it could come once every four, five, or even ten or fifteen days.

Whatever the origins of such special days, the Jews took a unique approach to the Sabbath. The fourth commandment received on Mount Sinai explains the meaning of the Jewish Sabbath. The Bible says that it commemorates the respite taken by God after His six days' labor of creation. "On the seventh day He stopped and was refreshed." "Refreshed" meant a combination of physical rest and spiritual replenishment. An entire cuisine, therefore, had to be created that could be cooked in advance of the Sabbath. The bustle on the Friday preceding the Sabbath eve ensures quiet and rest for the entire family, including the constantly working mother.

In religious homes, no fire for domestic use is lit on the Sabbath, because of the commandment: "Ye shall kindle no fire throughout your habitations upon the sabbath day" (Exodus 35:3). This means that it is not permissible to smoke, cook, or in any way burn anything. Cooking is considered one of the thirty-nine types of work forbidden on the Sabbath. For this reason, Sabbath candles are lit just before sunset.

In ancient times, fires made before the Sabbath had to keep burning as long as possible until they went out naturally. Slow-cooking dishes such as *cholents*, kugels, and the Yemenite *kubbanah* were devised for this reason. With modern gas and electric stoves, however, there is less of a problem, and warm foods can be eaten throughout the day of rest. Food that has been at least partially cooked before Shabbat can be warmed on a tin or aluminum sheet shaped to cover two burners and the dials of a stove or an electric warming tray. For example, the food should be partially cooked before the Sabbath starts. A coffee urn can be plugged in before the Sabbath falls and kept plugged in throughout the day. Or previously boiled hot water can be simmered on the tin throughout the day.

Since the Sabbath is a special day, festive foods have to be prepared. The feast traditionally includes wine, two loaves of bread, salt, and fish or meat. The elevation of one day in the week means three special meals: Friday evening, Saturday midday, and Saturday late afternoon before dusk. On this one day, observant families are together with no interruption. At leisure, people can savor their rest and their food. For this reason the *seudah shelishit,* the third meal, usually a light dairy or pareve meal, is extremely important. If one knows that it is a religious obligation to eat no fewer than three meals on the Sabbath, he will eat just enough at each meal to satisfy his hunger. And by savoring the Sabbath food, he will enjoy this day into his innermost parts.

Festive breads and baked goods, separating the Sabbath from the rest of the week, are prepared ahead for these three meals and have become an integral part of Jewish life. Thus, many American Jews, whether religious or not, are accustomed to eating a sweet braided challah and perhaps a *babka* on the Sabbath. For many, these special dishes are a reminder of the purity of the day of rest, as well as a remembrance of the historic gastronomic deprivation of Eastern European Jews who lived on black bread during the week.

For the rich it was never a problem to fulfill the Talmudic injunction of preparing three meals, but for the poor—and the majority of people have always been poor—this was a difficulty to be surmounted with imagination and inventiveness. Originally designed for the Sabbath, such foods as challah, gefilte fish, *petcha, cholent,* and kugel are the basis of most Jewish holiday fare.

Today, most Jews do not celebrate the Sabbath as our ancestors did. The great majority of those who *do* observe light candles, make kiddush, and celebrate the culinary side of Judaism on Friday night. The way each family spends the Sabbath is highly personal. Shabbat is a perfect reason for a family to slow down and spend time together going to synagogue, taking long walks, or merely hanging around the house. In places with large communities of young single Jews, Shabbat dinners are a time to gather with friends, a dinner party with the added dimension of religious meaning.

Everything slows down for Friday night. A pretty table is set with a white tablecloth, fresh flowers, white candles, good china, and a freshly baked challah. Most people, religious or not, are aware of the special feeling of that one day in the week.

Food of the Sabbath creates memories. The late Chaya Segal, from the Ukraine who was my Sunday school teacher in Providence, Rhode Island, recalled with relish how she raced home from school on Friday at noon to taste the turnovers or strudel her mother made from the scrapings of leftover challah dough.

To make the turnovers, a lump of leftover challah dough would be rolled out, spread with a tablespoon or so of prune or strawberry jam, and then folded over and sealed before the cookie was placed in a medium oven. If there was more dough left than usual, her mother would make a strudel. She would roll out one strip of dough, spread it with jam, cover it with another strip, and bake it in a medium oven for about twenty minutes.

With the challah aroma permeating the house, it was no wonder that small children could not wait for the Sabbath dinner to taste the Friday treat! You may want to continue this tradition in your own home by making such treats for your own children.

MENUS

FRIDAY DINNER

SEATTLE SEPHARDIC
Challah
Greek Fish with Plum Sauce
Sakau (Eggplant and Meat Casserole)
Fresh Fruit
Egg Cookies

OLD NEW YORK SEPHARDIC
Challah
Sephardic Cold Spicy Fish
Fassoulia (Sephardic String Bean and Meat Stew)
Green Salad
Fruit Cup with Sherbet

HUNGARIAN
Challah
Chicken Noodle Soup
Chicken *Paprikash*
Rice
Hungarian Cucumber Salad
Splendid Strudel

MINSK
Challah
Zamosc Gefilte Fish
Friday Night Brisket

Kosher Dill Pickles
Potato Kugel
Carrots
Hot Fruit Compote
Mandelbrot (Almond Bread)

HENRIETTA SZOLD, BALTIMORE
Challah
Chopped Chicken Liver
Stewed Fish with Lemon Sauce
Rice
Salad
Chocolate Cream

SATURDAY LUNCH

AMERICAN JEWISH
Challah
Chopped Herring Salad
Roast Chicken
Green Vegetable
Jerusalem Kugel
Tu Bi-Shevat Salad
"Jewish" Apple Cake

***DESAYUNO* (SEPHARDIC SATURDAY MORNING MEAL)**
Syrian Cheese *Sambusak*
Huevos *Haminados* (Hard-boiled Eggs)
Bulgarian Zucchini *Fritada* or
Spinach Soufflé
Cheese
Melons and Grapes
Yogurt
Cookies
Turkish Coffee

MOROCCAN MAIN MEAL
Pain Pétri (Moroccan Challah)
Moroccan Carrot Salad
Moroccan Eggplant Salad
Dafina
Fresh Fruit
Ghouribi (Moroccan Sugar Cookies)

EAST EUROPEAN MAIN MEAL
Challah
Hungarian-Style *Cholent*
Pineapple Noodle Kugel
Mandelbrot

SEUDAH SHELISHIT
Challah
Herring in Sour Cream
Fresh Fruit

SEUDAH SHELISHIT
Challah
Calves' Foot Jelly
Compote

CHALLAH

If a man says no more than "How beautiful is this bread! Blessed be He for having created it," that is sufficient blessing over the bread.

The Midrash

And the Lord spoke to Moses, saying: Speak unto the children of Israel, and say unto them: When ye come into the land whither I bring you, then it shall be, that, when ye eat of the bread of the land, ye shall set apart a portion for a gift unto the Lord. Of the first of your dough ye shall set apart a cake for a gift; as that which is set apart of the threshing-floor, so shall ye set it apart. Of the first of your dough ye shall give unto the Lord a portion for a gift throughout your generations.

Numbers 15:17–21

And they gathered it [manna] morning by morning, every man according to his eating; and as the sun waxed hot, it melted. And it came to pass that on the sixth day they gathered twice as much bread, two omers for each one; and all the rulers of the congregation came and told Moses. And he said unto them: "This is that which the Lord hath spoken: To-morrow is a solemn rest, a holy sabbath unto the Lord. Bake that which ye will bake, and seethe that which

ye will seethe; and all that remaineth over lay up for you
to be kept until the morning."

Exodus 16:21–23

Ada Baum Lipsitz of Boston believed she was "born making challah." Before she passed away at age eighty-four she made the sweet twisted loaf once a week. From the age of ten, she started making challah each Friday morning before going to school. While she was in class, her father would punch down the dough (her mother was an invalid) and store it in a cool place until the young girl returned. With the advent of the freezer, the late Mrs. Lipsitz made at least four loaves each Monday and sometimes fought insomnia by making additional loaves throughout the week. The week she died she made challahs and gave them to the doctor in the hospital.

Watching Mrs. Lipsitz make bread was quite an experience. She never measured the ingredients exactly, just took a pinch of this and a handful of that. Her fingers, usually in pain with arthritis, miraculously sprang back to life as she kneaded the dough.

Before shaping the dough, Mrs. Lipsitz tore off a piece about the size of an olive, recited a blessing over the bread, and put it into the oven. This piece of kneaded dough is a symbolic contribution of a loaf given to the priest in the days of the Temple, as commanded in the Bible.

After separating the portion, Mrs. Lipsitz braided the bread with deftness and speed. She then sprinkled sesame or poppy seeds on top, symbolic of manna (which resembled white coriander seed).

When the challah came out of the oven, shiny and sweet-smelling, Mrs. Lipsitz always reserved two loaves for her family's Friday night dinner table and two loaves for each of the other Sabbath meals. At each meal these loaves were covered with a white cloth so they would not feel shamefully ignored because the kiddush was not recited over them.

After the lights were kindled and the kiddush recited, one of Mrs. Lipsitz's sons recited *hamotzi*. He then cut a portion large enough to last throughout the meal. After breaking off a piece of bread, dipping it in salt, and tasting it, he distributed a morsel to each member of the family, who repeated his act.

Twisted white challah, rich in eggs and sweetened by sugar or honey and raisins, was originally much different from Mrs. Lipsitz's robust cakelike loaves.

THE SABBATH BREAD

"And thou shalt take fine flour, and bake twelve cakes thereof: two tenth parts of an ephah shall be in one cake" (Leviticus 24:5). God instructed Moses to place these round loaves—two rows of six *challot* each—on a table before Him in the tent of meeting: "Every Sabbath day he shall set it in order before the Lord continually; it is from the children of Israel, an everlasting covenant" (Leviticus 24:8).

After the Romans destroyed the Temple in Jerusalem in 70 C.E., the home table became a metaphor for God's table; it was likened to the altar in the Temple. And the Sabbath bread became a sacred offering from every family.

By the eighteenth century, when twisted breads had come into vogue in Central and Eastern Europe, the twelve round loaves of bread in Leviticus became two loaves with at least six humps from the braids in each. Some bakers still carefully braid the challah dough so that six humps will show in each of the two traditional loaves used on the Sabbath. There are several explanations for the two loaves. One is that they represent the double portion of manna that the Lord provided on the sixth day in the wilderness during the forty years of wandering, so there would be enough for the Sabbath and the Israelites would not need to collect it on the day of rest (Exodus 16:22–23). Another is that the two loaves represent two different versions of the Fourth Commandment. In Exodus 20:8, the words are to "remember the sabbath day, to keep it holy." In Deuteronomy 5:15, in the repetition of the Ten Commandments, the Jews are reminded that they were slaves in Egypt, but that "God took thee out thence by a mighty hand and by an outstretched arm; therefore the Lord thy God commanded thee to keep the sabbath day."

The Sabbath bread closest to that of the ancient Israelites is baked by Iraqi and many Sephardic Jews. It is a flat bread, more like pita, sometimes in a larger size than that of everyday bread. In many Israeli homes today, this Iraqi, Yemenite, or Kurdish flat bread sits side by side with the European sweet challah, and the breads are blessed together. The sweetened loaf, developed much later, was not just a Jewish phenomenon. The Greeks have an egg-rich braided bread at Easter; so do the Portuguese and the Russians.

And the food impresario George Lang recalls his mother's regular Friday night challah from Hungary—"elaborate . . . a bird with peppercorn eyes, grapes. It was wonderful, mellow, and had a slightly sweet dough."

Many challah traditions were lost as a result of the Holocaust and Soviet religious suppression. When I visited the Soviet Union a few years before its breakup, I kept searching for a sweet Russian challah. In Tbilisi, at the home of a *chazzan* (cantor) from one of the few remaining synagogues, I tasted a homemade round white loaf, with no sweetening. In Moscow, contrary to my expectations, I found no challah. Nor did I see any in Vilnius. But someone translated a small item for me from a Lithuanian newspaper. "Remember that challah bread," it read. "How we used to like it. Perhaps now that there is perestroika some bakery will bake it again for us." They did not. The Jewish bakers of Lithuania are no more.

Jerusalem is the city I explored, starting one morning at five o'clock, to find the ultimate challah.

My odyssey began at an Iraqi bakery in the Bukharan quarter, one of the oldest neighborhoods outside the Old City, built and financed in the late nineteenth century by Jews from Bukhara in Central Asia. The wood-fired oven of this hole-in-the-wall bakery included a concave clay cover. The dough, stretched by hand, was placed on a gigantic pot holder and then pressed onto that clay cover, to be peeled off a few minutes later, when cooked. This crisp flat bread, popular in the holy city, is eaten by Iraqis for all meals, even the Sabbath. Although it includes leaven, it is not much different from the earliest matzah of the ancient Jews, and is most like the bread offered in the Temple of Jerusalem.

A few blocks away I visited Nahama, a Persian bakery, with a more sophisticated wood-fired oven. Here the bakers were forming the same dough as the Iraqis into more bulbous oval shapes, pressing their fingers into the tops, and then transferring the loaves to long wooden paddles, which they used to put the loaves into the oven and then remove them. Challah for Persians, I learned, like the bread of the Iraqis, is just a different form of their everyday bread. "Go around the corner for your sweet challah," advised a customer.

My next stop was in a narrow alley at Lendner's Bakery, which specializes in Romanian-style challah. Matti Lendner, a third-generation baker, showed me his white brick, turn-of-the-century, wood-fired oven. A baker was working in the pit created below the door of the oven.

Matti Lendner is continuing a tradition started by his grandfather, Moshe Dov Lendner, who came as an early religious pioneer to bake bread in Jerusalem at a time when most religious Jews went there to die. Moshe Lendner conveniently located his bakery next to his synagogue. Every day at 3:00 a.m., he heated the sanctuary before he mixed his dough. Then he returned to pray with other congregants while the dough was rising.

Lendner's challah incorporates yeast, sugar, water, and flour. In Jerusalem at the turn of the century, when people were poor and mostly dependent on outside contributions, eggs and sugar were out of the question. "In my family's part of Romania," said Matti as he shellacked his loaves with a mixture of cornstarch and water, "challah rarely included eggs. It was already a luxury to have a bread with white flour for the Sabbath. Most Jerusalem challot today do not include eggs."

"BAKING AND PRAYER ARE VERY COMPATIBLE"

Berish Brizel

Still in search of a crusty egg challah, I walked toward Brizel's Bakery on ultra-Orthodox Mea Shearim Street. Black-garbed men in their long coats and *peyot* (curled sidelocks) and women wearing long-sleeved dresses and black stockings, their heads covered with a scarf or *sheitl* (wig), were rushing along. Brizel's Bakery, in its 8- by 10-foot selling space, was already packed with customers clutching their robust challahs, strudels, *fluden,* and cheese Danish.

Berish Brizel, in his mid-sixties, dressed in an apron and sporting a long beard and *peyot,* found time to talk before he rushed off to study at the yeshiva at 7:30. "Baking and prayer are very compatible," said Mr. Brizel, who had already returned from the dawn prayer, where he goes between dough risings.

He told me that his grandparents came to Palestine at the turn of the century from Raisha, Galicia, today part of southern Poland. Like many wives of religious Jews, his mother worked while his father, a rabbi, studied the Torah. During the British Mandate, from 1917 to 1948, Mrs. Brizel made cheese and butter for Jewish Jerusalemites and the British soldiers and baked challah and pastries for her family at home.

In 1948, during the siege of Jerusalem, when foods had to pass through a barricade, the driver who brought them milk was killed. Being a practical businesswoman with a family to feed, Mrs. Brizel turned her cake-baking hobby into a business. "Everyone in the family helped out," recalled Berish Brizel. "And that is how we learned, including my father. A rich challah has to include eggs. The loaf also has to be brushed twice with an egg wash, allowing the coating to dry between brushings, and then baked in the oven. It is tricky to do that because the challah has already risen. You have to be careful. But by doing this you'll get that beautiful chestnut color."

THE ULTIMATE CHALLAH

*From Brizel's Bakery
and Jack Wayne*

MAKES 2 LOAVES. (P)

This is what I call the ultimate challah. Adapted from Brizel's Bakery in Jerusalem, the bread was perfected with the help of Jack Wayne of West Bloomfield Hills, Michigan, who comes from a long line of bakers in Lodz, Poland, once a center of Jewish customs and traditions. Zingerman's Bake House in Ann Arbor, Michigan, makes a variation of this crusty, chestnut-colored loaf and mail-orders it throughout the United States.

When you are making this challah, be sure to perform the mitzvah of setting aside about an ounce of the dough.* You can throw it away, or wrap it in aluminum foil as some religious bakers do and place it in the oven. Some people save all these challah-offerings and burn them right before Passover. Then take another piece of dough, fill it with jam as they did in Eastern Europe, and bake it for the hungry adult or child who, smelling the aroma of fresh bread, can't wait for the Sabbath to begin.

This recipe calls for two kinds of flour. Bread flour includes more gluten, helpful in the braiding. However, if you can find only all-purpose flour, use that. It also calls for ½–¾ cup of sugar, because I like my challah less sweet than many

*Technically, the separation of challah with a blessing, according to the Talmud, refers only to dough using flour that weighs at least 3 pounds 11 ounces. If the flour weighs less than 2 pounds 11 ounces, you do not have to separate the challah at all, and if it weighs more than 2 pounds 11 ounces and less than 3 pounds 11 ounces, you can separate it without a blessing. The challah is usually blessed after the flour, yeast, water, and other ingredients are mixed.

challah eaters, even in my family! If you are going to use just one loaf, perform another mitzvah—give away the second. If you are making a month of challahs, as I sometimes do, double the recipe and freeze several just after braiding them. Take them out of the freezer 5 hours before glazing and baking.

1 scant tablespoon (1 package) active dry yeast	5 cups bread flour
1¾ cups lukewarm water	3½ cups unbleached all-purpose flour (approximately)
½–¾ cup sugar	1 tablespoon salt
½ cup vegetable oil	Poppy or sesame seeds for sprinkling
3 large eggs	

THE DOUGH:

1. In a large bowl, dissolve the yeast in the warm water. Add the sugar and the oil and mix well with a whisk or a wooden spoon. Beat in 2 of the eggs, 1 at a time; then gradually stir in the bread flour, 2 cups of the all-purpose flour, and the salt. When you have a dough that holds together, it is ready for kneading.

2. To knead by hand, place the dough on a lightly floured surface. Knead well, using the heels of your hands to press the dough away and your fingers to bring it back. Continue, turning the dough, for about 10 minutes, or until the dough is smooth and elastic, adding the remaining 1½ cups of all-purpose flour or as needed.

   To knead by machine in an electric mixer fitted with the dough hook, knead for 5 minutes on medium speed, or until smooth. You can also process half the dough at a time in a food processor fitted with the steel blade; process for about 1 minute.

3. After kneading, place all the dough in a large oiled bowl, cover with plastic wrap, and let it rest in a warm place for 1 hour, until almost doubled in size. You can also put the dough in an oven that has been warmed to 150 degrees for a few minutes and then turned off.

4. When the dough is almost doubled in size, remove it from the bowl and punch it down—the rougher you are, the more the dough likes it. Return it to the bowl, cover it again, and let it rise in a warm place for 30 minutes more. Or, if you have to go out, let the dough rise slowly in the refrigerator several hours or overnight and bring it to room temperature when ready to continue.

BRAIDING AND BAKING THE CHALLAH:

5. To make a 6-braided challah, take half the dough and form into 6 balls. Roll each ball with your hands into a strand about 14 inches long and 1½ inches wide. Pinch the strands together at one end and then gently spread them into 2 groups of 3. Next, take the outside right strand over 2 to the middle empty space. Then, take the second strand from the left to the far right. Regroup to 3 on each side. Take the outside left strand over 2 to the middle and the second strand from the right over to the far left. Continue this method until all the strands are braided. The key is to always have 3 strands on each side so that you can keep your braid balanced. Make a second loaf the same way. Place the braided loaves in greased 10- by 4-inch loaf pans or on a greased cookie sheet with at least 2 inches in between.

   To make loaves symbolizing the 12 shewbread, the consecrated loaves placed on the altar in the Temple of Jerusalem, shape one half of the dough into 12 tight balls and press them together in the bottom of a greased 10- by 4-inch loaf pan. Repeat with the second half of the dough in another pan.

6. Let the challah loaves rise another hour, uncovered. Fifteen minutes before putting the loaves in the oven, beat the remaining egg and brush it gently over them. Five minutes later, lightly brush them again. Then sprinkle with poppy or sesame seeds and let dry a few minutes.

7. Preheat the oven to 400 degrees. Bake the loaves on the middle rack of the oven for 10 minutes. Then reduce the temperature to 375 degrees and bake

for 30 minutes more. Turn off the oven and leave the loaves in 5 minutes longer to get a dark-golden crust. Remove and cool on a rack.

Note: Practice braiding first with Play-Doh, using strands of different colors.

VARIATION: ZINGERMAN'S BAKE HOUSE HOLIDAY TIP

Soak ¾ cup dark raisins and ¼ cup yellow raisins in 6 tablespoons dark rum for 1 hour or more. Add the rum-soaked raisins with any leftover rum to the dough after 5 minutes of kneading, adding a few tablespoons more flour to absorb the liquid. If you are using a mixer or food processor, work the raisins in by hand.

"HEAVENLY" CHALLAH

Andra Tunick Karnofsky

A few years ago I attended kiddush after Sabbath services at Aitz Hayim, a synagogue "Without Walls" located in a community center in Highland Park, Illinois. The lay leader placed a three-pound challah in the middle of the group, where a number of people held it. Then, after he said the blessings, he asked the gathering (about sixty of us) to chant the *hamotzi,* the traditional prayer over the bread, together while either holding the challah or touching someone who was. The idea is to connect—to provide an unbroken physical and spiritual chain within the group, bridging the secular and the spiritual with joy. We then tore the challah apart, all participating equally, saying, "Raise the challah when you say the blessings. Elevate it."

"People touching each other creates a wonderful connectedness," said Andra Tunick Karnofsky, one of the congregants and the baker of the whole-wheat challah. "By the time we eat, we are physically close together and can continue the spirit of the blessings, the service, and Shabbos."

Andra, a psychologist, has been supplying her synagogue and many local stores with her Heavenly Challah since 1991. "I always loved cooking," she said. "As the eldest child with a grandmother who was a great cook, the legacy was handed down to me."

Her particular passion for baking challah began fifteen years ago, when her husband, Keith, was a Hillel rabbi at the University of Rhode Island. "We invited students for Shabbos," she said. "It was in the early eighties, and I wanted my foods to be natural. When I made cookies, I put in whole-wheat grains and wheat germ, so when I made challah, it seemed sad to be serving an all-white bread. I decided to enrich it with whole-wheat flour." Later, in Boston, St. Louis, and Chico, California—wherever the rabbinate took Andra and her husband— she still baked challah and invited people over for the Sabbath. "People liked the challah and encouraged me to sell it," she said. "One of the appeals of baking for me is that it is a transformation. You take a variety of elements in their natural form and you create something completely new and different. It has little grains but becomes part of the greater whole. And so the love you put into the dough is incorporated into the bread."

One special addition to Andra's challah is her team of baker's helpers. As a behavioral specialist at Lambs Farm, a community for retarded adults in Libertyville, Illinois, she contracts with Lambs Farm to make her bread at the farm's bakery on Wednesdays and Fridays with the assistance of from five to fifteen of the adults. "So it's a double mitzvah."

HEAVENLY WHOLE-WHEAT CHALLAH

From Andra Tunick Karnofsky

MAKES 2 LOAVES. (D OR P)

"When I first started making challah, people either loved it or were offended by the whole wheat," Andra said. "It was supposed to be white." She sees it this way: "My grandmother made white challah, but she didn't have the bleached white flour we just buy in a bag. It had to be sifted; it was expensive, a treat for the Sabbath. Today you buy the flour for the bread and it is white. It takes more effort to incorporate other ingredients, which is what makes whole-wheat challah special today. In our society, it is a reversal because of our American eating habits."

If you like, you can substitute all egg whites for the whole eggs. But then add 1 tablespoon of vegetable oil so the bread won't be too dry.

1 cup plus 1 teaspoon warm water

2 scant tablespoons (2 packages) active dry yeast

3½ cups unbleached all-purpose flour

½ cup sugar

1½ cups whole-wheat flour, preferably stone-ground

2 teaspoons salt

¼ pound (1 stick) unsalted butter or pareve margarine, at room temperature

3 large eggs

2 tablespoons poppy or sesame seeds for sprinkling

THE DOUGH:

1. In a large bowl, mix together 1 cup of the water, the yeast, 1 cup of the all-purpose flour, and ¼ cup of the sugar. Set aside for 20–30 minutes—Andra feels that making this "sponge" helps the yeast add an extra tangy flavor to the bread.

2. In the bowl of an electric mixer fitted with the dough hook, place the sponge mixture and 2 more cups of the all-purpose flour, the remaining ¼ cup sugar, the whole-wheat flour, and the salt. Mix well at a low speed. Gradually add the butter or margarine and 2 of the eggs, 1 at a time. While adding the remaining ½ cup of all-purpose flour as needed, gradually increase the speed of the mixer and continue mixing about 10 minutes, until the dough becomes smooth and elastic.

3. Place the dough in a large, lightly oiled bowl and turn so all the sides are coated with oil. Cover with a cloth and let the dough rise 1–2 hours, until doubled in size. You can also refrigerate the dough and let it rise slowly overnight. Punch it down, remove it to a floured board, and knead until the air pockets are pushed out.

BRAIDING AND BAKING THE CHALLAH:

4. Divide the dough in half. Set aside one half and divide the other into 4 equal portions. Roll each piece with your hands into an even strand about 15 inches long and place the 4 strands side by side. Pinch the upper ends firmly together to connect them. Beginning from the right and working toward the left, take the outside strand and weave it over the adjacent strand, under the next strand, and over the last strand on the left. Proceed in the same over-under fashion, moving downward row by row, always weaving from right to left,

until the ends are reached. Connect the ends by pinching them together as you did in the beginning and tuck them under the braided loaf. Form the second loaf the same way. Place both on a greased cookie sheet 2 inches apart.

5. In a small bowl, beat together the remaining egg with the teaspoon of water. Brush the braided loaves with the egg wash.

6. Cover the loaves loosely with a towel or plastic wrap and let them rise for 1 hour more, or until doubled in size.

7. Preheat the oven to 350 degrees. Brush the loaves again with the egg wash and sprinkle with the poppy or sesame seeds.

8. Bake on the middle rack of the oven for 35–45 minutes, or until golden. The loaves are done if they sound hollow when tapped.

SEASONAL VARIATIONS

Knead the following ingredients into the dough during step 2, after adding the eggs. Owing to the moisture found in some of the ingredients, more flour may be needed.

Thanksgiving and fall: 1 cup frozen cranberries tossed in 2 tablespoons sugar, or 1 cup peeled and diced apples sprinkled with cinnamon sugar.

Winter: 1 cup diced dried apricots or golden raisins plumped in hot water for 10 minutes, then drained and dried.

February, for Washington's Birthday: 1 cup frozen whole Bing cherries, coarsely chopped.

Spring and summer: 1 cup frozen blueberries or diced fresh peaches.

As an optional glaze for challah with fruit, melt ¼ cup apricot jam with 1 tablespoon water. Brush the melted jam mixture over the baked challah.

ONION POPPY SEED ROLLS

Adapted from Rose Zawid

MAKES 12 ROLLS. (P)

I have always wanted to find this recipe. It used to be served in bakeries on the Lower East Side. Now each Friday I try to make it with half my challah dough.

1 scant tablespoon (1 package)
    active dry yeast
1½ teaspoons plus ½ cup sugar
¾ cup lukewarm water
    (approximately)
¼ cup plus 3 tablespoons
    vegetable oil

3 large eggs
1½ teaspoons salt
4–4½ cups all-purpose flour
½ medium onion, diced
2 tablespoons poppy seeds
½ teaspoon coarse salt

1. In a large bowl, dissolve the yeast and 1½ teaspoons of the sugar in the warm water.
2. Whisk ¼ cup of oil into the yeast, then beat in 2 of the eggs, 1 at a time, with the remaining sugar and salt. Gradually add the flour. When the dough holds together, it is ready for kneading. (You can also use a mixer with a dough hook for both the mixing and kneading).
3. Turn the dough onto a floured surface and knead until smooth. Clean out the bowl and grease it, then return the dough to the bowl. Cover with plastic wrap and let the dough rise in a warm place for 1 hour until it almost doubles in size. The dough may also rise in an oven that has been warmed to 150 degrees and turned off.
4. Punch down the dough, cover, and let rise again in a warm place for another 30 minutes. Roll out the dough to a rectangle about 12 by 18 inches or as thin as you can.
5. Sprinkle the onion, the poppy seeds, and the coarse salt over the dough. Leave a 1-inch border along the edges.
6. Using a pastry brush, brush the border of the dough with oil. Then roll the

dough up from the long side into a jelly roll. The dough will be very malleable. Pinch the ends closed.

7. Preheat the oven to 350 degrees and grease 12 muffin tins with the remaining oil.

8. Using a dough cutter, cut the dough into at least 12 rounds and place the rolls into the tins, cut side on top. Mix the remaining egg with a little water and brush over the rolls. Let rise another 30 minutes.

9. Bake for 20–25 minutes, or until golden. Remove from the oven and serve warm.

LOW-CHOLESTEROL CHALLAH

MAKES 2 LOAVES. (P)

A contradiction in terms, perhaps, but this one-egg low-cholesterol challah is delicious. Sonia Greenberg worked on this recipe for many years while living in Kalamazoo, Michigan. It was printed in the 1966 *Cook's Tour of Kalamazoo* cookbook.

2 scant tablespoons (2 packages) active dry yeast	1½ teaspoons salt
	7–8 cups all-purpose flour
2 cups lukewarm water	2 large eggs
¼ cup sugar	3 tablespoons vegetable oil

1. Mix the yeast with the water and 1 tablespoon of the sugar. Combine the remaining sugar, salt, and 7 cups of the flour in a large bowl. Place the yeast mixture in the center of the dry ingredients and stir into the flour. Add 1 egg and the oil and knead, adding additional flour if necessary to form a medium-soft dough.

2. Let rise, covered, until doubled in size, about 1½ hours. Punch down, divide in half, and divide each half again into 3 even portions. Braid 2 loaves and place 2 inches apart on a greased cookie sheet. Let rise again until doubled in size.

3. Preheat the oven to 350 degrees.

4. Brush the loaves with an egg wash made with the remaining egg and a little water. Bake for about 45 minutes or until the loaves sound hollow when tapped with a knife.

BERCHES

(My Great-Grandmother's Potato Challah)

MAKES 2 LARGE LOAVES. (P)

Birkat Adonai hi ta-ashir. (The blessing of the Lord, it maketh rich.)
Proverbs 10:22

Berches is the Judeo-German oblong loaf of twisted bread eaten on the Sabbath. Unlike the traditional sweet challah we know in this country, *berches* is often a bread with a slightly sourdough taste and a crunchy crust. My father ate this as a child in Augsburg, Germany, and so did Jews I have interviewed who lived as far away as Budapest. This particular recipe is that of my great-grandmother, Rose Bernheim, of Augsburg.

A popular explanation of the name *berches* is that it is a corruption of the Hebrew word *birkat* (blessing) from the verse in Proverbs quoted above. Both *birkat* and *ta-ashir* are words derived for the twisted form of bread. *Taatscher* is a corrupt form of *tartcher* and a diminutive of *tart* or *torta* ("twisted" in Italian). The above verse is still engraved on knives used on the Sabbath to cut the challah.

Berches, like *Berges* in northern Germany among non-Jews, was the bread offered to Berchta, or Perchta, the Teutonic goddess of fertility. In ancient times women would offer their hair to her. When this practice became obsolete, it was replaced by a symbolic offering of the hair in the form of a loaf of intertwined braids. It is a moot point whether or not *berches* was indeed a Jewish version of this practice. (Other scholars say the twisted loaf rather represents interlocked arms.)

Note: If you need this challah for Friday evening, you can start the dough about eight o'clock Thursday night to let it rise slowly overnight. Finish the next morning.

6–8 cups bread or unbleached all-purpose flour	2¼ pounds cooked, mashed potatoes (about 3 cups), still lukewarm
2 yeast cakes or 2 packages dry active yeast	1½ teaspoons salt
½ cup lukewarm water	Poppy seeds

1. Place the flour in a large bowl, making a well in the middle. Stir in the yeast and water. Add to the well a small amount of the flour, about 3 tablespoons. Cover and let the "starter" stand in a lukewarm place until doubled in size (about 30 minutes).
2. Add the potatoes, salt, and more lukewarm water if needed. Knead the dough about 10–12 minutes, or until it pulls away from the bowl and is firm. Alternatively, divide in fourths and whirl in a food processor for 1 minute, using the steel blade. Put the dough in a greased bowl and cover with a cloth. Place in a medium-warm, draft-free spot and let stand until the dough has doubled in size (3–5 hours).
3. When the dough is ready, punch it down, place it on a floured wooden board, and split it into 4 parts. Make a long loaf of 1 part and divide 1 other part into 3 pieces. Roll the 3 pieces into long ropes as thick as a thumb and braid them. Place the braid on top of the long loaf, pinching it down to attach it. Repeat with the 2 remaining parts. Place on a greased cookie sheet. Cover the challah and let rise once more for about 1 hour.
4. Preheat the oven to 350 degrees.
5. When ready to bake, sprinkle the top with water and then with poppy seeds.
6. Bake 45 minutes to 1 hour, or until the challah is nicely browned and sounds hollow when tapped with the knuckles.

Note: You can also divide the dough into 4 portions, 2 larger than the others. Divide the larger portions into 3 pieces and braid. Then divide the smaller portions into 4. Braid 3 of the pieces and place on the larger braid. Roll out the last piece and press down lengthwise on the braid. Repeat.

YEMENITE *KUBBANAH*

(Sabbath Overnight Bread)

From Zohar Cohen-Nehemia Halleen

MAKES 1 *KUBBANAH*. (D OR P)

This is an updated version of the Yemenite Sabbath morning bread, traditionally made with flour and water and cooked in a pot in the embers of a fire overnight. Although special aluminum *kubbanah* pots are sold in Israel, any 6-cup or larger ovenproof casserole with a cover will do.

With the bread, you can bake the Sephardic Sabbath *huevos haminados* for *desayuno* (breakfast). Wrap some hard-boiled eggs, in their shells, in aluminum foil and perch them on top of the pot if possible, or alongside. (Traditionally, the shells are first colored by simmering the eggs in water with coffee grounds or onion peel.) Serve the *kubbanah* with the eggs, cut-up tomatoes, and *zhug*, a Yemenite hot sauce, or *helbeh*, a fenugreek mixture (see page 178).

1 scant tablespoon (1 package)
    active dry yeast
1½ cups plus 2 tablespoons
    lukewarm water
1 tablespoon sugar
4–5 cups bread flour or
    unbleached all-purpose flour

1 tablespoon black caraway seeds*
1 tablespoon salt
¼ pound (1 stick) unsalted butter
    or pareve margarine
5 hard-boiled eggs in their shells

1. Mix the yeast in 1½ cups of the water with the sugar. Place 4 cups of the flour in a bowl and make a well in the center. Pour the yeast mixture into the well and sprinkle in the caraway seeds. Using your hands, mix well to incorporate the flour and the seeds.

*Black caraway seeds, also called *chernuska,* are members of the pepper family. You can buy them at health-food stores or Middle Eastern markets.

2. In another bowl, pour the additional 2 tablespoons of water. Place the dough in the water and let it sit, covered with a damp towel, for 1 hour in a warm place.

3. Punch the dough down and knead it, gradually adding the remaining 1 cup of flour and the salt. Here you can cover the dough and refrigerate it until you are ready to complete the final risings and bake the bread. Or let the dough rise once more, covered, for another hour.

4. Preheat the oven to 400 degrees and melt the butter or margarine in a metal *kubbanah* pan or 6-quart casserole fitted with a lid.

5. Punch the dough down one more time and divide it into 4 balls. Place the balls in the casserole side by side, rolling them in the butter to coat them. Cover with the lid and let the dough balls rise another 30 minutes.

6. Bake the bread, covered, for 45 minutes on the lowest rack of the oven. Then lower the oven temperature to 150 degrees.

7. Wrap the hard-boiled eggs in aluminum foil. Place the eggs on top of or alongside the covered *kubbanah* pan and bake overnight, or at least 8 hours. Serve the bread hot, as is or dipped in soup, with diced tomatoes, *zhug,* or *hilbe.*

Note: If you prefer to make 2 *kubbanahs,* just use smaller covered casseroles and divide the dough into 8 pieces.

JERUSALEM *BOYOS*

(Pastries Stuffed with Potatoes or Spinach)

From Zohar Cohen-Nehemia Halleen

MAKES 24 *BOYOS.* (D OR P)

The first time I tasted a flaky *boyos,* filled with spinach and served with a hard-boiled egg, I was in the office of the caretaker of an old synagogue in Izmir, Turkey. I was instantly determined to find a recipe for it. A cross between a croissant and a knish, this flaky snail-shaped pastry (using the same dough as in *burekas*) is a Friday night must, served with a white bean soup, in many Bulgarian, Turkish, and other Ladino Jerusalem homes. It is also a Saturday morning breakfast specialty. Sometimes *boyos* resemble potato knishes in shape.

Make the puff pastry yourself or use a shortcut version with prepared puff pastry.

THE PUFF PASTRY:

6 cups unbleached all-purpose flour
1 tablespoon salt
1 teaspoon sugar
3 tablespoons cider vinegar
¾ cup vegetable oil

1½ cups ice water, or as needed
1 pound (4 sticks) unsalted butter or pareve margarine, at room temperature
Vegetable oil for rolling
Filling of choice (see below)

1. Place the flour, salt, sugar, vinegar, and oil in a food processor fitted with the steel blade. Then, bit by bit, add the ice water as you are pulsing until the dough forms a ball and, as Zohar says, it "feels as soft as your earlobe."

2. Remove the dough to a lightly greased bowl and let it rest, covered with a towel, for 30 minutes. Divide it into 6 pieces. Roll each piece out on a lightly floured work surface to a rectangle 6 by 10 inches.

3. Gently spread 5⅓ tablespoons (⅔ of a stick) of the butter or margarine on top of each piece of dough. Fold the dough in half from the long side, then fold in half again the other way, so you have a small rectangle about 3 by 5 inches. Repeat this step with the other 5 pieces of dough. Wrap each in plastic wrap and refrigerate overnight.

4. Preheat the oven to 375 degrees and remove 1 piece of the dough from the refrigerator. Using a pastry cutter or a knife, cut the dough into 4 equal pieces. Place 1 piece on a lightly floured board. Roll it as thinly as possible to a rectangle about 6 by 10 inches. Spread one of the fillings over the dough as instructed below. Roll up the filled dough as you would a jelly roll, from the longer side. Take the end of the jelly roll and coil inward with your hands to make a "snail," tucking the end piece under the dough. Repeat with the remaining dough.

5. Place the *boyos* on 2 ungreased baking pans with a rim to catch any excess butter or oil and bake on the middle rack for 25–30 minutes, or until golden brown. Drain them immediately on racks set over the baking pans.

Note: You can also make bite-size *boyos*—great for parties. In step 4, divide each piece of dough into 8 pieces instead of 4. Spread each piece with 1½ tablespoons potato or 2 tablespoons spinach filling, and proceed as above.

POTATO FILLING:

4 large potatoes (about 3 pounds), peeled and boiled
1 pound cream cheese
½ cup Bulgarian feta or any hard tangy cheese

2 large eggs
Salt and freshly ground pepper

1. In a bowl, mash the potatoes and add the cream cheese, feta, eggs, and salt and pepper to taste. Mix well.

2. Spread 3 heaping tablespoons of the filling over each piece of dough. Roll and bake as above.

SPINACH FILLING:

20 ounces (2 bags) fresh spinach, washed well and dried

4 ounces goat cheese, crumbled
Salt and coarsely ground pepper

1. Remove the stems and chop the spinach as finely as possible—a crucial step for this recipe.
2. Spread 4 heaping tablespoons of the spinach and 1 teaspoon of the cheese over each piece of dough. Sprinkle with salt and pepper to taste, and roll and bake as above.

A TEACHER OF BAKERS

Michael London

In Eastern Europe, itinerant bakers used to drive with a horse and buggy to distribute baked bread from the cities to the shtetls. Michael London, pastry chef and owner of Mrs. London's Bakery in Saratoga Springs, New York, is not exactly an itinerant baker, but this legendary guru earns his living training other professionals to make Old World breads and baked goods. "One of my goals is to rescue the Jewish traditions in baking and to make them available to all," he said as he tossed flour across the tops of unbaked bialys. "Personally, bread goes to the heart of Judaism, because one needs to quiet the mind, to allow the windows of the soul to open to Adonai, God, and other larger forces."

Michael talks about bread in a spiritual, almost mystical way. "We make some of our breads in an ancient manner," he said. "They are made from starter, which we make and replenish without commercial yeast. Dough is a living thing." In a throwback to the religious heave-offering, he takes his best baked loaf of the day and offers it to the fire. "Baking is alchemy," he said. "It's very important for me to be integrating the four elements—earth, air, fire, and water—and to be enlisting the support of the spirit behind them."

Brooklyn born, he grew up with a hit parade of dishes—kugel, *kneidlach,* and such desserts as his Nana's Galicianer prune and nut roll (see page 313). Later, in the tumultuous 1960s, Michael, then a literature professor, traded in words for wheat and a whisk. "I was a dislocated, estranged, alienated sort that didn't know what he wanted to do, but didn't want to teach literature anymore," he said.

In the early 1970s, he wound up baking bread at Ananda East, a natural food bakery in Greenwich Village, where he developed his Pumpernickel Rye Bread (see page 209). On his days off, he and his wife, Wendy, also a baker, visited bakeries. "We followed every bakery that Mimi Sheraton wrote about," he said. "We tasted and tried to duplicate the recipes."

Far ahead of the current bread-baking trend, Michael decided that the best way to really learn was to apprentice with some of the great bakers of New York. "I first went to Mr. Greenberg at William Greenberg, Jr.," he said. "He told me I was completely out of my gourd because I had a master's degree, but I kept on going back to him." Five months later Mr. Greenberg said, "Michael, at four on Wednesday afternoon you have to show up." Although Michael had jury duty that day, he realized this was a pivotal moment in his life. He showed up.

He watched Mr. Greenberg decorate his famous wedding cakes, and learned how to make *schnecken* (see page 193) from Andrew Martin, a baker at Greenberg's. "Honey helps with the taste and the caramelization," he said. (Mr. Greenberg uses only brown sugar and butter in his.)

After William Greenberg, Jr., Michael worked at Eclair Bakery, the Viennese bakery that was home to refugees following World War II. "At one a.m. on my 'lunch break,' a wonderful Austrian baker, John Richter, taught me how to make the many forms of *kuchen,* the basics of *babka,* and how to seal *kugelhopfs,*" he said. "For me, Eclair was a unique opportunity, because I worked on a shift with many Eastern European bakers who were on the verge of retiring." (The original Eclair Bakery closed in 1996.)

Later, when he moved to upstate New York, Michael learned the art of hand-rolled kaiser rolls from Rudy Cohen in Saratoga Springs. The Londons opened their highly successful Mrs. London's Bakery and Café there, using many of the tricks learned from the old-timers.

Today, Michael crisscrosses the country, teaching other bakers his techniques. He has certainly made an impact. At the Pittsburgh airport, bearing bags of bread, he was stopped by a flight attendant. She told him that she had just tasted a wonderful challah in Memphis. It was from one of his licensees.

NEW YORK BIALYS

From Michael London

MAKES 16 BIALYS. (P)

"When I was a kid, bagel bakeries made bialys. Bagels spread but bialys didn't," said Michael London during a bialy-baking session. "Once I met a guy driving a taxi whose cousin worked at Kossar's Bialystoker Kuchen on Grand Street. I asked if I could watch the bialy-baking process. The cabbie told me to talk to Tony. I did, and worked that night." Kossar's, one of the last bakeries in this country to specialize in bialys, is a place I also visited, also at night. What follows is Michael's rendition with my very great approval.

I suspect that, as we know it, the word "bialy," which means "white" in all Slavic languages, is of American inspiration. I have yet to find a baker born in Poland or Russia who ever heard of a bialy before coming to this country. Canadian bakers and Parisian bakers have never heard of them either, although they both make *pletzel,* like their bagels, with an egg.

The origin of the bialy may forever remain unsolved, but this is my take on it:

In Poland and Russia, Jews ate a Bialystoker *tsibele pletzel kuchen,* a flat onion bread originally from the city of Bialystok, Poland. It came in two sizes—a larger version, called a *pletzel,* and a smaller version, called a *pletzelach.* My guess is that when immigrants were working in bagel bakeries in New York they made a form of *pletzel* that intrigued their American bosses. "What is it?" one might have asked. "A *pletzel.*" Then the boss would have continued, "*Pletzel,* it sounds too much like 'pretzel.' Where does it come from?" The reply may have been "Bialystok." The lightbulb went on. "That's it! How about 'bialy'?" And so the bialy was born.

Made with the same ingredients as New York bagels—salt, water, yeast, and flour—but in different proportions, a good bialy demands a long, slow rising period. The end result will have a pleasing texture. The center is indented by a thumb and forefinger and filled with diced, sweated onions and sometimes poppy seeds before the bialy is quickly baked in a very hot oven.

1 scant tablespoon (1 package) active dry yeast	4 teaspoons salt
1¼ cups cold water	1 tablespoon vegetable oil, preferably safflower
5 cups high-gluten flour or bread flour	¾ pound onions, peeled and diced
	2 teaspoons poppy seeds

1. Dissolve the yeast in the water.
2. Place 4 cups of the flour and 3 teaspoons of the salt in the bowl of an electric mixer fitted with the dough hook. Add the yeast and water to the flour and process for 10–12 minutes, gradually adding the remaining 1 cup of flour if the dough is too sticky. (This is a dough that needs to be kneaded a long time.) Put the dough in a large, greased bowl, cover with a cloth, and let it rise for 2 hours.
3. Punch the dough down and scrape it away from the sides of the bowl with a plastic scraper. Cover again with plastic wrap and let it rest for another hour.
4. In a skillet with a cover, heat the oil, add the onions, and sweat them, covered, on low heat for about 20 minutes, or until soft. If you choose, you can microwave the onions in a small bowl, covered with plastic wrap, for 5 minutes. Add the poppy seeds and the remaining 1 teaspoon of salt.
5. Divide the dough into 16 pieces and form them into balls, remembering to dust your hands, but not the work surface, with flour. Cover the dough balls

with plastic wrap and let them relax for 1 more hour in a warm place. You don't want this dough to dry out. If it does, it will not expand properly in the oven, nor will it color properly.

6. Preheat the oven to 450 degrees.
7. Remove the plastic wrap, flatten the balls, and dust flour over the bialy rounds, using a side swing as if throwing a curve ball. The characteristic of a good bialy is that it is well coated with flour. Place your thumb and forefinger into the center of each to make a depression, not a hole.
8. Place a heaping tablespoon of the onion–poppy-seed mixture in the center of each bialy.
9. Place the bialys on a greased cookie sheet and bake on the middle rack of the oven for 10–15 minutes, or until slightly golden.

SEPHARDIC COLD SPICY FISH

(*Pescado Helado*)

SERVES 6–8 AS AN APPETIZER. (P)

We remember the fish, which we were wont to eat in Egypt for nought.
Numbers 11:5

There dwelt men of Tyre also therein, who brought in fish, and all manner of ware, and sold on the sabbath unto the children of Judah, and in Jerusalem.
Nehemiah 13:16

Fish has always been a mainstay of the Jewish diet. Jewish history tells us how, during their long journey in the Sinai to the promised land, the Israelites longed for the fish first tasted in Egypt. Later, at the time of Nehemiah, so much sea fish was sold in Jerusalem that the gate nearby was called "the Fish Gate."

From earliest times fresh seafood markets surrounded the Sea of Galilee. During the Roman period, fresh fish for the Sabbath was in such demand that the Romans imposed a high tax for the right to fish in the lake.

Eating fish symbolizes the hope of redemption for Israel and reminds us of the mercies of God. In Genesis, God blesses man and fish several times, creating a mystical triad. He urges them to "be fruitful and multiply." From this, fish came to symbolize fertility and immortality. The defeat of the Leviathan, the great monstrous fish mentioned in Job, is used as the symbol of glory to come in the Messianic Age, when good will triumph over evil. At that time the Leviathan will be caught and the flesh given to the faithful.

In folk traditions, a woman who ate a fish found inside a larger fish would become pregnant. A virgin should be married on the fourth day of the week and have intercourse on the fifth day, when the blessing of the fish is pronounced. For Moroccans, the seventh day of the wedding feast is "fish day," when the groom sends the bride a plate of fish—which her mother throws at the groom's feet. After he takes a bite of the fish, the bride steps over a fishnet and symbolically becomes pregnant. In Sarajevo, Yugoslavia, after the wedding-ring ceremonies, relatives arrive carrying fish, the heads decorated with flowers and the bellies garnished with tinsel. The bride then hops over each fish in the hope that she soon will become pregnant. To this day, North African Jewish women wear fish amulets around their neck.

Although the Talmud does not command the eating of fish on Friday night, it is nevertheless strongly suggested. From Talmudic times, Orthodox Jews have been eating fish, meat, and wine on Friday night and at each of the other two meals of the Sabbath. The Talmud describes the joy of eating fish on the Sabbath: "Wherewith does one show his delight therein? . . . With a dish of beets, a large fish, and cloves of garlic."

The Talmudic combination of fish, garlic, and beets is today most often found in eating gefilte fish—but not always. Jews throughout the world eat variations of fish recipes on Friday night.

The same delights of a spicy fish can be found elsewhere, however. A recipe that is a possible carryover from as far back as the Middle Ages is the following for cold spicy fish. Handed down in the Sephardic family of the late Emily Nathan, it may have originally been used in Spain as an appetizer on Friday night or to start holiday meals. The dish may very well have been served the first

Friday night that Emily's forebear, Abraham De Lucena, spent in New Amsterdam, when twenty-three Sephardic Jews established a settlement in 1654. There have been subtle changes in the recipe throughout the years to adjust to special tastes. The tomato juice and cayenne pepper were probably later additions, picked up when Emily's ancestors were in Brazil prior to their arrival on this continent.

Note: Have the fish dealer cut a whole fish through the backbone into steaks about 3 inches wide. The backbone must be left in the fish. Ask for several fish heads with the eyes left in and the skeleton for natural gelatin.

One 4½-pound striped bass, rockfish, pickerel, yellow pike, or any firm fish (see Note)
Coarse salt
1 teaspoon cayenne pepper, or to taste*

6 cups tomato juice (or more)
1 bay leaf
1 medium onion, sliced
2 tablespoons lemon juice, or to taste

1. Rub the fish steaks with coarse salt and about ½ teaspoon of cayenne and let stand for a few hours in the refrigerator.
2. Bring to a boil enough tomato juice to cover the fish skeleton and heads. You can put the heads in a cheesecloth, if you like, to extract after the fish is done. Some people, however, like to eat them.
3. Season the tomato juice mixture with bay leaf, onion, lemon juice, and the remaining ½ teaspoon of cayenne. There should be enough cayenne to make it sharp and hot.
4. Simmer, covered, for 15 minutes.
5. Add the steaks to the liquid, bring to a boil again, and simmer, covered, until the fish flakes easily with a fork, about 12 minutes.
6. Remove the fish steaks and heads (if desired), place in a bowl, strain the liquid, and pour it over. Add the onions if you like. Let cool and refrigerate overnight.

*Cayenne pepper can be omitted and about ½ cup fresh parsley added, as served in Turkey.

GEFILTE FISH

On an enormous silver platter a great fish reposed in a bed of parsley; it was complete and perfect from head to tail, with eyes of carrots and capers, and gleaming scales of gelatin.

"Why, it's the most wonderful thing I ever tasted!" a lady once said, and Mother beamed. "It's not a bit like gefüllte fish," the lady continued. Mother stiffened; that was not the comment she wanted at all: her fish was the apotheosis of gefüllte fish.

Someone asked Mother how it was made; she began a rather vague explanation about chopped carp and whitefish and egg, but Father took over.

"Made?" he said. "You might as well ask how a salmon is made. Every Friday morning the gefüllte fish swarm down the Hudson in schools of thousands and tens of thousands. The orthodox Jews stand on one bank with nets, and the reform Jews on the other bank with poles—they don't think nets are sporting. Of course the orthodox side catches twice as many as—"

"Dan," Mother said, and she motioned to the maid to pass the cucumbers. These were always served with the fish; they were cut in long, thin, spaghetti-like strips and soaked in a wonderfully pungent thin white sauce.

Felicia Lamport, *Mink on Weekdays, Ermine on Sunday*

Surely no holiday food is more Jewish than gefilte fish. Yet it was not eaten until the late Middle Ages.

When the Jews migrated to Eastern Europe, fresh fish was hard to come by. And they wanted just a little bit for their Friday evening meal—to enjoy the delights of the Sabbath. Since nearly all the Jews were extremely poor, they learned to invent dishes for people of limited means. During the week their diet consisted of potatoes, salt herring, onions, and dark bread. Fresh fish was reserved for the Sabbath. Living near the North Sea, they could use pike, carp, buffel, or other inexpensive freshwater fish. But these fish spoil quickly. A fish stretcher—gefilte fish—was therefore concocted so that all the members of the family could have at least a small taste for the Friday meal. The women learned to scrape the flesh away from the skin and bones, to add chopped onions, seasoning, and bread or matzah crumbs. Egg was added and the fish poached in much the same way *kneydlakh* is. The fish broth could be used again for a *milchig* dish of fish chowder during the week.

To locate the earliest written gefilte fish recipe, I pored through more than five hundred books on fish in a collection donated to Harvard University in 1915. I found not one recipe from anywhere in the world remotely resembling gefilte fish.

Elsewhere, in Mrs. Hertz's German cookbook of 1867, I saw a recipe resembling gefilte fish. And in the first American-Jewish cookbook, the *Jewish Cookery Book,* published by Esther Levy in 1871, there is a recipe for a fish cake.

Leon Hirschbaum, a Jewish-cookbook buff in Brooklyn, sent me the earliest recipe for gefilte fish in English. It is for stewed codfish balls. (Codfish was substituted for the freshwater fish of Eastern Europe, and the recipe was probably brought by an immigrant to England.) It comes from an 1874 book entitled *The Easy and Economical Book of Jewish Cookery,* written by Mrs. J. Atputel, cook to the Baroness Lionel de Rothschild.

STEWED FISH BALLS WITH EGG SAUCE

Take 2 pounds of cod and free it from all the bones; chop it and season it with pepper, salt, grated nutmeg, and a little of the rind of a lemon chopped fine, parsley and marjoram, a little soaked bread, with the water drained from it. Mix well together with an egg, make them into nice-sized balls the size of an apple. Slice in the stew-pan a large onion, 3 tablespoonfuls of salad oil, let it fry, add a teacupful of boiling water, let it boil up, put in the balls. When done beat in a basic 3 eggs, strain the juice of 2 large lemons, with a little dried saffron and a little chopped parsley. Stir and mix it all well together, dish them up by first taking out the balls, then strain the sauce over them. Garnish with parsley; 3 or 4 tomatoes added to the balls is a great improvement and makes it a pretty dish.

ZAMOSC GEFILTE FISH

MAKES 24 LARGE PATTIES. (P)

Carp in Poland had a fine clean taste, never "muddy." It was poached, sautéed au bleu, or baked—the latter version sometimes stuffed with a farci made of the carp's milt and liver, mushrooms, truffles, parsley, seasonings, eggs and bread crumbs. The stuffed fish would be sewn up with cotton thread, wrapped in a sheet of buttered white paper and baked in a moderately hot oven. Karp po Zydowsku, "in the Jewish style," was popular all over Poland. Diced carrots, chopped onions, chopped celery, diced celery root, and chopped parsley root would be simmered in salt water and butter, and seasonings (bay leaves, cloves, peppercorns, salt) would be added. Before the vegetables were done, the thick slices of carp were put on top and left steaming for another half-hour. The carp was served hot, or cold with an aspic made of the strained sauce into which some housewives would put additional fish heads.

Joseph Wechsberg, *Gourmet* magazine, February 1975

The gefilte fish in Joseph Wechsberg's mouthwatering description is unfortunately a dish of the past. Today, most people buy frozen or bottled brands. Good cooks, however, insist on preparing the homemade variety for Friday night and the holidays. My late mother-in-law, Peshka Gerson, made it twice a year, at Passover and Rosh Hashanah. She used her mother's recipe, handed down orally, from Zamosc, Poland. Her only concession to modernity was making individual patties rather than stuffing the filling back into the skin as described by Wechsberg. In addition, her filling was less elaborate.

Years ago, when I asked Peshka for her recipe, two of her sisters-in-law were present. They all agreed that the rule of thumb is one pound of fat fish to one pound of thin. They also preferred the Polish custom of adding a little sugar. (Lithuanians say sugar is added to freshen already unfresh fish. Needless to say, Lithuanians do not add sugar to their gefilte fish.) Peshka, Chuma, and Rushka disagreed, however, on the seasonings. Chuma insisted on more salt, and Rushka explained that a little almond extract would do the trick. They both took me aside, promising to show me the "real" way to make gefilte fish. I have used their two suggestions as variations on Peshka's basic recipe. Make your fish Lithuanian or Polish, with sugar or without, but just remember—it's the carrots and horse-radish that really count!

I have been making this recipe since the mid-1970s. The only difference is that I cook the fish for twenty minutes. My mother-in-law cooked it for two hours!

STOCK:

4 stalks celery, cut in 4-inch slices
3 onions, sliced*
6 carrots, sliced on the bias
8 cups water, or enough to cover bones with 1 inch to spare (use less rather than more)

Bones of fish (and heads, if desired)
1 tablespoon salt
½ tablespoon freshly ground pepper
1 tablespoon sugar

FISH:

3 pounds carp (meat)
1½ pounds whitefish, pickerel, or rockfish (meat)
1½ pounds yellow pike or buffel (meat)
6 onions*
2 tablespoons salt, or to taste
6 eggs

3 tablespoons sugar
½–1 cup matzah meal
¾ cup water
1 teaspoon almond extract or ¼ cup ground almonds (optional)
1¼ teaspoons pepper
Horseradish (bottled or fresh)

Note: The ratio of fish can be adjusted according to taste and availability. The less carp and the more whitefish, the more delicate the flavor and the lighter the dish. Each fish market will have its own suggestions for the most flavorful and eco-nomical mix. Today most markets will grind the fish for you and give you the heads, bones, and skins in a separate package.

*If desired, the onion skins can be reserved and added later to the stock to flavor and darken it.

1. Place all the stock ingredients in a large kettle with a cover. Bring to a boil, then partially cover and reduce the heat to a simmer. While waiting for the pot to boil, begin preparing the fish.
2. In a wooden bowl, add to the ground-up fish all the other ingredients listed under *Fish,* carefully chopping very fine and blending. You can also use the grinder on a mixer. Wet your hands and form the fish into fat, oval-shaped patties, carefully sliding each into the simmering stock.
3. Simmer over a low flame slowly for 20 to 30 minutes or for 2 hours. Allow to cool in the pot and carefully remove all the patties, placing them on a platter. After the fish has been removed, strain off the cooking liquid. This stock should then jell when chilled; if it does not, simply add a package of unflavored gelatin, following instructions on the package.
4. Serve the chilled gefilte fish with the jellied fish stock, horseradish, and of course the carrots.

GREEK FISH WITH PLUM SAUCE

(Pescado con Abramela)

SERVES 4–6 AS A MAIN COURSE AND 6–8 AS AN APPETIZER. (P)

Seattle's Pike Place Market is famous for its fresh salmon. One of the most popular shops is the City Fish Market, owned by the Levy brothers, Sephardic Jews from the island of Marmora, whom we filmed for *Jewish Cooking in America.*

Today, there are over three thousand Sephardim in Seattle, with two synagogues. The older Bikur Holim congregation is from Marmora and Fikirdayi; the newer, from the island of Rhodes.

On one trip to Seattle, I visited the Bikur Holim synagogue and stopped to talk with the late Lisa Benaroya, the wife of the rabbi. She was one of the prime movers behind their *Sephardic Cooking,* one of several Sephardic synagogue cookbooks published in this country. (Others are from Los Angeles, Atlanta, Houston, and Deal, New Jersey.) While talking about the special recipes from her native Marmora, she fed me *biscochos* (egg cookies), which she deftly molded each week for her grandchildren.

Although I am quite familiar with Sephardic cooking, the unusual combination of ingredients described in Mrs. Benaroya's recipes intrigued me, especially the Friday night fish dishes. We have all heard of the typically Greek fish with lemon sauce. But what about fish poached in rhubarb and tomatoes, greengage plums, or sour (unripe) grapes? These are favorite recipes of this picturesque Seattle community.

Eager to try these tantalizing dishes, I hurried down to the City Fish Market and spoke to Jack Levy. "Try the white salmon," he insisted. "It is less expensive and tastier than the red." Try making the following fish with plum sauce with salmon, snapper, sole, or rockfish for your Friday night meal.

6–7 greengage or red plums,
   peeled and diced
4 tomatoes, peeled and diced
1 tablespoon fresh flat-leaf
   parsley, chopped
Juice of 1 lemon

1 teaspoon sugar
Salt and pepper
2 pounds salmon steaks or red
   snapper or sole fillets (salted
   and drained)

1. Simmer the plums and tomatoes in a saucepan, covered, until soft (about 20 minutes). Do not overcook.
2. Remove from the heat and add the parsley, lemon juice, sugar, and salt and pepper to taste.
3. Preheat the oven to 400 degrees.
4. Let the mixture sit until lukewarm and then add the fish.
5. Bake in a saucepan or baking dish, uncovered, for 15–20 minutes. Serve cold as an appetizer or as a main course with rice.

Variation: To make fish with rhubarb sauce, simmer 2 cups sliced rhubarb, ½ cup tomato sauce, 3 tablespoons oil, 1 teaspoon sugar, salt to taste, and ½ cup water, covered, for about 30 minutes, or until the rhubarb is tender. Then add the fish and proceed with steps 3–5 above.

CHOPPED HERRING SALAD

SERVES 8 AS AN APPETIZER. (P)

When I spent Shabbat with friends in London, they started their Sabbath meal with chopped herring. Later, I discovered the same recipe in the only cookbook I know of written by a rabbi, *Kitchen Blues,* by Rabbi Lionel Blue of London (published by Victor Gollancz, 1987). The Reform (the British equivalent of Conservative) clergyman was cookery correspondent for the Catholic newspaper *The Universe* and a popular BBC cooking personality. Rabbi Blue, whose book blends anecdotes, humor, theology, and recipes, insists that he ministers through food. "I think if you enter people's kitchens you can get to their hearts. The best place to counsel people is in the kitchen, the comfiest place in the house," he preaches. "People feel secure there. There is great ministry in giving people a biscuit and a cup of tea. It helps people cope with life."

One 12-ounce jar pickled herring
3 slices pickled onion from the
     herring jar, or raw onion
3 slices brown bread, decrusted,
     soaked in water, and squeezed
     very dry

1 large apple, peeled and cored
1 tablespoon vegetable oil
1 teaspoon sugar
1 teaspoon salt
½ teaspoon pepper
3 hard-boiled eggs

1. Chop and mix all ingredients, reserving some egg for garnish. Do not use any of the pickling liquid from the herring or the dish will be too sharp.
2. Spread the chopped herring in a thin layer on a platter. Rabbi Blue advises, "To lessen the sad gray look of the fish (which should not put you off), scatter with the remaining chopped egg." Eat with thick white bread or with challah.

ISRAELI EGGPLANT SALAD

MAKES 3 CUPS. (P)

There is a saying in the Middle East that until a woman knows how to prepare 101 eggplant dishes, she is not ready to marry. At the beginning of the Middle Ages, Arab, and possibly Jewish, merchants brought the eggplant with them from the East. Since that time it has been the most versatile vegetable in the eastern Mediterranean. It has been known for centuries as far north as Russia and Bulgaria.

It is probably fair to say that Jerusalem has become the eggplant capital of the world, with each immigrant bringing a favorite recipe. Pickled eggplants and eggplant salads are spiced with tomatoes and green peppers; oniony *baba ghanouj* with *tahina* (sesame-seed paste); and moussaka with ground meat. Soups and cakes are made from eggplants. There used to be a restaurant in Tel Aviv, Melekh ha-Matzilim (King of the Eggplants), that boasted over seventy different eggplant recipes on its menu. Try these two Israeli eggplant salads, which must be made a day or two in advance to heighten the taste.

Note: The first two steps of this and the following eggplant and tomato salad are identical, and therefore it is a good idea to make both at the same time. They go well together as hors d'oeuvres with bread or crackers.

Vegetable oil for frying	1 clove garlic, minced
1 medium eggplant, unpeeled	3 tablespoons mayonnaise, or to
Salt	taste
½ large onion, peeled and sliced in	Juice of 1½ lemons
thin rings	Pepper

1. Pour about 2 inches of oil into a heavy frying pan and heat to 375 degrees.
2. Cut the eggplant in half lengthwise and cube the flesh into ½-inch squares. Sprinkle with salt and fry half of the eggplant at a time. When it is golden, remove it with a slotted spoon to a glass or ceramic bowl. Add the onion rings.

3. Blend in the garlic, mayonnaise, lemon juice, and salt and pepper to taste. Adjust the seasoning. Let sit overnight and serve with hot bread.

EGGPLANT AND TOMATO SALAD

MAKES 3 CUPS. (P)

Vegetable oil for frying
1 medium eggplant, unpeeled
Salt
½ large onion, peeled and sliced in thin rings

3 tablespoons tomato paste
3 tablespoons water
2 tablespoons catsup
1 clove garlic, minced
Pepper

1. Pour about 2 inches of oil into a heavy frying pan and heat to 375 degrees.
2. Cut the eggplant in half lengthwise and cube the flesh into ½-inch squares. Sprinkle with salt and fry half the eggplant at a time. When it is golden, remove it with a slotted spoon to a glass or ceramic bowl. Add the onion rings.
3. Add the tomato paste, water, catsup, garlic, and salt and pepper to taste. Let sit overnight before serving.

HUNGARIAN GREEN PEPPER
AND TOMATO SALAD

SERVES 6. (P)

With little or no refrigeration and often only impure water available until the twentieth century, ordinary people did not risk eating fresh vegetables that couldn't be peeled or shelled. Cucumber, beet, or cabbage salads were about the only ones used in Eastern Europe, and cooked salads featuring eggplant or broiled peppers were served in many Mediterranean countries. Lettuce, the base of most crisp salads we eat today, had to be cleaned in sterilized water and eaten immediately. Tomatoes were considered inedible in the raw state and were used only in purees.

Taboos surrounded many of these foods, especially the tomato. Until about 1900, many people believed the red fruit to be poisonous like its relative, the deadly nightshade.

It seems that Jews were especially superstitious about the tomato. One Jewish lady from Poland relates how she feared buying this new blood-red fruit. Grown by Gentiles in fields surrounding her shtetl, tomatoes seemed to grow on crosses. In time, however, these fears were dispelled.

2 green peppers	¼ cup white vinegar
3 tomatoes	2 teaspoons sugar
1 red onion	½ cup olive or vegetable oil
Salt	

1. Remove the white ribs and seeds from the green peppers and cut lengthwise into slices.
2. Slice and remove the seeds from the tomatoes.
3. Thinly slice the red onion.
4. Combine the salt to taste, vinegar, and sugar, and slowly whisk in the oil. Pour over the green peppers, tomatoes, and onion, arranged in a glass bowl.

HUNGARIAN CUCUMBER SALAD

(Uborkasalata)

SERVES 4–6. (P)

2 medium or large cucumbers

1 teaspoon salt

Pinch of sugar

¼ cup white vinegar

Dash of garlic powder

½ cup water

Sweet paprika

Black pepper

1. Peel the cucumbers and slice them very thin. Sprinkle with salt and let stand for 30–60 minutes with a plate and a 5-pound weight on top. Squeeze out the water on a paper towel.
2. Combine the sugar, vinegar, garlic powder, and water. Add the cucumbers and marinate for a few hours. To serve, sprinkle paprika on half of the salad and black pepper on the other half.

Note: Instead of garlic powder, a thinly sliced onion may be used.

GERMAN-STYLE CUCUMBER SALAD

SERVES 4–6. (P)

This is an old family recipe that my aunt Lisl (see page 158) made frequently when I was growing up.

2 cucumbers

1 teaspoon salt

2 tablespoons mayonnaise

1 teaspoon prepared mustard

¼ teaspoon garlic powder

Salt

1 tablespoon chopped fresh dill

   (optional)

1. Peel the cucumbers and slice them very thin. Sprinkle with salt and place in a colander for 30 minutes. Wash off the salt with cold water and press to extract the remaining liquid.
2. Mix the mayonnaise and mustard and add to the cucumbers. Sprinkle with garlic powder and salt to taste. Add fresh dill, if using. Mix well. Chill.

MARINATED MUSHROOMS

MAKES ABOUT 2 CUPS. (P)

When I lived in Jerusalem, a predawn, post-rain sport was hunting wild mushrooms in the Judean Hills. It was always necessary to include a mushroom expert in the group who could distinguish the poisonous from the edible varieties. When we returned to the city, we would quickly prepare a fresh mushroom omelet for breakfast.

In the Ukraine, Christian peasants knew how to differentiate edible from inedible varieties of wild mushrooms. They would go into the forest after a rain in the dark hours before dawn hunting for wild mushrooms in the rich dirt of the forest and selling them in the local marketplace. Housewives who would buy large quantities of these mushrooms would then string them on a line and air-dry them for later use. The famous mushroom and barley soup usually included not fresh but dried mushrooms, so tasty as flavoring agents.

In the United States, until recently we were accustomed to eating only one type of mushroom, the white *Agaricus campestris,* which is farmed mostly in Pennsylvania and distributed around the country. Now we have such a variety, but white mushrooms or cremini are perfect for this tasty appetizer.

1 pound fresh mushrooms	1 tablespoon prepared mustard
1 small onion, peeled and sliced in rings	1 teaspoon chopped fresh flat-leaf parsley
⅓ cup red wine vinegar	1 tablespoon chopped fresh dill
⅓ cup salad oil	¼ teaspoon salt
1 tablespoon brown sugar	3 peppercorns

1. Steam the mushrooms for 1 minute.
2. In a saucepan over medium heat, bring to a boil the onion, vinegar, oil, sugar, mustard, parsley, dill, salt, and peppercorns. Simmer, uncovered, for a few minutes.
3. Place the mushrooms in a glass or ceramic bowl and add the marinade. Let marinate in the refrigerator at least 24 hours, stirring occasionally. Serve with toothpicks.

KOSHER DILL PICKLES

MAKES ABOUT 150. (P)

What would the Lower East Side be without Guss's Pickles? And what would a kosher deli be without pickles? Although pickles are mass-marketed quite successfully, there is still a nostalgic taste sensation in reaching into a wooden barrel, pulling out a wet, garlic-smelling pickle, and slurping it down, dripping it over the floor and one's chin.

While we lived in Cambridge, Massachusetts, I loved sampling the pickles at Savenor's, the grocer and butcher whom Julia Child made famous on her *French Chef* show. At the entrance to Savenor's, there was a huge wooden barrel filled with pickles twelve months a year. Jack Savenor's brother-in-law, Max Baskies, learned to make the following Polish kosher dill pickles at his mother's knee over fifty years ago. For a smaller quantity, see the recipe on page 231.

50 pounds pickling cucumbers (Boston or Chicago variety)	2 ounces fresh dill
	1 pound pickling spice
3 pounds kosher salt	3 ounces garlic, minced
15 quarts hot water (about)	1 pint cider vinegar

1. Find an old wooden barrel, preferably one that contained olives from Portugal or Spain.
2. Wash the cucumbers and place them in the bottom of the barrel.
3. Mix the kosher salt (which Max feels makes the best brine) with enough hot

water to make the salt dissolve. Add the dill, pickling spice, garlic, and vinegar. Pour the brine on the cucumbers.

4. Add enough hot water to cover, close with a wooden top, and let stand 3 days. Then taste. In the summer the cucumbers pickle faster than in winter. Max uses no sodium benzoate or aluminum sulfate.

CHOPPED CHICKEN LIVER

MAKES ABOUT 2 CUPS. (M)

For the king of Babylon standeth at the parting of the way, at the head of the two ways, to use divination; he shaketh the arrows to and fro, he inquireth of the teraphim, he looketh in the liver.

Ezekiel 21:26

Before Nebuchadnezzar approached the land of Israel, he stood at the parting of the ways and, using means of divination, determined which way he should go— to Jerusalem or to the capital of the Ammonites. Archaeologists have found models of livers at Megiddo and Hazor dating back as far as 1400 B.C.E.

One might assume that the ancients thought the liver to have a life of its own, that it was the soul of man. The reason might be in its shape or in the fact that it contains so much blood, which is life itself. In prayer Jews often say, "*Nefesh habasar bedam hu,*" "The life of the flesh [Hebrew soul] is in the blood."

With blood considered the seat of life, it is easy to understand how it became an object of sacred awe. Because of the liver's excess blood, salting does not suffice in koshering; fire is also needed.

Whatever the ancient origins, chopped chicken liver has become a Jewish specialty, and every mother has her own version. Here is my mother's, coarsely chopped in a wooden bowl with a hand chopper. Some people prefer a smoother pâtélike consistency. Grated egg yolk may be served on top, delicatessen-style. Onion and pepper may be omitted. Although not traditional, tarragon is a pleasant herb to add to this dish.

½ pound chicken livers
½ cup chopped onion
½ cup chopped celery
2 tablespoons chicken fat or
    pareve margarine

2 hard-boiled eggs
Salt and freshly ground pepper

1. Broil the livers* lightly and quickly, and then sauté them with the onion and celery in chicken fat or margarine until the onions are golden (about 5 minutes).
2. Place the mixture in a wooden chopping bowl and chop with the eggs until smooth. Or you can place it in a food processor, fitted with a plastic blade, and spin for a few seconds until the mixture is well blended and fairly smooth. Do not overblend.
3. Add salt and pepper to taste. If the mixture seems dry, add additional chicken fat or margarine.

VEGETARIAN CHOPPED LIVER

MAKES 2 CUPS. (P)

The dairy restaurant, an American-Jewish phenomenon, is perhaps a precursor of many of today's health-food restaurants. One of the most famous was Ratner's, located on Delancey Street in New York. It boasted an endless array of pickles, bagels, onion rolls, bialys, herring, borscht, chopped hard-boiled eggs with fried mushrooms and onions, and much more. Salads included mock chopped liver made from cooked millet, green beans, or eggplant. Eggplant is also an economical replacement for meat as in eggplant schnitzel, for caviar in eggplant caviar, and for chopped liver in this Friday night vegetarian dish.

---

*According to kashrut, liver must be cut open across its length and width and placed with the rent part downward over the fire, so that the fire will draw out all of the blood. Before broiling, it is washed and lightly salted. It must be broiled until it is edible and then washed 3 times so that the blood is rinsed off. It must be broiled with a forked utensil or over a grate so that the blood is consumed by the fire or drained off. After it is koshered, it can be sautéed.

1 medium eggplant

¼ pound (1 stick) butter or pareve
   margarine

1 medium onion, minced

2 hard-boiled eggs

Salt and pepper

1. Slice the eggplant in ¼-inch circles. Sauté it in butter or margarine until golden on both sides.
2. Sauté half of the minced onion.
3. Grind the eggplant, fried and raw onions, and eggs in a food grinder or processor.
4. Add salt and pepper to taste. Refrigerate. Remove from the refrigerator 30 minutes before serving.

HERKIMER CHICKEN SOUP

MAKES 12 CUPS TO SERVE 6. (M)

Chicken soup, prepared and eaten on Shabbat and holidays, was made by cooking all of the chicken parts and innards, excluding the head and lungs, in a pot of water, with onions, carrots, and salt. The feet of the chicken were added to the soup to give it a rich flavor. When cooked in water, the skin of the feet came off, settled on the bottom of the pot, and gave the soup a nice color and rich flavor. If an extra piece of meat or chicken were available, it would be added to the soup. Often the skin from the neck of the bird was filled with fat, flour, raw chopped potatoes, cooked potatoes, or cooked grains. Each end was sewn together and the neck was cooked in the soup. The heart was also added to the soup. In the summer, various fresh vegetables, such as parsley root or parsley leaf, might be added. Some women added millet or other grains, or even something special, such as farfl, lokshn, or cooked rice. If extra ingredients were added to the basic soup, they would be added from the onset of the cooking.

Amy Snyder, Columbia University master's thesis on the
cooking of a Jewish lady from Lagev, Poland

The late Judith Rush lived in Herkimer, New York (population 9,000). Mrs. Rush and her late husband were one of the town's forty Jewish families. Determined to keep kosher in Herkimer, Mrs. Rush traveled an hour to Syracuse or an hour and a half to Albany to purchase her kosher meat. Mrs. Rush has been immortalized by her granddaughter, Becky Mode, in *Fully Committed,* a play about a restaurant: "You see, people think that an elderly person is not going to check the bill. But I did! I was in business thirty-five years as vice president of the Rush Furniture Company in Herkimer, New York—" said Mrs. Rush.

4 quarts water, or more to cover
1 whole onion, peeled
4 parsnips, peeled and left whole
1 chicken, preferably stewing or large roaster, with skin, cut up
½ cup celery leaves

2 tablespoons fresh flat-leaf parsley
2 tablespoons fresh or 2 teaspoons dried dill
1 tablespoon salt
¼ teaspoon pepper
6 peeled carrots, cut in 1-inch chunks, plus 1 left whole

1. Bring all the ingredients except the carrots to a boil. Cover and simmer gently for 3 hours.
2. Skim off the skin that forms at the top.
3. Add the carrots and simmer 1 hour more, or until everything falls apart.
4. Strain and serve with noodles or matzah balls. Cut the whole carrot into slices and serve in the soup.

CALVES' LIVER SOUP

SERVES 4–6. (M)

This soup was served on Friday nights on the German side of my family. It is a good example of how German Jews changed a rich cream of liver soup to adhere to the dietary customs. The non-Jewish equivalent includes cream and butter. My grandmother used palmin, a coconut oil eaten before margarine was invented.

½ pound calves' liver

3 tablespoons pareve margarine

Salt and freshly ground pepper

½ teaspoon dried tarragon
  (optional)

1 small onion, diced

1 tablespoon chopped fresh
  flat-leaf parsley

2 tablespoons flour

1½ quarts beef or chicken broth

2 egg yolks, beaten

1 teaspoon Cognac (optional)

Croutons made from 3 slices
  toasted bread

1. Lightly broil and slice the liver. Then sauté it in 1 tablespoon of margarine for 10 minutes. Add salt and pepper to taste and tarragon, if using. Remove from the pan.
2. In a heavy saucepan, sauté the onion in the 2 remaining tablespoons of margarine. When the onion is golden, add the parsley and the liver. Cover and simmer over low heat for 5 minutes.
3. Add the flour, mix thoroughly, but don't let the flour brown. Slowly add the beef or chicken broth. Let simmer, covered, for a few minutes, until thickened.
4. Before serving, strain the soup through a cheesecloth and whip in the egg yolks mixed with Cognac, if using.
5. Serve with toasted croutons.

HENRIETTA SZOLD'S STEWED FISH
WITH LEMON SAUCE

SERVES 4–6. (D OR P)

Henrietta Szold, founder of Hadassah, was known for her scholarship, translations, leadership ability, and a number of other laudable activities. Expertise in cooking was not one of them. Yet she knew how to cook, and in her exacting way typed out many of the favorite family recipes, which one of her nieces kindly shared with me.

Her strudel recipe calls for a "supperplateful of sugar and cinnamon" and a quart of flour. "Liver for entrée" is known to us as chopped liver. A most interesting recipe is for *ganef,* a barley and farina stuffing for the back of a goose.

An especially tasty dish is stewed fish with lemon sauce, which was usually served as a main course on Friday nights. This particular recipe is not typically German (their Friday night fish was usually sweet-and-sour). I was surprised to find it cited as well by a number of other German-Jewish women from old Baltimore families. Puzzled by this coincidence, I searched for an answer.

An old friend of the Szold family told me that Baltimore's German-Jewish community was extremely close-knit. Although few of the women themselves actually cooked, they all guided their Irish maids in the kitchen. *The "Settlement" Cook Book,* first published in 1901, was then the rage in the German-Jewish circles. One hostess must have served this boiled fish with Sephardic lemon sauce on a Tuesday or Friday (fish market days) and then passed the recipe on to her friends. To this day, many German-Jewish families of Baltimore, including the remaining Szolds, serve stewed fish with lemon sauce on Friday night, the second night of Passover, and other special occasions.

One 4-pound rockfish, striped bass, sea trout, salmon, or halibut, cleaned, cut in steaks, with the head and tail still attached	1 teaspoon ground ginger
	Pepper
	2 tablespoons butter or pareve margarine
	2 tablespoons flour
Salt	2 cups fish bouillon (recipe below)
2 quarts water (approximately)	
1 medium onion, sliced	2 egg yolks, beaten
2 carrots, sliced	Juice of 1 lemon
2 stalks celery with leaves, sliced	Lemon slices and chopped fresh flat-leaf parsley for garnish
6 large sprigs of flat-leaf parsley	
1 teaspoon white peppercorns	

1. Clean the fish and let it stand in salt several hours. (Some Jewish cooks feel that stewed fish has a better taste if it is salted when it is cleaned and allowed to stand awhile. Then, before stewing, the salt is rinsed off.)*

---

*It is really not necessary to salt fish in this way. Very religious Jews might feel, however, that fish should be treated as meat and salted. Also, there is a Jewish superstition about salting food to keep away the evil eye.

2. Place the fish in a flat wide dish or fish poacher and add enough cold water to cover. Remove the fish and add the onion, carrots, celery, parsley, peppercorns, ginger, and salt and pepper to taste. Bring to a boil to make a bouillon of all the ingredients but the fish. After the bouillon has simmered until flavorful, about 15–20 minutes, return the fish to the poacher, leaving enough bouillon to come halfway up the fish. Bring the bouillon to a boil, reduce the heat, and simmer the fish 10 minutes for each inch of thickness. Let simmer until the fish is soft or white, about 20 minutes. A large fish might take longer.

3. Carefully remove the fish. Allow it to cool. Skin and bone it and set aside. Reserve 2 cups of bouillon.

4. Make a velouté sauce by melting the butter or margarine, adding the flour, cooking for 2 minutes, and then pouring in the 2 cups of fish bouillon. Stir thoroughly until smooth. Add some of the hot sauce to the well-beaten egg yolks, whisking so as not to cook the eggs, and pour the mixture back into the sauce; beat carefully. Add the lemon juice to make the sauce creamy. Don't let the sauce boil again or the eggs will curdle.

5. Pour the sauce over the fish and garnish with lemon slices and chopped parsley.

Note: The court bouillon can include lemon, more or less celery, onions, or carrots. Some recipes call for sugar and vinegar as well.

FRIDAY NIGHT BRISKET

SERVES 12. (M)

You could smell the roast all over the house, it had so much garlic in it. A roast like that, with fresh warm twist, is a delicacy from heaven. And when you consider that we had some fresh dill pickles, and a bottle of beer, and some cognac before the meal and cherry cider after the meal—you can imagine the state our guest was in.

Sholem Aleichem, "Tit for Tat"

In the ancient world, garlic was known as an aphrodisiac, and the phrase "to eat garlic" was therefore a euphemism for sexual intercourse. Since a husband is supposed to fulfill his marital obligation to his wife—at least on Friday night—rabbis have suggested that more garlic and less salt be used in dishes at the Sabbath meal. Thus, Jews became known as "garlic eaters."

Foods can be divided into two categories—those that "chill" the body and therefore have a quieting effect on procreative powers and those that "heat" the body and awaken sexual desires. Salt is in the first category, garlic and onion in the second.

Early in history, Jews became addicted to garlic. In the desert they mourned the garlic, onions, leeks, and melons they had eaten in Egypt. Manna contained all the flavors found in the world except those of onion and garlic. These last two were excluded, as they were considered harmful to pregnant women.

The Romans, too, considered garlic an aphrodisiac. At their festival of Ceres, Cerealia, garlic was eaten. Serbians still use garlic as a remedy against witches and demons, and the custom is prevalent among Jews in Northern Europe of using garlic to avert the effects of the "evil eye."

I tasted this delicious brisket one Rosh Hashanah at the home of Lynn and Wolf Blitzer. The very American sauce is based on a recipe that Lynn learned from her late mother in Buffalo, New York. Through the years Lynn has added her own touches, using julienned carrots, adding more and sometimes less ketchup. I've added garlic, and you can personalize the recipe, as well.

One 6-pound brisket	1½ cups ketchup
2 packages onion soup mix	1½ pounds carrots
6 cloves garlic	

1. Preheat the oven to 350 degrees.
2. Place the meat fatty side up in a baking dish large enough to hold it comfortably. Sprinkle the onion soup mix over the meat. Cover with the ketchup and 2 cups water. Crush the garlic cloves, and add to the liquid. The meat should be almost covered with the liquid.
3. Cover with aluminum foil and bake for 3½ hours.
4. While the meat is cooking, peel the carrots, and cut them lengthwise into thin sticks. Cut the carrots in half. Place them on top of the brisket, cover, and bake for another hour.

5. Set the brisket and carrots aside to cool before refrigerating overnight. The next day, skim off the fat from the meat. Remove the brisket to a cutting board and slice thin across the grain.

6. Return the brisket to the baking dish and re-cover with the carrots. To reheat, preheat the oven to 350 degrees. Put the sliced brisket and the carrots in the oven and bake for another hour, or until the brisket is heated through. Serve with noodles.

CHICKEN *PAPRIKASH*

SERVES 4–6. (F)

A Hungarian Jew is Hungarian—especially in the kitchen—except for the omission of two Hungarian cooking basics. Goose fat or, now, suet or lard are replaced by margarine or vegetable oil for milk dishes. A dollop of sour cream does not adorn such favorites as Hungarian goulash, stuffed cabbage, or chicken *paprikash*. But poppy seeds and paprika still decorate many dishes, and salads are flavored with vinegary dressings. Chicken *paprikash* with rice and cucumber salad or green pepper and tomato salad are typical and typically delicious Hungarian Friday dinner dishes.

2 large onions, minced
2 tablespoons chicken fat or
   vegetable oil
2 green peppers, seeded and sliced
2 tomatoes, quartered (optional)
2 tablespoons Hungarian sweet
   paprika

1 fresh hot pepper or a few
   sprinkles of crushed red
   pepper
Salt
1 large, plump fryer, cut into
   pieces
2 cups long-grain white rice

1. In a Dutch oven, sauté the onions in the chicken fat or oil until golden brown. Add the green peppers and brown slightly. Add the tomatoes, if using, paprika, and hot pepper, mixing well and making sure the paprika does not burn.

2. Salt the chicken and add it to the above. Mix and cover. Let the chicken render its own juices, simmering until tender (about 50 minutes). You may have to add water.

3. When the chicken is cooked, move it to one side of the Dutch oven, or remove it to a warm plate, and add the rice. Mix with the pan juices; add water if the pan juices do not cover the rice by about 1 inch. Add salt to taste. Cover and simmer about 20 minutes, until the rice is cooked.

STUFFED CHICKEN

SERVES 6–8. (M)

Chicken has always been a typically Jewish main course for Friday night. This chicken has a stuffing of bread and green peppers under the skin. I first tasted it in Israel, but it is a standard Hungarian dish. The crunchy addition of cornflakes makes it American.

2 large onions, chopped
¼ cup vegetable oil or margarine
1 green pepper, seeded and
    chopped
4 stalks celery with leaves, finely
    chopped
2 tablespoons minced fresh flat-
    leaf parsley

Salt and freshly ground pepper
1 small loaf white bread with
    crusts removed
2 eggs
1 cup crushed pareve cornflakes
8 chicken breast halves, with skin
3 cloves garlic
1 teaspoon paprika

1. Sauté the onions in 3 tablespoons of the oil. Add the green pepper, celery, parsley, and salt and pepper to taste, and continue cooking until the green pepper is soft. Let cool.
2. Soak the bread in water. Squeeze out the water and combine the bread with the sautéed onion mixture.
3. Mix in the eggs and then fold in the crushed cornflakes.
4. Preheat the oven to 350 degrees.
5. Wash and dry the chicken breasts and rub with garlic. Sprinkle with salt, pepper, and paprika.

6. Stuff the filling under the skin of each breast and brush the top with the remaining 1 tablespoon of oil.

7. Place in a 9- by 13-inch or similar casserole and bake, uncovered, in the oven for 30–45 minutes, or until golden brown.

Note: The leftover stuffing can be placed in aluminum foil and cooked alongside the chicken.

FASSOULIA

(Sephardic String Bean and Meat Stew)

SERVES 6–8. (M)

This string bean and meat casserole, coming from the heyday of Sephardic Jewry, is probably one of the oldest Jewish recipes in this country. Handed down through the generations of the New York Nathan family, whose first relatives landed on American soil in 1654, it probably came with them in oral form during their flight from Spain via Brazil, where they picked up the allspice. Every other recipe I have ever seen for this dish—known as *fassoulia* in Arab countries—includes tomatoes, which makes me think this recipe antedates the others. After the Nathans' departure from Spain, tomatoes were introduced to the Old World from the New. Jews who stayed in Spain or fled to the various parts of the Turkish Empire added the new fruit. By the time the Nathans might have added tomatoes, the recipe had become such a symbol of their past that it remained pretty much intact.

Given the fact that Nathan ancestry includes poets Emma Lazarus and Robert Nathan, Supreme Court Justice Benjamin Nathan Cardozo, and Annie Nathan Meyer, founder of Barnard College, consider yourself in good company if you serve the following recipe. Try it in the original Nathan form or with the later addition of tomatoes. Both ways, it has become a family favorite in my home (and we are no kin to the Sephardic Nathans).

3 pounds lean brisket, chuck,
  shoulder steak, or breast
  deckel
1 clove garlic
Salt and pepper
2 tablespoons vegetable oil
4 whole black peppercorns

½ teaspoon whole allspice, or
  to taste
2 cups water or 1 cup water
  and 1 cup tomato juice or
  sauce
12 small onions
2 pounds fresh string beans

1. Rub the brisket with garlic and season well with salt and pepper. Brown on all sides in a little oil.
2. Place the peppercorns and allspice in a cheesecloth and add to the meat with 1 teaspoon of salt.
3. Simmer, covered in 2 cups of water, with the onions for 2½ hours or more. Let stand until cool and skim off the fat.
4. Remove the tip ends and string the beans if necessary. Add to the meat and simmer slowly, covered, 30 minutes more, or until tender.

MOROCCAN MEATBALLS

(Kofta)

MAKES 18. (M)

When Americans think of meatballs, it is most often in terms of the Italian or Swedish variety. As did so many other foods, however, meatballs originated in the Middle East. Arab and Jewish merchants and later the Crusaders spread the word to Europe of how easy and tasty it is to combine ground lamb, beef, or veal with onions, garlic, bread crumbs, and spices. These balls are then usually simmered in a sauce. By tasting the spices in each meatball, it is easy to discern from which country and even sometimes from which town the recipe came. Iraqi Jews, for example, tend to add cumin and turmeric; Greeks use oregano and potatoes; and Persians introduce a combination of turmeric and such novel ingredients as ground nuts, rice, apricots, or prunes. The following recipe comes from Morocco. Its ingredients include cumin, garlic, and bread crumbs or matzah meal. It is often served on Friday night with a variety of salads.

MEATBALLS:

1 pound ground beef
2–3 cloves garlic, minced
Salt and pepper
1 egg

¼ cup matzah meal or bread
    crumbs
1 teaspoon ground cumin

SAUCE:

¼ cup vegetable oil
Salt and pepper
1 teaspoon ground cumin
1 teaspoon paprika

⅛ teaspoon crushed red pepper
    (optional)
½ cup water
Juice of 1 lemon (optional)

1. Mix together all the ingredients for the meatballs. Roll into walnut-size balls.
2. Combine the ingredients for the sauce.
3. In a heavy saucepan, bring the sauce to a boil. Add the meatballs and simmer in the sauce, uncovered, until cooked, about 20 minutes.

CALVES' FOOT JELLY

(Petcha)

SERVES 6–8. (M)

Petcha, or calves' foot jelly, made from the cheeks and bones of the calf, is often eaten as a main dish in summer at noon on the Sabbath or, in winter, as an appetizer or with the third meal. Called *drelies* in Galicia, *pacha* in Iraq, and *pilse* in Romania, it is *fisnoga* in Russia. The Yiddish for foot is *fus*. The Russian for foot is *noga*. Russian Jews combined both these words into *fisnoga*, literally "foot-foot."

What is the custom of eating calves' foot jelly on the Sabbath? In the days of redemption, even the feet—the lower extremities of the body—will be elevated on high. Since the Sabbath affords the faithful a taste of the World to Come, "food made of feet" is eaten in anticipation.

There may also be a more practical reason for eating the calf's foot. It is an inexpensive cut of meat. Jews in Eastern Europe were generally very poor. This delicacy was just one more way of stretching a little bit of meat to be eaten on the Sabbath. It is similar to "souse" or "headcheese" made in the South from pigs.

The late Rose Siegel, originally from Minsk, told me how her mother prepared *fisnoga*. In winter she would often leave it in the oven overnight and serve it at noon as a gravy with kasha, followed by a brisket or chicken. In summer she would serve it cold, as it is in the following recipe.

I rarely see people preparing *petcha* these days. But one Purim, at the home of klezmer musician Andy Statman, I saw someone bring him a platter of *petcha* as a *shalach manos,* or Purim gift.

2 large onions, sliced	3–4 cloves garlic, minced
1 cow's or 2 calves' (preferred) feet, cleaned and cut into large pieces—ask your butcher to do this	1½ teaspoons salt
	½ teaspoon pepper
	3 hard-boiled eggs, sliced
	Lemon slices

1. Put the sliced onions in a large soup pot. Add all the other ingredients except the eggs and lemon slices.
2. Cover with water and boil slowly until the meat falls away from the bones, about 3 hours, adding water as needed to keep all the ingredients covered.
3. Turn off the heat and remove the meat. Clear the meat and the jellylike substance from the bones. Grind the meat and place in the bottom of a deep glass pie plate or bowl. Strain the soup over the ground meat to cover, using about 2 cups of liquid. Place the sliced eggs in the liquid; they will fall to the bottom.
4. Refrigerate until firm. Cut into squares and serve cold with lemon slices.

Variation: Some people separate the egg whites and yolks, mixing the whites with the meat and the yolks with the gravy. *Petcha* can also be served warm, topped with a hot egg sauce made from 6 eggs, water, salt, sugar, and lemon, diluted, after thickening, with a little chicken soup.

DAFINA

(Moroccan-style Cholent)

SERVES 8–10. (M)

Go now to the flock, and fetch me from thence two good kids of the goats;
and I will make them savoury food for thy father, such as he loveth.

Genesis 27:9

Rebecca's savory stew that Jacob fed to Isaac may have been a precursor to *hamim* ("hot" in Hebrew) or *cholent,* the long-simmering stew traditionally served at noon on the Sabbath. The original version would have included olive oil, chickpeas or lentils, meat, water, onions, garlic, herbs, and leeks. Because of the prohibition against lighting a fire on the Sabbath, the *hamim,* as far back as the second century, was hermetically sealed and placed in a very low oven, originally the remaining hot embers of a fire begun on Friday afternoon, and opened at noon Saturday after the morning services. When the Jews left Palestine, they brought this dish with them. With the local ingredients available in different countries, the stew changed character. The lamb or kid changed to beef, tongue, or calves' feet; the lentils became white, black, or navy beans. Potatoes, eggs, carrots, and barley were all local changes, as was the addition of rice. *Cholent* can be made in a pot in a low oven, or easily in a Crock-Pot.

The following recipe for Moroccan *dafina* (meaning "hidden") came to Casablanca from Spain at the time of the Inquisition. An Egyptian version would include a calf's foot instead of a tongue, and a Brazilian version would have black beans rather than chickpeas.

Hamim is one example of how a Jewish dish influenced the great national cuisine of a country. In Spain, *cocido madrileño* is a national dish. Its ingredients classically include chicken, beef, veal, bone marrow, chorizo sausage, a ham joint, blood sausage, fresh pork fat, and salt pork fat. Chickpeas, potatoes, carrots, cabbage, garlic, and leeks are also included. Sound familiar? It is a descendant of *dafina* similar to the one in the following recipe. Peter Feibleman, author of Time-Life's *Spanish Cookery,* related that during the Inquisition it was necessary for every Spaniard to show his adherence to Christianity. While Muslims and Jews ate no pork for religious reasons, a "pure" Christian ate pork once a day, preferably in public. Even at home he could be caught off guard, for anyone who came unexpectedly to share his *cocido* could see clearly from the pork in it that this was the house not of an infidel but of a "pure believer in the true faith." Thus, hard-boiled eggs, symbolic of the eternity of life, were quickly replaced by large quantities of pork and pork fat.

It has been suggested by many that New Amsterdam Jews, taking the *dafina* across the ocean, lent this recipe to the Pilgrims for—you guessed it—baked beans. Baked beans became, with the addition of salt pork and navy beans, the long-simmering New World stew eaten on Saturday nights.

The following *dafina* recipe from Morocco is outstanding. The meat loaf—made from ground walnuts, ground beef, cinnamon, and sugar—is a marvelous Moroccan addition. The stew is sealed tightly and cooked for about eighteen hours, and the result is a melt-in-your-mouth meal that can be served in three courses. The broth becomes a soup with the addition of thin, vermicelli-like *fidellos* noodles. Then come the vegetables, and finally the meat course. Having identified *hamim* and *cholent* as stews so heavy only Alka-Seltzer and a good long nap could cure them, I was pleasantly surprised at how absolutely savory —and light!—this stew was. Just follow it with a light fruit dessert rather than a heavy kugel. Try it next Sabbath or for your next winter dinner party.

1 cup chickpeas that have been
    soaked in water overnight
Salt and pepper
¼ teaspoon turmeric
½ teaspoon ground mace
1 entire head garlic, peeled
1 onion, sliced
One 4-pound top rib, breast of
    beef, or brisket
1 pound ground beef
½ cup sugar
1 teaspoon cinnamon

¼ teaspoon ground cloves
10 eggs
1 beef tongue (optional)
2 cups rice, uncooked
½ cup vegetable oil
6–7 yams or sweet potatoes,
    peeled and halved
10–12 whole boiling potatoes,
    peeled and halved
4–6 dates, pitted
Water

1. Using a large 9-quart casserole with a tight-fitting lid, place the chickpeas on the bottom. Sprinkle with salt, pepper, turmeric, and mace.
2. Place the garlic cloves, onion, and brisket on top of the chickpeas. Sprinkle again with salt and pepper.
3. Mix the ground beef, sugar, cinnamon, cloves, and 2 of the eggs and form into a meat loaf. Wrap tightly with aluminum foil and place next to the meat.
4. If using tongue, place that in with the rest of the meat.
5. Put the rice loosely in a piece of cheesecloth and close tightly. Place on top of the meat. Pour the oil over the rice.
6. Surround the rice with the yams or sweet potatoes, the white potatoes, the dates, and the remaining whole, unpeeled 8 eggs. Sprinkle again with salt and pepper.
7. Add water up to the top of the potatoes, about ¾ full. Bring to a boil, cover, and simmer 1 hour on top of the stove. Add more water, as necessary, to keep it ¾ full.
8. Preheat the oven to 250 degrees and place the *dafina* in the oven. Leave overnight or for at least 10 hours. Do not open until ready to serve. Place the vegetables in one dish, the meat in another, the rice in a third, and the broth in a fourth as your soup course.

HUNGARIAN-STYLE *CHOLENT*

SERVES 8. (M)

The rabbi and the Catholic priest in a village of Hungary were very friendly. The priest complained to the rabbi that he could not sleep. The rabbi suggested a *cholent* recipe as a cure for insomnia. A few days later when they met again, the rabbi asked the priest how the *cholent* was. The priest replied, "I understand how you fall asleep from this dish, but what puzzles me is: How do you get up?" According to George Lang in his classic *Cuisine of Hungary,* from which this story is excerpted, barley was added to this soupy stew in Hungary; the closer to the Austrian border, the less barley and the more rice was included. The Central European version originated during the Middle Ages in the Rhineland and was called *schalet* by German Jews. Rice with beans or peas was the basic vegetable in *cholent*; later, in Poland and Russia, potatoes, barley, and brisket appeared. The amount of meat depended on the wealth of the family.

Each town and in fact each family of Central and Eastern Europe had its special *cholent* recipe. There were said to be over three hundred varieties.

The word *cholent* and the German *schalet* come from the old French word *chald,* or the modern French *chaud,* for warm. This, of course, was a translation from the Hebrew *ham,* also meaning warm. Another theory is that the word comes quite simply from the Yiddish *shul ende,* or end of synagogue, since that is when the *cholent* is eaten. The second explanation sounds more to me like a play on the words of the first.

The *cholent* was hermetically sealed in an iron pot to retain the juices during its long cooking. A piece of cloth or cheesecloth would be placed around the top of the casserole, or a dough made from flour and water would be pressed between the cover and the top of the casserole. After it was sealed, the *cholent* was either placed in the oven at home or taken to the baker, where each saucepan was marked with the name of the owner. The baker locked all the community pots in his oven and allowed the fire to go out. To retain the heat, he often sealed the door with lime.

After synagogue, small boys brought the meal home. Dessert kugels and *schalets* were also cooked in a similar manner, often inside the *cholent* pot.

To make carrying permissible on the Sabbath, the entire town (if it was small enough) was surrounded with a string or wire. The *eruv,* that is, the enclosure of the village by wire for the Sabbath, made the village like one household, within which carrying is permissible. If the fence broke, the *cholents* were handed from person to person to the house.

This Hungarian *cholent* recipe was given to me by the late Alex Lichtman, the owner of Mrs. Herbst's Bakery in New York.

2 cloves garlic, finely chopped
1 medium onion, diced
⅓ cup chicken or goose fat or
    vegetable shortening
2–3 quarts water
1½ cups dried small white or lima
    beans, uncooked

½ cup pearl barley
1 smoked beef tongue (available at
    kosher markets)
1½ tablespoons hot paprika
1 large ripe tomato, quartered
2 stalks celery, quartered

1 whole parsley root and greens
(turnips can be substituted)
1 pound breast of beef or brisket
2 slices flanken (beef short ribs),
cut into 3 pieces each

2 unbroken eggs, in the shell
1½ tablespoons salt
Pepper
Stuffed goose neck (optional—
see page 82)

1. Preheat the oven to 250 degrees.
2. Sauté the garlic and onion in the chicken or goose fat or vegetable shortening.
3. Using a heavy 5–6-quart casserole, combine the garlic and onion with all the remaining ingredients, starting with about 8 cups of water. Bring to a boil on top of the stove.
4. Cover and place in the oven. Bake for 6 hours or overnight. After the cholent has been cooking about 2 hours, stir and check if there is enough water. If not, add 2 cups more. If, later, it needs more water, add about ½ cup at a time. Serve in large soup bowls.

Note: Traditionally this dish was cooked overnight and then eaten at noon the next day. The Orthodox could not open the pot and therefore started with more water than I have in this recipe. I make it in advance, cool it, skim the fat off, and then reheat it.

STUFFED GOOSE NECK

(*Toltott Libanyak*)

SERVES 6–8 AS AN APPETIZER AND 4 FOR A MAIN COURSE
(IN THE *CHOLENT* RECIPE IT WILL SERVE 8). (M)

This is another example of using all the parts of the meat—in this case, the neck. It was made as an appetizer or added to the *cholent*.

1 whole large goose neck (remove skin from neck and clean inside and out)	1 teaspoon paprika
	½ clove garlic, crushed
	1 cup flour
1 small onion, chopped	1 teaspoon salt
¾ pound goose meat	1 egg
7 ounces goose fat	1 cup chicken broth

1. Grind together any remaining meat from the goose neck, plus the onion, goose meat, and 4 ounces of the goose fat. Grind again.
2. Combine the ground goose mixture with the paprika, garlic, flour, salt, egg, and the remaining 3 ounces of goose fat, which has been melted. Mix well.
3. Fill the skin of the goose neck with the stuffing. Sew the narrow end. Fill with more stuffing and sew the other end. Sew any other openings.
4. Preheat the oven to 400 degrees.
5. In a small casserole, place the chicken broth and the stuffed goose neck. Bake, uncovered, in the oven for about 30 minutes, making sure to brown the goose neck on each side. Serve alone or add to the previous *cholent* recipe. Serve hot or cold. Slice like a sausage.

LOKSHEN NOODLES

Adapted from Debbie Klatskin

SERVES 4. (P)

Debbie makes these noodles with her children. This is a wonderful tradition for them to remember as they get older and a wonderful skill to achieve. Although Debbie uses her hands, you can also use a food processor and a pasta machine.

3 cups unbleached all-purpose flour (approximately)	3 eggs
	½ teaspoon kosher salt

1. On a clean countertop form 2 cups of the flour into a pile. Make a well in the center. Carefully break the eggs into the well and sprinkle the salt on top of the flour. Work the eggs into the flour with your hand or a fork until a soft dough is formed, adding flour as needed.
2. Knead the dough for 20–25 minutes. Cover the dough with plastic wrap and let it rest on the counter for 15–30 minutes.
3. On a floured surface roll out the dough with a floured rolling pin until it is approximately ⅛ inch thick. Let the dough rest again for another 10–15 minutes.
4. Use your fingers to stretch the dough and lift it up until it begins to become transparent (but not as thin as strudel dough). Then, once again on a floured surface with a floured rolling pin, roll the dough out until it is even thinner, about 9 by 12 inches. Using a knife, cut the dough into irregularly shaped noodles about 2 inches long. (You can also use a pasta machine for this.)
5. Bring a pot of either salted water or chicken soup to a boil. Drop the noodles into the boiling water or broth and boil until cooked, approximately 6 minutes. Taste to see if the noodles are al dente. Drain the noodles and place them in a bowl with hot steamy broth. Serve immediately or refrigerate and serve later.

PINEAPPLE NOODLE KUGEL

SERVES 8. (P)

In Eastern Europe, kugel was the official Sabbath dessert after a hot *cholent*. Made of *lokshen* (noodles) or soaked white bread mixed with beaten eggs and liberally dotted with raisins, sugar, spices, and shortening, it was baked until it was firm, brown, and fragrant. The kugel could be baked simultaneously with the *cholent*. A covered earthenware pot holding the kugel was placed in the center of the iron *cholent* pot. Then the *cholent* potatoes or beans were arranged to fill the empty space around this centerpiece. Cooked inside the *cholent* pot, the kugel came out moister than if it had been baked alone. With the heavy main course and the heavy dessert, it is no wonder that Sabbath afternoons were (and for many still are) literally days of rest.

The following kugel—my husband's favorite—can be prepared for dessert or as a starch with roast or broiled chicken on the Sabbath or any day.

Vegetable oil
16 ounces broad noodles
9 eggs
6 tablespoons pareve margarine,
    melted and cooled to room
    temperature
¾ cup sugar

One 8-ounce can crushed
    pineapple with juice
1½ teaspoons vanilla extract
1½ teaspoons cinnamon
One 15-ounce can pineapple rings
Cherries

1. Preheat the oven to 350 degrees and grease a 9- by 13-inch baking dish with the oil. Boil the noodles in salted water for half of the time recommended on the package. Drain and rinse in cold water.
2. In a large bowl, combine the eggs and margarine. Beat well. Add the sugar, crushed pineapple and juice, vanilla, and cinnamon. Mix well. Add the noodles.
3. Pour the kugel in the prepared dish. Place the drained pineapple rings on top, with a cherry in the middle of each ring.
4. Bake for 40–60 minutes, until golden.

Note: You can decrease the number of eggs, but the result will be less fluffy. To make a dairy pineapple kugel, use 3 eggs, ½ pound pot cheese, 1 cup sour cream, and 1 cup milk.

JERUSALEM KUGEL

(Sweet and Peppery Spaghetti Pudding)

SERVES 8–10. (P)

In Mea Shearim, the religious quarter of Jerusalem, it is said that this eighteenth-century sweet and spicy kugel originally came from the Gaon of Vilna and his followers.

2 teaspoons salt, or to taste	4 eggs
16 ounces capellini or other thin spaghetti	1½–2 teaspoons freshly ground black pepper
½ cup vegetable oil	1 teaspoon cinnamon
¾ cup sugar	

1. Preheat the oven to 350 degrees and grease a Bundt pan.
2. Place 1 teaspoon of salt in about 3 quarts of water and bring to a boil. Add the spaghetti and cook until al dente, about 5 minutes, or according to package directions. Drain well and set aside in a saucepan.
3. In a medium saucepan, heat the oil and ½ cup of the sugar. Stir constantly until the sugar turns very dark, almost black (about 10 minutes).
4. Very carefully pour the hot caramel into the spaghetti and mix well. Cool slightly.
5. Combine the eggs, remaining salt, pepper, cinnamon, and remaining ¼ cup of sugar and add to the pasta mixture, tossing well. Transfer to the Bundt pan and bake, uncovered, until golden brown on top—1 to 1½ hours. Remove from the oven, turn kugel upside down on a serving plate, unmold, and serve.

EXCITING NOODLE KUGEL

SERVES 4–6. (D)

When my mother was just about my age, she edited *Regard Thy Table,* put out by the Larchmont Temple in Larchmont, New York. One of her favorite recipes in this charming book is Exciting Noodles, basically a savory noodle kugel with onions and sour cream. It can be prepared in advance and served for Friday or Saturday dinner if you are having a fish or vegetarian meal.

8 ounces medium-wide noodles
1 cup cottage or pot cheese
Salt
Dash of Tabasco sauce
1 tablespoon Worcestershire sauce

1 clove garlic, chopped
2 cups sour cream
1 onion, finely minced
Grated Parmesan cheese

1. Preheat the oven to 350 degrees and grease a 1½-quart casserole.
2. Cook the noodles until tender. Drain and combine with the cottage or pot cheese, salt, Tabasco, Worcestershire sauce, garlic, 1 cup of the sour cream, and onion.
3. Pour into the prepared casserole. Bake until brown and crusty on top. Serve with grated Parmesan cheese and additional sour cream.

CATHERINE PANTSIOS'S NOODLE PUDDING

MAKES ABOUT 24. (D)

At Zola's Restaurant in San Francisco, the husband-and-wife chef team like to include traditional recipes. This savory kugel is a perfect accompaniment to a poached salmon for a Friday night dinner.

8 ounces fine egg noodles
⅓ pound unsalted butter
1 cup small-curd cottage cheese
8 ounces cream cheese, softened
5 eggs

2 cups milk
Grated zest of 2 lemons
2 tablespoons caraway seeds
Salt and freshly ground pepper

1. Preheat the oven to 350 degrees and grease two 12-cup muffin tins.
2. Cook the egg noodles until tender. Drain and toss with the butter.
3. Blend together the cottage cheese, cream cheese, and eggs.
4. In a large bowl combine the noodles and butter with the egg-cheese mixture. Add the milk, lemon zest, caraway seeds, and salt and pepper to taste. Mix well.
5. Bake in the muffin tins for 1 hour or until puffy and slightly browned.

POTATO KUGEL

SERVES 8–10. (M OR P)

The potatoes never failed us. . . . For each meal, they looked different and tasted different. Once in a great while she [Tanta Malka] even managed a spoonful of chicken fat to flavor them with. For days afterward the smell of chicken fat would linger with me. And I'd even dream about it in my sleep. But the main stand-by for flavoring and trimming was the onion. There was no limit to its uses and versatility and there was no meal without it. Sliced, browned, or cooked, it was there. But onion or no onion, there was always the appetite. It was like a curse.

Yuri Suhl, *One Foot in America*

In the poorer shtetls of Eastern Europe, four eggs would have been a luxury in a potato kugel. The baking powder in the following recipe, an American addition, adds a lightness to the potatoes.

4 eggs
8 medium Idaho potatoes, peeled
1 large onion, peeled
6 tablespoons matzah meal
1½ teaspoons baking powder

2 teaspoons salt
¼ teaspoon pepper
¼ cup melted chicken fat or
  pareve margarine

1. Preheat the oven to 375 degrees and grease a soufflé dish.
2. Break the eggs in a medium bowl and set aside.
3. Grate the potatoes and onion in a food processor or by hand. Pour into a large strainer. Drain the liquid and combine the potatoes and onions with the eggs. Stir thoroughly and add the matzah meal, baking powder, salt, pepper, and chicken fat or margarine. Turn into the soufflé dish and spread evenly.
4. Bake in the oven, uncovered, for 30–45 minutes, until golden brown.

BULGARIAN ZUCCHINI *FRITADA*

(Simple Soufflé)

SERVES 4. (D)

Saturday breakfast after early morning synagogue is a special meal for the Sephardim. *Desayuno*—as this meal is called—has a quality all its own. *Huevos haminados* (hard-boiled eggs cooked in coffee grounds and onion peels to make the eggs brown) are served with buttery *burekas* filled with eggplant, spinach, or cheese. *Fritada,* a low egg soufflé with vegetables and feta or farmer cheese, is another easy dish to prepare. The following is an outstanding *fritada* recipe from Bulgaria.

1 pound zucchini, sliced thin
Salt
½ medium onion
2 tablespoons butter
8 ounces farmer or feta cheese

2 tablespoons chopped fresh dill
3 eggs
¼ cup grated Parmesan or
  kashkaval cheese

1. Set the sliced zucchini in a colander and sprinkle with salt. Let sit for at least 30 minutes. Squeeze out as much water as possible. Sauté the onion in butter and add the zucchini, cooking a few minutes. Transfer to a bowl and let cool.
2. Preheat the oven to 375 degrees and grease a 9-inch pie plate.
3. Crumble the farmer or feta cheese and add to the zucchini. Add salt if necessary. Sprinkle with dill.
4. Beat the eggs and add to the vegetables, mixing well.
5. Place the zucchini mixture in the pie plate and sprinkle with the Parmesan or *kashkaval*.
6. Bake for 45 minutes, or until golden brown.

LEBANESE RICE WITH SOUR LEMON SAUCE AND EGGPLANT

(Riz-au-Hamod with Eggplant)

SERVES 6–8. (M)

The following recipe is listed as Egyptian, Syrian, or Lebanese in various Middle Eastern cookbooks. This particular version of rice with sour lemon sauce and eggplant came from Annie Simonian Totah. Her Jewish husband, Sammy, was the number one student at the American University of Beirut and she, an Armenian, number two. The two fell in love, overcoming religious and ethnic differences. Annie learned this recipe from her Syrian-born mother-in-law. It is served on Friday nights. The chicken broth in this recipe was traditionally made from the necks, giblets, and wing bones of the chicken.

2 cups rich chicken broth or water

1 tablespoon vegetable oil

Salt and pepper

2 small cloves garlic, minced

2 tablespoons fresh parsley, chopped

2 stalks celery with leaves, chopped

1 tablespoon sugar

Dash of cayenne pepper

Dash of paprika

Juice of 2 lemons

1 medium eggplant or 2–3 dwarf eggplants, peeled and thickly chopped

2 cups uncooked rice

1. Place the chicken broth or water in a medium saucepan.
2. Add the oil, salt and pepper to taste, garlic, parsley, celery, sugar, cayenne, and paprika. Bring to a boil and add the lemon juice. (Use more lemon juice if desired.)
3. Add the eggplant. Simmer, uncovered, until the eggplant is soft, about 20 minutes.
4. Meanwhile, cook the rice. Serve the eggplant over the rice with broiled or roasted chicken and a green salad.

PICKLED PEACHES

Early Jewish settlers in this country also ate pickles, although a different sort from the kosher pickles described above. Abigail Franks of New York wrote letters to her son David, who was studying in England. She would send him preserved foods—fish, meat, strawberries, apples, and vegetables, including artichokes and cauliflower. In a letter from the year 1736, she wrote:

> I have sent you two Caggs of pickles one is 15 gallon filled with peper and the other ten with Mangoes Peaches and a few peper to fill up the Cask when you receive them take the Peaches and Mangoes from the peper and put fresh vinegar to them and that will take of the strength of the peper.

And here is the earliest recipe for pickled peaches I could find in this country. It is taken from Esther Levy's *Jewish Cookery Book* of 1871.

TO PICKLE PEACHES—Take a quarter of a pound of sugar to one pint of vinegar and scald the peaches, they should not be quite ripe; put them with some mace, allspice, cloves and nutmeg; when boiled take out the spice, and put the peaches in a jar; observe that the vinegar covers them, and put them away in a dry cool place. Pears and plums can be pickled the same way.

WILLIAM GREENBERG, JR.'S *SCHNECKEN*

With Help from Michael London

MAKES 24 REGULAR OR 48 MINI *SCHNECKEN*. (D)

William Greenberg, Jr., master of wedding cakes and *schnecken*, used to hold court in his carriage-trade shop at 1100 Madison Avenue in Manhattan. Growing up in the town of Lawrence, Long Island, he learned to bake from his aunt Gertrude. "At thirteen I started selling my cookies to my classmates, and then I graduated to baking for the Five Towns Woman's Exchange, in Cedarhurst. I sold *schnecken*, cookies, apple turnovers, and mocha tarts. Anything I liked to bake, I sold," he said. Even during a short stint in the army, where he was—what else?—a cook, he has been baking his entire life. Until he sold the business, Mr. Greenberg used to come into the Madison Avenue shop every day, don an apron over his hallmark polo shirt, and decorate the special-occasion cakes he made for at least two generations.

Schnecken ("snail" in German), parent to the American sticky buns, are made from a rich yeast dough sprinkled with raisins and sometimes nuts. That dough is rolled up, then sliced and baked, as at Greenberg's, in butter and brown sugar. By today's standards this recipe is rich—and worth every one of those calories.

THE DOUGH:

¾ pound (3 sticks) salted butter,
 at room temperature
½ cup sugar
3 large egg yolks
1 cup sour cream
3 scant tablespoons (3 packages)
 active dry yeast

1½ teaspoons white vinegar
1 teaspoon vanilla extract
5½–6 cups unbleached all-
 purpose flour

THE GLAZE AND FILLING:

1 pound (4 sticks) salted butter
5 cups light-brown sugar, loosely
 packed
2 cups roughly chopped pecans

1 tablespoon cinnamon
2 cups raisins, soaked in warm
 water a few minutes and
 drained

THE DOUGH:

1. Place the butter and sugar in an electric mixer fitted with the paddle and cream at a low speed until smooth. Add the egg yolks, 1 at a time, then the sour cream, yeast, vinegar, and vanilla, mixing at medium speed for about 3 minutes, until well incorporated.

2. Replace the paddle with the dough hook and add the flour gradually, mixing at a low speed for about 10 minutes. The dough will be soft and slightly sticky. Remove it, dust with flour, and divide into 2 pieces. Press each piece into a rectangle about 2 inches thick. Cover each piece with plastic wrap and refrigerate overnight.

THE GLAZE:

3. The next day, cut 2 sticks of the butter into 2-inch pieces and place them in a food processor fitted with the steel blade. Add 1¼ cups of the light-brown sugar and process until smooth. Remove the mixture to a bowl. Repeat with the remaining butter and 1¼ cups more of the sugar. Spoon the creamed butter-sugar mixture into the bottoms of twenty-four 3-inch or forty-eight 2-inch muffin cups. Using a pastry brush or the back of a spoon, coat the inside of the cups completely with the butter mixture. At Greenberg's, a pastry bag is used to do this.

4. Scatter the nuts generously over the butter-sugar mixture in the muffin cups and pat down gently.

ASSEMBLING AND BAKING THE *SCHNECKEN*:

5. Remove the dough from the refrigerator. Roll each portion into an 8- by 13-inch rectangle about ¼ inch thick for the 3-inch cups and ⅛ inch thick for the 2-inch cups.

6. Sprinkle each sheet of dough with 1¼ cups light-brown sugar, 1½ teaspoons cinnamon, and 1 cup raisins. Press a rolling pin gently over the filling. Roll the dough up carefully and tightly from the long side.

7. Trim the ends of the rolls slightly and cut each into 12 slices, about 1 inch thick for the regular *schnecken* and ½ inch thick for the mini *schnecken*. Place in the muffin tins, cut side down, so that the swirls are face up. Press them down gently into the tins. Then let the *schnecken* rise, covered with plastic wrap, for 30 minutes.

8. Preheat the oven to 325 degrees and bake the *schnecken* on the middle rack until golden, about 40 minutes, resting the tins on top of a cookie sheet in case there are spills. Remove them from the oven and immediately invert them onto waxed paper.

VARIATION: A COFFEE CAKE

Greenberg's also made a sour-cream coffee cake from half the dough: Roll out to a rectangle about 8 by 12 inches, sprinkle with ¾ cup brown sugar and 1 teaspoon cinnamon. Roll up like a large jelly roll from the long side, cut into 3 thick slices, and place each one, seam side up, in a greased 9- by 12-inch baking pan. Bake in a 325-degree oven on the middle rack for about 40 minutes.

"WE WERE GLAD WE HAD A LITTLE BREAD"

Ben Moskovitz

"The only reason I keep doing what I am doing is I don't want my recipes to die," said Ben Moskovitz, owner and baker of Star Bakery in Oak Park, Michigan. "You have to baby everything. Nothing is just given to you. It's hard work." This spectacled seventy-four-year-old man, wearing a white apron, a white base-ball cap, and a wide smile, works in his bakery fourteen hours a day, starting at 5:00 a.m.

For years I had heard about Mr. Moskovitz and his Star Bakery. On several occasions Michigan congressman Sander Levin brought me (and others, many others!) shopping bags filled with Star Bakery's corn rye, *babka,* and *kichel.* "He's the genuine article," Sandy kept telling me, and he was right.

Born in Apsha, Czechoslovakia (now in Ukraine), a country town of about two hundred Jewish families at the foot of the Carpathian Mountains, Mr. Moskovitz grew up on a farm. In 1939, Apsha was occupied by the Hungarian army under German rule. In 1941, the Nazis took his parents away, and he was sent to work camps in Hungary, where he planted trees, worked in a kitchen, and made bullets. In 1949, the American Jewish Joint Distribution Committee brought him to the United States. This is his story from that long-ago time before the war:

"In Apsha, we were living from the farm. Everybody grew their own stuff. We had land and we lived on it, with horses, a cow or two or three, and stables. Every person had a big garden. Poultry and geese we had. It was a big family with everybody busy. I had five brothers and two sisters. After the war, three brothers and one sister remained. My uncle became a farmer in Argentina and my brother Jack has a big farm in Michigan and likes to cowboy around.

"Because we had two ovens at home in Apsha, we baked for our Jewish neighbors. The big oven had a square opening in the floor in front of it, and you would step down and work that oven. The smaller oven, built on top of it, you could work standing on the regular floor, and it was used twice a week, on Tuesday and Friday. We didn't charge for using our oven on Fridays because we were neighbors and it was our custom.

"The big one was used for matzah and once in a while for holidays. People brought their flour and we charged for the labor. The rabbi supervised.

"We ate chicken once in a while, soup Friday night, and fish when you could catch them. There was a river right in front of the house. We caught mostly white fish, like perch. We had gefilte fish occasionally. At Hanukkah time we ate the geese and made *schmaltz.* We had a ball.

"There were no bakeries in town. Sometimes a driver with a horse and buggy went to Solotfina ten kilometers away and picked up bread. It was a rye bread. We didn't have bread like here—99 percent of the Jews made their bread at home.

Where we lived there was a water mill where they ground the corn, all the same formula. We ate *malai,* corn bread. It was made from ground corn and worked on the basis of a sour with only corn flour. It was crumbly, sandy, and sour. We ate that all week. *Mamaliga* [Romanian cornmeal mush] was the daily food for breakfast. For many people, *mamaliga* was a substitute for bread. Some people kept it a whole day for all their meals. We bought three kilos of white flour and made challah for Shabbos.

"For Shabbos we had challah until the war. Once in a while we could get white flour. Only the rich ones could afford white bread the whole week. I was poor; sugar at six dollars a kilo was a luxury—we never bought sugar; we couldn't afford that. When you are hungry things are different. We didn't add nothing but I adored the challah, it was so delicious. I know challah is better here. Ours was made from flour, yeast, and water. I never had nothing else. When I came to America I realized it is a different world. There is no comparison."

CHOCOLATE *BABKA*

From Ben Moskovitz

MAKES 1 LARGE AND 1 SMALL OR 3 SMALL *BABKA* LOAVES. (D OR P)

A *babka* is a high cake, but "babka" is also a word for grandmother in Polish, Russian, and Yiddish. My mother-in-law remembers her mother baking chocolate *babka* like Mr. Moskovitz's for the Sabbath. "And if there was any left over," she said, "my mother would slice it thin, sprinkle sugar and cinnamon on top, and bake it in the oven for breakfast. We didn't have any toaster ovens then. Now that was a treat!"

When making Star Bakery's *babka* recipe, I use imported bittersweet chocolate for the filling. I have also given choices to make this recipe pareve or dairy. You can make it with high-gluten and cake flour, as Mr. Moskovitz does, or simply use all-purpose flour. However you decide to fill your *babka,* this is a wonderful recipe.

THE CAKE:

1 cup lukewarm milk or water

1 scant tablespoon (1 package)
    active dry yeast

5½ cups unbleached all-purpose
    flour (approximately)

½ pound (2 sticks) unsalted

butter or pareve margarine, at
    room temperature

⅔ cup sugar

1½ teaspoons salt

5 large eggs

1½ teaspoons vanilla extract

THE FILLING AND EGG WASH*

4 tablespoons (½ stick) unsalted
    butter or pareve margarine

¾ cup apricot jam or ¼ cup
    almond paste

1 cup leftover cake or pound-cake
    crumbs

¾ cup chopped almonds
    (optional)

9 ounces good bittersweet
    chocolate, preferably
    imported

1 large egg, beaten

1 tablespoon water

THE STREUSEL:

3 tablespoons sugar

6 tablespoons unbleached all-
    purpose flour

3 tablespoons unsalted butter or
    pareve margarine

THE CAKE:

1. Place the milk or water, yeast, and 2 cups of the flour in the bowl of an electric mixer fitted with the paddle. Mix for about 1 minute on low speed until well incorporated. Transfer this "sponge" to another bowl. Cover with a towel and let it sit for 1 hour, until doubled in size.

2. Cream the butter or margarine and the sugar in the bowl of the electric mixer. Add the sponge, salt, eggs, and vanilla, and continue mixing at a low speed until incorporated, about 3 minutes. Gradually add the remaining 3½ cups of the flour and work the ingredients for 12–15 minutes on low speed until the

*See also the apple filling on page 98.

dough is smooth, adding more flour as needed. The dough will be soft. Remove the dough from the bowl. Divide it into 3 pieces and dust the pieces with flour. Cover each loosely with plastic wrap and refrigerate overnight.

3. The next day, remove the dough from the refrigerator and let it sit for about 20 minutes while you prepare the filling. Dust a work surface with flour. Shape 1 piece of the dough with your hands into a rough oblong, adding more flour if needed, and roll it out into a rectangle about 8 by 12 inches, ¼ inch thick.

FILLING AND ASSEMBLING THE *BABKAS*:

4. Melt the butter or margarine and place it in a food processor fitted with the steel blade. Add the apricot jam or almond paste and the cake crumbs and process until smooth. Spoon one-third of the filling onto one of the dough rectangles and spread it with a spatula, leaving a ½-inch border all around. Sprinkle with one-third of the almonds. Grate the chocolate in the food processor and sprinkle one-third of it over the dough, leaving the borders. Brush the borders with the egg mixed with water to help seal the *babka.*

5. Roll the dough up like a jelly roll from the longer side, close the ends, and then gently twist the roll into a spiral. Fit this into a greased 9- by 5-inch loaf pan. Fill and roll up the other 2 rectangles of dough. Either twist them as above and put them in loaf pans, or make 1 large *babka.* To make a large *babka,* link 2 rolls (not twisted) end to end in a circle in a greased 9- or 10-inch *babka* or Bundt pan, seam side up, and press the ends together.

MAKING THE STREUSEL AND BAKING THE *BABKAS*:

6. Using your fingers, combine the sugar, flour, and butter or margarine and sprinkle one-third on top of each *babka.* Let the *babka*s rise over the tops of the pans, about 1 hour.

7. Preheat the oven to 350 degrees.

8. Bake the *babka*s on the middle rack for 45 minutes, or until the streusel is golden brown. Mr. Moskovitz says to press on the dough. If your finger goes in easily, the *babka* is not done.

VARIATION: APPLE FILLING

1 pound flavorful apples, peeled,
    cored, and coarsely chopped
    (about 2 apples)

2 tablespoons sugar
½ teaspoon cinnamon

1. On a lightly floured board, roll out one-third of the dough to a rectangle 6 by 18 inches. Mix the apples, sugar, and cinnamon in a small bowl. Cover half of the dough with the apple mixture, leaving bare a rectangle 6 by 9 inches, and leaving a ½-inch border all around. Brush the border with the egg wash. Fold the uncovered half of the dough over the half with the apples, pinch the edges to seal, and gently twist the dough along the 6-inch ends, as you would wring out a towel.
2. Place the dough in a greased 9- by 5-inch loaf pan and proceed as you did with the chocolate *babka* in making the streusel and baking.

KUCHEM-BUCHEM

(Cocoa-dipped Babka Rolls)

From Jeannie Lazinsky

MAKES 9 *KUCHEM-BUCHEM*. (D OR P)

Babka dough can be twisted into all kinds of wonderful shapes. One outrageously delicious variation is *kuchem-buchem,* clusters of *babka* dough filled and rolled in cocoa and then baked. It comes from Jeannie Lazinsky of Baltimore, Maryland. *Kuchem-buchem* is one of those marvelous made-up Yiddish rhyming names.

¼ pound (1 stick) unsalted butter or pareve margarine, at room temperature
¼ cup Dutch-process unsweetened cocoa

¾ cup sugar
2 cups *babka* dough (one-third of the *babka* dough recipe on page 96)

1. Melt the butter or margarine and mix it with the cocoa and sugar.
2. Take the dough from the refrigerator and knead it for about 5 minutes.
3. Divide the dough into 9 pieces and shape them into balls. Take a teaspoon of the cocoa mixture and, using your fingers, press it into the middle of one of the balls and gently reshape the ball. Repeat with the other balls of dough. Place the remaining cocoa mixture in a wide bowl and roll the balls of dough in it. Then fit them side by side into a greased 8- by 8-inch pan. Cover and let the balls of dough rise in a warm place for about 1½ hours.
4. Preheat the oven to 350 degrees and bake the *kuchem-buchem* on the middle rack for 25–30 minutes, or until firm outside.

KICHEL

(Bow Tie Cookies)

From Ben Moskovitz

MAKES ABOUT 70 *KICHEL*. (P)

Kichel, coming from the same root as *kuchen* in Yiddish, means "cookie" and is either sweet or savory. This particular version, rolled in sugar before baking, is very light—it melts in your mouth. "On Saturday night in Apsha, before the war, people had tea and *kichel,*" said Ben Moskovitz while making this recipe.

5 large eggs
½ teaspoon vanilla extract
⅔ cup vegetable oil
1 teaspoon sugar, plus 1 cup for
    rolling

2⅓ cups high-gluten or
    unbleached all-purpose flour
1 teaspoon salt

1. Place the eggs, vanilla, oil, 1 teaspoon sugar, the flour, and salt in the bowl of an electric mixer fitted with the paddle and blend on low speed until incorporated; then beat on high for 5 minutes.
2. Remove the paddle and scrape the batter down the sides of the bowl. Rest the dough in the bowl, covered, until soft and spongy outside, about 1 hour. Then remove it from the bowl—it will be sticky—and make a ball out of it.
3. Preheat the oven to 350 degrees and grease 2 cookie sheets.
4. Sprinkle a work surface with ½ cup of the sugar, about ⅛ inch deep. Place the dough in the center, flatten it slightly with a rolling pin, and sprinkle the dough liberally with remaining ½ of sugar. "Don't be bashful with the sugar," says Mr. Moskovitz. Roll the dough to a thickness of ⅛ inch, a rectangle about 18 by 12 inches. Then, using a pastry cutter or a dull knife, cut the dough into strips ¾ inch wide and 2 inches long. Lift each strip, twist in the middle to make a bow tie, and place on the cookie sheets, leaving ½ inch around each strip.
5. Bake the *kichel* for 25–30 minutes on the middle rack of the oven, until the

cookies are hard to the touch on all corners and golden brown. (If using 1 oven, put the cookie sheets on the top and center racks; then switch them midway.) To test for doneness, break a *kichel* in half. If it is doughy or too soft, it is not done yet. Return to the oven for a few minutes more.

UKRAINIAN *KAMISH BROIT*

MAKES ABOUT 36. (P)

This easily prepared zwieback-type cookie was always on hand in Ukrainian-Jewish households. It is served at any time for unexpected guests and is perfect on a Sabbath afternoon.

1½ cups unbleached all-purpose flour
½ teaspoon salt
1 teaspoon baking powder
3 eggs, at room temperature
1 cup plus 2 teaspoons sugar
¼ cup corn oil

¼ cup orange juice
1 teaspoon vanilla extract
1 cup chopped almonds or walnuts, or half nuts and half raisins or chopped dates
1¼ teaspoons cinnamon

1. Preheat the oven to 350 degrees and grease two 9- by 5-inch loaf pans.
2. Sift the flour, salt, and baking powder into a bowl.
3. Using a beater or food processor, beat the eggs until fluffy. Add 1 cup of the sugar and beat until the mixture turns pale yellow.
4. Mix together the oil, orange juice, and vanilla. Stir into the eggs, alternating with the flour mixture. Blend in the nuts or fruit-nut mixture.
5. Cover the bottom of the loaf pans with a little of the batter. Sprinkle with a little cinnamon and repeat until all the batter and 1 teaspoon of the cinnamon are used up.
6. Bake for 30 minutes. Cool, turn out of the pans, and cut into ½-inch slices.

7. Turn up the oven to 400 degrees. Arrange the slices on a baking sheet. Combine the remaining 2 teaspoons of sugar and ¼ teaspoon of cinnamon. Sprinkle on cookies. Return to the oven and brown for about 10 minutes, or until golden.

MANDELBROT

(Almond Bread)

MAKES 3 LOAVES. (P OR D)

Particular tea drinkers have always on their 5 o'clock tea tray a special kind of sugar. This is made from the beet and comes in thin oblongs better suited to tiny teacups than are the usual cubes. It is claimed, too, by connoisseurs, that this sugar gives just the right flavour.

New York Jewish Messenger, May 12, 1899

And with this sugar, most probably first brought to these shores by Marrano Jews in the seventeenth century, a sweet is always eaten. *Mandelbrot* is a typical cookie for Saturday afternoon tea. This recipe is a perfect accompaniment to a fruit dessert.

½ pound (2 sticks) unsalted
    pareve margarine or butter,
    softened
1½ cups sugar
4 eggs
1 teaspoon vanilla extract
½ cup whiskey or brandy
4 cups unbleached all-purpose
    flour

4 teaspoons baking powder
1 teaspoon salt
1 cup raisins
1 cup grated unsweetened
    coconut
½ cup chopped walnuts
1 cup slivered, blanched, and
    toasted almonds

1. Preheat the oven to 350 degrees and grease and flour 3 pans approximately 4½ by 10 inches.
2. Cream together the margarine or butter and sugar.
3. Beat the eggs well and combine slowly with the margarine or butter. Add the vanilla and whiskey. If the mixture looks curdled, add a little of the flour.
4. Sift the flour with the baking powder and salt. Add to the margarine or butter mixture. Mix well.
5. Blend in the raisins, coconut, walnuts, and almonds and turn the dough into the prepared pans.
6. Bake about 30 minutes, until done. Cool and slice thin. Arrange on a baking sheet and place in a 400-degree oven for a few minutes until golden brown.

"JEWISH" APPLE CAKE

MAKES 1 CAKE. (P)

I came across the identical listing for "Jewish" Apple Cake in two local Maryland cookbooks—one the *Favorite Recipes from Trinity Church* in St. Mary's City and the other *Mrs. Kitching's Smith Island Cookbook* (1981). Mrs. Kitching, who until recently ran a popular boardinghouse, got this recipe from her grandmother who lived on Smith Island, population 550, all her life. It might be considered Jewish because there is oil rather than butter or lard in the batter. In any event, the crumbly exterior and moist texture reminded my husband of all the Polish-Jewish cakes his mother and aunts made during his childhood.

5 large apples (Granny Smith, Golden Delicious, Gala, or Jonathan), unpeeled
Juice of 1 lemon
2 teaspoons cinnamon
2 cups sugar
4 eggs, at room temperature

1 cup vegetable oil
½ cup orange juice, at room temperature
2 teaspoons vanilla extract
3 cups unsifted flour
1 tablespoon baking powder
½ teaspoon salt

1. Preheat the oven to 350 degrees. Grease a 10-inch tube pan and dust with flour.
2. Core and cut the apples into thin slices. Place in a large bowl, toss with the lemon juice, and sprinkle with the cinnamon and 5 tablespoons of the sugar.
3. Beat the eggs and gradually add the remaining sugar, oil, orange juice, and vanilla.
4. Sift together the flour, baking powder, and salt. Add to the wet mixture and mix thoroughly with a spoon.
5. Pour one third of the batter into the pan. Layer with one third of the apples. Repeat for 2 more layers, ending with apples on top.
6. Bake for 1½ hours, until golden on top. Let sit a few minutes and then run a knife gently around the sides of the mold. Cover with a plate and invert to remove from the pan.

PEAR KUGEL

SERVES 4–6. (D OR P)

The following kugel is an unusual dessert recipe I found in the 1947 *Community Cookbook* of Congregation B'nai Israel in Woonsocket, Rhode Island. I was fortunately able to contact Mrs. Coleman Falk, who chaired the writing of this excellent collection of authentic Jewish recipes. During the war years, she and a number of other ladies observed the older members of their community making dishes. Thus, they were able to write down and preserve an oral tradition. The recipe calls for steaming the kugel in water, but it could very well be steamed inside a *cholent* pot in the traditional way described on page 80.

FILLING:

3 pears, peeled, cleaned, and sliced	Pinch of salt
½ cup sugar	½ cup raisins
1 teaspoon cinnamon	4–5 prunes, washed, soaked,
Pinch of nutmeg	pitted, and diced

DOUGH:

1½ cups flour

¼ teaspoon salt

2 teaspoons baking powder

1 teaspoon sugar

1 egg

4 tablespoons (½ stick) butter or
  pareve margarine

3 tablespoons ice water
  (approximately)

1. Mix all the filling ingredients and set aside.
2. Preheat the oven to 250 degrees. Grease a 2-quart round baking dish.
3. Sift the flour, salt, baking powder, and sugar together. Add the egg and 2 table-spoons of butter or margarine and work into a medium-loose dough with your hands or a food processor. Add a little water if too stiff. If too loose to roll, add a little flour (the softer the dough, the better). Knead into a round ball. Roll out about ⅛ inch thick.
4. Sprinkle the filling mixture all over the dough. Dot with the remaining 2 tablespoons of butter or margarine. Fold the outside edges in toward the center, pinching into the shape of a ball. With a wide spatula, transfer to a baking dish.
5. Set this dish into a larger pan filled with enough hot water to come halfway up the sides of the kugel dish. Cover the kugel tightly and bake 4 hours or overnight. Remove the cover for the last 30 minutes. As the water evaporates in the outer pan, add more water so that the kugel will brown slowly and not burn. Alternatively, you can bake the kugel for 1 hour at 375 degrees, without the water bath.

HOT FRUIT COMPOTE

SERVES 8. (P OR D)

This recipe originated in Eastern Europe as a simple fruit compote, with honey, water, and dried fruits. Transplanted to the United States—where more glamorous ingredients are available—it has become a fancier dish.

4 cups canned mixed fruits,
    drained, with juice reserved
½ pound dried prunes
½ pound dried apricots
¼ cup brown sugar
½ cup brandy

Juice of ½ lemon
½ teaspoon cinnamon
12 dried macaroons, crumbled
4 tablespoons (½ stick) pareve
    margarine or butter

1. Preheat the oven to 350 degrees and grease a 2½-quart covered casserole.
2. Fill the casserole with the drained canned fruits, prunes, apricots, brown sugar, brandy, lemon juice, and cinnamon. Add the reserved juice to barely cover the fruit. Cover and bake for 30 minutes.
3. Sprinkle the crumbled macaroon over the top. Dot with margarine or butter and bake 15 minutes more, uncovered. Serve hot or cold.

CHOCOLATE MOUSSE TORTE

SERVES 12. (D OR P)

It is traditional to serve some sort of kugel, or pudding, on the Sabbath. This pudding cake is to remind us of the manna, which was covered with dew. It was supposed to be white, like coriander seed. Just as manna was considered a delicacy in the desert, mousse, a rich pudding, has become a dessert delicacy for us. This chocolate mousse torte comes from Sharon Hoffman, owner of Panache Chocolatier in Kansas City. The recipe, which can also be used at Passover, first appeared in a slightly different version in *Beyond Parsley,* the Kansas City Junior League's award-winning cookbook of 1984. I have found different versions in Hungary, Mexico, and Israel.

5 ounces pure bittersweet chocolate	½ pound (2 sticks) unsalted butter or pareve margarine, at room temperature
3 ounces semisweet chocolate	
1 cup sugar	8 eggs, separated

1. Preheat the oven to 325 degrees and grease and flour a 9-inch springform pan.
2. Melt the chocolates in a double boiler. Combine the sugar, butter or margarine, and melted chocolate; mix well and let cool. Add the egg yolks, 2 at a time, beating after each addition.
3. Whip the egg whites until stiff. Gently fold the egg whites into the chocolate mixture.
4. Pour ¾ of the batter into the springform pan. Bake 35 minutes, or until a toothpick inserted in the center comes out clean. Let the cake stand at room temperature until cool. Spread the remaining batter on top.
5. Refrigerate or freeze until serving time. Serve cold, frozen, or at room temperature.

HAVDALAH SPICES

The Emperor asked Rabbi Joshua ben Hananiah, "What gives your Sabbath meal such an aroma?" He replied, "We have a spice called Sabbath which is put in the cooking of the meat, and this gives it its aroma." The Emperor said, "Give me some of this spice." He replied, "For him who keeps the Sabbath, the spice works; for him who does not keep it, it does not work."

Sabbath 119a

As soon as the first stars are seen in the sky the Havdalah candle is lit. Two separate candles usher in the Sabbath; the Havdalah candle has at least two and usually three entwined wicks that come together as we enter the new week with the experience of Shabbat strengthening us.

In cooking for the Sabbath and other holidays, we sometimes forget the importance of using real "spice and spirit." Spices form an essential part of the Sabbath in the Havdalah service after sunset. First there is a blessing over the wine, which symbolizes joy; then the spices are blessed. Any aromatic spice or seasonal flower will do. Cinnamon and cloves are traditional. The spices symbolize the spiritual riches of the Sabbath and are sniffed before replacing them in the *hadas,* or receptacle. These spices are to cheer the soul—so saddened with the departure of the Sabbath.

ROSH
HASHANAH

ROSH HASHANAH

And God said: "Let the earth put forth grass, herb yielding seed, and fruit-tree bearing fruit after its kind, wherein is the seed thereof, upon the earth." And it was so. And the earth brought forth grass, herb yielding seed after its kind, and tree bearing fruit, wherein is the seed thereof, after its kind; and God saw that it was good.

Genesis 1:11–12

Go your way, eat the fat, and drink the sweet, and send portions unto him for whom nothing is prepared; for this day is holy unto our Lord.

Nehemiah 8:10

The Jewish New Year, the anniversary of the Creation, is a time for self-examination and repentance. It comes ten days before Yom Kippur, the day on which divine judgment is sealed. The shofar—a horn of a ram or one of the four other animals specified in the Talmud, whose tradition in Jewish history stems from the time when God permitted Abraham to substitute a ram for Isaac as a sacrifice—is sounded. Blowing the ram's horn has become a symbol of the complete faith of Abraham and of the Jewish people.

The ancient peoples had no organized New Year but rather calculated the year from the new moon nearest to the beginning of the barley harvest in spring (at Passover) or to the ingathering of the fruits (Sukkot) in autumn. Rosh Hashanah—the time of the new moon close to the latter holiday—was eventually adopted as the beginning of the festal year. Today it is one of the great solemn days of the Jewish faith.

The Rosh Hashanah table is laden with delicacies representing optimism for a sweet future. Dishes abound with honey, raisins, carrots, and apples—all seasonal reminders of hope for the coming year.

No sour or bitter dishes have a place on this joyous table. Moroccans, for example, will not eat black foods such as olives or eggplants, whose color and possible bitter taste might augur evil for the coming year. Lebanese will not eat salty or lemony foods, and Bulgarians prefer to eat sweet-and-sour foods.

Some Eastern European Jews—those from the Ukraine—will not serve cucumbers, pickles, horseradish, or even walnuts or almonds. The sourness of the first three is obvious, but the reason the nuts are avoided is less so. The total numerical value of the letters of the Hebrew word for walnut, *egoz*, is seventeen, equivalent to the numerical value of the Hebrew word for sin, *het*. Almonds might be avoided because, historically, the almond branch of Aaron's rod included sweet almonds on one side and bitter on the other. As long as Israel walked in the ways of the Lord, sweet almonds were fresh (moist); but when they departed from the right path, the bitter ones ripened. Thus, at the day of judgment the superstitious would avoid all nuts. (In addition, nuts and almonds stimulate an increased flow of saliva, which interferes with the recital of prayers.)

Because of the original harvest-festival character of Rosh Hashanah, it is natural that, for the ancients, the symbolic foods would be chosen from those fruits and vegetables abundant at that time of year.

Both Sephardic and Ashkenazic Jews say a blessing over an apple dipped in honey. "May it be Thy will to renew unto us a good and sweet year." On the second night, another new fruit (a pomegranate when available) evokes the blessing: "In the coming year may we be rich and replete with acts inspired by religion and piety as this pomegranate is rich and replete with seeds." Either a new fruit of the season is eaten or a new garment is worn on the second night at the kiddush, because new fruits and garments rate the Sheheheyanu prayer, the blessing for new experiences.

In addition to the above fruits, Sephardic Jews say blessings over other seasonal foods. Pumpkins, fenugreek, leeks, onions, beets, turnips, gourds, quinces, and zucchini all grow rapidly in the early fall and are considered symbolic of fertility, abundance, and prosperity.

Moroccan Jews dip a date in anise seeds, sesame seeds, and powdered sugar. "As we eat this date, may we date the new year that is beginning as one of happiness and blessing and peace for all mankind."

Most important is the cooked head of a fish or lamb. The head expresses the hope that the New Year will see the Jewish nation redeemed and at the head of the nations of the world, rather than at the tail as a small, downtrodden people.

Before these symbolic foods are blessed, the meal begins with the blessing over the wine and the round challah for a full year. The foods selected for the meal are usually colorful and sweet. Carrots, prunes, honey, apples, and sweet potatoes are all present. The carrots, prunes, honey, and apples in the recipes that follow are all seasonal reminders of the hope for a good New Year. Jews throughout the world bake sweets with honey, *mit lechig* in Yiddish, for this holiday.

One of my favorite meals of the year is lunch after the first day of Rosh Hashanah. I invite a few close friends and family to a buffet after synagogue. After blessing the round challah for a full year, dipping an apple in honey, and saying a prayer over a date, a custom I learned from the Israeli ambassador, we linger over lunch—gefilte fish, brisket, salads, *zwetschgenkuchen,* honey cake, or Edda Servi Machlin's version of *teyglakh.*

MENUS

GERMAN
Berches (Potato Challah)
Herkimer Chicken Soup with
Nockerln
German Sweet-and-Sour Carp
Roast Goose
Carrots
German-style Cucumber Salad
German Potato Salad
Zwetschgenkuchen
Splendid Streusel

MIXED SEPHARDIC
Pain Pétri
Greek *Rodanchos* (Squash Strudel)
Egg-Lemon Soup
Grilled Fish
Lebanese Stuffed Zucchini with
Apricots
Meat *Sambusak* (meat-filled)
Green Salad
Fresh Fruit: Grapes, Apples,
Plums
Almond Macaroons

RUSSIAN

Four-Hundred-Year-Old Challah

Zamosc Gefilte Fish

Chicken Soup with Matzah Balls

Roast Beef or Turkey
with Stuffing

Pineapple Noodle Kugel

Green Beans

Baked Apples

Heidi Wortzel's Honey Cake

MOROCCAN

Pain Pétri (Moroccan Challah)

Seven Vegetables

Baked Whitefish

Dates Dipped in Anise, Sesame
Seeds, and Sugar

Apple Dipped in Honey

Moroccan Lamb *Tagine* with
Prunes and Almonds

Moroccan Carrot Salad

Meat *Pastels*

Fresh Fruit

Moroccan *Cigares*

MY ROSH HASHANAH BUFFET

Ultimate Challah

Zamosc Gefilte Fish

My Mother's Brisket

Pineapple Noodle Kugel

Zwetschgenkuchen

FOUR-HUNDRED-YEAR-OLD CHALLAH

MAKES 6 LOAVES. (P)

One of the most symbolic foods at Rosh Hashanah has become the round challah. This spiral of bread, often studded with raisins or saffron, recalls the image of prayer rising heavenward. Usually the bread is formed in a circle, to signify the desire for a long span of life. It can be braided into a long challah and then twisted into a circle; the dough can be divided into a braided circle topped by a smaller circle, or twisted spiral fashion into a circle with the end of the spiral on top, symbolically ascending to heaven.

In certain towns of Russia, the round challah was imprinted with the shape of a ladder on the top. This ladder symbolizes the ascent to God on high. A Midrash, or explanatory rabbinic story, states that on Rosh Hashanah, the "Holy One, blessed be He, sits and erects ladders; on them He lowers one person and elevates another . . . that is to say, God judges those who will descend and those who will ascend."

In the Ukraine, perhaps in Kolikow, a town known for bread, bread for the holidays is baked in the form of a bird, symbolizing the protection of God's people, as stated in Isaiah 31:5: "As birds hovering [over their fledglings], so will the Lord of hosts protect Jerusalem." Jews from Lithuania bake challahs topped with a crown, in accordance with the words of the great liturgical poet Eleazar Kalir: "And thus let all crown God."

This particular recipe comes from Mark Talisman, one of our capital's finest cooks. He learned how to make this challah from Russian-born Esther Becker of Cleveland. When Talisman was administrative assistant to Ohio congressman Charles Vanik, he helped Mrs. Becker solve a difficult problem. One day this elderly lady with long braided hair came to see Talisman when he was visiting his family in Cleveland. Like every Jewish mother since antiquity, she came bearing a gift—this time a huge, expertly braided challah—and asked what she could do to repay him for helping her. "Teach me to make your bread," said Talisman. Now, a woman like Esther Becker "feels" her ingredients rather than measures them, so Talisman devised a fail-safe system to record the recipe. He placed soft plastic lids over the mixing bowls to rescue and measure the proportions before Mrs. Becker could add each new ingredient.

Talisman has varied the recipe slightly by using a food processor and hard wheat flour. This challah was made on Friday mornings in Mrs. Becker's family in Russia and has been handed down by word of mouth for generations.

Before eating the round challah this Rosh Hashanah, don't forget the blessing over the bread, and instead of dipping it into salt as is done on Friday nights, dip it, for the Days of Awe, in honey. Then say the blessing over a honey-dipped slice of apple: "May it be Thy will to renew unto us a good and sweet year."

3 tablespoons (3 packages) active
    dry yeast
2½ cups very warm (not
    lukewarm) water
Pinch of sugar
15 cups all-purpose flour
1½–2 tablespoons salt
½–1 cup honey

6 extra-large eggs
½ cup vegetable oil
½ cup cinnamon and sugar
    mixture (optional)
1¼ cups raisins (optional)
Egg and water for glazing
Sesame seeds

1. In a large glass container, dissolve the yeast in 2 cups of the water. (It is important that the water not be lukewarm, especially in winter.) Add a pinch of sugar. Stir with a plastic or wooden spoon to mix the yeast. Wait about 5 minutes until the yeast has a head on it, like beer.

2. Mix the flour and salt. Place on a floured flat surface and make a well in the center. Using a wooden or plastic spoon, put the yeast mixture in the well and begin slowly to stir flour from the inner edge of the well into it.

3. Add the honey to the well and stir in more flour from the edge of the well. Break the eggs one by one and stir into the well. Stir the oil into the well. Blend the remaining flour with the ingredients in the well. The dough should be sticky. If it is not, add more water, a little at a time, until sticky.

4. Either knead by hand for about 10–15 minutes, until the dough is smooth and shiny, or divide the dough into 6 parts and run each part in the food processor, using the steel blade. When the dough forms a ball—about 1 minute—it is done. Knead the individual balls together by hand. If it is too sticky, add a little flour to the mixture in the food processor; if it is too dry, add a little water. The finished dough should be tacky to touch.

5. Place the dough in a lightly greased bowl. (Use margarine for greasing in the winter.)

6. Heat the oven to its lowest setting. Turn the oven off, place the dough in the oven, and let it rise until doubled in size. This should take 45–60 minutes. Take care not to let it over-rise.

7. Punch the dough down and divide it into 6 equal pieces. Shape each piece into a ball.

8. Take 3 of the balls, knead well, shape in 3 oblong balls, and place in 3 greased loaf pans.

9. If desired, you can roll out the fourth ball into a rectangle, sprinkle with cinnamon and sugar, and spread a cup of raisins over it. Pressing the raisins gently into the dough, roll it, starting at the shorter side, jelly-roll fashion, and press the dough together into an oblong form. Place in a fourth loaf pan.

10. With the remaining 2 loaves (or all 6 if you prefer), make your Friday night or Rosh Hashanah challah. Work the remaining ¼ cup raisins into the dough at this point, if desired. Divide each ball into 4 pieces. Make a ball of each piece. Then pat the ball down very hard with your hand. Roll, jelly-roll fashion, once, press down, and roll again. Then, with your hands, roll out to make a rope about 12 inches long. Repeat with all the remaining balls.

11. Place 4 ropes side by side. Press the top ends together and start braiding. Take one outside rope, place it over the nearest one and then under the next. Then, before braiding the opposite outside rope, pull the braids tight. This is important, because it makes the braids higher during baking and thus gives a lighter, higher loaf. Continue braiding and tuck in the ends.

12. For Rosh Hashanah and the first Saturday of each month, gently work the braids into a circle and pinch the ends together. If you want a spiral effect, see the *Pain Pétri* on page 119.

13. Brush the challah with the egg mixed with water and sprinkle with sesame seeds. Place on a greased cookie sheet. If you prefer, the round challah may be put in an 8–9-inch round pan.

14. Cover all the loaves and let rise again, about 1 hour (or less), until the loaves come above the top of the loaf pans.

15. Preheat the oven to 375 degrees.

16. Glaze the challah again with egg mixed with water. Bake in the oven for 30 minutes, or until golden. Cool on racks before slicing. Wrapped tightly, this

bread will last through the week—until you run out and it is time to start baking all over again.

Note: If you would like to make a saffron challah for Rosh Hashanah, add ⅛ teaspoon of powdered saffron at the end of step 1.

You can also reduce the vegetable oil to ¼ cup and add more water.

PAIN PÉTRI
(Moroccan Challah)

MAKES 5 LOAVES. (P)

Years ago, I tasted this flavorful, almost cakelike challah spiked with anise at the home of Moroccan Jews. Recently, in Paris, I went to a Jewish Moroccan bakery, hoping to taste the bread once again. Alas, this second generation of Moroccan Jews, raised in Paris, had Ashkenazied the bread. They called it Moroccan, but it tasted like traditional European challah and there was no anise flavor.

In Morocco, as in most Middle Eastern countries, bread for centuries has been bought daily from special bakeries rather than made at home. On the Sabbath and special holidays, however, Jews knead their own sweet bread. With the French colonization of Morocco at the beginning of the twentieth century came an overwhelming desire on the part of Moroccan Jews to adopt everything French—their speech, manners, and cuisine. Today, recipes for Jewish holidays include French rather than Spanish names. Moroccan challah was once called *pan de casa,* or "bread of the house," in Hakitia, a mixture of Spanish, Hebrew, and Arabic. In French, the Sabbath bread is called *pain pétri,* or "kneaded bread," since the women spend a great deal of time kneading it to achieve its perfect smooth, light texture. For the Sabbath and Rosh Hashanah, it is studded with sesame and anise seeds. For Yom Kippur eve, raisins and blanched almonds are also added. The bread is often braided in intricate, delicate designs for the Sabbath; it is usually a circle for Rosh Hashanah.

You can either make this by hand or use a food processor.

7–8 cups unbleached all-purpose flour	1 teaspoon salt
⅓ cup sugar	1 tablespoon sesame seeds
3 eggs plus 1 yolk	1 tablespoon anise seeds
⅓ cup plus 1 tablespoon vegetable oil	1½ scant tablespoons (1½ packages) active dry yeast
	1½ cups warm water

1. Place 7 cups of flour in a huge bowl. Make a well in the center and place the sugar, 3 eggs, ⅓ cup of oil, salt, and sesame and anise seeds in the well. Dissolve the yeast in the warm water, then add it to the well.
2. Using your hands, gradually work in the flour with the ingredients in the well. Add more flour as needed. When a medium-stiff dough is formed, knead on a wooden board for about 20 minutes.
3. Form the dough into a ball, turn it in a greased bowl to coat the surface, and cover with a towel. Let rise in a warm place for 30–40 minutes, or until doubled in size. Punch down and knead once more. Divide the dough into 5 pieces. Either shape each into a round ball or make a long piece of it and twist it into a spiral with the end of the dough at the high point in the center. Cover and let rise for about 1 hour, until doubled in size.
4. Preheat the oven to 375 degrees. Cover a cookie sheet with aluminum foil.
5. Remove the dough to the cookie sheet. Brush with the remaining egg yolk mixed with the tablespoon of oil and bake for 35 to 45 minutes.

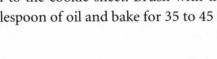

PARISIAN *PLETZEL*

From Finkelsztajn's

MAKES 8 *PLETZEL*. (P)

This Parisian version of a Bialystoker *tsibele* (onion) *pletzel*, also called onion *zemmel*, onion *pampalik*, or onion board, is very similar to an Italian *focaccia*. Try this flat bread sprinkled with rosemary, and you will see how very close it is.

1 cup lukewarm water
1 scant tablespoon (1 package) active dry yeast
4–5 cups unbleached all-purpose flour
2 large eggs
¼ cup plus 2 tablespoons vegetable oil

1 scant tablespoon sugar
2 teaspoons salt
½ cup cold water
1 medium onion, diced (about ¾ cup)
2 tablespoons poppy seeds
Kosher salt

1. Mix the water with the yeast in a large glass bowl. Add 4 cups of the flour, the eggs, ¼ cup of oil, the sugar, and the salt to the yeast mixture. Stir well, then turn the dough out onto a work surface and knead for about 10 minutes, or until smooth, adding more flour if necessary. Let the dough rise, covered with a towel, for 1 hour in a greased bowl. You can also leave the dough in the refrigerator for several hours or overnight.
2. Preheat the oven to 375 degrees and grease 2 cookie sheets.
3. Divide the dough into 8 balls and roll or flatten them into rounds about 5 inches in diameter. Place 4 *pletzel* on each cookie sheet and gently press down the centers. Brush with water and sprinkle each with about 2 tablespoons of diced onions, leaving a ½-inch border. Drizzle the remaining 2 tablespoons of oil over the onions and sprinkle with the poppy seeds and some kosher salt. Let sit for 15 minutes, uncovered.
4. Bake the *pletzel* for 20 minutes, switching from the top to the middle rack after 10 minutes, or do them in 2 shifts on the middle rack. Then stick them

under the broiler for 1 minute, keeping a sharp eye on them, to brown the onions. If you don't have a broiler, raise the heat to 550 degrees and put each sheet on the top rack for 2 minutes or so.

ALGERIAN SWISS CHARD *BESTELS*

(Turnovers)

MAKES 12 TURNOVERS. (P)

This Algerian-Jewish dish, served at Rosh Hashanah, comes from Leone Jaffin's *150 Recettes et Mille et un Souvenirs d'une Juive d'Algérie* [150 Recipes and 1,001 Memories of an Algerian Jew] (Encre Edition, 1980).

2 pounds Swiss chard or spinach, washed	1 dozen 5-inch egg-roll wrappers (see Note)
2 hard-boiled eggs, mashed	1 egg, slightly beaten
Salt and freshly ground pepper	Peanut oil for frying

1. If the Swiss chard leaves are small, leave them whole. Otherwise, remove the stems and keep the leaves; cut them up. If spinach is used, remove and discard the stems; the leaves should remain whole. Blanch the leaves for 15 seconds in a large pot of boiling salted water. Drain completely, pressing to get rid of the water.

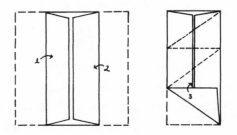

2. Mix the leaves with the hard-boiled eggs. Season with salt and pepper to taste.
3. Place a heaping tablespoon of stuffing in the bottom center of each square wrapper. Fold the right and left sides of each wrapper toward the center, covering the filling and forming a long rectangle. Fold the bottom left corner of the rectangle over and up to form a pocket. Fold the top left corner over and down to cover the pocket. Seal shut with water or a thin film of beaten egg.
4. Fry in about 2 inches of hot peanut oil. Drain and serve.

Note: You may substitute 3-inch wrappers for the 5-inch and use a heaping teaspoon of filling.

GREEK *RODANCHOS*

(Squash Strudel)

MAKES ABOUT 12. (P)

Although most Sephardic Jews say blessings over dates, pomegranates, gourds, leeks, an apple dipped in honey, and the head of a fish or lamb before commencement of the Rosh Hashanah meal, they prepare these foods in a variety of ways. For example, Moroccans bake sweet vegetables (see page 141) and Greeks twist squash into strudel dough and leeks into *kioftes de prasses.* The squash strudel recipe follows; the leek patties can be found on page 383.

One 2-pound butternut squash	2 teaspoons cinnamon
5–6 tablespoons sugar	¼ cup vegetable oil
	16 sheets phyllo dough

1. Preheat the oven to 350 degrees and grease a cookie sheet.
2. Slice the squash in half lengthwise, scoop out the seeds, and place, cut side down, in a pan with a little water. Cover with aluminum foil and bake for 30 minutes, or until soft. Drain and scoop out the flesh of the squash; puree it.

3. In a saucepan combine the squash, sugar, cinnamon, and 1 tablespoon of the oil. Stirring constantly, heat over a low flame until all the liquid evaporates, and then set aside to cool.

4. Taking 1 sheet of phyllo at a time while keeping the rest covered, fold the sheet in half. Brush with oil. Then place 2 heaping tablespoons of the filling along the long side. Close the phyllo, rolling jelly-roll fashion.

5. Being very careful, twist the long roll and then roll it up like a snail, with the outside end tucked under. Brush with the remaining oil and place on the cookie sheet.

6. Continue until all the filling is used up.

7. Bake for 20–25 minutes, or until golden brown. If, at the end of the time, the *rodanchos* are not yet golden, raise the heat to 375 degrees for a few minutes.

GERMAN POTATO SALAD

SERVES 10–12. (P)

Potatoes have become such an integral part of Jewish cuisine that we forget what a gastronomic newcomer this root vegetable is. Brought to Europe from South America in the eighteenth century, potatoes were introduced into Prussia by Frederick the Great. In 1774 he distributed free seed potatoes to reluctant peasants and ordered the planting of the vegetable to help relieve a famine. Little by little, people began to eat the potato.

My late father could not remember a major meal without potatoes from his youth in Germany. There was potato bread, potato pancakes, potato soup, potato dumplings; roasted, boiled, and fried potatoes; as well as hot and cold potato salads. This is my aunt Lisl's Bavarian cold potato salad, which was always a part of the Rosh Hashanah meal.

3 pounds potatoes, scrubbed
    and halved
⅓ cup vegetable oil
½ cup water

1 pareve vegetable bouillon cube
    (optional)
1 teaspoon salt
½ teaspoon black pepper

1 clove garlic, crushed and peeled

½ teaspoon sugar

1½ tablespoons red wine vinegar

½ medium onion, finely sliced

Hard-boiled eggs (optional)

Mayonnaise (optional)

Fresh flat-leaf parsley (optional)

Fresh chives (optional)

1. Steam the potatoes in a small amount of water for about 20 minutes, or until cooked through but not mushy. While hot, peel and slice them.
2. Pour the oil over them and mix well. Let stand for about 10 minutes.
3. In a small saucepan, bring to a boil the water, bouillon cube, if using, salt, pepper, garlic, sugar, and vinegar. Pour the hot liquid over the salad and add the onion.
4. Mix well, add the optional ingredients if desired, and let stand. Serve at room temperature.

Variation: To make an Italian salad, add to the above potato salad 4 ounces cut-up party-snack herring in wine sauce; 8 ounces canned cubed red beets; ½ medium apple, sliced; some mayonnaise; and, if you like, some walnuts.

BAKED WHITEFISH

(*Moroccan Pescado Blanco*)

SERVES 8–10 AS A FIRST COURSE. (P)

On Rosh Hashanah, as on Friday nights, fish is served to start the festive meal. Fish represents immortality, fertility, and the special relationship between the Jewish people and the Torah. There is such a close connection between Jews and the fish in the water that after the afternoon services on the first day of Rosh Hashanah it is customary to perform the Tashlih (throwing-away) ritual near a body of flowing water, preferably containing fish. Observant Jews go to a river or seashore abounding in fish because "man is likened to a fish who may be caught in the net of trouble if he fails to watch his conduct." One Tashlien custom is to throw bread crumbs from their pockets into the water, symbolically throwing off their sins, to be carried away by the stream. This act, based on an ancient one of throwing bread to the spirits in the water, became popular in Judaism in fourteenth-century Germany. The ceremony is supposed to recall the sacrifice of Isaac by Abraham.

All Jews have their traditional fish recipes. Moroccans serve a whole baked whitefish with the head attached. The head is often served first to the head of the table, and the fish is mentioned in the special blessing prior to the commencement of the meal. German Jews eat sweet-and-sour carp or salmon. And of course there is the Eastern European gefilte fish.

I love this recipe and make it these days with a large fillet of salmon instead of a whole fish.

One 5-pound whole whitefish, trout, or rockfish, gutted and split down the center, or a 4-pound fillet
½ cup chopped fresh flat-leaf parsley
½ cup chopped fresh cilantro
1 entire head of garlic, peeled and minced

4 medium tomatoes, sliced in rings
½ red pepper, sliced in rings
3 lemons, sliced in rings
½ teaspoon saffron threads
¼ cup vegetable oil

1. Preheat the oven to 350 degrees and place the entire fish in a glass or earthenware baking dish.
2. Stuff the fish with most of the parsley, cilantro, and garlic and scatter around the fish the remaining parsley, cilantro, and garlic, the tomatoes, red pepper, and lemons. If you are using a fillet, just cover the fish with all the herbs and vegetables.
3. Dissolve the saffron in about ½ cup of boiling water and let it sit for a few minutes. Then sprinkle the saffron water over the fish and tomatoes.
4. Pour the oil around the fish and tomatoes. Bake, uncovered, for 20–30 minutes, or until golden and crisp.

GEWETCH DI PESHCADO

(Balkan Striped Bass)

SERVES 8. (P)

Balkan-born Suzy David, author of *The Sephardic Kosher Kitchen* (Jonathan David Publishers, 1985), has long been known as one of Israel's finest cooks. Her book features favorite recipes along with tidbits about Sephardic food customs. When she was growing up, for example, she kept from fainting at Yom Kippur with a quince (not an apple or an orange, as is the Ashkenazic custom) studded with cloves. The following recipe from her book is a perfect fish dish for the Rosh Hashanah period—the head is included for good luck, and the fish is surrounded by fresh vegetables that are abundant during the harvest period.

6 tablespoons olive oil

2 yellow onions, peeled and sliced into thin rings

2 celery stalks, chopped coarsely

2 carrots, scraped and thinly sliced

2 green peppers, seeded and sliced into thin rings

2 pounds tomatoes, peeled, seeded, and sliced

2 ounces raw green peas

2 ounces fresh string beans, sliced diagonally

Salt

1 teaspoon black pepper

2 bay leaves

5 whole allspice

½ teaspoon sugar

4 tablespoons chopped fresh flat-leaf parsley

2 large potatoes, parboiled, peeled, and thinly sliced

3–4 pounds fresh striped bass, cleaned and sliced into 2½-inch-wide steaks, head reserved

1 lemon, thinly sliced

1. Preheat the oven to 375 degrees.
2. In a large, heavy skillet, heat 4 tablespoons of the oil and sauté the onions, celery, carrots, and pepper rings for 5 minutes. Remove with a slotted spoon to a large mixing bowl.
3. Cook the tomatoes in the skillet for 1–2 minutes, then add the peas and the

string beans. Continue cooking for another 3–5 minutes. Remove with a slotted spoon to the mixing bowl and add 1½ teaspoons of salt, the pepper, bay leaves, allspice, sugar, and 2 tablespoons of the parsley. Combine well.

4. Spread the vegetable mix on the bottom of a deep baking dish, large enough to hold the vegetables and fish. Insert the potato slices among the vegetables and arrange the pieces of fish, including the head, on top. Drizzle another 2 tablespoons of oil over the fish. Sprinkle salt over the fish, place the lemon slices on top, and sprinkle with the remaining parsley. Cover with aluminum foil and bake for 20 minutes. Uncover and bake another 15 minutes. Serve warm or cold.

GEFILTE FISHBALLS

MAKES ABOUT 20 FISHBALLS
1½ INCHES IN DIAMETER. (P)

In assimilated America, the prosaic gefilte fish is sometimes disguised. One Jewish resort in Lakewood, New Jersey, dubs it "fresh stuffed deepwater fish en glace." Cracow's renowned Wierzynek Restaurant features on its elegant menu "carp Jewish-style" for its American visitors. A Brookline, Massachusetts, French restaurant serves *"poisson farci en glace."* Some hostesses change the name to "chilled fishballs."

Delle Sacks of Belmont, Massachusetts, calls her family recipe "gefilte fishballs." She learned how to make gefilte fish from her Austro-Hungarian mother in the Bronx. Besides serving it at family gatherings and on holidays, Delle often used this hors d'oeuvre at parties she and her husband, Albert Sacks, former dean of the Harvard Law School, gave for faculty and students. Today you can substitute the frozen gefilte fish mix for fresh fish.

One 4–5 pound haddock (fillets, cut and ground) plus the head, skin, and bones—if only smaller fish are available, you can add 1–2 more fillets
2 quarts plus ½ cup water

1–2 large onions, peeled
Several sprigs of flat-leaf parsley
6–7 large carrots, peeled
5 tablespoons sugar
4 teaspoons salt

Freshly ground pepper
1 small onion, grated
1 egg
2 tablespoons matzah meal or
    cracker crumbs

1. Put the head, skin, and bones of the haddock in a large soup pot. Cover with water to about 2 inches over the bones (about 2 quarts). Add the peeled onions and parsley. Cut the carrots on a diagonal and add them to the pot. Bring to a boil. Add 4 tablespoons sugar, 3 teaspoons salt, and pepper to taste. Remove the scum and simmer.
2. If your fishmonger did not grind the fish for you, grind it now, in your food processor or using the grinding attachment on your mixer, and place in a bowl. Add the grated onion, egg, matzah meal, 1 teaspoon salt, pepper, 1 tablespoon sugar, and ½ cup water. Mix well.
3. Dip your hands in cold water and form balls 1½ inches in diameter (tinier if you want them for appetizers). Drop the balls in the simmering stock and bring to a boil again. Then simmer, covered, for 1 hour.
4. Remove the balls carefully and then extricate the carrots. Pour the liquid stock through a strainer and chill. The bones can be discarded.

For an hors d'oeuvre, serve each tiny fishball with a toothpick on a round of carrot, using horseradish as a dip. As a first course or summer luncheon dish, serve fishballs with carrots, some fish stock, a sprig of parsley, horseradish, and challah.

GERMAN SWEET-AND-SOUR CARP

SERVES 6. (P)

My father's family that hails from Bavaria has its own symbolic foods for this festival, many of which have been with our ancestral family in Bavaria for centuries. His family served such dishes as sweet-and-sour carp, chicken soup with *nock-*

erln (egg drops), and for dessert *zwetschgenkuchen* (plum tart) and apple strudel, streusel, or kuchen.

In Germany the main course would have been roast goose with cabbage salad, potatoes, and carrots. From this first very young goose of the season, my grand-mother would begin saving the *schmalz* for cooking oil until Passover.

To authenticate the dishes handed down from Bavaria, I was fortunate to find the well-worn book of favorite recipes my grandmother Lina Bernheim Nathan compiled as a young bride over a hundred years ago. The following sweet-and-sour carp and *nockerln* are the first dishes my father recalls relishing. His grand-mother Rose Bernheim served them each and every Friday night and on Rosh Hashanah.

One 3½-pound carp, pike, trout, or salmon	1 medium onion, sliced in rings
Salt	1 bay leaf
4 cups water, or enough to cover the fish	1 teaspoon whole peppercorns
	½ cup raisins
½ cup red wine vinegar	5 whole cloves
1 lemon, sliced and seeded	½ cup brown sugar
	4–5 gingersnaps or *lebkuchen*

1. Clean, slice, and salt the whole fish, cutting through the bone. Let stand several hours or overnight. (My grandmother preferred using winter or chicken carp, which is a rich or fatter oily fish with lighter meat, to summer carp for this dish; she always included the head and bones for stock, as they add flavor to the sauce.)

2. Place the fish in the pan and add water to cover. Remove the fish and set aside. Add the vinegar, lemon, onion, bay leaf, peppercorns, raisins, 1 tablespoon salt, and cloves to the water in the pan and bring to a boil. Add the fish to the liquid and let simmer, uncovered, for 10 minutes.

3. Add the brown sugar and gingersnaps (the gingersnaps add color to the sauce).

4. Simmer 10–15 minutes more, until the fish is done. The fish should be light and firm to the touch, and the flesh should leave the bones easily.

5. Remove the fish from the liquid; skin and separate the meat from the bones. Arrange on a platter.

6. Boil the liquid 15 minutes longer and let cool. Then strain, removing the onions and raisins from the strainer. Pour the liquid over the fish and garnish with the raisins and onion rings. Refrigerate until the sauce jells. Serve as an appetizer the following day.

NOCKERLN (EGG DROPS) FOR CHICKEN SOUP

MAKES ENOUGH FOR 2 QUARTS OF SOUP. (M OR P)

My father loved this dish made by my aunt Lisl. These loose dumplings are a quick addition to soup.

2 tablespoons melted chicken fat or pareve margarine	7–8 tablespoons flour
4 eggs	Salt

1. Let the melted chicken fat or margarine cool a bit and add the eggs, 1 at a time, beating after each addition.
2. Add the flour slowly while continually beating with a whisk or spoon. Add salt to taste.
3. Drop the *nockerln* into boiling soup (see recipe, page 65) by placing a small amount on the tip of a teaspoon, putting the spoon in the soup, and leaving it in for a moment.
4. Boil for 10 minutes and serve.

TOMATO-VEGETABLE SOUP

SERVES 6. (M)

In 1937 a group of Chicago Jewish housewives decided to write and publish a cookbook to benefit the Jewish Community Center of Chicago. All board members of the Women's Auxiliary of the Center, they thought this way of collecting funds would be preferable to direct solicitation. How right they were! The nonkosher book, entitled *Thoughts for Food,* would include the women's best recipes for entertaining. To avoid favoritism, the authors' names would remain anonymous. Sixty-seven years later, the now famous *Thoughts for Food* series, including *Thoughts for Buffets, Thoughts for Festive Foods,* and *Thoughts for Good Entertaining,* sold over a quarter of a million copies. To this day, very few people know who the authors are and who receives the benefits.

Elaine Frank of Winnetka, Illinois, was one of the founding authors of the series. A well-known hostess, she shared with me her tomato-vegetable soup, which appears in *Thoughts for Buffets* and which she served her family each year on the eve of Rosh Hashanah.

1 beef soup bone with meat or	1½ cups sliced onion
1 veal knucklebone	1½ cups diced carrots
5 cups water	2 potatoes, diced (optional)
¼ cup fresh flat-leaf parsley,	3 cups solid-pack tomatoes
chopped	2 teaspoons salt
1½ cups celery, cut into pieces	½ teaspoon pepper

1. Simmer the soup bone in the water for about 2 hours, covered, over a low flame, skimming the fat.
2. Add the parsley, celery, onion, carrots, potatoes, if using, tomatoes, salt, and pepper.
3. Simmer, covered, another hour, or until the vegetables are cooked. Adjust the seasonings.

HONEY-ORANGE CHICKEN

SERVES 6–8. (M)

Everyone has a favorite holiday chicken recipe. This one, with a happy combination of honey, orange, and fresh ginger, is mine—a perfect beginning for a sweet New Year.

2 eggs	½ cup vegetable oil
2 teaspoons water	1 cup hot water
1 cup bread crumbs or matzah meal	¼ cup honey
	1 cup orange juice
1 teaspoon salt	2 tablespoons grated fresh ginger
⅛ teaspoon pepper	or ¾ teaspoon ground ginger,
Two 3-pound fryers, cut up	or to taste

1. Preheat the oven to 325 degrees.
2. Beat the eggs with the 2 teaspoons of water in one bowl. In another bowl, mix the bread crumbs or matzah meal with the salt and pepper.
3. Dip the chicken in the egg mixture and then in the bread crumbs.
4. Heat the oil in a heavy skillet and brown the chicken on all sides. Drain on paper towels.
5. Combine 1 cup of hot water with the honey, orange juice, and ginger. Place the chicken in a casserole and cover with the mixture.
6. Cover and simmer in the oven for 45 minutes, basting occasionally. Serve with rice and a tossed green salad.

MOROCCAN VEGETABLE AND MEAT STEW WITH COUSCOUS

SERVES 10–12. (M)

It is traditional for North African Jews to eat couscous at noon after the morning service of Rosh Hashanah. Couscous is one of the world's famous long-simmering stews. Some of the same vegetables blessed in the evening services the night before are included in the couscous itself, as well as in the accompanying sweet vegetable dish. They include carrots, leeks, onions, zucchini, pumpkin, and turnips. The following couscous, unlike that of Algeria, is a sweet stew, perfect for a sweet New Year.

Chickpeas, another tradition at Rosh Hashanah, are included in the couscous. It was thought that the moonlight caused these beans to grow, and the moon is associated with the flow of water and hence with "merit and favor." *Kara,* the Hebrew word for chickpeas, implies that they are cold (*kar*) on the inside. Therefore, chickpeas are taken to symbolize the cooling down of God's stern judgment. Eastern European Jews also eat chickpeas at Rosh Hashanah, but alone, sprinkled with salt and pepper, as on page 296.

The following couscous recipe and the sweet vegetable dish on page 141 are those of Ginette Spier, a Moroccan kosher cooking teacher who now lives in Paris. Her recipes are from her home in Fez, the culinary capital of Morocco.

Read this recipe through carefully before beginning. Use your imagination with the vegetables.

⅓ cup dried chickpeas

1 pound carrots, peeled and halved lengthwise

1 small cabbage, cored and quartered

1 pound leeks, cleaned and sliced lengthwise in medium pieces

3 large onions, quartered

2 white round turnips, peeled and quartered

1 large green pepper, sliced lengthwise and seeds removed (optional)

3 pounds top rib, flanken, breast *deckel,* or chuck

2–3 meat bones
Salt and pepper
½ teaspoon turmeric (optional)
¼ teaspoon ground ginger
    (optional)
½ teaspoon saffron (if using
    thread type, soak in ½ cup
    boiling water for 5 minutes
    and pour in)
4 quarts water, or to cover
4 tomatoes, quartered and peeled
    (optional)

3 medium zucchini, sliced in thick
    pieces
1–1½ pounds acorn squash or
    pumpkin, peeled and sliced in
    2-inch pieces
1 pound couscous (never steam
    more than this at once)*
2 cups water with 2 teaspoons salt
¼ cup pareve margarine, melted

1. Soak the chickpeas overnight in enough water to cover.
2. Using the bottom part of a large *couscoussier* (a deep soup kettle) or your own improvisation, put in the soaked chickpeas, carrots, cabbage, leeks, onions, turnips, green pepper, if using, meat, meat bones, salt and pepper to taste, turmeric and ginger, if using, and saffron. Cover with water. Bring to a boil and simmer, covered, for about 2 hours, or until the meat is tender.
3. Remove the vegetables and meat to a warm plate.
4. Keep the stock in the bottom part of the *couscoussier* and add the tomatoes, if using, zucchini, and squash or pumpkin. Let boil and cover with the top part of the *couscoussier* or a sieve. (To retain the steam, tie a cloth or towel between the 2 parts.) Add the couscous. When the steam comes through the couscous, lower the heat to a simmer. Using your hands, continue to stir the couscous for 15–20 minutes, separating the lumps or grains with your hands. It won't be too hot.
5. Turn off the heat and remove the couscous to a deep dish. Sprinkle with some of the salt water and let set until absorbed. Repeat the sprinkling process once or twice. Cover.
6. Thirty minutes before serving, return all the vegetables and meat to the stock and let boil again. Return the couscous to the top half of the steamer and let steam for 10–15 minutes.

*If you'd prefer, follow the preparation directions on the couscous package.

7. To serve, use a large dish. In the center, place the sliced meat and the vegetables. Surround with the couscous, which has been moistened with the melted margarine. Sprinkle lightly with some stock, and serve the rest of the stock in a gravy bowl.

This can be served as is or with the sweet potato–vegetable dish on page 141. All beef, all lamb, all chicken, or a combination thereof can be used in this recipe. The same goes with the vegetables listed. Cumin is a common Moroccan spice. A dish of *harissa,* or hot sauce, can also be included, as well as blanched and sautéed almonds. The couscous can be served in the meat dish or separately, piled like a pyramid and garnished with toasted almonds and raisins.

Algerian couscous would include *kofta,* or meatballs with green peppers and tomatoes embedded in the meat and then fried, as in my recipe in *The Flavor of Jerusalem.* The broth would be served separately. The couscous would be hotter, with several spicy salads. This version from Fez is lighter and more delicate.

MOROCCAN LAMB *TAGINE* WITH PRUNES AND ALMONDS

SERVES 8–10. (M)

On the first night of Rosh Hashanah, bitter pickled olives are sometimes distributed to worshippers in Moroccan communities as they depart from the synagogue. This is a reminder to have faith in God, as asserted in the Talmud: "Let my sustenance be as bitter as the olive in the divine charge, rather than sweet as honey in the charge of flesh and blood."

For the first night of Rosh Hashanah, the late Mercedes Bensimon, formerly of Casablanca and a great cook, symbolically served tongue with green (never black) olives. Like many Moroccans, she was superstitious, especially at the New Year. On the second night she prepared a lamb *tagine,* or stew, with prunes and almonds. Although the prunes are black, they are sweet, so she could prepare this dish for the second—but never the first—night. Lamb is served to symbolize the ram of Isaac. Moroccan Jews do not avoid nuts at Rosh Hashanah, as is seen from this delicious recipe.

2 pounds onions, chopped
½ cup plus 2 tablespoons
    vegetable oil
2 tablespoons honey
1 teaspoon cinnamon
2 tablespoons sugar
4 pounds lamb, fat removed, cut
    into 1-inch cubes

3½ cups water
2 pounds dried prunes, which
    have been soaked in water for
    1 hour
½ pound (1 cup) blanched
    almonds

1. Cook the onions in ½ cup oil over a very low flame, stirring occasionally, until they are tender, limp, and almost black (about 1 hour). Combine with the honey, cinnamon, and sugar. Set aside.

2. Using the additional 2 tablespoons of oil, sauté the lamb until browned. Then add ½ cup water, cover, and simmer over a very low flame for 1½ hours, stirring occasionally, until the meat is very tender. Each time you stir, you may need more water, as much as 3 additional cups, to keep the lamb covered.

3. Add the onions and the soaked prunes to the meat. Simmer, covered, 20 minutes more.

4. Toast the almonds in a frying pan over medium heat, watching carefully and stirring constantly. Just before serving, sprinkle them over the meat. Serve with rice.

PERSIAN *FESENJAN*

(Pomegranate-Walnut Chicken)

SERVES 4–6. (M)

Thy lips are like a thread of scarlet.
And thy mouth is comely.

Song of Songs 4:3

Thy temples are like a pomegranate split open
Behind thy veil.

Song of Songs 6:7

The pomegranate (literally: apple with seeds) is one of the oldest and most beloved fruits known to mankind. Israelite secret agents brought these fruits, along with grapes and figs, from the "land of milk and honey" to the Jews wandering in the desert.

From antiquity the pomegranate has been a widely cultivated fruit throughout the countries of the Middle East. Since the time of King Solomon, the pulp of the pomegranate has been not only eaten raw, but squeezed to make fresh and cooling summer drinks. The large number of seeds found in each fruit and its bright red color make it a sign of fertility, especially at the time of Rosh Hashanah. In Israel today, Yemenite Jews will have an entire centerpiece of pomegranates at the New Year. My mother-in-law welcomed the rare pomegranates in prewar Poland, which voyagers brought from the Middle East. At the New Year they were almost as precious as the *etrog* (citron).

One of the prize Iranian dishes is *fesenjan*, the ancient *khoresh* or stew made from meat, pomegranates, and walnuts. This delicacy can be made from duck, partridge, chicken, lamb, or veal hind shin, shoulder, or ground beef. It is expensive in this country because of the high price of imported pomegranate juice; it is costly in Iran because of the expense of imported walnuts. A treat reserved for all festival dinners, *fesenjan* is especially appropriate for Iranian Jews and Jews throughout the world to eat at Rosh Hashanah, when the prayer is said: "In the coming year may we be rich and replete with acts inspired by religion and piety as the pomegranate is rich and replete with seeds."

One 3½-pound chicken, cut up	2 cups pomegranate juice or
2 tablespoons vegetable oil	½ cup pomegranate
1 medium onion, chopped	molasses
2 cups walnuts, ground	1 tablespoon tomato paste
⅓ cup hot water	Salt and freshly ground pepper
2 tablespoons lemon juice	2 tablespoons sugar

1. Brown the chicken in the oil and remove to drain on a paper towel.
2. Brown the chopped onion in the same oil.
3. In another pan, brown the walnuts, stirring constantly, without using any shortening. When brown, add the onion. Then slowly add the hot water so that the mixture does not stick. It should not be too liquid—more like a paste. Then add the lemon juice, pomegranate juice, tomato paste, salt and pepper to taste, and sugar, stirring with a spoon. When well mixed, add the chicken.
4. Bring the mixture just to the point of boiling (not a fast boil). Decrease to a simmer and let cook, covered, until the chicken is very tender, about 45 minutes. If the sauce is not thick enough, remove the chicken and boil the liquid down until the desired thickness is reached, stirring as it cooks. When ready to serve, place the chicken on a dish, pour the sauce over, and serve with a *chelou*.

CHELOU

(Crunchy Persian Rice)

SERVES 3 PERSIANS OR 6–8 AMERICANS. (P)

To Iranian Jews more than any others, a meal is not a meal without a rice dish such as *chelou* or *polou* or pilaf.

Chelou is a simply cooked, oiled rice that is baked in the oven or on top of the stove in such a way as to form a crunchy crust in the bottom of the pan. *Chelou* is always served with meat dishes having a thick sauce, called *khoreshes.* A pilaf, on the other hand, consists of cooked, drained rice mixed with a vegetable, fruit, fowl, meat, or nuts. Oil or butter is used to coat the rice; saffron, chopped almonds, pistachios, or spices are the usual flavoring.

Fesenjan is traditionally served with a *chelou.* This particular recipe, served at Rosh Hashanah, comes from the late Mohtaran Shirazi, originally of Teheran. When she made the *chelou* for me, she prepared a *khoresh* of dried herbs—such as parsley, the greens of leeks, or mint—simmered with a small amount of meat and a dried lime. This took me back to the time of the ancient Israelites who, with few foods available to them year-round, saved every bit they did not eat. Instead of discarding their leek greens and unused limes, they collected them and dried them in the sun for several days. The dried herbs and fragrant limes provided a base for sauces when fresh foods were not in season.

The difference between Iranian *chelou* and our rice is that each grain of rice in the *chelou* comes out feathery, fluffy, and separate. It is essential to cook the rice in a great deal of water. As a general rule, one pound of rice should be covered with hot water to a depth of 8–10 inches. Try the following *chelou* recipe this Rosh Hashanah with the *fesenjan* or any of the other chicken or stew dishes in this book.

1 pound long-grain rice	½ teaspoon turmeric
3 tablespoons salt	2 russet potatoes, peeled and
6 tablespoons vegetable oil	sliced about ¼ inch thick

1. Fill a 6-quart saucepan with water and bring to a boil. Add the rice and salt. Boil, uncovered, for 7–10 minutes over high heat. Stir the water occasionally, being careful not to break the rice grains. Taste the rice to see that it is done. Remove immediately, drain, and rinse in lukewarm water to remove excess starch and salt.

2. Heat a heavy-bottomed 4-quart saucepan with 4 tablespoons of the oil mixed with ½ cup hot water. Add the turmeric. Then place the potatoes on the bottom of the saucepan. Pour the rice into the pan; cover with a cloth and a lid. Let simmer over a low flame for about 10 minutes.

3. Mound up the rice in the center of the pan and make a deep hole in the center of the mound. (This hole allows the rice to steam.) Sprinkle about 2 more tablespoons of oil with ½ cup hot water all around the rice. Cover and simmer for about 20 more minutes.

4. When ready to serve, uncover the pan and stir the rice gently with a spatula to make it fluffy. Turn the rice out in a mound onto a warm serving dish. Then remove the crust and potatoes from the bottom of the pan and serve separately, or heap the potatoes on the rice on the serving platter.

MOROCCAN SWEET POTATOES AND VEGETABLES

SERVES 10–12. (P)

This accompanies the couscous on page 134. I love this dish at Rosh Hashanah with brisket. I microwave the squash and sweet potatoes.

4 large onions, sliced thickly
2 tablespoons vegetable oil
One 15-ounce can chickpeas, drained
1 pound acorn squash, pumpkin, or carrots, peeled, cubed, and microwaved for 5 minutes

1–2 sweet potatoes or yams, peeled, cubed, and microwaved for 5 minutes
¼–⅓ cup raisins
¼ cup sugar
2 teaspoons cinnamon

1. Preheat the oven to 375 degrees and grease a 9- by 13-inch casserole.
2. Sauté the onions in the oil until golden.
3. Place the chickpeas and onions in the bottom of the casserole. Cover with the remaining vegetables and raisins. Sprinkle with the sugar and cinnamon, and add a little oil, if desired.
4. Bake for 30 minutes, covered, and another 20 minutes, uncovered, or until well browned. Serve with Moroccan couscous (page 134) or a simple roast.

LEBANESE STUFFED ZUCCHINI WITH APRICOTS

SERVES 6–8. (M)

As the apple [apricot] tree among the trees of the wood,
So is my beloved among the sons.
Under its shadow I delighted to sit,
And its fruit was sweet to my taste.

Song of Songs 2:3

It is said that in King Solomon's palace there was a room painted with murals showing apricot trees in full bloom. Their fruit was so golden and lifelike that guests could smell the sweet aroma.

Known as "golden apples," apricots were first brought to the Middle East from Armenia at the time of Noah. Today in the Middle East, apricots are still a living treasure, as they are ripe for such a short time. It is only natural, then, for Jews in these countries to celebrate the New Year with dried apricots in their symbolic dishes. This recipe for zucchini stuffed with meat and rice and cooked with dried apricots is a sweet seasonal start to the New Year, both in the Middle East and in the United States, with our often bumper crop of zucchini.

In the Middle East the light green squash are squatter than our zucchini, so you may have to cut the zucchini in half. I make this dish at least once a year.

6–8 medium zucchini
1 cup rice
1 pound ground lamb or beef
Salt and pepper
½ teaspoon cinnamon (optional)

2 tablespoons pine nuts (optional)
1 cup dried apricots (about 30),
 soaked in water overnight and
 split (reserve the water)
Juice of 1 lemon, or to taste

1. Using an apple corer, scoop out the pulp from the zucchini, making sure to keep the outer skin intact and to leave one end closed. Reserve the pulp for another use.
2. Combine the rice, lamb or beef, salt and pepper to taste, and cinnamon and pine nuts, if using. Blend well.
3. Stuff the zucchini ¾ full.
4. Place half of the apricots open side down in a heavy casserole. Cover with the stuffed zucchini and top with the remaining apricots. Squeeze lemon juice over all.
5. Pour 1 cup of the reserved water from the apricots over the zucchini. Cover and simmer over low heat for 1½–2 hours, until the zucchini are tender. If needed, add more of the reserved apricot water.

MOROCCAN CARROT SALAD

SERVES 8-10. (P)

Today carrots are probably, with apples and honey, the most symbolic food served at Rosh Hashanah. Since carrots were one of the few sweet-tasting vegetables accessible to the poor Jews of Russia and Poland, they became *the* vegetable substitute for the pumpkin and gourd.

Mohrrüben in German and *mern* in Yiddish mean carrot. The Yiddish word also means "to increase" or "to multiply." Thus, by eating carrots at Rosh Hashanah, the Jew reiterates the hope that the Jewish nation will increase greatly in numbers and merit during the coming year. This hope is based upon the promise stated in the Bible as part of the covenant God made with Abraham:

"And He brought him forth abroad, and said, 'Look now toward heaven, and count the stars, if thou be able to count them'; and He said unto him: 'So shall thy seed be' " (Genesis 15:5).

Carrots cooked whole and then sliced into circles resemble coins in color and shape. Carrots, then, signify an increase in numbers and wealth—i.e., a yearning for a prosperous year. Carrots are cooked in kugels, cakes, *tsimmes,* salads, stews, and even candies for Rosh Hashanah.

I always serve this carrot salad at Rosh Hashanah. It's easy and can be made ahead, and everyone likes it. I serve it with a roasted pepper salad as well.

2 pounds carrots	½ cup lemon juice
3 cloves garlic, peeled and minced	Salt
2 teaspoons paprika	2 tablespoons chopped fresh flat-
Hot pepper to taste	leaf parsley
1 tablespoon ground cumin	3 tablespoons olive oil

1. Peel the carrots and boil them in water for about 20 minutes, or until barely tender. Cool and cut into thin rounds.
2. Place the carrots in a mixing bowl and add the remaining ingredients, except the parsley and oil.
3. Cover and refrigerate until thoroughly chilled. Before serving, sprinkle with the parsley and oil.

ANNA SIEGEL'S CARROT PANCAKES

SERVES 6–8. CAN BE USED AS A VEGETARIAN ENTRÉE

AT PASSOVER OR ANYTIME. (P)

Mark Siegel, Democratic Party activist, and his wife, Judy, serve this holiday dish, a hand-me-down from Mark's mother, Anna. One of their family traditions is the dispute about the origin of the recipe: is it Galician or Italian? After all, what would a Jewish family be without a vigorous discussion! The Siegels serve it each year at Rosh Hashanah. Although I think it is good at Hanukkah, Judy disagrees. But she does serve it at Passover.

2 green peppers, diced	½–1 cup matzah meal
¼ cup vegetable oil plus oil for frying	Salt
	16 ounces tomato sauce
6 medium carrots, peeled and quartered	2 tablespoons sugar
	¼ cup water
6 eggs	

1. Sauté the green peppers in ¼ cup oil. Drain and set aside.
2. Place half of the carrots and 3 of the eggs in a food processor. Grate medium fine. Remove and repeat with the remaining carrots and eggs. The carrots should be the consistency of potato pancake batter. Add matzah meal and salt to taste until patties can be formed for frying.
3. Heat a thin film of oil to 375 degrees in a frying pan. Add a heaping table-spoon of batter. Fry until light golden on both sides. Repeat with the rest of the batter. Drain the pancakes well on paper towels. Layer in a large casserole.
4. Mix the tomato sauce with the sugar, green peppers, and water. Pour the sauce over the pancakes and bake, uncovered, in a 325-degree oven for 30 minutes. This dish is even better the second day. It also freezes well.

CARROT CAKE

SERVES 8–10. (D)

The following carrot cake perfectly illustrates the evolution of baking techniques over the last hundred years. Prior to 1850 in Europe, the leavening of baked goods depended on yeast or sour milk and baking soda. Cream of tartar was another possibility but was imported from Italy. With the invention of baking powder or monocalcium phosphate in the United States in 1869, immigrant Eastern European women quickly learned new ways to make cakes. Prior to the advent of baking powder, this particular cake was probably denser than it is today. The eggs may have been separated and the whites beaten stiff, with cream of tartar added, to make the cake rise a bit higher. The cream cheese frosting is certainly a twentieth-century addition.

3 cups sifted all-purpose flour	1½ cups vegetable oil
2 teaspoons baking powder	3 cups grated raw carrots
2 teaspoons baking soda	(1 pound)
½ teaspoon salt	4 eggs
2 teaspoons cinnamon	½ cup chopped walnuts
2 cups sugar	

1. Preheat the oven to 350 degrees. Grease and flour a 10-inch Bundt or tube pan.
2. Sift the flour together with the baking powder, baking soda, salt, and cinnamon.
3. In another bowl, combine the sugar and oil and mix thoroughly. Add the carrots and blend well.
4. Add the eggs, 1 at a time, to the carrot mixture, beating well after each addition. Fold in the nuts. Then gradually add the flour mixture, blending well.
5. Pour the batter into the prepared pan. Bake for 1 hour, or until a toothpick inserted in the center comes out clean. Cool before frosting.

FROSTING:

3 ounces cream cheese, softened	2 cups confectioners' sugar
4 tablespoons (½ stick) butter or	1 teaspoon lemon juice
pareve margarine, softened	

When the cake is cool, blend together the above ingredients and frost.

HEIDI WORTZEL'S HONEY CAKE

(Lekakh)

MAKES 2 LOAVES. (P)

So David and all the house of Israel brought up the ark of the Lord with shouting, and with the sound of the horn. . . . And he dealt among all the people, even among the whole multitude of Israel, both to men and women, to every one a cake of bread, and a cake made in a pan, and a sweet cake.

II Samuel 6:15, 19

The Jewish sweet tooth can perhaps be traced as far back as King David! In Hosea 3:1, the "sweet cake" is identified as a raisin cake.

An ancient sweet raisin cake is a logical description since "honey," as used in the Bible, referred to the honey and jam extracted from honeycombs, dates, grapes, figs, and raisins. The only bees found in biblical Israel were of the ferocious Syrian variety. They had to be smoked from their hives, so extracting honey from their combs was never an easy task.

During the Roman period, the more docile Italian bees were introduced to the Middle East. Gradually the image of the bee changed to that of a gentler, tame insect, with bee honey becoming a more commonly used food item. The honey and its comb were at that time precious commodities. They were eaten alone, added to drinks, used in cooking, and valued for medicinal properties.

Lekakh, Yiddish for honey cake, is the traditional Eastern European cake served on the first night of Rosh Hashanah and is eaten as a sweet throughout the period between Rosh Hashanah and Simhat Torah. It is also served at the birth of a boy, at weddings, and generally at all happy occasions.

When I first published this recipe, it appeared in the *New York Times* to raves coast to coast.

1 cup strong coffee

1¾ cups honey

3 tablespoons Cognac (optional)

4 eggs

¼ cup vegetable oil

1¼ cups dark brown sugar

3½ cups sifted all-purpose flour

1 tablespoon baking powder

1 teaspoon baking soda

1 teaspoon cinnamon

¼ teaspoon ground cloves

¼ teaspoon ground nutmeg

½ teaspoon ground ginger

½ cup chopped toasted almonds
   or walnuts

½ cup white raisins

¼ cup chopped candied citron
   (optional)

1. Preheat the oven to 300 degrees. Generously grease and flour two 9- by 5-inch loaf pans.
2. In a 2-quart saucepan, combine the coffee and honey and bring to a boil. Let cool, then stir in the Cognac, if using.
3. In a large mixing bowl, beat the eggs. Stir in the oil and brown sugar.
4. In another large mixing bowl, sift together the flour, baking powder, baking soda, cinnamon, cloves, nutmeg, and ginger. Stir in the nuts, raisins, and citron, if using.
5. Stir the flour mixture and honey mixture alternately into the egg mixture. Pour the batter into the loaf pans and bake for 70 minutes, or until the cakes are springy to the touch. Do not serve for 24 hours, so that the flavor of the honey has a chance to develop.

APRICOT HONEY CAKE

From Ben Moskovitz

MAKES 1 CAKE. (P)

"One thing I cannot get in my head," said Ben Moskovitz, owner of Star Bakery in Oak Park, Michigan. "Was the food better growing up in Czechoslovakia or were the people hungrier there? My mother made a honey cake for the holiday, and it was so delicious. Honey was too expensive for us, so my mother burned the sugar to make it brown. Here I use pure honey, but I still think my mother's cake was better and I know I am wrong. The taste of hers is still in my mouth."

Mr. Moskovitz's European honey cake follows, with a few of my American additions. Other European Jewish bakers interviewed for this book also bake with white rye flour and cake flour when we would use all-purpose flour. I have included both choices.

½ cup dried apricots, roughly
   chopped
¼ cup dark rum
2 large eggs
1 cup clover honey
⅓ cup vegetable oil
Grated zest and juice of 1 lemon
Grated zest and juice of 1 orange
⅓ cup sugar
1 teaspoon salt

⅓ cup apricot jam
1¾ cups white rye or unbleached
   all-purpose flour
¼ cup cake or unbleached all-
   purpose flour
½ teaspoon baking soda
½ cup slivered almonds or
   roughly chopped walnuts or
   cashews

1. In a small bowl, soak the apricots in the rum for at least 30 minutes.
2. Preheat the oven to 350 degrees and grease a 10- by 5-inch loaf pan.
3. In a mixing bowl, beat the eggs with a whisk. Stir in the honey, oil, grated lemon and orange zests and juice, and the sugar, salt, and apricot jam.
4. Sift the 2 flours and the baking soda into another bowl.
5. Strain the apricots, reserving the excess rum.
6. Add the flour alternately with the rum to the honey cake mixture. Fold in the apricots. Scoop the batter into the prepared pan and sprinkle with the nuts.
7. Bake on the lower oven rack for 50–55 minutes, or until the center of the cake is firm when you press it. Remove from the oven and cool on a rack.

CHOCOLATE LOVERS' HONEY CAKE

From Andra Tunick Karnofsky

MAKES 1 CAKE. (P)

This decidedly American chocolate–chocolate-chip honey cake is included in the Rosh Hashanah gift packs Andra Karnofsky sends to college students. She uses mini chocolate chips so they won't sink to the bottom.

2 ounces unsweetened chocolate	2 large eggs
2 cups unbleached all-purpose flour	3 tablespoons vegetable oil
	¾ cup honey
½ teaspoon baking soda	⅔ cup light-brown sugar
1 teaspoon baking powder	½ cup orange juice
1½ teaspoons cinnamon	1 cup mini chocolate chips

1. Preheat the oven to 350 degrees and grease a 9- by 5-inch loaf pan. Melt the unsweetened chocolate over simmering water in a double boiler or microwave for 1 minute. Set aside.
2. Sift into a mixing bowl the flour, baking soda, baking powder, and cinnamon and set aside.
3. In a larger bowl, beat the eggs and add the oil and honey. Then add the brown sugar and melted chocolate.
4. Alternately add the dry ingredients and the orange juice. Stir in ¾ cup of the chocolate chips.
5. Pour the batter into the loaf pan. Sprinkle the remaining ¼ cup chocolate chips over the top.
6. Bake on the lower rack of the oven for 50–55 minutes, or until a toothpick inserted in the center comes out clean. Cool on a rack for about 15 minutes. Gently run a knife around the edges to loosen the cake, then remove it from the pan.

SARAH WERNICK'S *TEYGLAKH*

This is a Lithuanian recipe for *teyglakh,* little pieces of fried dough dredged in honey, eaten by Jews on happy occasions: Rosh Hashanah, Sukkot, Simhat Torah, Hanukkah, Purim, weddings, and *brits.* The honey that is used for cooking the dough is not thrown away but can be used as the base for several honey cakes and sweet-potato *tsimmes.*

SYRUP:

1 pound honey

¾ cup water plus more if needed

2 tablespoons lemon juice

2 cups sugar

DOUGH:

6 eggs

3 tablespoons vegetable oil

1 tablespoon ground ginger

½ teaspoon salt

1 teaspoon baking powder

3½ cups all-purpose flour plus
  ½ cup or more for rolling
  dough

GARNISH:

¾ cup slivered almonds

½ cup whole glacéed cherries

½ cup sesame seeds
  (approximately)

1. Line 2 cookie sheets with aluminum foil and oil lightly. Set aside. In a large, heavy pot (at least a 6-quart capacity), mix together the honey, water, lemon juice, and sugar. (This pot size may seem too large; however, the syrup would overflow a smaller pot later in the recipe.) Heat to boiling.
2. While the honey syrup is heating, beat together the eggs, oil, ginger, and salt until blended. Sift together the baking powder and 3½ cups flour. Add to the egg mixture to form a sticky dough. Cut into 8 pieces. Dust each piece with flour and roll between your hands until the dough forms a rope about ¾ inch in diameter. Slice each rope into about 10 slices, ¾ inch thick. Add to the boil-

ing syrup, reduce the heat, and simmer slowly for about 1 hour. It is important to cook the dough for the full time.

3. At the end of the first 30 minutes, the *teyglakh* will be an attractive golden
   color, but they will not be hard and crisp. Further cooking will improve their
   texture and make them a beautiful dark mahogany color.

4. Stir gently every 10 minutes or so during the cooking period. If the liquid
   seems close to evaporating, add more water, about ⅓ cup at a time. Ten minutes before the end of the hour, add the almonds and cherries. Stir frequently
   until done, to make sure that the syrup doesn't burn. When the cooking is
   complete, remove the pan from the heat. Immediately place the *teyglakh,*
   almonds, and cherries on the oiled pans, keeping as much of the leftover
   syrup as possible in the pot.

5. Separate the *teyglakh* so that they don't stick together. Stir the sesame seeds
   into the leftover syrup, adjusting the quantity to the amount of syrup that
   remains, if necessary. Pour onto a greased cookie sheet to shape. When the
   sesame-syrup mass cools enough to be handled, form it into spheres the size
   of gumballs. Work quickly but carefully: the syrup is extremely hot at first but
   will become too hard to shape as it cools. Form the *teyglakh* into pyramids—
   one large or several small—and decorate with the cherries, sesame balls, and
   slivered almonds.

Note: Teyglakh keep very well and make an excellent gift. If it is necessary to cover
them, use lightly oiled aluminum foil. Some cooks roll the finished *teyglakh* in
finely chopped nuts or coconut, which makes them less sticky. Others form the
teyglakh dough into shapes, such as spheres or knots. They can be stuffed with
bits of nut or dried fruit before they are cooked.

"IN OUR SOUL, IN OUR HEART, WE NEVER FORGOT WE WERE JEWS"

Edda Servi Machlin

For years I've admired the work that Edda Servi Machlin, author of the two-
volume *Classic Cuisine of the Italian Jews,* has done in bringing to the American
public the food and stories of her family in Pitigliano as well as recipes of other

Italian Jews. One hot August afternoon I visited her at home in the town of Croton-on-Hudson, New York. For lunch, she served a meal from Volume 2, including a delicious molded fettuccine and *fruste,* a crusty bread that she bakes often for her husband, Gene, and their two daughters. Her house, hugging a hill, has a grape arbor on the back deck that annually becomes a *sukkah,* and there is a garden resplendent with zucchini, tomatoes, and salad greens and fresh herbs.

Baking for Mrs. Machlin is second nature. And so are the memories, exuberantly told. As we ate, we talked about the crucial period in her life between November 1943 and June 1944, when "we ran for our lives." Her parents and younger brother were taken to an Italian concentration camp near Siena. "In our soul, in our heart, the four of us still free—my two older brothers, younger sister, and I—never forgot that we were Jews," she said. "We became beggars, often living with peasants from farm to farm. But whenever the peasants celebrated, we made Jewish delicacies. At every opportunity I cooked. For the first time ever we ate polenta, something my mother had thought of as peasant food. Sometimes we had to knock on doors and people gave us bread and cheese just to send us away."

CECIARCHIATA TEYGLAKH

From Edda Servi Machlin

SERVES 8–12. (P)

Ceciarchiata means "chickpeas" or "little bits" in Italian. This festive circle of *teyglakh* is similar in nature to the French *croquembouche*, although it's a crown, not a mountain. It is a spectacular centerpiece with its clusters of dough and nuts, and is totally addictive.

3 large eggs, slightly beaten
2 cups unbleached all-purpose
  flour plus more for dredging
½ teaspoon salt
1 cup olive or vegetable oil
1 cup honey

½ cup toasted and coarsely
  chopped hazelnuts (see Note)
2 teaspoons grated lemon zest
1 tablespoon lemon juice
1 cup toasted and coarsely
  chopped almonds (see Note)

1. Put the eggs, flour, and salt in a bowl and stir to make a soft dough. Turn out on a floured working surface and knead the dough 1–2 minutes. Shape it into a ball, flatten it with your hands, and sprinkle it lightly with flour.
2. Roll the dough out to a rectangle about ¼ inch thick. With a sharp knife or a pizza cutter, cut into ¼-inch-wide strips and dredge these long strips in flour. Then cut them into chickpea-size bits, and again dredge with flour to prevent them from sticking to each other. Scoop up the bits in a large sifter and shake to remove the excess flour.
3. Heat the oil in a small saucepan or wok and fry a handful of the bits at a time until lightly golden, stirring so they are an even color. Drain on paper towels and cool. You can also bake them, one third at a time, on an ungreased cookie sheet on the middle rack of a preheated 400-degree oven for 7 minutes.
4. Bring the honey to a boil in a 6-cup heavy casserole and simmer over moderately high heat for 3 minutes. Add all the dough balls, the toasted and chopped hazelnuts, and the lemon zest and juice. Cook over lower heat 7 minutes longer, stirring constantly.

5. Spread the toasted almonds over an oiled round heatproof serving platter and pour the hot mixture on top. Let it settle for a few minutes. When the mixture is cool enough to be handled, shape it into a circle with the help of a spoon and your moistened hands. Let it cool thoroughly at room temperature. It will harden a little. The *teyglakh* can be eaten either by breaking off pieces with your fingers or by cutting it into 2-inch segments.

Note: Mrs. Machlin suggests toasting whole hazelnuts and almonds by preheating the oven to 450 degrees and placing the nuts on a cookie sheet on the middle rack. Roast for 4–5 minutes, shaking the pan a couple of times. Watch them carefully, so they don't burn. Allow the nuts to cool for at least 10 minutes before chopping them very briefly in a blender or food processor.

MOROCCAN *CIGARES*

MAKES 50. (P)

Dainty finger pastries oozing with honey syrup are great delicacies in the Middle East. These *cigares,* shaped like rolled cigarettes, are served in Moroccan-Jewish homes on special occasions. In Casablanca, the late Mercedes Bensimon made her own paper-thin wrappers. In Washington, she discovered that Chinese wonton wrappers are convenient substitutes.

25 wonton-roll wrappers
3 cups blanched ground almonds
2½ cups sugar
1 egg
1 tablespoon orange-blossom
    water

Grated zest of 1 lemon
2 cups vegetable oil, or more
½ cup water
2 tablespoons honey

1. One hour before beginning, remove the wonton wrappers from the freezer. Cut each in half.
2. Combine the almonds, 1½ cups of sugar, and the egg. Mix well and add the

orange-blossom water and lemon zest. Combine well. Place 1 heaping teaspoon of the filling in the center of each wrapper and roll up like a jelly roll.
Moisten the ends to secure.

3. Fill a heavy frying pan with 4 inches of oil. Heat the oil and drop the *cigares* in,
    a few at a time. When they are light gold in color, turn and then remove with
    a slotted spoon. Drain on paper towels.

4. In a small, heavy saucepan, bring the remaining 1 cup sugar and ½ cup water
    to a boil over a high heat, stirring until the sugar dissolves. Add the honey.
    Cook briskly, undisturbed, until a small bit dropped into ice water immedi-
    ately forms a soft ball or until the syrup measures 240 degrees on a candy
    thermometer. When the syrup cools to lukewarm, dip in the *cigares*. Drain off
    the syrup and place on a platter.

APPLES

At the commencement of the Rosh Hashanah meal, an apple, symbol of the
Divine Presence, is dipped into honey for a sweet year. Apples, however, were
originally small and sour, hardly the sweet forbidden fruit associated with the
Garden of Eden. (Contrary to popular opinion, the apple is not even mentioned
in the biblical story.) In fact, the soil and climate of ancient Israel were not suitable for them. The "apples" of antiquity were more likely either apricots or
quince. But since apples became popular in the Middle Ages, it has been traditional to associate them with the Garden of Eden and, more to the point, with
Rosh Hashanah.

My father told us that he would dip the apple in honey the first night of Rosh
Hashanah and eat figs the second night. On Yom Kippur the children brought an
apple or a lemon stuck with cloves to synagogue, to sniff in case they felt faint.
The fruit was saved and later hung in the sukkah.

The following two apple recipes are typical family favorites at Rosh Hashanah. The apple pie was originally a German kuchen, made of dough similar to
the *zwetschgenkuchen* on page 160. It became double crusted when my aunt Lisl
watched some of her American neighbors and friends bake.

AUNT LISL'S APPLE PIE

SERVES 6–8. (D OR P)

½ pound (2 sticks) butter or
    pareve margarine
2 cups all-purpose flour
6 tablespoons plus 1 teaspoon
    sugar
⅛ teaspoon salt
¼ cup plus 1 tablespoon cold
    water
5–6 apples (Granny Smith,

Jonathan, Gala, or other good
    baking apples), peeled, cored,
    and finely sliced
¼ cup raisins
Juice and grated zest of 1 lemon
½ teaspoon cinnamon
1 egg yolk
2 tablespoons grated almonds or
    walnuts

1. Using a food processor or pastry blender, combine the butter or margarine, flour, 2 tablespoons of the sugar, and salt. Mix well and slowly add the cold water. When a soft ball forms, divide in half, wrap in waxed paper, and refrigerate for about 1 hour, or until firm.
2. Preheat the oven to 450 degrees.
3. Combine the apples, raisins, 4 tablespoons of the sugar, lemon juice and zest, and cinnamon in a medium bowl.
4. Roll out half of the dough and press into a 10-inch pie plate. Fill with the apple mixture. Roll out the top crust and cover the pie. Seal the crust. Make a few air holes in the top with a fork. Brush the egg yolk over the crust and sprinkle with the nuts and the remaining teaspoon of sugar. Bake for 10 minutes, then reduce the oven temperature to 350 degrees and continue baking for 30 minutes, or until golden.

APPLE STREUSEL

SERVES 6–8. (P OR D)

⅓ cup sugar

½ teaspoon cinnamon

¼ cup orange juice

6 tart apples, peeled, cored, and
    sliced

¾ cup all-purpose flour

1 teaspoon baking powder

4 tablespoons (½ stick) pareve
    margarine or butter

⅔ cup brown sugar

1 egg

¼ cup chopped walnuts (optional)

1. Preheat the oven to 350 degrees.
2. Add the sugar, cinnamon, and orange juice to the apples. Mix lightly and place in a greased 1½-quart casserole.
3. Sift together the flour and baking powder.
4. Cut the margarine or butter into the flour and rub with your fingertips to a crumbly consistency.
5. Mix the brown sugar and egg. Stir the mixture, along with the nuts, if using, into the flour mixture. This is the streusel.
6. Sprinkle the streusel over the apple mixture. Bake 45 minutes, or until the apples are tender and the crust golden brown.

BAVARIAN BUGLES AND BAKING

Lisl Nathan Regensteiner

My aunt Lisl grew up toward the end of the German Empire in the Bavarian city of Augsburg. Each morning, in that world that is no more, the postman would get off his horse and sound his post horn to herald the arrival of mail. He often arrived at the same moment that the cook removed from the oven the buttery breakfast *schnecken*, which we know as sticky buns, one of the hallmarks of southern German baking.

Lisl Nathan Regensteiner was born into this charming world in 1899 and died ninety-four years later in Rhode Island. She was typical of a particular generation of middle-class European women who came of age between the two world wars. Baking was an integral part of their lives.

Like many middle-class girls at the time in Germany, Lisl and her older sister Trudel learned about baking from a shared Nuremberg miniature kitchen complete with replicas of tube pans and other baking items. It was used by three generations of young cooks—my grandmother, my aunts, and their daughters—as a toy and an educational instrument. Dressed in uniforms with white aprons and bonnets, the young ladies baked miniature fruit and nut *kuchen* and *torten* in the copper molds. Today, that kitchen resides in our home in Washington, D.C. A fourth generation, my three children, including my son, have grown up playing with its two hundred pieces.

Besides cooking in the miniature kitchen, my aunt learned to bake breads and butter-rich pastries for the family by watching her mother and grandmother. For the Sabbath her grandmother baked *berches* (the Sabbath bread) from flour, yeast, potatoes, salt, and water. Others, less fortunate, brought their loaves to the baker who, for a small fee, finished them off in his oven, built into the wall in a kitchen attached to his home.

In 1933, when Hitler became chancellor of Germany, the lives of Lisl, her husband, Ludwig, and their three children changed forever. Although Ludwig believed that Nazi rule would only be a passing nightmare, Lisl realized, by 1937, that the time had come to leave. Because my father, her younger brother, had left Germany in 1929 and was already an American citizen, he was able to arrange affidavits for the rest of the family to cross the ocean.

Like other immigrants in America, Lisl found herself using cooking and baking skills to feed at least ten family members, including her parents and her husband's brother and his family, who joined them in 1940. She also helped settle 135 less fortunate refugees. But unlike most refugees, she had had time to bring with her many family possessions, including cooking pots and pans and her grandmother's and mother's heirloom handwritten cookbooks of traditional Bavarian recipes, given to her on her wedding day.

These traditional recipes had come to America a hundred years earlier with the large wave of Bavarian immigrants in the nineteenth century. By the time my aunt arrived, the recipes, translated into English, had already been published and eventually Americanized in *The Joy of Cooking* and *The "Settlement" Cook Book.* A typical southern German special-occasion dessert like *igel torte,* an icebox cake made from ladyfingers, coffee, and cream with roasted almonds stuck into the cake like porcupine quills, was dubbed Porcupine Icebox Cake in *The "Settlement" Cook Book* and, in a later edition, Mocha Icebox Cake. As advertisers in America introduced new shortcuts and modern methods of baking, these recipes evolved, unlike in Europe, where they often stayed more classically the same.

I remember that when I was a child, Lisl's house often had the sweet smell of baking mixed with the pungent scent of my grandfather's ever-present cigars. Before my aunt even offered, I would cross the breezeway from the kitchen to the garage and open every single cookie tin to see what she had baked since my last visit. Each was filled with a different-color iced butter cookie, sometimes topped with scattered nuts.

I would watch while her fingers deftly shaped the dough into luscious cakes for our family gatherings. Her signature dishes were *gesundheitskuchen* (see page 487), a simple tea cake, and the plum-filled *zwetschgenkuchen,* which she reserved for Rosh Hashanah. "I have made these so many times, I don't even look in the book anymore," she once told me. When friends and relatives complained that they could not duplicate her recipes, she could never understand why. She said perhaps it was because she used tube and tart pans brought with her from Germany. I always suspected, however, that the real reason for the success of her baking had nothing to do with the pans she used. Her pastries were touched by compassion and love.

ZWETSCHGENKUCHEN

(Southern German and Alsatian Italian Plum Tart)

From Lisl Nathan Regensteiner

SERVES 6–8. (D OR P)

The following southern German and Alsatian *zwetschgenkuchen* is served traditionally at the high holidays in early fall, when the small blue Italian plums are in season. In southern Germany and Alsace the tart was made from *zwetsche* (in

French, *quetsche*), a local variety of these plums. My aunt Lisl always used a *mür-beteig* crust (a short-crust butter cookie dough) for this tart, and sliced each Italian plum into four crescent shapes. She lined the tart with bread crumbs and then apricot preserves, which protected the dough during baking, creating a crispy crust. She went light on the cinnamon, a spice she felt was overused in this country. (I agree with her.) She made an *apfelkuchen* in much the same manner. My aunt's results, simple to prepare, were simply delicious.

My mother learned to make this from my aunt. One of my fondest Rosh Hashanah memories is helping my mother arrange the plum slices one by one in this tart. I love this recipe and make it with peaches and blueberries at other times of year.

1 cup unbleached all-purpose flour	2 pounds Italian plums
Dash of salt	2 teaspoons dried bread crumbs
¼ cup sugar	⅓ cup apricot preserves
¼ pound (1 stick) unsalted butter or pareve margarine, chilled	1 tablespoon brandy
	½ teaspoon cinnamon
1 large egg yolk	Confectioners' sugar

1. To make the crust using a food processor fitted with the metal blade, pulse the flour, salt, and 1 tablespoon of the sugar together. Cut the butter or margarine into small pieces, add to the bowl, and process until crumbly. Add the egg yolk and process until the dough forms a ball, adding more flour if necessary.

   To make the dough by hand, use your fingers or a pastry blender to work the butter or margarine into the flour, salt, and 1 tablespoon of sugar until the mixture resembles coarse bread crumbs. Add the egg yolk and work the dough into a ball.

2. Remove the dough from the bowl, dust with flour, and pat into a flattened circle. Cover with plastic wrap and refrigerate for at least 30 minutes.

3. When you are ready to make the crust, dust your hands and the dough with flour. Place the dough in the center of a 9-inch pie plate and with your fingers gently pat it out to cover the bottom and go up the sides. Trim the crust and prick the bottom in several places with the tines of a fork.

4. Preheat the oven to 375 degrees.

5. Pit and cut the plums into fourths. Sprinkle the bread crumbs on the crust, then spoon the apricot preserves on top and drizzle with the brandy. Place the plum quarters on the crust in concentric circles, starting from the outside and working inward, so that each overlaps the next, into the center. Sprinkle with cinnamon and the remaining sugar. (At this point, if you wish, you can wrap and freeze the tart, to bake it later. Just remove it from the freezer 1 hour before baking.)

6. Place the tart in the oven and bake about 40 minutes, or until the crust is golden brown and the plums are juicy. Remove from the oven. Just before serving, sprinkle with confectioners' sugar.

FIG *FLUDEN*

From Finkelsztajn's

MAKES 16 SQUARES. (D OR P)

This is one of those recipes that has pretty much disappeared in the United States, but those who remember it rave about it. A *fluden,* which comes from *fladni* or *fladen,* "flat cake" in German, is just that, a flat, double- or often multi-layered flaky pastry filled with poppy seeds, apples and raisins, or cheese. It was originally common to southern Germany and Alsace-Lorraine, later spreading east to Hungary, Romania, and other Eastern European countries. Often flavored with honey, it is eaten in the fall at Rosh Hashanah or Sukkot and is symbolic, like strudel, of an abundant yield. I have tasted apple two-layered *fluden* at Jewish bakeries and restaurants in Paris, Budapest, Tel Aviv, and Vienna, sometimes made with a butter crust, sometimes with an oil-based one. But only in Paris, at Finkelsztajn's Bakery, have I tasted the delicious fig rendition, a French fig bar. (Figs, my father used to tell me, were often eaten in Germany as the new fruit on the second day of Rosh Hashanah.)

This recipe is a perfect example of the constant flux of Jewish foods. Today, with the huge population of Tunisian Jews in Paris, it is no wonder that the Finkelsztajn family spike their fig filling with *bou'ha,* a Jewish Tunisian fig liqueur used for kiddush, the blessing over the wine on the Sabbath. You can, of course, use kirsch or any other fruit liqueur instead.

THE DOUGH:

⅓ pound (10⅔ tablespoons) unsalted butter or pareve margarine, or half butter and half vegetable shortening, cut into tablespoon-size pieces

2 cups unbleached all-purpose flour
½ teaspoon salt
¼ cup ice water

THE FILLING:

4 cups water
2 tea bags
Grated zest and juice of 1 lemon
2 cinnamon sticks
3 cups dried figs, stemmed

⅓ cup sugar
2 tablespoons *bou'ha* or other fruit liqueur
1 large egg, slightly beaten

THE DOUGH:

1. Place the butter or margarine (or butter and vegetable shortening), flour, and salt in a food processor fitted with the steel blade. Process until crumbly and gradually add the water, continuing to process until a ball is formed. Wrap the dough in waxed paper and refrigerate for at least 30 minutes.

FILLING AND BAKING THE *FLUDEN*:

2. Bring the water to a boil, then lower the heat and add the tea bags, lemon peel and juice, and cinnamon sticks. Steep for 1–2 minutes and remove the tea bags. Place the figs in the water and poach for about 5 minutes.

3. Drain the figs and the lemon zest, reserving the poaching liquid. Then place the figs, lemon peel, sugar, and liqueur in a food processor fitted with the steel blade. Process but do not purée; you want the figs to have texture. Add a tablespoon or so of poaching liquid if the filling is too dry.

4. Preheat the oven to 400 degrees and grease a 9-inch square pan.

5. Roll out half of the dough to a ⅛-inch thickness. Put it in the bottom of the pan (it should not go up the sides) and trim off the excess dough. Prick the dough with a fork. Spoon in the fig mixture.

6. Roll out the second half of the dough and cover the fig mixture. Prick a few holes in the top and brush with the egg.

7. Bake the *fluden* for about 25 minutes, or until the crust is golden.

8. When done, cut the *fluden* into 16 squares. It is wonderful served warm, with whipped cream or ice cream. Or you can let it cool and eat it as you would a fig bar.

YOM
KIPPUR

YOM KIPPUR

Howbeit on the tenth day of this seventh month is a day of atonement; there shall be a holy convocation unto you, and ye shall afflict your souls; and ye shall bring an offering made by fire unto the Lord. And ye shall do no manner of work in that same day; for it is a day of atonement, to make atonement for you before the Lord your God.

Leviticus 23:27–28

Then went up Moses [to Mount Sinai] . . . and seventy of the elders of Israel; and they saw the God of Israel. . . . And upon the nobles of the children of Israel He laid not His hand; and they beheld God, and did eat and drink.

Exodus 24:9–11

Go thy way, eat thy bread with joy, And drink thy wine with a merry heart; for God hath already accepted thy works.

Ecclesiastes 9:7

We are all familiar with fasting on Yom Kippur. This one day is to be spent humbling the heart in repentance and atoning for sins so that we will be inscribed in the Book of Life for a good year. Yet what is the origin of this fast?

When the early Israelites first beheld the Holy Presence of God at Mount Sinai, they ate and drank. With excessive feasting, they forgot themselves and began to worship the Golden Calf of the heathens. When Moses saw this on his descent with the Ten Commandments, he broke the tablets. He returned to Mount Sinai and descended on the tenth day of Tishri (Yom Kippur) with the second tablet of the Ten Commandments to find his people fasting and repenting their great sin. Moses told them that God had accepted their sincere penitence and proclaimed that day as a day of forgiveness throughout all generations.

For thousands of years, on the tenth of Tishri, Jews have fasted and refrained from catering to their physical appetites. It has always been a day when the Jew devotes himself to spiritual requirements in order to be like the angels. Sexual intercourse, the wearing of leather shoes, washing the mouth, entering into money transactions, and anointing oneself with cream are also avoided. (Although most people are supposed to fast, pregnant and nursing women, the sick, and girls under twelve and boys under thirteen are all exempt.)

With the stress on fasting, how many of us are aware of the mitzvah involved in celebrating a substantial feast in the afternoon of the day prior to Yom Kippur? As important as it is to fast, so it is necessary to eat properly beforehand. It is more difficult to fast when accustomed to eating well. And on Yom Kippur it is important to feel hunger pangs, to remind oneself all the more of the difficult task of atonement. Originally the pre–Yom Kippur feast was at noon. In America today, most people eat a substantial but not excessive meal late in the afternoon.

On the eve of Yom Kippur, it is traditional for most Jews to eat chicken. Mild chicken and rice dishes are prefast foods the world over. This is also due in Judaism to the *Kapparot* ceremony, performed that morning, whereby one transfers one's sins to a cock or hen. The chicken is often boiled, but it does not have to be; it merely should not be highly spiced. Rice, carrots, and fresh fruit are also served. Not all of these foods are seasoned, to discourage thirstiness and indigestion throughout the long fast. No nuts are served, as they can cause excessive saliva and throat irritation, making the recital of prayers difficult. At the end of the meal it is customary to eat a morsel of bread and water as symbolic sustenance throughout the fast.

Unlike the "black fasts"—such as Tisha Be-av, mourning the destruction of the Temple—Yom Kippur is a "white fast." White is symbolic of purity in accordance with Isaiah 1:18: "Though your sins be as scarlet, they shall be as white as snow." In the synagogue a white *kitl*, or robe, is worn, the synagogue ark is draped in white, and the Torah scrolls are adorned with white mantles.

After the meal before sunset on the eve of the fast, in traditional homes a white cloth is spread over the dining-room table. On it are placed a Bible, a prayer book, and other sacred books, instead of the traditional Sabbath loaves of challah. The books are covered with a white cloth until the break-the-fast meal the following evening, as symbolic testimony that this holy day is being honored, not with food and drink, but with study and prayer. A candle is lit in memory of departed family members.

According to a Midrash, at the close of the Yom Kippur service a voice calls from heaven telling the faithful that their prayers have been heard. Confident that we have obtained forgiveness, we can rejoice and partake of a post-fast meal. This repast recalls the feast the high priests celebrated after Yom Kippur in gratitude for having been permitted to emerge from the Holy of Holies. Often in the United States today, close friends and family assemble for the post-fast feast. Usually a dairy meal is served, beginning with coffee and a sweet—sometimes just an apple dipped in honey—followed by herring or another salty food. From there on, it is up to the imagination of the hostess. Russian Jews often made *schnecken;* Moroccans, *fijuelas,* deep-fried pastries oozing with honey; Syrians and Egyptians make a cardamom cake; Yemenites, a ginger cake. Sephardim also serve eggs, the symbol of hope and life. Quinces, pomegranates, watermelon, or other seasonal fruits are also served. It is becoming more and more traditional in this country to serve a glorified dairy brunch with bagels, lox, cream cheese, herring, and kugel.

MENUS

FOR YOM KIPPUR EVE

MINSK
Challah
Herkimer Chicken Soup with
Matzah Balls
Boiled Chicken or Tasty Apricot
Chicken
Green Salad
Honey-Glazed Carrots
Baked Apples
Heidi Wortzel's Honey Cake

GREEK
Challah
Egg-Lemon Soup
Greek Stewed Chicken in Tomato Sauce
Fidellos Tostados (Toasted Pasta)
Salad
Watermelon

TO BREAK THE FAST

MOROCCAN
Fijuelas
Meat and Vegetable Soup
Fruit
Tea with Mint

RUSSIAN
Herring in Sour Cream
Apple Dipped in Honey
Lokshen Kugel
Lox with Cream Cheese Bagels
Schnecken or Honey Cake

FOR YOM KIPPUR EVE

MEAT KREPLAKH

MAKES ABOUT 60. (M)

Which came first—kreplakh, pirogi, ravioli, or wonton soup? Each country seems to have its own version of a filled egg-noodle dough, either fried or boiled in water or soup. Just for fun, we filmed an episode for my PBS show with a Chinese, an Italian, and a Jewish cook each making his or her own version of boiled pocket pastries. Most authorities think that this dish originated in China and worked its way via trade routes to the countries of the West. The Jews may have learned about kreplakh from the Chinese or the Italians. Maimonides traces cooked dough to Persia and the Middle East.

The word "kreplakh" itself comes from the French *crêpe*. Whatever the origin of the food, it requires effort and time to cut, fill, form, and enclose each of these three-cornered bits of dough filled with chopped meat. Thus, they are reserved for special occasions. I still recall how my mother-in-law would lovingly mold kreplakh for festive meals.

The meat of the kreplakh symbolizes inflexible justice; the soft noodle dough denotes compassion. The kreplakh are, then, a metaphor, a suggestion that the attribute of God's strict justice will be mellowed on the side of mercy.

These pockets of food where the meat is hidden inside the dough also refer to the hidden nature of the three days they are eaten. The day prior to Yom Kippur is a feast but not a full holiday; on Simhat Torah people dance and drink; and on Purim the name of God is never mentioned.

Traditionally served in a soup, these "Jewish wontons" can also be boiled and then fried in chicken fat. My mother-in-law serves them this way, as a starch with meat.

MEAT FILLING:

1 small onion, chopped   1 egg
¾ pound leftover brisket, chopped   Salt and pepper
1 tablespoon vegetable oil

1. Sauté the onion with the ground meat in the vegetable oil. Drain the excess fat.
2. Combine with the egg and salt and pepper to taste. Set aside.

NOODLE DOUGH:

3 eggs   2 tablespoons water
¾ teaspoon salt   2 cups all-purpose flour

3. Beat the eggs slightly. Add the salt, water, and enough flour to make a medium-soft dough. Knead well by hand or in the food processor. Divide the dough into 2 balls. Cover with a moist towel.
4. Working quickly, roll out 1 ball of dough very thin with a rolling pin and cut into 6 strips, each 1½ inches wide. Then cut into pieces 1½ inches square.
5. Place ½ teaspoon of the meat mixture on each square. Fold into a triangle and press the edges together firmly, using flour to bind them. Leave as is or press together two of the ends. Repeat with the second ball of dough.
6. Drop into boiling water and cook, uncovered, 15 minutes.

Note: After being formed, the kreplakh can be placed on a cookie sheet, frozen, and then transferred to plastic bags for freezer storage.

EGG-LEMON SOUP

SERVES 6. (M)

Greek and other Mediterranean Jews eat egg-lemon soup for their prefast and major holiday meals. Both kreplakh and the traditional matzah balls in chicken soup are foreign to them.

6 cups rich chicken broth	Salt
½ cup uncooked rice or dry	2 eggs
alphabet pasta	Juice of 1 lemon, or to taste

1. In a medium saucepan bring the broth to a boil. Add the rice or alphabet pasta and simmer, uncovered, until the rice or noodles are tender. Add salt to taste.
2. In a separate bowl large enough to hold all the ingredients, including the broth, beat the eggs well. Add the lemon juice and mix well. Add a little of the stock, beating constantly with a wire whisk. Slowly add the remainder of the soup, always stirring.
3. Return the soup to the saucepan, bring to a boil, and remove from the heat immediately. Adjust the seasoning and serve.

Note: At Passover the same soup is served with broken pieces of matzah or farfel replacing the rice.

YEMENITE HIGH HOLIDAY SOUP STEW

SERVES 10–12. (M)

For some two thousand years the Jews in Yemen—some living in agricultural communities and others in cities—isolated themselves from the rest of Jewry, adhering to their ancient ways. There are several legends regarding how the Yemenites separated from the Jewish mainstream, but the Yemenites themselves say they have been separated since the destruction of the Second Temple by the Romans in the first century, when most of the Jews were dispersed from Palestine and they veered off and headed south to the Arabian peninsula.

Yemenites believed that one day a great bird or a magic carpet would bring them all back to the Holy Land. In 1948 they felt that this belief was fulfilled when transport planes, in an airlift the Israelis called "Operation Magic Carpet," rescued 43,000 Yemenite Jews, carrying them from the desert to Israel.

The closest modern Jews can come to the roots of ancient Jewish gastronomy is to attend a holiday meal at a Yemenite home like that which I attended at the home of Rabbi Josef Zadok, the then eighty-seven-year-old head of Jerusalem's Yemenite Community and a master silver craftsman.

It is the custom of many Yemenites that a festive meal of meat and later a dairy meal of white cheese, honey, bread, and fruit precede the annual Yom Kippur fast. At 8:30 a.m. on the morning before Yom Kippur the festive meal was on the table: the holiday bread baked the morning of the meal, a soupy stew, symbolic spices, a bowl of fruits and nuts known as *ga'le*, and a tart grape juice. Presiding at the table in the family's living room above the jewelry workshop sat the bearded patriarch, barefooted and cross-legged on a pillow atop his usual corner bench at the dining table.

As the meal began, Rabbi Zadok took a goblet of the grape juice and made the first of a fourfold blessing, this one of the fruit of the vine. The sugarless grape juice, which the Zadoks called wine, had been prepared just a few days earlier.

Little sugar is used in the Yemenite diet. Yemenites eat little but well, preferring a diet of grains, nuts, and small amounts of meat including the genitals, tails, legs, bellies, and udders of lambs and cows. In Yemen roasted locusts are a special treat.

Over the *lakhoakh*, the festive bread, Rabbi Zadok recited the prayer thanking God for the fruits of the earth. Each person dipped the bread into a bowl of spicy sauce called *helbeh* (Arabic) or *rubiya* (Hebrew), meaning "be fruitful and multiply." The sauce is made from soaked fenugreek seeds, which symbolize fertility. According to a Yemenite legend, fenugreek is supposed to keep women plump and fertile. The fenugreek is combined with fresh tomatoes and *zhug*, the Yemenite hot sauce made from pepper, black caraway seeds, cumin, cardamom seeds, garlic, fresh coriander, and dried chili peppers.

The stew consisted of chicken, beef, vegetables, and yet another spice combination, *hawayij*. Rabbi Zadok pointed out that the only "new" ingredients of the stew were potatoes and tomatoes, brought to Yemen by the Turks in the seventeenth and eighteenth centuries.

Hot spice combinations such as the *zhug* and *hawayij* are as important to Yemenite cuisine, because of taste, as sauces are to the French. Although the rabbi's wife grinds her own, most Yemenites in Jerusalem today have a preferred merchant in the marketplace who specializes in grinding the spices, adding a little more of one or another spice depending on the family's taste preferences and the dish for which the spices are intended.

Before and after eating the stew, each person nibbled from the large bowl of *ga'le,* consisting of grapes, pomegranates, pecans, walnuts, and roasted peanuts and beans.

By 10:00 a.m. the meal was over. The rabbi sat back to rest a little and said, "Blessed be the Name. We have always eaten little but well of what God has given us. These are the foods of the harvest before us."

3 pieces beef marrow bone (about 2 pounds)

One 3-pound chicken, cleaned and quartered

3 pounds beef shoulder, ribs, or stew meat (fat removed), left whole or cut into pieces

5 quarts water (approximately)

10 to 12 cloves garlic, separated but unpeeled

2 large onions, peeled and quartered, or 9 small white onions, peeled

1 large white turnip, unpeeled but quartered

4 leeks or green onions, coarsely cut

3 celery stalks, cut in 2-inch pieces

1 medium zucchini or acorn squash, cubed

3 medium carrots, cut in 3-inch slices

1 large tomato, almost quartered but not cut apart at bottom

3 potatoes, peeled and diced

1 small bunch fresh flat-leaf parsley or fresh cilantro, woody stems trimmed

Salt

1 tablespoon *hawayij* spice combinations or to taste (see below)

1. In a large kettle, place the beef marrow bones and chicken with water to cover. Bring to a boil, then simmer until a froth forms. Remove the bones and chicken and discard the water. Clean the kettle.

2. Add the beef and bones and cover with water. Bring to a boil again, lower the heat, and add the unpeeled garlic cloves. (By being left unpeeled, they won't soften in cooking.) Add the onions, turnip, and leeks or green onions. Cook, covered, about 1½ hours, or until the meat seems relatively tender.

3. Remove the marrow bones, add the chicken, cover, and simmer another 20 minutes. Cool and leave as is overnight.

4. Before cooking, skim off the fat and add the celery, zucchini or acorn squash, carrots, tomato, and potatoes. Cover and simmer another 20 minutes. Just before serving add the parsley or cilantro, salt to taste, and *hawayij* and simmer for another 10 minutes. Remove the garlic and adjust the seasonings.

5. Place a bowl of soup at each table setting. Serve with pita or a pita-type bread and *helbeh* (see below.) Dip the bread into the *helbeh* and then into the soup, scooping up the meat and vegetables and the sauce.

HAWAYIϳ

(Yemenite Spice Combination)

MAKES ABOUT 4 TABLESPOONS. (P)

2 tablespoons whole black
    peppercorns
1 tablespoon black caraway seeds
1 teaspoon cumin seeds

1 teaspoon cardamom seeds
1 teaspoon saffron
2 teaspoons turmeric

Pound all the ingredients together using a mortar and pestle, or use a coffee grinder or a standard blender.

HELBEH

(Dipping Sauce Made from Fenugreek Seeds and Zhug)

MAKES ABOUT 1 CUP. (P)

2 tablespoons fenugreek seeds,
    ground
Water
¼ teaspoon *zhug* (see below)
Salt

1 tablespoon lemon juice, or to
    taste
1 puréed tomato or 1 tablespoon
    tomato paste (optional)

1. Cover the fenugreek seeds with water. Let sit overnight or at least 8 hours.
2. Pour off any remaining liquid, leaving a moist paste.
3. Using a wooden spoon, whip, little by little, up to ½ cup of water into the paste. Then combine the paste with the *zhug,* salt to taste, lemon juice, and, if desired, the tomato.
4. Adjust the seasonings to taste. It should be very spicy.

YEMENITE ZHUG

(Hot Sauce with Spices and Herbs)

MAKES ABOUT ¼ CUP. (P)

1 teaspoon black peppercorns
1 teaspoon black caraway seeds
1 teaspoon cumin seeds
Seeds from 3 to 4 cardamom pods

4 small fresh hot peppers
2 cloves garlic, peeled, or to taste
1 cup cilantro leaves or chopped
    watercress

1. Using a mortar and pestle, a grinder, or a blender, grind all the spices. Add the spices to the cilantro or watercress leaves and blend in a mortar or in a food processor. If using a blender, a little water may have to be added.
2. Store well sealed.

GREEK STEWED CHICKEN IN TOMATO SAUCE
(Pollo en Salsa de Tomat)

SERVES 4–6. (M)

The most superstitious custom associated with food in Judaism is that of the *Kapparot*, the expiation of sins or "scapegoat" offering. On the morning of the day prior to Yom Kippur, in religious communities a live fowl is swung around the head three times. These words are then recited: "This fowl is my substitute, this is my surrogate, this is my atonement." Some old texts even add, "May it be designated for death and I for life." In essence, this *Kapparot* ceremony is the transferral of our sins to the fowl, an ancient custom rife in sorcery. In ancient days the scapegoat was sent out into the desert, carrying the sins of the community. Babylonians employed their abundant rams, lambs, or goats, instead of the chickens used later in Eastern Europe. According to one account, after the fowl was slaughtered, the dead and dried entrails were thrown onto the roof.

Although this custom still prevails in some very observant communities, in the first edition of the *Shulhan Arukh,* around 1565, Joseph Karo wrote, "This is a silly custom and its observance should be checked." His opinion did not prevail, however, and his comment was never included in any other edition of the code of Jewish law.

My late mother-in-law described the *Kapparot* tradition in Zamosc, Poland. Early in the morning of the day prior to Yom Kippur, the fowl was whirled about the head of the penitent. Her father would whirl a rooster, her mother a hen, and she and her siblings a pullet or a cockerel. As a child, she was always frightened by the fluttering feathers. After the whirling, her mother would race to the *shohet* and have the fowls ritually slaughtered to make food for the meal prior to the fast. All the fowls would be cooked and any extras given to bachelor relatives or to the poor. Chicken soup would be made for the kreplakh and the boiled chicken eaten as a mild main dish.

In some homes a fish might be used if a fowl was not available. Since there were five children in my mother-in-law's family, seven fowls were whirled, but in larger families a donation to charity of about eighteen cents, or *chai*, might be substituted for each chicken. Today this custom of using a live fowl for the ceremony is not as common. Most people who observe this rite substitute money wrapped in a handkerchief and swing it around the head.

To this day, chicken and rice are prefast foods the world over. Even the poorest Jew tries to serve a chicken at least once a year, for the meal prior to the Yom Kippur fast. The following is a mild, typically Greek chicken dish served on the eve of Yom Kippur.

Salt

One 3-pound frying chicken, cut into 8 pieces

¼ cup olive oil

One 35-ounce can Italian whole tomatoes

1 onion, chopped

1 teaspoon dried oregano

1. Salt the chicken and sauté in the oil in a large skillet or pot. As the chicken begins to brown, add small amounts of water, letting the chicken cook until the water is absorbed. Remove all except 2 tablespoons of the oil.
2. Strain the tomatoes to remove the seeds and pour over the chicken. Add the onion and oregano. Cover and cook slowly for about 45 minutes, or until done. This dish is usually served with *fidellos* (thin noodles, see page 181) and braised leeks.

TASTY APRICOT CHICKEN

SERVES 6–8. (M)

This easy-to-make chicken is an American convenience recipe that a Russian-Jewish caterer shared with me. I tasted a similar one, with quince jam, at the home of Vivian and the late Simha Dinitz, Israeli ambassador to the United States.

Two 3½-pound broiling chickens, cut up into 8 pieces

Salt and pepper

1 clove garlic

½ pound apricot preserves

6 ounces Russian dressing

1 cup diced onion

1. Preheat the oven to 350 degrees.
2. Season the chicken well with salt and pepper and rub with garlic.
3. Mix together the apricot preserves, Russian dressing, and onion. Pour over the chicken and bake in the oven about 50 minutes, or until golden brown.

FIDELLOS TOSTADOS

(Toasted Pasta)

SERVES 6. (P)

Contrary to popular opinion, pasta was probably introduced to the seaports of Spain from China via the Middle East as early as the eleventh century and even possibly much earlier. By the early thirteenth century, fifty years before Marco Polo's journey to the East, the Jews of Spain were eating a threadlike noodle called *fidellos*, similar to angel-hair pasta.

Fidellos tostados is a typically Jewish dish found in Greece and other countries to which the Spanish Jews fled. It is basically a tomato noodle kugel, with the coils fried until golden brown before being softened in boiling water. Curiously, *fidellos* is now eaten throughout Latin America and has been introduced into the American pasta manufacturers' market to meet the demand of the great influx of Latin Americans. The following is an old Spanish-Jewish recipe.

One 12-ounce package *fidellos* or *fideos* (a vermicelli-like pasta)
½ cup olive oil

2 cups strained stewed tomatoes
3 cups water
1 teaspoon salt, or to taste

1. Panfry the *fidellos* coils in oil until golden brown. Set aside in another pan.
2. Add the tomatoes, water, and salt to the original pan, and boil. Add the *fidellos*. Simmer, semicovered, for about 10 minutes, stirring occasionally with a long fork to separate the coils and keep the noodles from sticking. Cook until the *fidellos* are tender and the liquid is absorbed.
3. Remove from the heat and let sit, covered, about 10 minutes before serving. Stir again. This dish goes well with stewed chicken in tomato sauce.

Note: Preparing this dish in advance improves the taste. Cover to reheat.

HONEY-GLAZED CARROTS

SERVES 6–8. (P)

A simple dish of honeyed carrots is a light vegetable for the prefast meal.

2 pounds carrots	½ cup honey
1½ cups water	Salt
2 tablespoons cornstarch	1 teaspoon ground ginger

1. Peel and cut the carrots into 1-inch rounds. Place in a pan with the water and bring to a boil. Reduce the heat, cover, and simmer until barely done, about 15–20 minutes. Drain, reserving 1 cup of the cooking water.
2. Dissolve the cornstarch in ¼ cup of the cooking water. Add to the carrots, with the remaining ¾ cup of cooking water, along with the honey and salt and ginger to taste. Stir over low heat until the mixture thickens. Remove promptly from the heat.

TO BREAK THE FAST

HERRING IN SOUR CREAM

MAKES ABOUT 3 CUPS. (D)

First she chopped the milk roe with onion—this was the appetizer. The herring brine was the base for a potato soup. The second onion was sliced and flavored with vinegar—the salad, to be sure. The herring itself was the roast, which she wrapped in a wet newspaper and then placed on the red coals in the range.

Sholem Asch, *The Mother*

Small fish in brine are good to eat after fasting.

Avodah Zarah 29A

In the poor Eastern European shtetl, a four-course meal could be made from a milk roe, herring, a potato, two onions, and a piece of day-old bread, as novelist Sholem Asch shows. This raw salt herring, often chopped with onion, an apple, a slice of bread, and a little vinegar, was distinctly the Polish-Russian-Lithuanian gift to Jewish cookery. Once a major part of the diet during the week, it has become for us a coveted hors d'oeuvre or Sunday breakfast dish.

After eating a sweet and tea to break the fast of Yom Kippur, it is traditional to eat herring to help restock the body with salt. In my family, herring with sour cream and red onions is served. I have added a bit of dill to this originally Polish dish. Another variation might include apples and nuts.

One 13-ounce jar herring in wine sauce
1 red onion, sliced in rings
¼ cup sour cream

2 tablespoons fresh lemon juice
1 tablespoon sugar
Sprig of dill, chopped (optional)

1. Drain the herring and remove the onions.
2. Replace the original onion rings with about 5 red-onion rings. Mix in the sour cream, lemon juice, and sugar. (The amount of sour cream and onion rings can vary according to taste and the number of guests.)
3. Place in a larger covered glass container and chill in the refrigerator for a few hours or overnight. Sprinkle with dill, if using, and serve with crackers. This will last for weeks in the refrigerator.

Variation: Omit the dill and add 1 chopped apple and ½ cup coarsely chopped blanched almonds.

MARK TALISMAN'S BAGELS

MAKES 20–24. (D)

You take a hole, and you put some dough around it.
Old Yiddish recipe for bagels

What is more Jewish—and American—than the bagel? Of all the foods handed down from our Eastern European forebears, who ate these buns as snacks in the afternoon, bagels have probably become the most universally popular.

Bagels, lox, and cream cheese with tomatoes and onions are not only break the fast, circumcision, and even Sunday-brunch Jewish favorites, they are standard fare for all American brunches. Green bagels are served on St. Patrick's Day, and this bread with a hole is served in first-class delicatessen lunches on airplanes. Twenty-four-hour bagel factories operate in many cities. Many bakeries even prepare bagel bread.

Symbolic of the endless circle of life, bagels were mentioned as early as 1610 in the community regulations of Cracow. These bagels were given to women in childbirth. (Today, doctors prescribe day-old bagels for teething infants.) The origin of bagels is, however, clouded in mystery. One theory traces them to 1683 Vienna, where bakers created stirrup-shaped buns in honor of their deliverance from the Turks by the King of Poland who was a riding buff; *buegal* is the Austrian word for "stirrup." Another theory is that "bagel" is a Yiddish corruption of Middle High German *bougel* or *beugel,* meaning "a twisted or curved ring or bracelet." A third theory is that bagels were invented as an economical food for poor people because the hole saved material!

A true bagel is made from white high-gluten wheat flour and is perfectly plain. The secret is to boil it in water to reduce the starch content as well as to give it an outer sheen and hard crust. There were also milk and egg bagels. Today there is an endless variety of rye, pumpernickel, whole-wheat, onion, poppy-seed, raisin, and even pizza bagels. Bagel mavens claim that the best bakery bagels are in Montreal, though people from Toronto claim that their twisted bagels are superior. For years Mark Talisman has been making bagels, getting up at dawn and rolling them out for friends and family.

2 tablespoons margarine	8 cups unbleached all-purpose
1 cup milk, scalded	flour (approximately)
2 scant tablespoons (2 packages)	1 tablespoon salt
active dry yeast	3 quarts water
Pinch of sugar	2 tablespoons kosher salt
2 cups warm water	Sesame, poppy, or caraway seeds

1. Melt the margarine in the scalded milk.
2. Dissolve the yeast with a pinch of sugar in the warm water.
3. Combine the 2 liquid mixtures in a large bowl and gradually blend in the flour and the salt until a soft, sticky dough is formed. (A food processor is fine to start this.) Knead well and place in a greased bowl. Cover and let rise in a warm place until doubled in size, about 1 hour.
4. Preheat the oven to 400 degrees. Boil the 3 quarts water with the kosher salt.
5. Knead the dough again on a floured board. Break off a piece about the size of a plum and roll out into a 5½-inch-long snakelike shape, tapering the dough at each end. Twist into a circle and press the ends together. Place on a floured board. Continue until all the dough is used up. Let stand, uncovered, until the dough begins to rise, about 10 minutes.
6. Drop the bagels one by one into the boiling salted water, boiling a few at a time. Cover and wait until the water boils again. With a slotted spoon, turn the bagels, cover again, and wait until the water boils, about 2 minutes. (The water gives the bagels a crunchy crust.) Remove to a greased cookie sheet.

7. Sprinkle with sesame, poppy, or caraway seeds and bake about 30 minutes, or until golden. These bagels freeze well.

Note: These will not be as hard as commercial bagels because no preservatives are used. They are deliciously crunchy on the outside and chewy inside.

LOX

The Jewish people have always liked salty foods. What was offered to God or His emissaries had to be pure. No sourness or rottenness, no food in a state of decay, fermentation, or dissolution would be appropriate. Perhaps this is the original reason Jews honor salt, a pure mineral. All sacrifices were strewn with it. The Dead Sea healed and purified because of its salt content. Newborn children were rubbed with it. Coarse salt is issued for clearing the blood out of meat, poultry, and even fish. A table is not ready for a meal without salt, a reminder of the Tabernacle.

Herring and lox are both salty fish greatly liked by Jews. Today, with freshly cut belly lox so expensive, many people buy precut lox. Salt is added as a preservative. Nova Scotia salmon is the more expensive, less salted variety.

"Lox," meaning "salmon," comes from the German word *lachs.* In the late nineteenth century, "lox" in the United States referred to salt-cured salmon from the Pacific Ocean. In this period before refrigeration, lox was not smoked but cured in a heavy brine as a preservative and then placed in large wooden casks. A large portion of this lox was shipped to Europe. Some remained in New York, where it was soaked in water before eating; it was enjoyed largely by the Jewish community of the Lower East Side. With the advent of refrigeration and freezing, salmon came in both a mild salt-cured or frozen form before being smoked.

The American addiction to bagels and lox comes from the dairy cafeteria, which draws on traditional Eastern European dairy and fish cuisine. It has crossed over to delicatessens and to such gourmet emporia as New York's Zabar's, which also carries smoked whitefish, sable, salmon, chub, and of course all kinds of pickled herring.

LOX, SOUR CREAM, AND CAVIAR MOLD

MAKES A BIT LESS THAN 1 QUART. (D)

1 tablespoon (1 envelope)
    unflavored kosher gelatin
¼ cup cold water
½ cup heavy cream
8 ounces cream cheese
1 cup sour cream
1 tablespoon Worcestershire sauce
Dash of Tabasco sauce
2 tablespoons chopped freeze-
    dried or fresh chives

1 teaspoon lemon juice
1 tablespoon chopped fresh flat-
    leaf parsley
1 tablespoon white horseradish,
    freshly grated or prepared
½ pound lox smoked salmon,
    coarsely chopped
4 ounces red salmon caviar

1. Soak the gelatin in the cold water. Add the heavy cream.
2. Blend the cream cheese and sour cream in a food processor or electric mixer.
3. Add the gelatin mixture, Worcestershire sauce, Tabasco, chives, lemon juice, parsley, and horseradish to the cream cheese mixture and combine well.
4. Blend in the lox and the caviar.
5. Rinse a 1-quart mold with cold water. Dry, then rub some vegetable oil inside. Fill with the mixture and chill for at least 12 hours.
6. When ready to serve, insert a sharp knife around the mold, wrap the mold with a towel dampened in hot water, place a plate on top, invert them, and unmold. Serve with sliced black bread.

LOX BRUNCH SPREAD

MAKES 1½ CUPS. (D)

½ cup finely minced onion
½ pound lox smoked salmon,
   shredded

3 teaspoons chopped fresh dill
4 teaspoons prepared horseradish
¾ cup sour cream

Mix all the ingredients well in a bowl, adjusting to taste. Let stand, covered, a few hours for the flavors to blend. Serve on thick slices of pumpernickel or bagels.

TADJINE AU POULET ET AUX COINGS
(Algerian Chicken Tagine with Quinces)

SERVES 4–6. (M)

For Algerian Jews quinces are a fruit of the fall season. Leone Jaffin, in her *150 Recettes et Mille et Un Souvenirs d'une Juive d'Algérie* (150 Recipes and 1,001 Memories of an Algerian Jew), tells of the chicken *tagine* with quinces that constituted the main course at the break-the-fast meal in her father's hometown of Algiers. She shared this recipe from her book with me.

1 large chicken, cut into 8 pieces
½ cup flour for dredging
½ cup peanut oil
Salt and freshly ground pepper
2 pounds onions, chopped

1 tablespoon sugar
2 pounds quinces
Juice of 1 lemon
Pinch of nutmeg
2 teaspoons cinnamon

1. Roll each piece of chicken in flour, shake off the excess, and brown in the oil. Remove to a plate lined with paper towels. Season with salt and pepper to taste.

2. In the same skillet add the onions with the sugar. Cook, stirring occasionally, until the onions are golden.

3. Meanwhile, peel the quinces, remove the seeds, and cut into 6 or 8 pieces depending on the size. Sprinkle with lemon juice.

4. Place the onions, chicken pieces, and then the quinces in a Dutch oven. Add the nutmeg and the cinnamon.

5. Cover tightly and let simmer on a low flame for 1½ hours. By the end of the cooking everything should be a golden pink, a little like the color of a quince compote. Add a little more cinnamon to taste and serve.

FIJUELAS

MAKES 24. (P)

This recipe came to McLean, Virginia, from Morocco, via four generations of Sultan Levy Rosenblatt's family who lived in Brazil. It is a crisp pastry that is eaten with Moroccan mint tea to break the fast of Yom Kippur and also at Hanukkah.

1 cup warm water	Vegetable oil for frying
2 egg yolks	2 cups sugar
2 tablespoons vegetable shortening or pareve margarine	1 cup water
1 teaspoon salt	1 teaspoon orange-blossom water
4 cups all-purpose unbleached flour	Cinnamon

1. Combine the warm water, egg yolks, shortening or margarine, and salt. Gradually add the flour, kneading gently as you go. Knead about 10 minutes, until you reach a firm dough. Cover with a towel and let rest for 1 hour.

2. When the dough has risen (it will not rise very much), break off a piece the size of a plum and flatten it out with the palm of your hand. Shape into a rectangle and roll it out in strips approximately 3 by 9 inches. It is easiest to use a

pasta machine for this. Otherwise, use a rolling pin. It should be almost as thin as phyllo dough. When it is as thin as possible, stretch it out gently. Place each piece of dough on a floured cookie sheet. Cover with a towel while making more. Continue until all the dough is used up.

3. In a heavy casserole, heat the oil to about 375 degrees. With a slotted spoon, place one end of the thin strip in the oil. As it cooks, it will roll up like a jelly roll. When it is golden brown, let it drain tilted on the edge of the pan. Drain again on a paper towel. You must work very quickly to cook and then drain it, so that it does not retain too much fat. Continue until all the pieces are completed.

4. Combine the sugar and water and boil until a syrup is formed, about 20 minutes. Add the orange-blossom water. Let cool somewhat.

5. Pour the syrup over the *fijuelas* and sprinkle with cinnamon. The *fijuelas* will last several weeks if covered.

ALMOND MILK

MAKES ABOUT 4½ CUPS. (P)

From being forbidden by their usage to mingle butter, or other preparation of milk or cream with meat at any meal, the Jews have oil much used in their cookery of fish, meat, and vegetables. Pounded almonds and rich syrups of sugar and water agreeably flavoured, assist in compounding their sweet dishes, many of which are excellent, and preserve much of their oriental character; but we are credibly informed that the restrictions of which we have spoken are not at the present day very rigidly observed by the main body of Jews in this country, though they are so by those who are denominated strict.

As a substitute for milk, in the composition of soufflés, puddings, and sweet dishes, almond-cream as it is called, will be found to answer excellently. To prepare it, blanch and pound the almonds, and then pour very gradually to them boiling water in the proportion directed below; turn them into a strong cloth or tammy, and wring it from them with powerful pressure, to extract as much as possible of it from them again.

Almond-cream: (for puddings, etc.) almonds, 4 oz.; water, 1 pint. For blancmanges, and rich soufflés, creams and custards: almonds, ½ pound to whole pound; water, 1 to 1½ pints.

Obs. As every book may not be quite aware of the articles of food strictly prohibited by the Mosaic law, it may be well to specify them here. Pork in every form; all varieties of shell-fish, without exception; hares, rabbits, and swans.

The above quotation comes from Eliza Acton's *Modern Cookery for Private Families,* published in London in 1845. Not only did this book include recipes for Roman Catholic fast days, it also provided a chapter with kosher recipes for Jewish households.

Almond milk is one of the first drinks known to mankind. It was, and still is, recommended for nursing mothers.

Before the advent of commercial bottled drinks, more naturally flavored beverages were prepared, especially in warm lands. To this day, Jews from the Middle East drink a variety of sweet fruit and nut beverages to break the fast of Yom Kippur. Persian Jews prepare *afshoreh seeb*, an apple drink with rose water; Lebanese prefer an apricot drink with nuts, similar to *amardin*, a sweet apricot drink with which the Muslims break the daily fast of Ramadan. Iraqi Jews drink *hariri*, or almond milk, because its white color symbolizes purity and it acts as a good lining to an empty stomach. Greek Jews call the almond milk *soumada*.

In a thickened state, it was used by Jews instead of cream sauce over fruit desserts with a meat meal. Although wealthy Russian Jews from Riga ate it over *kichel* or cranberry or rice pudding, it most probably originated with Sephardic Jews. The following is a Moroccan variation still used to this day.

4 cups water	1 cup sugar
1 pound blanched almonds	¼ cup orange-blossom water

1. Place 1 cup of the water in a blender or food processor. Add ½ cup of the almonds, ¼ cup of the sugar, and 1 tablespoon of the orange-blossom water. Whirl until pulverized.
2. Press the mixture through a cheesecloth. Then blend once more. Repeat the process 3 more times with the remaining ingredients. Combine the 4 batches.
3. Serve with ice and dilute with water until the desired consistency is reached.

MEAT AND VEGETABLE SOUP
(Harira)

SERVES 4–6. (M)

A meal without soup is no meal.
Berakhot 44

This rich soup is eaten by some Moroccan Jews for the meal after the fast of Yom Kippur. Basically an Arab dish to break the fast of Ramadan, it has been adapted by the Jews of southern Morocco to their diet. Except for the tomatoes in this recipe, the other ingredients are extremely old and could date back to the biblical period.

1 cup dried lentils
1 cup dried fava or lima beans
1 pound stewing meat, cubed
2 medium onions, chopped
¼ cup vegetable oil
1 pound tomatoes, peeled and
    chopped
1 bunch celery with leaves, finely
    chopped

2 tablespoons fresh cilantro or
    flat-leaf parsley
Salt and pepper
Water
2 tablespoons flour
Juice of 2 lemons
Lemon slices

1. Soak the lentils and fava or lima beans overnight.
2. In a heavy saucepan, sauté the meat and chopped onions in the oil. When the meat is brown, add the lentils, beans, tomatoes, celery, cilantro or parsley, and salt and pepper to taste. Add 4 cups of water and simmer, covered, for about 2 hours.
3. When the meat is tender and the beans soft, adjust the seasonings. Bring to a boil.
4. Mix the flour into about 2 tablespoons of cold water and stir into the boiling soup. Keep stirring to avoid lumps.
5. After 1–2 minutes, turn off the heat and add the lemon juice. Serve very hot with lemon slices.

SCHNECKEN

MAKES 48. (D)

If the benevolent eighteenth-century Russian Hasidic rabbi Levi Itzhak ben Meir of Berditchev, who judged his people with compassion-colored spectacles, were to look down on the New York food scene today, he would not be surprised to see his descendant, Marian Fox Burros, defending the American consumer. As food columnist for the *New York Times* and author of many cookbooks, Marian is involved in all aspects of cooking.

Through Marian's books she includes old Russian family favorites such as this cookie-like *schnecken*. "Schnecken" is a German word for "snails," and indeed the pastry—rolled up with nuts, cinnamon, and raisins—resembles snails. Rabbi Levi Itzhak's wife might well have made her *schnecken* from leftover strudel dough, however. Marian's recipe, a traditional break-the-fast treat, is one she watched her mother prepare. A variation of the original appears in her second book, *Freeze with Ease*, and is reprinted here.

3 cups all-purpose flour	1 cup chopped walnuts or pecans
½ pound (2 sticks) unsalted butter, softened	1½ cups sugar
	2¼ teaspoons cinnamon
3 egg yolks, slightly beaten	
1 cup light cream	
1 tablespoon (1 package) active dry yeast	

1. Mix the flour and butter until well blended.
2. Combine the egg yolks and cream.
3. Add the egg mixture to the flour and blend well. Sprinkle the dry yeast over the top of the dough and mix it in with your hands.
4. Divide the dough into 6 parts and wrap each part in aluminum foil. Refrigerate overnight.
5. Roll each piece of dough into a circle on a floured board, about ⅛ inch thick.
6. Preheat the oven to 325 degrees.

7. Combine the nuts, sugar, and cinnamon and then divide into 6 portions. Place one circle of dough on top of each of these portions. Press down, turn over, and repeat, so both sides are covered with the mixture. Cut each circle into 8 wedges, like a pie. Roll up each wedge, starting at the wide end.
8. Bake on a greased cookie sheet for 25 minutes, or until golden.

LOKSHEN KUGEL

SERVES 4–6. (D)

Since no cooking is permitted during the fast of Yom Kippur, foods must be prepared ahead of time. A sweet noodle kugel is a perfect beginning to a new year.

8 ounces broad noodles	½ pound cottage cheese
4 large eggs, separated	½ pint sour cream
¼ pound (1 stick) unsalted butter, softened	½ cup sugar
	¼ cup graham cracker crumbs

1. Cook the noodles according to the directions on the package. Drain.
2. Preheat the oven to 350 degrees.
3. Beat the egg whites until stiff peaks form. Combine the remaining ingredients, except the crumbs, and fold in the egg whites.
4. Transfer to a greased 1-quart round baking dish and sprinkle with graham cracker crumbs.
5. Bake 45 minutes, or until golden brown.

MRS. HERBST'S PASTRIES

Alex Lichtman

In 1905, Alexander and Bertha Herbst came to New York on their honeymoon from their native Budapest. Like over two million Jewish immigrants of that period, they decided to stay. Alexander, a cabinetmaker by trade, worked for fifteen years building Steinway pianos, including Toscanini's. On one Yom Kippur, the Steinway Company wanted him to work. A religious Jew, Mr. Herbst refused and quit. From there he started a variety of businesses: he built a newsstand at 79th Street and First Avenue and he opened a grocery store.

At the beginning of the Depression in 1930, he was fifty-five years old, broke, and jobless. He began a new career out of his kitchen with his wife, known as a fine cook throughout Yorkville, the Hungarian-German neighborhood on the Upper East Side around 86th Street, where the Herbsts lived. Each day at 4 a.m., the Herbsts started stretching and filling strudels with poppy seeds, nuts, cherries, apples, or cabbage. "My grandfather built a box that he strapped on his back with a space for trays of strudel," said Cissie Klavens, Mr. Herbst's granddaughter. "He delivered strudel to restaurants by subway until he had enough money for a small truck."

In 1935, Mrs. Herbst's Bakery, specializing in strudel, *pogacsa,* and *fluden,* opened on Third Avenue between 81st and 82nd Streets, catering to the carriage trade. "I remember the first time we visited Mrs. Herbst's Bakery and I saw chauffeurs coming in to pick up the fancy cakes and pastries," recalled George Greenstein, the author of *Secrets of a Jewish Baker.* "My dad, also a Hungarian baker, took me in the back and I stood there stunned because there were women pulling the strudel. We were all men in our bakery."

Eventually the Herbsts' daughter Elsie started helping out, delivering strudel to restaurants throughout Manhattan, including one where an immigrant from Satmar, Hungary, now Romania, was working. The young man, Alex Lichtman, had worked as a chef and pastry chef at several restaurants in New York City, and had chosen Mrs. Herbst's strudel to serve to his customers. Alex fell in love with Elsie, whom he soon married, and joined her family's promising business.

Until the Lichtmans retired in 1975, Alex did most of the baking and Elsie did the bookkeeping. As in many immigrant families, Alex brought his two brothers, Mano and Louis, to New York in 1938 and then taught them the business. Later they opened Louis Lichtman's Bakery, at 86th Street and Amsterdam Avenue.

Mrs. Herbst's closed in 1986 and Louis Lichtman's in 1987. Upon his retirement in 1980, Alex went to live at West Palm Beach's Century Village, where he taught a course, "Baking for Balabustas (housewives)." His dream was to write a cookbook, but he died before its completion. "My dad would come up to Newtown for two weeks and be planted in the kitchen, baking up a storm for all my friends," said Cissie. "My father's recipes were all in his head. Many were written down, but we can't find the recipe for his strudel. That may be lost forever."

HUNGARIAN *KUGELHOPF*

From Alex Lichtman

MAKES 1 KUGELHOPF. (D)

A cross between a brioche and a *babka,* the *kugelhopf* (also spelled *gugelhopf*) was made by Central European and Alsatian Jews. Unlike the classic Alsatian variety, made in an earthenware mold, this Hungarian version does not have candied fruit embedded in the dough. It is a perfect butter-rich cake to break the fast of Yom Kippur and is delicious any time of the year.

1 scant tablespoon (1 package) active dry yeast

⅔ cup warm milk

1 large egg

½ cup sugar

¼ teaspoon salt

½ teaspoon vanilla extract

2 cups unbleached all-purpose flour, or more as needed

¼ pound (1 stick) unsalted butter, at room temperature

2 teaspoons unsalted butter, melted

2 teaspoons cinnamon

2 tablespoons raisins

1 tablespoon warm water

1. Dissolve the yeast in the milk.
2. In the bowl of an electric mixer fitted with the paddle, mix the egg, ¼ cup of the sugar, the salt, and the vanilla. Add the yeast mixture, then gradually add the flour. Beat on low speed for 3 minutes, then turn to high speed until the dough leaves the sides of the bowl.
3. Place the dough in a pan dusted with flour, cover with a towel, and refrigerate for at least 15 minutes. The dough will be sticky. You can leave it for several hours.
4. On a floured board, roll out the dough to a 12- by 8-inch rectangle.
5. Spread all the soft butter over half the dough, measured from the shorter side. Fold the other half of the dough over the butter, sprinkling the board and the top of the dough with flour. Pinch the sides closed. Turn the dough 90 degrees and roll out to a rectangle again; then fold in half again.

6. Wrap the dough in plastic wrap, refrigerate for 15 minutes, and then roll it out and fold it in half twice more. Each time, roll it out in all 4 directions to 12 by 8 inches, turning it 90 degrees.

7. After the second folding, to a rectangle 8 by 6 inches, brush the top of the dough lightly with the melted butter. Cover with freezer paper or plastic wrap. Refrigerate at least 6 hours or overnight.

8. Roll the dough out to a rectangle about 10 by 8 inches. Mix the remaining ¼ cup sugar with the cinnamon and sprinkle on top of the dough, leaving a 1-inch border all around. Then sprinkle the raisins over the sugar. Roll the rectangle up tight, like a jelly roll, from the shorter side.

9. Grease well a 7-inch *kugelhopf* pan or 9- by 5-inch loaf pan.

10. Place one end of the roll against the other to form a circle and insert it into the *kugelhopf* pan, seam side up. If using a loaf pan, twist the dough once, holding the ends, so it resembles a bow tie and put it in the pan.

11. Let the *kugelhopf* rise, covered with a cloth, for at least 1 hour, until the dough is about double in size.

12. Preheat the oven to 350 degrees.

13. Brush the top of the *kugelhopf* with the warm water and bake for 45 minutes, or until the top is golden brown.

SUKKOT

SUKKOT

Three times thou shalt keep a feast unto Me in the year. The feast of unleavened bread shalt thou keep; seven days thou shalt eat unleavened bread, as I commanded thee, at the time appointed in the month Abib—for in it thou camest out from Egypt; and none shall appear before Me empty; and the feast of harvest, the first-fruits of thy labours, which thou sowest in the field; and the feast of ingathering, at the end of the year, when thou gatherest in thy labours out of the field.

Exodus 23:14–16

Sukkot, the Feast of the Ingathering, is at its best in Israel. There, after a hot, dry summer that has produced good crops, Sukkot marks, and has always marked, the successful harvest. The main features of the original celebration were the actual reaping of wheat, the gathering of grapes, and the ripening of olives, for which Palestine was famous. Olives are harvested in November, after Sukkot and the first rains.

In ancient times, special ceremonies were performed to induce the first rainfall of the year. One was the waving of branches of the four species of plants and trees that decorate the sukkah. They are the palm, the myrtle, the willow, and the citron, which produces a lemon-like fruit called *etrog* in Hebrew. There are many explanations for the four species. One is the following: The feminine *etrog*, shaped like a heart and symbolizing the hope of divine forgiveness for the mur-

muring and desires of our heart, is held in the left hand. In the right is the masculine *lulav,* or palm branch, symbolizing Israel's singlehearted loyalty to God, intertwined with the *hadas,* or myrtle, shaped like an eye and symbolizing the hope of divine forgiveness for greed and envy, and the *arava,* the willow, shaped like a mouth and symbolizing the hope of divine forgiveness for idle talk and falsehoods. In ancient times a combination of one feminine and three masculine symbols would bring rainfall. In the same way that these four plants cannot exist without water, the world must have rain.

People lived in trellis-roofed cabins throughout the period of harvesting. The booths were later reinterpreted as a reminder of the dwellings that the ancestors of Israel had lived in when they wandered in the wilderness on their journey from Egypt to the promised land. These booths protected farmers from the strong rays of the midday sun. This holiday then became a logical sequel to Passover and Shavuot, which commemorated the escape from bondage and the conclusion of the Covenant at Sinai. Of course, the Jews wandering in the desert probably never lived in wooden booths with green roofs. They dwelled in portable tents.

To this day, many Jews build a sukkah with wood or canvas and use branches of trees for the roof, as the sky must show through. In fact, sukkah-building kits, with instructions for building your own sukkah, have helped more families in preparing their own and even organizing sukkah-making parties. Friends help our family decorate the sukkah. I ask each guest to bring a decoration and a dish. Together, we dress the sukkah with fir branches, dried figs, pomegranates, and grapes—all evocative of the harvest and fall. Many families eat meals in the sukkah, especially on the first night and day. In case of a drizzle, the meal in the sukkah can continue, but if rain is falling in the food, the participants may retire to the house.

Seasonal fruits and vegetables—all symbols of plenty—decorate the branches and are prepared in daily dishes for the eight days of the festival. When the harvest festival first began, the foods included figs, dates, pomegranates, apricots, squash, romaine lettuce, onions, barley, and wheat bread, as well as freshly killed lamb.

The eighth day of Sukkot is Shemini Atzeret, when memorial services are held. On the next day, Simhat Torah, the Torah is carried around the synagogue and everyone dances. Drinking and eating are part and parcel of this joyous occasion when the annual cycle of the reading of the Torah is concluded. Go to any synagogue in your area to watch this colorful procession.

Throughout history Jews have built sukkot and celebrated Sukkot in many lands. In Eastern Europe seasonal fruits and vegetables included cabbage, cucumbers, sweet potatoes, and apples. Thus, dishes such as stuffed cabbage, pickles, *tsimmes,* and apple strudel are traditional at Sukkot there; kreplakh traditionally begin the Simhat Torah meal. In this country, vegetables such as zucchini, eggplant, and tomatoes are abundant in the fall. We have added our own dishes to the seasonal foods of our forebears. Since our American Thanksgiving festival was originally the English harvest festival, also observed in October, at the time of Sukkot, it is understandable that many dishes Americans serve for Thanksgiving can also be prepared for Sukkot.

A midrash teaches that in Sodom seven kinds of trees interlaced and grew one on top of the other: vine trees and fig, pomegranate, date, peach, almond, and other nut trees. With the destruction of Sodom these trees were laid waste and the land became the Dead Sea, salty and desolate. It was believed that, with the coming of the Messiah, Sodom would be rebuilt and its trees would bloom once more. It was also thought that those celebrating the Feast of the Tabernacles would then be given a place in the fruitful sukkot of Sodom redeemed.

MENUS

ORIENTAL
Syrian *Yaprak* (Stuffed Grape
Leaves with Apricots)
Turkish Stuffed Zucchini
Moroccan Carrot Salad
Baklava
Fresh Fruit

DURING THE WEEK
Romanian Eggplant and
Pepper Salad
Sukkot *Tsimmes*
Edna Rostow's Multigrain Bread
Ukranian Dill Pickles
Hot Fruit Compote
Aunt Eva's Cookies

HUNGARIAN
Berches (Potato Challah)
Mushroom and Barley Soup
Sweet-and-Sour Stuffed Cabbage
Cucumber Salad
Splendid Strudel

FRIDAY NIGHT
Chicken Soup with Matzah Balls
Turkey with Bread Stuffing
Sweet Potato *Tsimmes* with
Pineapple
Chestnuts and Prunes
Green Salad
Zwetschgenkuchen

THE SOUR AND THE MASH, RYES AND PUMPERNICKELS

"You don't have to be Jewish to love Levy's rye"—or any rye bread, for that matter. That you don't have to be Russian or Polish is more to the point. Rye needs a cold climate and was never grown in ancient Israel. It originated as a weed in parts of Asia where wheat was cultivated thousands of years ago. From here it was probably brought to northern Europe. Although "rye 'n injun," made from rye and cornmeal, was the staple bread of the early American colonists, it was Russian-Jewish bakers at the turn of the century and later advertising techniques that made rye bread so popular.

The earliest bread prepared by the Jews was made of flat cakes baked between layers of slow-burning camel dung, as in the Book of Ezra. They also parched the grain, like the reapers in the Book of Ruth. If they had a hearth, they roasted the dough in the ashes.

When the Jews settled down and began baking bread, they baked well. Their best bread was of wheat *kemach solet,* "essence of flour," from which they made Temple sacrifices to God and bread for the rich. Barley was used by the poor and for horse feed. To make barley palatable, ground lentils, beans, and millet were added.

At first, Jewish housewives and their daughters tended the ovens; later, maidservants helped. Later still, when Jews became city dwellers, men became bakers. In Jerusalem there is still a baker's street in the Old City. The first breads were small round loaves slightly raised in the center and about as thick as a finger. Three breads per person were eaten at each meal. Thus, at the meal Abigail prepared for David and his men, she served two huge jugs of wine and two hundred loaves of bread.

Nowadays rye bread, often considered inferior to wheat, is sometimes not eaten on holidays. But during the week of Sukkot it is perfectly acceptable with a hearty vegetable soup.

Black bread—rye bread made from dark, coarsely ground flour—is what poor Russian Jews ate during the week, with challah or white bread for the Sabbath. American rye is lighter, so we need coffee, cocoa, or blackstrap molasses to achieve the desired dark effect.

It takes an expert to prepare excellent rye bread. Rye flour is harder to handle than wheat. The dough is stickier, more difficult, and must be kneaded longer.

"In Poland we didn't have the white flour you have in the United States. We had a combination of flours. When I close my eyes, I see so many kinds of bread—rye bread, rolls, kaiser rolls, *razovanna* bread (a whole-grain health bread), round loaves of rye and pumpernickel bread with cracked grain, two kilos of wonderful bread, four-pounders that would last for three days and not get stale. The bread we baked back then was fantastic. We had black bread, too, but it wasn't like the Russian bread, more like the rye but darkened with molasses or coffee." So says Jack Wayne, son of a baker from Lodz, Poland, remembering his youth there. Mr. Wayne started baking in his parents' bakery at the age of six. He considers Zingerman's rye pumpernickel in Ann Arbor, Michigan, made with master baker Michael London's formula, the closest to what he grew up with in Lodz.

As Michael London told me during a baking session, the trick to making a good pumpernickel is in the sour and in the wet mash of leftover rye bread that goes into the bread. On New York's Lower East Side, before refrigerators, Jewish bakers left their moistened day-old bread in pickle barrels covered with cheesecloth and their sours in wooden proofing troughs. "The problem is, the mash molds easily," said Michael. "It was against the law in those days to use old soaked ryes." Had a health inspector seen the soaking bread, he would have made them throw it out.

THE SOUR

From Michael London

MAKES 6 CUPS. (P)

A good sour, a fermentation of flour and water caused by wild yeasts in the air, should be almost as stiff as the dough. "It should almost be like cement," said Michael. "It has a good smell, which builds up. The trick is to build it up successively until it cracks. I like to sprinkle rye flour on top when I start. When the flour cracks, I know it is ready. It can take from 18 hours to a day. There is a fine line between fermentation and putrefaction."

2 medium onions, coarsely chopped	4 cups water
1 tablespoon caraway seeds	5 cups medium rye flour, plus 1 tablespoon for sprinkling
1 scant tablespoon (1 package) active dry yeast	

1. Tie the onions and caraway seeds in a knotted cheesecloth bag.
2. Dissolve the yeast in 3½ cups of water in a small bowl and pour it over 4 cups of the flour in a large bowl. Stir to mix until it attains the consistency of wet cement. Submerge the cheesecloth bag of chopped onions and caraway seeds in the center of what will become "the sour." Sprinkle the tablespoon of rye flour over the surface. Cover loosely with plastic wrap and set aside overnight, unrefrigerated. The sour needs air to breathe, but not too much, or it will dry out.
3. The next day, remove the onion-caraway bag and discard it. The sour should smell somewhat acidic but not rotten after about 15 hours. At this point feed it (mix it) with the remaining 1 cup flour and ½ cup water, or enough to maintain the thick consistency. Cover again and let the sour sit until the area between the "cracks" in the dough spreads. You want to capture as much of its strength as possible.
4. After it rises again, in about 4 hours, you will have about 6 cups. You can begin to use it or continue to build it up (which increases the amount of sour). Use it in the bread now or refrigerate it. You should feed the sour once every 24 hours with at least 1 cup flour and ½ cup water. The sour can stay several days in the refrigerator without being fed, but, as Michael says, never take a sour for granted. It needs to be nourished.

PUMPERNICKEL RYE BREAD

Adapted from Michael London

MAKES 2 LOAVES. (P)

Sukkot is the time to start making pumpernickel. It's a great cold-weather bread, wonderful slathered with butter and served with good hot soup. Once you have mastered the sour, this bread is easy to prepare. Note that with this pumpernickel rye and the following Jewish corn rye bread you need very little yeast—the sour is the leavening agent.

I love making this bread, but if you'd rather, you can mail-order it from Zingerman's Bake House at www.zingermans.com.

5 slices day-old rye bread, crusts removed (about 2½ cups)

3 cups water

2 cups sour (page 207)

4 teaspoons blackstrap molasses or caramel coloring*

2 tablespoons sea salt

2 tablespoons coarsely ground caraway seeds (optional)

1 cup cracked rye or pumpernickel flour, plus additional for sprinkling

8 cups good bread flour, and more as needed

1 scant tablespoon (1 package) active dry yeast

1. In a bowl, crumble the day-old rye bread into 1 cup of water until the water is absorbed. Crumble it with your hands; this is what the old-time bakers did. It carries the character of yesterday's bread to today. Drain excess water.

2. In the bowl of an electric mixer fitted with the dough hook, put the rye bread mixture, the remaining 2 cups water, the 2 cups of sour, and the molasses or caramel coloring. Stir together at low speed until mixed, about 1 minute.

3. Add the sea salt and caraway seeds, if using. Gradually add the cracked rye or

*According to Michael, old-time bakers burned sugar to make the carmel coloring that gives New York pumpernickel rye its characteristic taste.

pumpernickel flour and the bread flour. Sprinkle the yeast in and stir about 5 minutes, until well incorporated, scraping down the sides of the bowl. Knead by hand for a few minutes. Place in a greased bowl and cover, letting the dough rise 1–1½ hours, until doubled in size.

4. Punch the dough down, and if it is still sticky, incorporate more flour as needed. Divide the dough in half, gently form 2 round or oblong loaves, and let them rest 10–15 minutes on a floured work surface. Remove the loaves to a floured cookie sheet, cover very loosely with plastic wrap, and let them rise for another 1½ hours, until doubled in size.

5. Preheat the oven to 400 degrees, set a rack in the middle, and put 6 ice cubes in a pan on the floor of the oven.

6. Since rye and pumpernickel love steam, brush or spray the loaves with water. Sprinkle some of the rye flour on top and then, with a single-edged razor or very sharp knife, make 5 cuts across each loaf, shorter ones on the ends, longer in the center. Bake the loaves for 45–50 minutes, or until they sound hollow when tapped with a spatula. To keep a shine, brush them afterward with water or with ½ cup water and ½ teaspoon of cornstarch.

JEWISH CORN RYE

Adapted from Ben Moskovitz

MAKES 2 LOAVES. (P)

"As every good baker knows, you can't rush. Each dough has its own character and some are more temperamental than others. If you wind up with a stiff sweet dough, you've probably used cold eggs. Let the dough warm up and it will be pliable again. Also, with a sour starter, it has to be babied constantly. The sour is the flavor. Corned beef has to be pickled and bread has to be babied. Make it simple and it will be delicious." That's the point, from Ben Moskovitz, owner of Star Bakery.

I have always wondered why American Jews call a very heavy and sour rye bread "corn bread." Somehow, the translation got garbled. In Yiddish, "corn" changed in meaning from "particle" to "small seed" and specifically "grain," so a corn bread could be any bread made with grain. Some say that the bread got its name because cornmeal is thrown on the baking sheet when it is baked.

Once you have made your sour, baking this corn rye is easy. Make one loaf with caraway seeds (for a stronger flavor) and one without. See which you prefer.

3 cups sour (page 207)	1½ tablespoons salt
7 cups bread flour	2 tablespoons caraway seeds
2¼ cups water	Cornmeal for dusting
1 teaspoon active dry yeast	

1. Place the sour in a large mixing bowl. Add 1¾ cups of the bread flour and ½ cup of water to keep it wet. Mix and scrape down the sides to keep them clean. Cover loosely with plastic wrap and let the mixture sit for 1 hour.

2. Scoop the mixture into the bowl of an electric mixer fitted with the dough hook. Sprinkle the yeast with the remaining 1¾ cups of water into the bowl. Then gradually add the remaining flour and the salt as you knead the dough at medium speed, about 5 minutes. If the dough is too stiff, add more water. When the dough no longer sticks to the dough hook, it is ready. Remove the dough, pat it into a round, and let it rise on a floured work surface for 20 minutes, uncovered.

3. Punch the dough down and divide it in half. Add caraway seeds to one half, and form both into balls or oblongs. Let them rise 1 more hour on a cookie sheet dusted with flour.

4. Preheat the oven to 400 degrees. You will know when the dough is ready to bake because its texture softens—it becomes soft like a balloon, and when you push on it with your finger, it springs back and does not leave a mark. Slash the loaves ⅛ inch deep a few times with a straight razor or very sharp knife. Put 5 ice cubes in a pan on the floor of the oven. Before you put the loaves in the oven, brush them with water.

5. Bake the loaves on the middle rack of the oven for 40–50 minutes, or until they sound hollow when you tap them on the top. When you remove the loaves, brush with water or with ½ cup water and ½ teaspoon cornstarch, if you want a shinier loaf.

EDNA ROSTOW'S MULTIGRAIN BREAD

MAKES 2 LOAVES. (P)

When Edna Rostow's children were growing up in New Haven, Connecticut, there was always a loaf of homemade bread set out on a board with a round of cheese nearby. "There are so many reasons for making bread besides the taste. It is good to come into a house and smell bread baking, and it is a good form of occupational therapy," says Mrs. Rostow, now in her eighties.

For Mrs. Rostow baking bread stems from her childhood memory of fresh European breads delivered to her parents' home in New Haven. "I hated American-bought bread except for the original Pepperidge Farm bread. I can remember the two wonderful challahs that were on my grandmother's table each Friday night. In the 1950s a number of us were experimenting with gourmet cooking, and I read about a nonfat bread made at Cornell University. That started me."

Now a grandmother of four, Mrs. Rostow has passed down her tradition of making bread to her daughter Jessica, who bakes the same multigrain bread for her own children, as does the author of this cookbook. I have through the years changed the amounts for busy cooks and to conform to my schedule. You can vary your "wheat germ mix" with bran, oat, and soy flakes, as well as lecithin, millet, oats, buckwheat, wheat bran, or cornmeal.

2 tablespoons (2 packages) active dry yeast	2 cups whole-wheat flour
3 cups water	1 tablespoon salt
1 tablespoon sugar	3 cups oatmeal
⅓ cup honey	2 cups toasted wheat germ
5½ cups unbleached all-purpose flour (approximately)	

1. Combine the yeast in the water with the sugar in a large bowl or the bowl of an electric mixer.

2. Stir in the honey and gradually add 5 cups of the all-purpose flour and all of the whole-wheat flour, salt, oatmeal, and wheat germ. Mix well and add as much all-purpose flour as needed to make a semi-stiff dough.
3. Let rise in a greased and covered bowl for at least 1 hour, or until doubled in size.
4. Preheat the oven to 350 degrees and grease two average-size baking pans.
5. Punch down and divide into 2 loaves. Place in two bread pans and bake for 40 minutes, or until the loaves sound hollow when tapped.

A SYRIAN JEWISH PASTRY SHOP IN BROOKLYN

The sign outside reads "Mansoura Middle Eastern Pastries." In the window there are trays of baklava, nougat, and Turkish delight.

As you enter the door, a bell rings and Josiane Mansoura or her husband, Alan, emerges from the back room where they've been busy making baklava, rolling up *ka'ak* (pretzel-like rings), modeling some other Syrian delicacy, or talking on the telephone in Arabic, Hebrew, French, or English. Today the candy made from apricots and rose water is being stuffed with pistachio nuts before being rolled in sugar, and the jam made from Chinese squash is being stirred.

For two generations in this country, the Mansoura family has been catering primarily to the 30,000-strong Syrian Jewish community, most of whom have some family ties to Aleppo, Syria, and now live along Ocean Parkway in Brooklyn. For hundreds of years before that, the Mansouras, first in Aleppo, and then in Heliopolis, a suburb of Cairo, were crafting the same delicacies.

"Both Farouk and Nasser were customers, but still we had to leave Egypt," said Alan, who came to this country in 1961. "King Farouk used to send his limo to buy our Syrian ice cream [made from vanilla, cream, and *sahlab,* a ground orchid root]. Nasser, too, came into the store." And no wonder. The Mansouras are proud of their pastries and take the time together, often with their three children, to hand-produce each one. Until recently, the large table in the back room was used to stretch phyllo dough for baklava and *burekas.* When commercial phyllo became available, Alan's father, now deceased, stopped making it.

On a recent visit we were interrupted several times by Mexican and Panamanian Sephardic Jews placing orders for the Turkish delight and apricot-pistachio candy. Other customers in this Egyptian, Syrian, Lebanese, and Israeli community also dropped in. "You know, even if I had a million dollars," said Josiane, "I wouldn't give up working at this place. I like to see people, I like to talk, and I like to sit in the back room until the doorbell rings."

SYRIAN *KA'AK* (PRETZEL-LIKE RINGS)

From Mansoura Middle Eastern Pastries

MAKES 76 KA'AK (P)

These crisp, pretzel-like rings—flavored with anise, cumin, black caraway seeds, and *mahlep* (ground cherry-pit centers) and dipped in sesame seeds—are a staple in Syrian Jewish homes. A must to break the fast of Esther, the day before Purim, they are also eaten after Yom Kippur as a sign that a circular year of life has just begun.

Ka'ak and Eastern European onion or poppy-seed *kichel* are considered in Judaism to be "journey cakes," so small that a *motzi*, the blessing of the bread, need not be recited before they are eaten.

Also called *biscochos* (in Spanish) and *crozettes* (in French), these pretzel biscuits are found in every Sephardic community throughout the world. Sometimes flavored with fennel and fenugreek (Iraq), anise (Spain), or coriander (Egypt), these crisp biscuits with a hole, probably the forerunner of bagels, make a perfect snack food or cocktail appetizer.

Josiane Mansoura from Brooklyn's Mansoura Middle Eastern Pastries sometimes adds 2 tablespoons of Parmesan cheese to her recipe and shapes the dough into long "bread sticks." She occasionally adds ¼ cup of sugar for a sweetened version.

½ cup lukewarm water
1 scant tablespoon (1 package) active dry yeast

1½ teaspoons salt
4 cups unbleached all-purpose flour

¼ pound (1 stick) pareve
    margarine or vegetable
    shortening, at room
    temperature
1 tablespoon anise seeds*
¾ teaspoon cumin seeds*

¼ teaspoon black caraway seeds*
¼ teaspoon *mahlep* (ground
    cherry-pit centers)
    (optional)*
1 large egg
Sesame seeds for dipping

1. In a small bowl, stir the water with the yeast.
2. Put the yeast mixture, salt, flour, and margarine or shortening in a food processor fitted with the steel blade or an electric mixer fitted with the dough hook. Process or mix until a soft dough is formed, about 1 minute for the food processor, 5 minutes for the mixer.
3. Grind the anise, cumin, and black caraway seeds, plus the *mahlep* if using it, in a coffee grinder used for spices until well mixed but not pulverized. (Or use a mortar and pestle.) Then add to the dough.
4. Place the dough in a greased bowl, cover it loosely with plastic wrap, and leave in a warm place to rise for 30 minutes.
5. Preheat the oven to 350 degrees and lightly grease a cookie sheet.
6. Divide the dough into 38 small balls, a little less than walnut size. Then roll each ball with your palms, against a board, into a pencil-thin, snake-like piece about 10 inches long and ½ inch wide. The dough should feel like modeling clay. Cut into 5-inch lengths and connect the 2 ends of each length to make a ring with a wide hole.
7. Break the egg into a wide bowl and beat well. Place the sesame seeds in another bowl. Dip the whole *ka'ak* first in the egg and then in the sesame seeds. Place on the cookie sheet. Make all the *ka'ak,* then bake in batches on the middle rack of the oven 20–30 minutes, or until light brown and firm. Or use 2 cookie sheets and bake on the middle and lower racks, switching about 12 minutes into the baking.

*Available at Middle Eastern markets.

CABBAGE STRUDEL

SERVES 8–12 AS AN HORS D'OEUVRE
OR VEGETABLE ACCOMPANIMENT. (D OR P)

Cabbage, one of the oldest known vegetables, was highly regarded by Jews for both nutritive and medicinal purposes.

Because the grapevine and the cabbage plant were said to loathe one another, cabbage came to be thought of as a prevention against intoxication. If a man ate cabbage while drinking, he would not become inebriated. It was also thought to be a cure for hangovers.

It is no wonder, then, that Hungarians traditionally prepare cabbage strudel for Simhat Torah and Purim, the two holidays when drinking and revelry take place. This scrumptious dish can be served as an elegant hors d'oeuvre, a vegetable accompaniment to goose, chicken, or pot roast, or, sprinkled with confectioners' sugar, as a dessert. I first tasted it with caraway seeds in Jerusalem at the enchanting home of Josef Tal, the famous Israeli composer.

1 head cabbage (2 pounds)	1 tablespoon sugar
2 teaspoons salt	1 teaspoon cinnamon
¼ cup vegetable oil	8 phyllo sheets
1 medium onion, coarsely chopped	6 tablespoons butter or pareve margarine, melted
Freshly ground black pepper	½ cup fine bread crumbs
1 teaspoon caraway seeds	1 egg white

1. Remove the core and shred the cabbage, using a food processor or grater.
2. Sprinkle with the salt and let stand about 15 minutes. Squeeze out the excess water.
3. Place the oil in a heavy frying fan. Brown the onion until golden. Remove and begin sautéing the cabbage (you will probably have to do this in 2 batches), cooking carefully until wilted.

4. Combine the cabbage and onions. Sprinkle with the pepper, caraway seeds, sugar, and cinnamon. Adjust the seasoning to taste.

5. Preheat the oven to 350 degrees.

6. Cover a pastry board with a cloth. Take 1 phyllo sheet at a time and cover the rest with a damp towel to prevent drying. Lay the sheet on the board and brush with melted butter or margarine, sprinkling on 1 tablespoon bread crumbs and some pepper. Lay the next phyllo sheet on top and cover with the identical combination. Continue until you have 4 layers of phyllo leaves and topping. Along the longer side of the phyllo, spoon out half of the cabbage filling about 4 inches from the edge of the dough. Fold the edge over the cabbage. Then, using both hands, lift the cloth and let the cabbage roll fall over and over itself, jelly-roll fashion, until the filling is completely enclosed in the pastry sheet. Place, seam side down, in a greased jelly-roll pan. If the roll is too long, cut it with a serrated knife to fit your pan.

7. Repeat the above process with the remaining 4 phyllo sheets, bread crumbs, cabbage, and pepper.

8. Brush the crust with additional melted butter or margarine. Then brush with egg white that has been stirred slightly.

9. Bake 45 minutes, or until golden. Slice thin and serve immediately. Or serve lukewarm as a dessert, sprinkled with confectioners' sugar.

Note: After the rolls have been formed, you can freeze them on cookie sheets and then remove them to plastic containers for freezer storage.

MARINATED EGGPLANT SALAD

MAKES 8 CUPS. (P)

Superstitions surround the eggplant, the purply black fruit in season at Sukkot. Because of its dark color, some Moroccan Jews will not serve it for Rosh Hashanah. Other Europeans believe that eggplants must be salted to get rid of the bitter and sometimes evil juices. If you select smooth, dark-skinned fruits that are light to the touch, the eggplants will not be bitter. I rarely salt eggplants before using them.

Vegetable oil for frying	One 28-ounce can tomatoes
3 green peppers	5 tablespoons cider vinegar
1 medium eggplant	1 large clove garlic, minced
1 medium onion, sliced in thin rings	Salt and pepper

1. Pour about 2 inches of oil in a heavy frying pan and heat to 375 degrees.
2. Quarter the green peppers, remove the seeds, and cut each quarter in 3 pieces. Deep-fry in the oil. Drain and place in a ceramic or glass bowl.
3. Quarter the eggplant lengthwise and slice thinly across the width. Deep-fry the slices in 2 batches. Drain. Add to the green peppers.
4. Add the onion rings to the eggplant mixture.
5. Roughly chop the tomatoes and add to the eggplant, along with 2 tablespoons of the juice from the can.
6. Add the vinegar, garlic, and salt and pepper to taste, and blend well.
7. Adjust the seasoning, cover, and serve several days later. The longer the marination period, the tastier the salad.

ROMANIAN EGGPLANT AND PEPPER SALAD

MAKES ABOUT 2 CUPS. (P)

Bulgarian Jews use mostly green peppers in their salads; Russians use all eggplant. Serbians use more eggplant than green pepper, and Romanians more green pepper than eggplant. Whatever your choice, just remember to prick the eggplant before putting it in the oven—otherwise, it will explode!

1 large eggplant	2 medium onions, chopped fine
2 green peppers	1 clove garlic, crushed
2 red peppers	¼ cup vegetable oil

3 tablespoons white vinegar
2 teaspoons salt
1 tablespoon sugar

1. Preheat the oven to 450 degrees.
2. Prick the eggplant with a fork and bake with the peppers on a cookie sheet in the oven until charred, about 20 minutes. Alternately, they can be rotated over a gas grill until charred on the outside. When cool, peel the eggplant and the peppers.
3. Chop the eggplant and peppers and mix with the onions and garlic. Add the oil, vinegar, salt, and sugar. Adjust the seasoning and let marinate at least 1 day. Serve alone or as a dip with crackers. This will last about 1 week, covered, in the refrigerator.

BREAD STUFFING FOR TURKEY

STUFFS A 14-POUND TURKEY. (M)

Just as the first pilgrims to America probably did not eat the tough, wild, dark-meated, forty-pound turkey covered with ticks available at the time of the first Thanksgiving, but rather lobster, clams, and venison, so the Jews in the desert ate whatever wild game they could find, perhaps venison or quail. There was no poultry as we know it in the Middle East until the fifth century B.C.E.

Brought to Europe in 1523–24 from Mexico by Turkish merchants (very possibly Sephardic Jews) going to the eastern Mediterranean, the turkey was dubbed the "Turkish bird" by the English. The French in turn called the bird the *coq d'Inde*, meaning "Indian cock" (the West and East Indies being one and the same in most people's minds in those days), which shortened to *dinde* or *dindon*. In Hebrew, too, turkey is called *hodu*, meaning India. In India they called turkey "Peru," which at least is geographically closer to the truth, although the turkey originated in North, not South, America.

The following stuffing recipe is a standard American-Jewish variety made from day-old challah. It comes from Fran Monus, a nutritionist and fine cook from Youngstown, Ohio.

¼ pound (1 stick) pareve margarine or ½ cup chicken fat

1 cup sliced onions

1 cup diced celery with leaves

½ loaf challah, toasted golden brown, cubed, and dried

Sautéed turkey livers

Sautéed turkey hearts, cut in small pieces (optional)

1 teaspoon poultry seasoning

¼ cup chopped fresh flat-leaf parsley

2 teaspoons salt

¼ teaspoon black pepper

2 eggs

1. Melt the margarine or fat in a frying pan. Add the onions and celery and cook until tender.
2. Soften the dried bread with water, then press the water out.
3. Add the bread, livers (and hearts, if desired), poultry seasoning, parsley, and salt and pepper to the vegetables. Add the eggs and mix lightly.
4. When filling the bird, do not pack the stuffing tightly—leave room for expansion during cooking.

PERSIAN RICE AND FRUIT STUFFING

STUFFS A 12–14-POUND TURKEY. (P)

While Eastern European Jews use bread and potatoes as fillers for most foods, Persian Jews use rice. The following rice stuffing with dried fruits is from Teheran. (Baghdad Jews would use almonds, rose petals, nutmeg, and cloves.) It is served on many festive occasions (including Passover, when rice is permissible for Persians) and is perfect for a large gathering inside a sukkah.

1 cup uncooked long-grain rice

1 tablespoon vegetable oil

3 spring onions, chopped

¼ cup sliced prunes

¼ cup sliced dried apricots

¼ cup chopped fresh flat-leaf
parsley

Salt and pepper

½ teaspoon cinnamon

½ teaspoon turmeric

1 cup water

1. Rinse and soak the rice in hot water for 30 minutes.

2. Drain the rice and sauté with the onions in the oil for a few minutes, until the onions are golden.

3. Add the prunes and apricots, parsley, salt and pepper to taste, cinnamon, turmeric, and 1 cup water. Simmer for about 10 minutes, or until the rice is almost cooked.

4. Meanwhile, prepare the turkey for stuffing. Stuff the turkey and roast as you normally do.

SWEET-AND-SOUR PICKLED TONGUE

SERVES 6–8. (M)

And Abraham hastened into the tent unto Sarah, and said: "Make ready quickly three measures of fine meal, knead it, and make cakes." And Abraham ran unto the herd, and fetched a calf tender and good, and gave it unto the servant; and he hastened to dress it.

Genesis 18:6–7

When the ministering angels visited Abraham, he prepared a feast for them. The "calf tender and good" refers to three oxen. Why three? According to Rashi, Abraham wanted to give each angel a great delicacy—a tongue with mustard. So it is that tongue has been a special treat for the Jews from Banquet Number One.

In Germany, Jewish cooks learned how to make sweet-and-sour sauces (with mustard, of course!). This recipe, traditional at Sukkot, comes from the German side of my family. So few people serve tongue these days. I love it!

One 4-pound pickled beef tongue	1 tablespoon mustard
2 tablespoons vegetable oil	3 tablespoons red wine vinegar
5 tablespoons tomato sauce	⅓ cup brown sugar

1. Parboil the beef tongue 4 times, changing the water each time to make it less salty.
2. Then simmer the tongue in water, uncovered, about 3 hours. If the tongue is small, it may fit in a pressure cooker and will take only 45 minutes to cook. Test with a fork; when it is tender, take it out of the water and peel while hot.
3. Mix the oil, tomato sauce, mustard, vinegar, and brown sugar. Simmer in a saucepan, uncovered, for 10 minutes. Slice the tongue and pour the sauce over it.

MOUSSAKA

(Eggplant and Meat Casserole)

SERVES 6–8. (M)

This recipe comes from Liliane Sivan, the wife of the former Israeli ambassador to Denmark. It is a kosher rendition of the famous Greek moussaka, which includes cheese with the meat. Eggplant casseroles like this are traditional in Israel today and have their roots in Romania, Greece, and Turkey.

1½ medium onions, finely chopped	6 large tomatoes, peeled and chopped
2 cloves garlic, finely chopped	1 teaspoon dried basil
½ cup vegetable oil	1 teaspoon dried oregano

Pinch of sugar

1 pound ground lamb

½ pound ground beef

½ teaspoon ground nutmeg

2 tablespoons chopped fresh flat-
leaf parsley

Salt and pepper

3 medium eggplants

1. Sauté the onions and garlic in ¼ cup oil until golden. Divide into 2 parts and place half in a large heavy saucepan. To this part add the tomatoes, ½ teaspoon basil, and ½ teaspoon oregano. Cover and simmer over low heat for 1 hour. Add the sugar.

2. To the other part of the onion mixture, add the ground meat and the remaining ½ teaspoon basil and oregano. Brown the meat, but do not overcook. Add the nutmeg, parsley, and salt and pepper to taste. Set aside.

3. In a heavy frying pan, using the remaining ¼ cup oil, fry the unpeeled eggplants that have been thinly sliced lengthwise and wiped dry. As the slices become golden brown on each side, remove them to a paper towel to drain off the oil. (An alternative method that I have discovered is to oil a cookie sheet, then brush each eggplant slice with oil and broil until golden on each side. This method takes half the time and uses much less oil.)

4. Preheat the oven to 350 degrees.

5. Place 1 layer of eggplant in a 2-quart casserole. Add some of the cooked tomatoes, then some of the meat mixture, and continue in layers until the ingredients are used up, ending with a layer of tomatoes.

6. Bake, uncovered, until brown on top. It can take up to 1½ hours. It is best to cook the casserole for 45 minutes the night before serving and then another 45 minutes the next day. Recooking improves the flavor.

SAKAU

(Eggplant and Meat Casserole)

SERVES 6–8. (M)

Similar to the preceding recipe for moussaka, this eggplant dish comes originally from the island of Marmora, via the Sephardic community of Seattle. I like the look of rolled eggplants in the casserole.

2 medium eggplants	1 teaspoon pepper
3 eggs	2 tablespoons uncooked rice
½ cup oil (for frying the eggplant)	½ teaspoon sugar
1 small onion, chopped	¼ cup water
2 tablespoons chopped parsley	¾ cup tomato sauce
1 pound ground beef	1 tablespoon chicken fat or pareve
1 teaspoon salt	margarine (optional)

1. Peel and cut the eggplants lengthwise into slices about ½ inch thick. Beat 2 eggs slightly. Dip the slices in the beaten eggs and fry in the heated oil on both sides until brown. Set aside.
2. Brown the onion in the same oil. Add the parsley. Remove from the heat.
3. Combine the remaining egg with the ground beef, salt, pepper, and rice. Add to the onion pan and brown.
4. Preheat the oven to 350 degrees.
5. Place a teaspoon or so of meat mixture at one end of each slice of fried eggplant. Roll up the slices jelly-roll fashion. Arrange them in a baking dish and sprinkle sugar over them.
6. Add the water, tomato sauce, and chicken fat or margarine, if using. Bake for about 35 minutes.

SWEET-AND-SOUR STUFFED CABBAGE

SERVES 6–8. (M)

Call it *holishkes*, *praches*, or just plain stuffed cabbage. Symbol of plenty, it is traditional at Sukkot. It is just as tasty the second day, especially on a cold winter's evening. There are probably as many different stuffed-cabbage recipes as there are towns in Central and Eastern Europe.

While many stuffed vegetables filled with meat and rice come from the Middle East, stuffed cabbage was known in Hungary prior to the Turkish occupation of the seventeenth century. It can be assumed that it was even then an ancient Hungarian dish.

However, Hungarian stuffed cabbage is not sweet and sour like that of Poland and Russia. The late Ada Baum Lipsitz, originally from Russia, experimented with her sweet-and-sour version for more than sixty years. Doctored up for American tastes, it is delicious! In the second edition of this book, I removed the frozen lemonade, one of Mrs. Lipsitz's tricks. I have had so many complaints through the years about its omission that I am using her original recipe in this edition. Her other trick is to freeze the cabbage for at least 2 days. Then you don't have to boil the cabbage leaves.

1 large cabbage	¼ cup catsup
2 pounds ground beef	3 eggs
½ tablespoon salt	½ cup uncooked rice
½ teaspoon pepper	1 medium onion, grated
½ teaspoon garlic powder or 1 clove garlic, peeled and chopped	

SAUCE:

One 28-ounce can tomatoes
One 16-ounce can tomato sauce
Salt and pepper
2 large onions, sliced
½ teaspoon garlic powder or
    1 clove garlic, peeled and
    chopped

½ cup catsup
One 12-ounce can frozen
    concentrated lemonade
¼ cup brown sugar
½ cup raisins

1. Freeze the cabbage for 2 days. Defrost it the night before cooking. This ensures soft, tender leaves and saves the step of boiling the cabbage.
2. Combine the ground beef, salt, pepper, garlic powder, catsup, eggs, rice, and grated onion; set aside.
3. In a saucepan, combine the tomatoes, tomato sauce, salt and pepper to taste, onions, garlic powder, catsup, lemonade, brown sugar, and raisins. Bring to a boil and let simmer until the cabbage rolls are ready to be cooked.
4. Preheat the oven to 300 degrees.
5. Remove the core from the head of cabbage. Separate the leaves. Place 1 heaping tablespoon of the meat mixture on each leaf. Tuck the ends in and roll up. Place in a 6-quart casserole.
6. Pour the sauce over the cabbage. Bake, covered, for 4 hours and then uncovered for 1 hour. This is even more delicious the second day.

TURKISH STUFFED ZUCCHINI

SERVES 6. (M)

With the continually escalating price of meat and poultry, and with frequent medical findings demonstrating that the American diet is unhealthily meat-oriented, more and more people are inserting additional vegetables into their diet. Sephardic Jews have been combining meats, vegetables, and grains for centuries. Originally courtly food at the time of the Ottoman Empire, stuffed grape leaves, zucchini, eggplant, onions, and tomatoes have become everyday cuisine throughout the Middle East.

This Turkish zucchini stuffed with rice and meat is based on a recipe from *Cooking the Sephardic Way*, put out by Temple Tifereth Israel in Los Angeles, with my own variations.

7 medium fresh ripe tomatoes, peeled, seeded, and finely chopped, or 2½ cups canned tomatoes, drained and chopped

1 cup freshly chopped onion

2 teaspoons salt

Freshly ground black pepper

6 medium zucchini or other summer squash, about 7–8 inches long

1 pound lean ground lamb or beef

⅔ cup uncooked long-grain white rice

2 teaspoons chopped fresh mint or 1 teaspoon dried mint

2 tablespoons chopped fresh flat-leaf parsley

¼ teaspoon ground nutmeg

½ teaspoon ground allspice

2 tablespoons dried currants or raisins

2 tablespoons pine nuts or chopped almonds

1. Combine the tomatoes, onion, 1 teaspoon salt, and pepper to taste in a heavy casserole large enough to hold the zucchini in 1 or 2 layers. Stirring frequently, bring to a boil over high heat. Reduce the heat to low, cover, and simmer for 20 minutes.

2. Scrub the zucchini under cold water. Pat dry and cut about 1 inch off the stem end. With an apple corer, carefully tunnel out the center of each zucchini, leaving a shell 1 inch thick all around.

3. Combine the meat, rice, mint, parsley, remaining 1 teaspoon salt, nutmeg, allspice, currants, pine nuts, and freshly ground pepper to taste. Spoon the stuffing into the squash, tapping the bottom end lightly on the table to shake the stuffing down. Fill the squash completely.

4. Lay the zucchini flat in the tomato sauce. Bring to a boil over high heat. Reduce the heat, cover tightly, and simmer for 30 minutes, or until the squash shows only the slightest resistance when pierced with the point of a sharp knife.

This can also be served with an egg-lemon sauce. Eggplants, green peppers, or onions can replace the zucchini.

SUKKOT *TSIMMES*

SERVES 6. (M)

A *tsimmes* is a fruit-and-vegetable stew eaten on the Sabbath and at Sukkot. My husband's family, from Poland, eats a carrot *tsimmes* without meat. The following recipe includes meat, fruit, and vegetables, and I think it is a happy combination of many traditions in Eastern Europe. In Yiddish, "to make a *tsimmes*" means to make a big fuss over someone. For other *tsimmes* recipes, see pages 229–31 and 371–72.

2 pounds flanken or chuck, cut into stewing pieces	2 white potatoes, peeled and quartered
1 tablespoon salt	½ pound large prunes
3 medium onions, sliced	½ pound dried apricots
2 tablespoons chicken fat or pareve margarine	¼ cup brown sugar
Water or beef bouillon to cover	Dash of nutmeg
2 large sweet potatoes, peeled and quartered	½ teaspoon cinnamon
5–6 large carrots, peeled and thickly sliced	Zest and juice of 1 orange
	Salt and pepper

1. Sprinkle the meat with the 1 tablespoon salt and brown with the onions in chicken fat or margarine.
2. Add water or bouillon to cover and simmer, uncovered, for 1 hour.
3. Preheat the oven to 350 degrees.
4. Place the meat, onions, and juices in a 4-quart casserole, surrounded by the sweet potatoes, carrots, white potatoes, prunes, apricots, brown sugar, nut-

meg, cinnamon, and orange juice and zest. Cover with additional water or beef bouillon. Cover and bake 1 hour.

5. Uncover, season with salt and pepper to taste, and cook an additional 2 hours, or until the liquid disappears and the top turns crusty.

A recipe from Vilna includes dumplings made from 2 cups flour, 2 eggs, 1 large grated white potato, 1 tablespoon chicken fat, salt and pepper to taste, and ½ cup water. These ingredients are combined and then steamed in the middle of the *tsimmes.*

SWEET POTATO *TSIMMES* WITH PINEAPPLE

SERVES 6–8. (D OR P)

This typical Thanksgiving dish, which my mother serves, is perfect for Sukkot. The marshmallows are obviously a very American addition to an essentially Eastern European recipe. If Thanksgiving falls near Hanukkah, as it does occasionally, you can mold leftover sweet potatoes into patties and fry them.

4 sweet potatoes
2 tablespoons butter or pareve
    margarine
One 8-ounce can crushed
    pineapple, undrained

½ teaspoon salt
1 tablespoon brown sugar
Paprika or marshmallows

1. Boil the sweet potatoes in water to cover in their skins until cooked. When done, cool, peel, and mash. Stir in the butter or margarine followed by the pineapple, salt, and brown sugar. This recipe can be prepared ahead of time up to this point.
2. Preheat the oven to 400 degrees and grease a medium casserole.
3. Spoon in the mixture. Heat 15 minutes. Remove from the oven. Either sprin-

kle with paprika or, for a sweeter taste, place the marshmallows on top, pressing gently into the sweet potatoes, and cook 10 minutes more, or until the marshmallows are golden brown.

ABUELITA'S MEXICAN *TSIMMES* CON CARNE

SERVES 8. (M)

This Mexican *tsimmes* shows how Jewish foods pick up the gastronomical characteristics of each country—beef, carrots, chicken fat, and beans, cilantro, mangoes, and chili powder.

2 pounds beef chuck, thinly sliced
1 tablespoon flour seasoned with
    salt and pepper
5 tablespoons rendered chicken
    fat or vegetable oil
2 carrots, peeled and thinly sliced
1 medium onion, thinly sliced
2 cloves garlic, finely chopped
1 cup puréed ripe mango
One 14-ounce can chopped
    tomatoes, with juice

2 tablespoons chili powder, or to
    taste
1 teaspoon coarse salt
1 teaspoon freshly ground pepper
¼ teaspoon cinnamon
One 28-ounce can red kidney
    beans, drained, liquid reserved
1 teaspoon sugar
1 tablespoon finely chopped fresh
    cilantro

1. Preheat the oven to 350 degrees.
2. Dredge the beef slices in the seasoned flour and shake off the excess. In a large skillet heat 3 tablespoons of chicken fat or oil. Add the meat and brown it quickly. Remove the meat to a large covered casserole or baking dish. Add the remaining 2 tablespoons of chicken fat or oil to the skillet. Add the carrots, onion, and garlic, and sauté, stirring, until the vegetables are soft but not brown. Add these to the meat.
3. Combine the mango purée with the tomatoes and chili powder, and add to

the casserole. Sprinkle the salt, pepper, and cinnamon over everything and add the beans.

4. Dissolve the sugar in the reserved liquid from the beans and pour enough into the pot to half-cover the stew. You may have to add more water.

5. Cover and bake 1–1½ hours, or until the meat is tender. Adjust the seasoning.

6. To serve, sprinkle with the chopped cilantro and serve with cooked kasha or rice.

UKRANIAN DILL PICKLES

MAKES 6 QUARTS. (P)

[Merrymakers] invade the homes of the well-to-do householders and treat them to an elaborate Simchas Torah kiddush. . . . The unwilling hosts have no choice but to bring out the best brandy and wine and set the table with food. If they don't, the revelers will get it themselves. They know where everything is kept. They can find their way to the oven, they can drag the preserves out of the cupboard, they can go down to the cellar and bring up the cherry wines, the pickled melons and the cucumbers that the wealthy housewives have prepared for the winter.

Sholem Aleichem, *Tevye's Daughters*

For those pickle enthusiasts who want to pickle in small quantities, try this Ukrainian recipe. Ukrainian Jews serve the pickles all year long—except at Rosh Hashanah, for fear that their sour taste might lead to a "sour" year.

4 quarts water
½ cup kosher salt
¼ cup white vinegar
40–50 small pickling cucumbers,
    depending on size

12 cloves garlic
2 tablespoons pickling spice
6 heads of dill

1. In a large pot, boil the water. Add the salt and boil 2 minutes. Let cool for 5 minutes. Then add the vinegar and let the mixture cool for 3–5 hours.
2. Wash the cucumbers twice in cold water. Dry with paper towels.
3. Fill 6 sterilized 1-quart jars with the cucumbers.
4. To each jar, add 2 cloves garlic, halved, and 1 teaspoon pickling spice.
5. Fill each jar with the water mixture. Place a large twig of dill in each jar and keep semicovered for 2–3 days. When the jar starts to bubble, let it bubble a day or two, removing the foam daily. Then cover tightly and put it in a cool place.

MANNA CATERING'S CAULIFLOWER WITH POMEGRANATE MALTAISE

SERVES 6. (D)

New York City's Manna Catering has been in the vanguard of contemporizing kosher cuisine. "We do work with Jewish symbols," said Dan Lenchner, co-owner chef with his wife, Joni Greenspan. "We like to work with food that has traditional value like apples, honey, and pomegranates, but we refuse to cook the traditional Jewish 'K' foods—kugel, knishes, kreplach, and kasha. They have become kosher-catering clichés." Lenchner sees these foods as at-home foods for the holidays, not dress-up foods for kosher events. "I love *cholent* and *tsimmes*, but they do not present well," he explained. And for the new brand of Jewish chefs, presentation is almost as important as taste. The following cauliflower maltaise and fig soufflé are symbolic fall dishes for a sukkah party, updated for the contemporary taste.

1 fresh pomegranate or ⅔ cup
    pomegranate juice with a few
    seeds reserved for garnish
1 medium-size head of
    cauliflower, cut into flowerets

3 egg yolks
1 tablespoon cold water
Salt and pepper
¼ pound (1 stick) cold unsalted
    butter, cubed

1. Gently roll the pomegranate, pressing to pop the seeds under the skin. Make a hole and pour the juice into the measuring cup.
2. Cook the cauliflower for approximately 3 to 4 minutes in rapidly boiling salted water. Test for doneness—don't overcook. Cauliflower should retain its crispness. Plunge the cauliflower into cold water, and then drain well.
3. For the pomegranate maltaise: Over a very low flame, in a double boiler, whisk the yolks, water, and salt and pepper to taste until smooth. Whisk in the cubed butter, a bit at a time, stirring constantly and adding more only when the previous addition has been completely incorporated. The sauce should be thick and creamy. Stir in the pomegranate juice. Adjust the seasoning. To serve, spoon 2 or 3 tablespoons of sauce over the flowerets and garnish with the reserved seeds. Serve warm or at room temperature, keeping the maltaise in the top of a double boiler over warm water. This sauce also works well with asparagus.

FIG SOUFFLÉ

SERVES 6. (P)

Figs, like pomegranates, are one of the seven species found in the ancient land of Canaan. I have always loved figs in any form. For me, nothing tastes as good as the sun-kissed ones found in Israel in the summer. Try Manna Catering's fig soufflé.

10 medium fresh figs, peeled and puréed to produce 1 cup, or 10 dried figs, soaked in water and puréed
2 egg yolks

10 tablespoons sugar
4 egg whites
1 tablespoon honey
2 tablespoons lemon juice

1. Preheat the oven to 400 degrees. Butter a 4-cup soufflé mold.
2. Whisk the egg yolks and 5 tablespoons of the sugar until the mixture lightens in color.

3. In another bowl beat the egg whites and 2 tablespoons of the sugar to soft peaks. Then add 3 tablespoons of sugar and beat to firm peaks.
4. Mix 4 tablespoons of the fig purée into the yolk mixture and then, in thirds, fold in the whites.
5. Fill the soufflé mold ¾ full and bake for 10–12 minutes. Do not open the oven door.
6. While the soufflé is baking, add the honey and lemon juice to the rest of the fig purée.
7. Serve the soufflé in its dish as soon as it comes out of the oven. Pour the sauce over the top at the table.

AUNT EVA'S COOKIES

MAKES 4 LOAVES OR 48 SLICES. (D OR P)

The following cookie recipe comes from my great-aunt Eva, whose parents came from Cracow, Poland. It is basically a thin pastry dough spread with jam or cocoa and cinnamon and rolled up jelly-roll or strudel fashion. After it is cooked, finger-size cookies are cut. This cookie has its origins in the German strudel of the following recipe. Other fillings for this and similar doughs might include apples or cheese.

12 tablespoons (1½ sticks) butter
    or pareve margarine
½ cup plus 1 tablespoon sugar
2 eggs
1 teaspoon vanilla extract
2½ cups unbleached all-purpose
    flour

1 tablespoon baking powder
Pinch of salt
1 cup apricot preserves or
    ¼ cup cocoa and 1 teaspoon
    cinnamon

1. Using a food processor, electric mixer, or wooden spoon, cream the butter. Add ½ cup sugar and mix well. Add the eggs, 1 at a time, followed by the vanilla. Slowly add the flour, baking powder, and salt. Knead the dough well.

2. Form the dough into 4 balls, cover with plastic wrap, and place in the refrigerator overnight.

3. Preheat the oven to 350 degrees and grease a cookie sheet.

4. Roll each ball of dough into a flat rectangle about ⅛ inch thick. Spread with the apricot preserves or a mixture of cocoa, cinnamon, and the remaining 1 tablespoon sugar. Roll jelly-roll fashion. (The easiest method is to flatten the dough on a pastry cloth, then lift the edge of the cloth so that the dough rolls into a long cylinder.)

5. Place 2 of the rolls on the cookie sheet, leaving room between them, as they will spread and flatten out. Repeat with the other 2 rolls on another baking sheet. Bake in batches on the middle rack of the oven. Or bake the 2 sheets on the middle and lower racks, about 20–30 minutes, until golden brown, switching pans halfway through. When cool, slice at an angle at about 1½-inch intervals, making finger-length slices.

STRUDEL, ART FROM THE AUSTRO-HUNGARIAN EMPIRE

Strudel dough has one of the most interesting culinary histories. First made in Bavaria or in Austria in a thicker version, it was later perfected in Hungary, where East, in the form of thin stretched dough brought by the Turks, met West.

In the late Middle Ages, German peasant women prepared a dough made of flour, water, and perhaps oil or butter. They filled it with fish or cabbage and ate it as a main dish on meatless Fridays or when meat was not available. Later, they made a sweet by filling the dough with apples, cottage cheese, plums, poppy seeds, or cherries. Jewish women followed suit.

The dough was shaped in two ways. Either two pieces of dough sandwiched a filling, or it was rolled out paper-thin, spread on one side with filling, and rolled—jelly-roll fashion—secured, and baked. As the Jews moved eastward from Germany into Poland and Russia in the late Middle Ages, they took this dough with them and used the sweet version as a basic dessert.

When this strudel reached Hungary, sometime in the sixteenth or seventeenth century, it met with a still thinner, finer dough, brought with the Turkish invasion. Hungarian bakers then learned how to make this phyllo dough, which they called *rétes*. They soon became the world's masters at stretching and pulling the dough gently over a table. They filled the *rétes* with the sweets of the Germans and rolled it up, jelly-roll fashion, rather than layering it and filling it with the nuts and honey or the spinach and sour cheeses of the Easterners. Unlike the Germans, the Hungarians also filled theirs with ground nuts and, even better, apricot preserves, long known throughout the Middle East. When the filled *rétes* reached the coffeehouses of Vienna and Budapest, they became known as strudel.

In 1939–40, when people could still leave Yugoslavia, a well-known chef taught many hopeful emigrants how to prepare intricate pastries so that they might be able to support themselves abroad. And when Diana Kennedy, the writer of Mexican cookbooks, wanted to learn to stretch strudel, she, like a whole generation of women (and some men) in Mexico City, took a class with Elisabeth Rosenfeld, one of those emigrants from Yugoslavia. Elisabeth's sister Aranka had been her teacher in the art of making strudel.

SPLENDID STRUDEL

Adapted from Elisabeth Rosenfeld

MAKES TWO 15-INCH-LONG STRUDELS, 6–8 SERVINGS EACH. (D OR P)

First the dough is mixed, thrown against a work surface, and set to rest until it is as flexible as taffy. Then the dough is placed in the middle of a large, cloth-covered table sprinkled with flour, patted out flat, and stretched with the fingers and the back of the hand until it is so thin you can read a newspaper through it. Holes do appear, but they are quickly patched up. The dough is finally sprinkled first with melted butter, then with fruit (or cheese or a savory), and the excess dough is trimmed from the edges. The dough is then rolled up to form a 3-inch roll—the strudel—and baked.

Strudel is one of the Austro-Hungarian Empire's great gifts to the world. Mrs. Rosenfeld, like other refugee women, earned a living from her skill.

For years I have been stretching strudel in my own home with my children. Before our elder daughter went off to college, she made an annual strudel for her school's auction and also gave strudels as gifts to her teachers. Making strudel is a cooperative enterprise, the culinary equivalent of a quilting bee. You need more than one person to stretch, preferably four. As the dough is carefully rolled out and then gradually pulled with the back of your hand and your fingers, it is a time to talk. The high-gluten flour and the warm butter or oil help to activate the dough, enabling it to stretch. Some people add vinegar as well, but Mrs. Rosenfeld did not. In Yugoslavia, she grew up using a goose feather to spread the melted butter on top of the roll as she turned the strudel; today we use a pastry brush.

This is a recipe for the adventurous. If you prefer the shortcut way, use the recipe on page 239, with bought phyllo dough.

2½ cups high-gluten flour	Pinch of salt
1 large egg yolk	¾ cup warm water
10 tablespoons (1 stick plus 2 tablespoons) unsalted butter or pareve margarine, melted, or warm vegetable oil	¼ cup dry bread crumbs
	Filling of choice (see below)
	Confectioners' sugar for sprinkling

THE DOUGH:

1. Place a glass or ceramic bowl in a 150-degree oven while preparing the strudel dough.

2. If you are making the dough by hand, place in a large bowl the flour, egg yolk, 5 tablespoons of the melted butter, margarine, or oil, the salt, and the water. Mix thoroughly, adding more flour if the dough is too sticky. Then remove the dough from the bowl and work it by hitting it on a table sprinkled with flour until it no longer sticks to your fingers and you have a dough that is soft and elastic.

   If you are using a food processor, fit it with the steel blade and put in the flour, egg yolk, 5 tablespoons of the melted butter, margarine, or oil, the salt, and the water and pulse, adding more flour if needed, until you have a smooth, soft dough.

3. Remove the warmed bowl from the oven and grease with some of the melted butter, margarine, or oil. Grease the dough, too; then place it on a board sprinkled with flour and cover with the bowl. Allow the covered dough to rest in a warm place for 30 minutes. (This is a technique I have found over and over in old cookbooks.) Now prepare the filling (see pages 239–41), so it is ready after you've stretched the dough.

STRETCHING THE DOUGH:

4. Cover a 5-foot-long table with a clean sheet and sprinkle the sheet with flour. Using a rolling pin, roll out the dough gradually until it measures about 10 by 20 inches. Then, using 2, 3, or 4 people spaced evenly around a table, gently lift the dough with the palms of your hands. Carefully extend the dough with the tips of your fingers, then with the backs of your hands, until it is as thin as possible in all places, measuring about 30 by 30 inches. (This is not a recipe for long fingernails.) Trim off the thick edges of the stretched dough with a knife; let the dough sit for about 4 minutes. This waiting period is important, since it helps make a crisper strudel. Don't worry about tears—just patch them up with the leftover dough. Give the rest to children to sprinkle with sugar and cinnamon and then bake.

FILLING AND BAKING THE STRUDEL:

5. Leaving a 2-inch border all around and a 4-inch-wide strip up the middle, drizzle some melted butter, margarine, or oil over the dough; then sprinkle on the bread crumbs, and finally spread the filling over the dough.
6. Preheat the oven to 375 degrees; line a 12- by 15-inch baking pan with aluminum foil (you need the foil for removing the strudel).
7. With the help of the sheet, and with the bare strip of dough perpendicular to you, carefully and tightly roll up the strudel like a jelly roll. Using a sharp knife or a pastry scraper, divide the long strudel into two 15-inch strudels at the point in the center where the strudel dough is unfilled, twist the open ends to close, and cut off the excess dough at the ends. Carefully, using both your hands or 2 sets of hands, remove the 2 strudels to the lined pan. Brush again with the butter, margarine, or oil.
8. Bake the strudels on the middle rack of the oven for 35 minutes, or until golden.
9. Sprinkle with confectioners' sugar and cut into slices 3 fingers thick, about 1½ inches. Serve warm; for a dairy meal, serve with with vanilla ice cream, whipped cream, or vanilla frozen yogurt.

Note: If you want to bake them later, you can freeze the unbaked strudels, wrapped. Remove from the freezer 30 minutes before baking. Then bake as above and serve warm. You can also form and bake the strudels early in the day, and then reheat them at 375 degrees for 10 minutes just before serving.

VARIATION: SHORTCUT STRUDEL

MAKES 2 STRUDELS, 12–14 SERVINGS. (D OR P)

4 sheets prepared phyllo dough
¼ pound (1 stick) unsalted butter
   or pareve margarine, melted

Filling of choice (see below)
Confectioners' sugar

1. Preheat the oven to 375 degrees and grease a jelly-roll pan.
2. Take 1 sheet of phyllo and spread it out on a work surface. (Cover the rest of the dough while working the sheet.) Brush with the melted butter or margarine. Place a second phyllo sheet on top. Brush with butter or margarine.
3. Spread half of the filling mixture over the entire surface of the phyllo, leaving a 1-inch border. Starting with the long side, carefully roll the phyllo, jelly-roll fashion, ending with the seam on the bottom. Brush the top with more butter or margarine and place in the jelly-roll pan. Repeat steps 2 and 3 with the 2 remaining phyllo sheets.
4. Bake the strudels on the middle rack of the oven for 35 minutes, or until golden. Just before serving, sprinkle with confectioners' sugar. Serve warm. For a dairy meal, serve with ice cream, frozen yogurt, or whipped cream.

Note: You can freeze these strudels wrapped, after assembling them. Remove from the freezer 30 minutes before baking them.

APPLE FILLING:

MAKES FILLING FOR 2 STRUDELS. (P)

10–12 Granny Smith, Jonathan, or
   other good baking apples,
   peeled, cored, and grated
   (about 10 cups)
Juice of 1 lemon
⅓ cup raisins (optional)

Grated zest of 1 lemon
2 teaspoons cinnamon
1 cup sugar
½ cup coarsely ground walnuts or
   almonds (ground in a food
   processor)

1. Sprinkle the grated apples with lemon juice and place in a colander over a plate until ready to use. Press the apples to release any excess moisture. This is important to a successful strudel.
2. Mix the apples with the raisins, if using, and lemon zest in a bowl.
3. Following the instructions in step 5, page 238, spread the apple mixture over the bread-crumb layer on the stretched strudel dough and dust with the cinnamon. Sprinkle the sugar and then the ground nuts over the apples and cinnamon. Roll and bake as on page 238.

CHERRY FILLING:

MAKES FILLING FOR 2 STRUDELS. (P)

10 cups sour cherries, pitted, or five 16-ounce cans sour cherries, well drained

2 cups sugar
½ cup ground almonds or walnuts

1. Place the pitted cherries in a colander over a plate until ready to use.
2. Following the instructions in step 5, page 238, scatter the cherries over the bread-crumb layer on the stretched-out strudel dough. Sprinkle with the sugar and finally the ground nuts. Roll and bake as on page 238.

Note: You can use other cooked fruits, such as rhubarb. Just make sure you drain them very well to remove as much liquid as possible.

SWEET CHEESE FILLING:

MAKES FILLING FOR 2 STRUDELS. (D)

2 large egg yolks
2 large eggs, separated
1½ cups sugar
1 pound plus 5 ounces farmer cheese

1 cup sour cream
Grated zest of 1 lemon
½ cup raisins

1. In a food processor fitted with the steel blade, purée 3 of the egg yolks with half of the sugar, the farmer cheese, and ½ cup of the sour cream.
2. Add the lemon zest and raisins; pulse briefly to mix them in. Remove the mixture to a large bowl.
3. Beat the egg whites until stiff, gradually adding the remaining sugar, and then gently fold them into the yolk mixture.
4. Following the instructions in step 5, page 238, spread the filling over the bread-crumb layer on the stretched strudel dough. Roll as above.
5. In a small bowl, combine the remaining ½ cup sour cream with the remaining egg yolk and mix well. Spread this over the top of the rolled-up strudel and bake as on page 238.

APFELBUWELE
(German Apple Boy)

MAKES 2 *APFELBUWELE* OR

1 *APFELBUWELE* AND 1 STOLLEN. (D OR P)

Apfelbuwele ("little apple boy" in German), sometimes called *schalet,* was the favorite Sabbath eve and Sabbath noon dessert in southern Germany. According to some, it was to remind the Jews of the many-layered manna eaten in the desert. The *buwele* was basically a yeast strudel or stollen dough filled with apples, rolled jelly-roll fashion, and then twisted into a ring before it was baked in a heavy black pot. Like manna, the *buwele* had many layers and sometimes had many tastes during the fall harvest festival, with other fruits such as pears, peaches, and plums in abundance. Most of the time, however, it was filled with the apples stored in the fall and usually available until February or March. This is my father's family recipe.

DOUGH:

8 cups flour

2 yeast cakes or 2 tablespoons (2 packages) active dry yeast

1 teaspoon salt

1 tablespoon plus 1 cup warm milk or water

1 cup sugar

¼ pound (1 stick) butter or vegetable shortening

1 teaspoon vanilla extract

Grated rind of 1 lemon

3 eggs plus 2 yolks, slightly beaten together

FILLING:

6 medium Granny Smith, Gala, or Jonathan apples, peeled, cored, and diced

½ cup raisins

¾ cup sugar

½ teaspoon cinnamon

1 tablespoon butter or vegetable shortening

1. Place 7 cups of the flour in a large bowl. Make a well in the center and stir in the yeast, salt, and about 1 tablespoon of warm milk. Sprinkle with the sugar.
2. Melt the butter or vegetable shortening in 1 cup warm milk or water.
3. Add the vanilla, lemon rind, eggs, and egg yolks to the well.
4. When the butter is melted, add to the flour mixture.
5. Knead the dough by hand until shiny and smooth, adding the remaining 1 cup flour as needed. Or divide the dough into thirds and whirl in a food processor, using the steel blade, until the dough is shiny and a ball is formed. Cover and let rise in a warm place for 2 hours, or until doubled in size.
6. Preheat the oven to 350 degrees and grease a jelly-roll pan or a 10-inch round pan with high sides.
7. Divide the dough in half. Reserve one half and roll out the other on a floured board into a rectangle about 24 by 18 inches. The dough should be about ⅛ inch thick. Then gently pull the corners with your hands to make the dough still thinner.
8. Mix the apples, raisins, sugar, and cinnamon and spread over the dough, leaving a 1-inch border around the edges.
9. Dot with the butter.
10. Carefully roll the dough, jelly-roll fashion, tucking the ends under. When the roll is completed, either leave as is and transfer to the prepared jelly-roll pan, or carefully form the *apfelbuwele* into a ring and place, seam side up, in the prepared round pan.
11. Bake for 30 minutes, or until golden. As the *apfelbuwele* starts to cook, the juice from the apples will accumulate. Occasionally brush the crust with this juice to form a glaze.
12. When finished, let sit a few minutes and then carefully, using a spatula, loosen the crust from the pan. If using the round pan, cover with a plate and then turn over. Tap the pan, and the *apfelbuwele* should fall out. Turn once again. Serve warm with ice cream or whipped cream.

With the remaining dough, you can do a variety of things. Of course, you can make another *apfelbuwele*. Or you can make a stollen by filling the dough with ½ cup raisins and ½ cup candied fruits before the rising and working into the dough; you twist the stollen like a challah. Or you can roll out 2 rectangles and fill with raisins, cinnamon, sugar, and nuts or your favorite fruits. For this last variety, just bake a shorter time and make a confectioners' sugar glaze for the top.

"MY DAUGHTER, THE JEWISH PASTRY CHEF"

Ann Amernick, the assistant pastry chef for Presidents Carter and Reagan, is like that cousin you haven't seen for years yet you can start talking with right away. And no wonder. She comes from a warm Russian-Jewish family that values a sense of humor. Her mother, Helen Silverberg, her aunt Bea Goldberg, and her sister Abby Lazinsky, all of whom live in Baltimore, travel fifty miles to Ann's home in Chevy Chase, Maryland, every Wednesday to help paint gum-paste leaves, buds, and flowers onto the special-occasion cakes she bakes. Their payment is pride in a daughter, niece, and sister who was the first Jewish female assistant pastry chef in the White House.

"When my mother started out, her buds were terrible," said Ann. "Now she's the bud expert. Every time one of my cakes is in a photo or a magazine, she rushes to see the buds. She no longer cares about the text about me."

Wednesday is the day to catch up on family history and old stories. One of Ann's favorites is about the time the kitchen was made kosher for the late Menachem Begin, then prime minister of Israel. It's a favorite of mine, too, so I'm repeating the story, which first appeared in *Jewish Cooking in America*. As Ann tells it: "For some reason the kosher caterer the White House wanted to use was not acceptable, so at the last minute the entire White House kitchen had to be kashered. I arrived early that day and came into the kitchen and saw three tiny *mashgichim* [kosher inspectors], shorter than I am, less than five feet, holding blowtorches as big as they were. They spent the entire day wandering around the kitchen burning and covering surfaces with aluminum foil. The kitchen was terribly hot with the activity between kashering and cooking. Roland Mesnier, the pastry chef, was desperately trying to get the sorbets made and one of the *mashgichim* was following him around with the blowtorch. Every time Roland turned around, the *mashgichim* were there. While some of the cooks had a partial understanding of kashrut from past experience in hotels and lessons in cooking school, the reality in the White House was another story. I felt it was a historic moment, and at the same time it was comical."

Ms. Amernick, a self-taught pastry chef, started out as a child in Baltimore watching her mother cook. "My mother made great blintzes," she said. "From her I learned the way to pour the tiniest bit of mixture in the pan, roll it around, and pour off the excess; so later I felt totally competent making crêpes." As a child,

Ann was always fascinated with food. "I would go down into our knotty-pine basement with the wet bar and act as a waitress for my sister and brother. I would bring them little tiny dishes and little tiny cups of ginger ale. I loved doing it."

Ann's specialties are rich cakes and pastries, which she bakes at Amernick's and at Palena Restaurant, where she prepares the dessert. I purposely had dairy bat mitzvah meals for both my daughters so the dessert would be one of Ann's cakes decorated with pastiches of their interests.

MARYLAND STRUDEL WITH DRIED FRUIT

From Ann Amernick

MAKES 4 STRUDELS, ABOUT 40 PIECES. (D)

"In this recipe I used my aunt Molly's strudel as a base. It was more of a mock sour cream–based strudel, like the one in Marian Burros's *Elegant but Easy Cookbook*," said Ann. "I think it's much easier to work than regular strudel." She also thinks this filled strudel tastes better after it's been baked and frozen or even just refrigerated a day or two. "Then the flavors of the raisins, nuts, and jam have a chance to age, like a fruitcake." Her strudel is filled with the kinds of nuts and dried fruits that are hung, and eaten, in a sukkah—raisins, walnuts, and dried cranberries or cherries.

THE DOUGH:

½ pound (2 sticks) unsalted
    butter
2 cups plus 1 tablespoon
    unbleached all-purpose flour

1 cup sour cream
1 tablespoon sugar

THE FILLING:

1½ cups golden raisins
1½ cups dark raisins
3½ cups finely chopped walnuts
1 cup sweetened dried cranberries
    or cherries

24 ounces apricot preserves,
    puréed in a food processor or
    blender
4 teaspoons cinnamon

THE DOUGH:

1. Using an electric mixer fitted with the paddle, mix the butter, flour, sour cream, and sugar on the lowest speed, until well blended. The dough will be very soft.
2. Divide the dough into 4 balls, cover each with plastic wrap, and refrigerate for 3 hours or overnight.

FILLING AND ASSEMBLING THE STRUDEL:

3. Preheat the oven to 325 degrees.
4. When the dough is ready to roll, mix the raisins, walnuts, and cranberries or cherries in a medium bowl and set aside.
5. Remove the dough from the refrigerator 1 piece at a time, and knead briefly. With a floured rolling pin, roll out each dough piece into a 9- by 12-inch rectangle.
6. Spread one-fourth of the puréed preserves over the top of the dough, leaving a ½-inch border all around. Sprinkle with one fourth of the fruit-nut mixture. Dust with 1 teaspoon of the cinnamon. Roll the dough up from the long edge for 1 turn. Fold the edges in and continue rolling. Place the roll, seam side down, on a parchment-lined baking sheet. Fill and roll the remaining 3 pieces of dough.
7. Bake the strudels on the middle rack of the oven for 45 minutes, or until golden brown. As soon as they come out of the oven, score them at 1-inch intervals with a serrated knife, then cut 1-inch slices with a regular knife. It is important to cut the strudel while still hot; otherwise the dough will crumble completely. After the strudels cool, you can freeze them, tightly wrapped.

"EMBALMING" AN *ETROG*

The Jewish ladies, it would seem, are in some particulars quite as fanciful as Christians; and they particularly covet the possession of a citron that has been offered at the Feast of the Tabernacles as an emblem of fertility and

plenty. Therefore, the husbands, brothers, fathers and sons are eager to pur-
chase; and hence the price for these consecrated citrons is often more than
double the original cost.

1842 Scripture Herbal, London

The *etrog,* known as Adam's apple and the apple of paradise, is the bitter citron fruit carried in the left hand as one of the four species at Sukkot.

Known in ancient Egypt and possibly brought to Palestine from India at the time of Alexander the Great, the *etrog* has always been admired for its beautiful color, perfect shape, and fragrant aroma, rather than for its taste, which is extremely bitter. During the period of the Second Temple, it was an ornamental motif on coins, the walls of synagogues, and mosaics. Although *etrogs* in general were abundant from the biblical period, an especially beautiful one was always hard to come by and therefore expensive.

A perfect *etrog* must conform to certain rules. If the larger part is covered with scars; if its nipple is removed; if it is peeled, split, or perforated so that any part is missing, it is invalid. Potential purchasers scrutinize the fruit very carefully for defects.

Throughout the centuries and the great dispersals, Palestinian Jews have sold *etrog*s to those living in Spain, Russia, Germany, and elsewhere to fulfill the mitzvah of Sukkot. Until the end of the nineteenth century, a center for *etrog* cultivation was also the island of Corfu, whose Jewish population, under Venetian and later French rule, acted as the broker of goods between Venice and the Levant.

After the holiday of Sukkot was over, the *etrog*'s thick skin was eaten pickled in vinegar or boiled to a pulp. A perfume was extracted from its peel, which was also highly valued as an antidote for snakebite. If you have a leftover *etrog,* add it to grapefruit and orange peel for citrus preserves. (This confection was made in ancient times, but it is rather bitter.) A folk custom relates that a woman who bites into an *etrog* will become pregnant within a year. So beware!

You can "embalm" your *etrog* and use it throughout the year at the Havdalah ceremony, as Dov Rosen of Jerusalem does. Here is his method. Use the embalmed *etrog* as our ancestors did, not only for Havdalah, but to relieve hunger pangs at Yom Kippur and as a good-luck charm during childbirth.

RULES FOR "EMBALMING" AN *ETROG:*

1. The *etrog* should be firm, not soft; smooth, not rough. One of small or medium size is recommended. Special care should be taken not to cut the upper protuberance, i.e., the nipple narrowing toward the pistil.

2. The cloves should be of the type normally used for cooking, hard and dry, with their tops intact. Only after they have been inserted all the way up to (but not including) their heads should the buds be detached by a finger or tool.

3. Each clove must be inserted in a separate perforation. No perforation should touch another, for otherwise a hole will form. Each clove must touch the next; this will prevent shrinkage. Here is the rule: The nearer the perforations to one another, the closer will the cloves be to one another, and the better for the *etrog.*

4. Any one of a variety of instruments may be used for making the perforations, as long as it is pointed and narrow.

5. The perforations should not be deep. This will prevent juice from seeping out, keep the cloves from moving, and force them to remain rigid.

6. After the "embalming" operation is completed—i.e., the entire *etrog* is covered completely with cloves—it should be left exposed to the air, preferably in the sun, for several days. When the fruit begins to harden, it should be placed in an etrog box, which should be kept closed. To preserve the *etrog* even better, it is advisable to line the bottom of the box with the remains of the cloves.

HANUKKAH

HANUKKAH

Now upon the same day that the strangers profaned the temple, on the very same day it was cleansed again, even the five and twentieth day of the same month, which is Kislev. And they kept eight days with gladness, as in the feast of the tabernacles, remembering that not long afore they had held the feast of the tabernacles, when as they wandered in the mountains and dens like beasts. Therefore they bare branches, and fair boughs, and palms also, and sang psalms unto him that had given them good success in cleansing his place. They ordained also by a common statute and decree, That every year those days should be kept of the whole nations of the Jews.

2 Maccabees 10:5–8

Can you guess, children, which is the best of all holidays? Hanukkah, of course. . . . You eat pancakes every day. . . . Mother [is] in the kitchen (rendering goose fat, mixing batter for pancakes).

Sholem Aleichem, "Hanukkah Money"

On Kislev 25 in the Jewish calendar, Jews throughout the world light the first Hanukkah candle. The holiday commemorates the Maccabean victory over Antiochus of Syria some twenty-one centuries ago. Going to cleanse and rededicate the Temple, the Maccabees found only enough sacred oil to light the menorah for one day. But a miracle occurred, and one day's supply lasted eight. For each of the eight nights of Hanukkah, therefore, an additional candle is inserted, from right to left, and lit by the *shammas* (or helper), from left to right, until an eight-candled menorah is aglow. After the candle ceremony, it is traditional to sing songs, play with the dreidel (spinning top), open presents, and eat latkes (fried pancakes) and other fried foods.

The Eastern European origin of latkes becomes apparent in contemporary distinctions between the Ashkenazic and Sephardic communities' celebrations of Hanukkah. Edgar Nathan III, president of the Spanish and Portuguese Synagogue of New York and a descendant of one of the first American Sephardic families, cannot remember a latke tradition in his family. It was, after all, not until the sixteenth century that potatoes were discovered and brought from Bolivia and Peru to Western Europe. By that time, the Nathans, because of the Inquisition, had left Spain.

The oil used for this frying relates, of course, to the end of the olive pressing at this time of year. Hanukkah is replete with desserts fried in or made with oil. Greek women claim that their *loukomades*—deep-fried puffs dipped in honey or sprinkled with powdered sugar—resemble the cakes the Maccabees ate, while Persian Jews prefer *zelebi*, a snail-shaped, deep-fried sweet. Israeli *sufganiyot*, which have replaced most of these sweets today as a celebratory treat, are basically raised jelly doughnuts and were probably adapted from the Greek *loukomades* and Austrian *pfannkuchen*.

The symbolism behind the pancakes is threefold. Made initially of flour and water, they served as a reminder of the food hurriedly prepared for the Maccabees as they went to battle before their military victory. The oil in which the pancakes are prepared symbolized the cleansing and rededication of the Temple after it was defiled by the Assyrians. The third meaning, added in medieval times, was one I was never told as a child: the latkes symbolized the cheesecakes the widow Judith served the Assyrian general Holofernes before she cut off his head, thus delivering her people from the Assyrians. The latkes signify the victory of her chastity and humility over the lust and pride of Holofernes, who would have had the Jews slaughtered had Judith not fed him so well and given him so much wine that he fell asleep.

Originally, Hanukkah was a solstice festival and commemorated the Maccabean saga. It was in the Middle Ages that it evolved from a distinctly minor Temple festival to a major family one, during which the *Shulhan Arukh* forbids fasting and mourning and encourages singing and rejoicing. It was about that time that the deep-fried sweet emerged, which later, in Eastern Europe, became the famous latke that we know and love today. Of course, in America today, Hanukkah has taken on more importance, celebrated so close to Christmas.

MENUS

FRIDAY NIGHT EASTERN EUROPEAN
Russian Vegetable Meat Soup
My Mother's Brisket
Potato Latkes
Applesauce
Green Salad
Kupferlin

FESTIVE CENTRAL EUROPEAN
Consommé
Roast Goose with Chestnut and Apple Stuffing
Romanian Fried Noodle Pudding
Endive, Grapefruit, and Avocado Salad
Apple Streusel

MOROCCAN
Moroccan Eggplant Salad
Fez-Inspired Spinach or Beet Top Salad
Moroccan Carrot Salad
Couscous
Moroccan Sweet Potatoes and Vegetables
Fijuelas
Ma'amoul (Nut-filled Cookies)
Moroccan *Cigares*

BRUNCH

Gravlaks or Pickled Salmon

Omelettes

Ada Shoshan's Apple Latkes

Tu Bi-Shevat Salad 448

Fruit-Filled Russian Coffee Cake 274

DAIRY

Mushroom and Barley Soup

Romanian Zucchini Potato Latkes

Applesauce and Sour Cream

Sufganiyot (Jelly Doughnuts)

Rugelach (Cream Cheese Cookies)

SAM THE ARGENTINE BAKER'S MEDIUM RYE BREAD

MAKES 2 LOAVES. (P)

Sam the Argentine Baker was a Washington legend. Born in Russia and raised in Argentina, he came to Washington and opened the city's finest bread bakery until he retired to Israel in 1974. Years ago, on a visit to Washington, Sam spent several days making empanadas, knishes, challah, pizza, and rye bread at my home. He probably had the strongest fingers I have ever seen, for he took only a few moments to knead the following rye bread. His movements appeared effortless. It was only when I tried to repeat his recipe that I learned how very talented he was.

2 tablespoons (2 packages) active
   dry yeast
1½ teaspoons sugar
2½ cups lukewarm water
1¼ pounds all-purpose flour
   (5 cups)

¾ pound rye flour (2¾–3 cups)
¼ pound rye bran* (1 cup)
1¾ teaspoons salt
3 tablespoons vegetable oil

1. Dissolve the yeast with the sugar in 1 cup of lukewarm water. Set aside. (In winter, make sure the temperature in your kitchen is at least 65 degrees.)
2. On a marble or pastry board, place 4 cups of all-purpose flour, 2 cups of rye flour, and the bran. Make a well and put in the yeast mixture. Work the wet ingredients into the dry, using your hands and a pastry scraper. Add 1½ cups more water and the salt and oil. Slowly work in the remaining cup of all-purpose flour and ¾ cup rye flour. (Dividing the dough in 3 and using a food processor is an easy alternative.) When you have added the flour, the dough will be sticky, heavy, and difficult to manage. Scrape under the dough, folding it over. Using your hands, continue to lift and fold, adding more flour as needed and scraping the board. Knead for about 5 minutes, until the dough is soft, velvety, and elastic.

*If you cannot find rye bran, whole wheat will do.

3. Shape the dough into a ball, dust with flour, and place in a bowl. Cover and let rise in a draft-free place until doubled in size. This will take ¾–1½ hours, depending on the heat of the room.

4. Punch down the dough, knead, and make 2 balls from it. Shape into oblong loaves and place on a greased cookie sheet. Cover and let rise about 30 minutes more, or until the loaves rise somewhat.

5. Preheat the oven to 400 degrees.

6. Using your hands, spread a little oil on the dough. With a razor make 4 flat, evenly spaced slits across each loaf.

7. Place the cookie sheet on the next-to-lowest rack of the oven. Bake 10–12 minutes. Then lower the heat to 350 degrees and bake about 45 minutes more, until the loaves sound hollow when tapped. If your oven does not seem too hot at 400 degrees, keep it that high.

Sam checked the loaves periodically and kept turning them around for even baking. Sam believes that rye bread should be eaten the next day. "When it's too fresh it's like a stone in the stomach."

POTATO LATKES

SERVES 8–10. (P)

What exactly is the Hanukkah-latke connection? "Latke" is the Yiddish word for pancake. According to Webster's, it probably goes back to the Greek *elaion* (olive oil). *Kartoflani platske* is still the term used to describe a potato pancake eaten in the Ukraine. It is the same food that the Jews living in the Pale of Settlement in the seventeenth century probably adapted for Hanukkah. Because their daily diet consisted of potatoes and bread, they wanted to include a special dish cooked in oil to symbolize the main miracle of Hanukkah. This potato pancake, already used by Ukrainians with goose for Christmas, seemed a good and relatively inexpensive choice. Because Hanukkah falls at the season when geese are plentiful, goose fat was an obvious and inexpensive substitute for the original olive oil.

For American Jews intrigued with the gastronomic side of Judaism, Hanukkah appears to be the preferred holiday. It is difficult to equal the taste of brown, crisp potato latkes. Can gefilte fish, matzah balls, *haroset,* or even hamantashen compare with them? Certainly not. Moreover, every latke lover seems to know how to make these potato pancakes—whereas admirers of, say, gefilte fish may be forced to an outside source—and has strong opinions about them. One will swear by a medium grater, another by the larger variety, and modernists by the grater blade on the food processor. Some prefer pepper; others, salt. Some add apples; others, grated zucchini, carrots, or parsley. Some insist on grated and others on sautéed onions. And then, of course, there are the purists who contend that only old potatoes and bruised knuckles will do.

Latkes have become a versatile delicacy. They can be made from buckwheat, or potatoes with a touch of flour. They can be served for breakfast, brunch, lunch, dinner, or as cocktail party fare. They can be eaten plain or fancy, with sugar, applesauce, sour cream, or even chicken soup.

10 medium russet or baking
     potatoes
2 medium onions
2 large or 3 medium eggs
¼ cup unbleached all-purpose
     flour, bread crumbs, or
     matzah meal

Salt and white pepper
Vegetable oil

1. Peel the potatoes if the skin is coarse; otherwise, just clean them well. Keep them in cold water until ready to prepare the latkes.
2. Starting with the onions, alternately grate some of the onions on the large holes of the grater and some of the potatoes on the smallest holes. This will keep the potato mixture from blackening. Press out as much liquid as possible and reserve the starchy sediment at the bottom of the bowl. Return the sediment to the mixture.*
3. Blend the potato mixture with the eggs, flour, and salt and pepper to taste.
4. Heat 1 inch of oil in a frying pan. Drop about 1 tablespoon of mixture for each latke into the skillet and fry, turning once. When golden and crisp

---

*The steel blade of a food processor or the grating blade are less painful ways of grating the potatoes and the onions. The blade makes a smooth consistency and the grater a crunchy one.

on both sides, drain on paper towels. Serve with yogurt, sour cream, sugar, or applesauce.

Note: People are always asking me about freezing potato latkes. You can! After making them, place them on a cookie sheet, freeze, and remove to a plastic bag. When ready to serve, place in a 450-degree oven for several minutes. I don't recommend refrigerating latkes—they turn out soggy. Make them early in the day, drain, leave them out on a cookie sheet, and reheat before serving.

ROMANIAN ZUCCHINI POTATO LATKES

MAKES 18 LARGE PANCAKES TO SERVE 6–8. (P)

2 pounds zucchini   Vegetable oil
2 large russet or baking potatoes   ¾ cup matzah meal
1 medium onion   Salt and pepper
3 large eggs

1. Peel the zucchini and grate down to the seeds (discard the seeds). Squeeze out the liquid.
2. Peel the potatoes and grate into the zucchini. As in the previous recipe, remove the liquid. This is important!
3. Grate the onion and add to the zucchini mixture. Add the eggs, 1 teaspoon of oil, and the matzah meal, starting with ½ cup meal and continuing to add more if necessary, until there is body to the mixture. Season with salt and pepper to taste and blend well.
4. In a large, heavy frying pan, heat a thin film of oil until almost smoking. Using a large oiled tablespoon, spoon round portions of zucchini mixture into the pan and brown on both sides. Serve hot with sour cream or applesauce.

Note: You can also add carrots, parsley, and dill to this recipe.

RUSSIAN *PASHTIDA*

(Panfried Potato Latkes)

THE NUMBER THIS RECIPE FEEDS DEPENDS
ON HOW MANY LATKES WERE EATEN THE NIGHT BEFORE. (P)

Leftover potato latke batter
   (page 258)
Handful of raisins (less or more
   depending on the amount of
   leftover batter)

Dash of cinnamon
Vegetable oil

1. Squeeze the water from the leftover potato mixture, which will probably have turned black overnight. Discard the water.
2. Add the raisins and cinnamon.
3. Heat the oil in a medium frying pan and cover with the potato mixture. Cook until golden. Then cut across the middle and gently turn each half to brown on the other side. *Pashtida* can be eaten as a starch with the meal or as a dessert.

APPLESAUCE

MAKES ABOUT 1 QUART. (P)

What would potato latkes be without applesauce? This is my own recipe, which I especially like because the apples are cooked in their skins, there is very little sugar, and it is easy!

4 pounds apples
1 lemon
2 cinnamon sticks

½ cup apple juice, cider, or water
Honey, brown sugar, or maple
   syrup

1. Quarter the apples and the lemon. Place the apples, seeds, and peels in a heavy pot with the cinnamon sticks. Add the apple juice, cider, or water.
2. Cover, bring to a boil, and then simmer over low heat, stirring occasionally to turn the apples and make sure they do not stick. You may want to add some liquid. Cook about 20 minutes, or until the apples are soft. Remove the cinnamon sticks.
3. Put the sauce through a food mill and adjust the seasoning by adding honey, brown sugar, or maple syrup to taste.

ADA SHOSHAN'S APPLE LATKES

MAKES APPROXIMATELY 36 LATKES. (D OR P)

This is a recipe found frequently in Israel.

2 eggs, well beaten
1½ cups orange juice, yogurt, or milk
2 cups all-purpose flour
1 teaspoon baking powder
Dash of salt

¼–½ cup sugar depending on taste
3 medium apples, peeled and coarsely grated
Vegetable oil for frying
Confectioners' sugar

1. Mix the eggs with the orange juice, yogurt, or milk in a bowl.
2. In a separate bowl combine the flour, baking powder, salt, and sugar. Add the dry ingredients to the egg mixture along with the grated apples. Heat a thin layer of oil in a skillet. Allowing 1 large tablespoon of batter per latke or pancake, drop into the hot oil. Cook about 2 minutes on each side, or until slightly golden.
3. Drain on paper towels, sprinkle with confectioners' sugar, and serve.

ROMANIAN BEET BORSCHT

MAKES ABOUT 2 GALLONS. (P)

The following Romanian beet borscht, from *The Best of Beth Israel,* published in Milwaukee in 1983, is a recipe clearly handed down from someone's mother or grandmother. In Romania, the root vegetables in the recipe, such as parsnips and beets, were stored in a cold cellar in winter. The pot roast that cooks in the simmering broth was probably roasted with potatoes and garlic and served for the Shabbat meal.

Serve the borscht with a loaf of dark bread for a Hanukkah party.

4 pounds bones, beef neck or shank bones with marrow and lots of meat
Salt
3 pounds pot roast or brisket
2 onions, peeled and sliced
1 bunch carrots, peeled and grated
One 16-ounce can stewed tomatoes
Two 12-ounce cans tomato paste and 2 cans water
One 32-ounce can tomato sauce
One 18-ounce jar sauerkraut

2 bunches beets, peeled and grated
2 parsnips, peeled and grated
1 small cabbage, shredded
5 stalks celery with leaves, chopped
1 green pepper, cored and seeded
1 large bunch dill, chopped
Onion salt to taste
½ teaspoon sour salt (ascorbic acid)
1 lemon, cut in half
2 tablespoons brown sugar
Boiled potatoes, optional

1. Place the bones in a soup pot with cold water to cover by 2 inches. Add salt to taste and simmer 2 hours. Strain into a 2-gallon pot. Add the brisket or pot roast and 12 more cups of water. Bring to a boil and skim. Reduce the heat. Add the onions and simmer 1 hour, uncovered.
2. Add the remaining ingredients and simmer, partially covered, another hour, or until the meat is tender. Remove the lemon and the bones. Cut the meat into small pieces and return to the soup.
3. Add boiled potatoes to the borscht when serving.

Note: You can cut up the meat in the soup or remove the meat, spread with mashed garlic and freshly ground pepper, roast in the oven with potatoes until brown, and serve as a separate dish.

IRENE YOCKELSON'S
SWEET-AND-SOUR CABBAGE SOUP

SERVES 8. (M)

This recipe comes from cookbook author Lisa Yockelson's late mother, Irene. "My mother always used top rib and plain water, although I enrich the soup with a mixture of beef broth and water. I think it makes a more well-rounded, full-bodied soup." Lisa remembers eating the soup throughout the year and especially at Hanukkah.

2 pounds top rib
1 quart beef broth
1 quart water
3 cups canned tomatoes, finely chopped, with their juice
1 cup tomato sauce
2 pounds cabbage, coarsely shredded or very thinly sliced

2 onions, diced
1 teaspoon sour salt (ascorbic acid)
1 teaspoon salt
½ teaspoon freshly ground black pepper
2 tablespoons sugar
3 tablespoons golden raisins

1. Combine the top rib, broth, and water in a 10-quart soup pot or kettle. Bring to a boil over moderate heat and after 5 minutes skim off all the gray residue that has risen to the top. Add the tomatoes, tomato sauce, cabbage, onions, sour salt, salt, black pepper, and sugar.
2. Return to a boil, stirring occasionally, then cover and simmer 3 hours, until the meat is very tender. Stir in the raisins, set the lid to the pot slightly askew, and simmer 20 minutes. Taste and adjust the seasoning, adding additional salt and pepper as necessary.
3. Serve the soup with boiled potatoes, a side of meat accompanied by a good strong horseradish, and dark bread.

RUSSIAN VEGETABLE MEAT SOUP

SERVES 8–10. (M)

"Substance" and "authority" are words to describe Jewish soups. Why else would chicken soup be called Jewish medicine? No insipid bouillons or consommés for us hearty eaters! Try this Russian-style vegetable soup at Hanukkah. Soak up the gravy with the Russian rye bread on page 256.

3 carrots	½ cup dried lima beans
2 medium white potatoes	½ cup dried green split peas
1 sweet potato	½ cup large whole barley
4 quarts water	½ pound fresh string beans, diced
2 pounds top rib, cut in 1-inch chunks	4 ribs celery, diced
One 2-ounce package dry mushrooms or 1 cup sliced fresh mushrooms	Salt and pepper to taste

1. Grate the carrots, white potatoes, and sweet potato on the large holes of a grater, or use the grating or steel blade of a food processor.
2. Bring the water to a boil and add all the ingredients. Cover and simmer about 2 hours, stirring occasionally. If, when finished, you prefer a thinner soup, add more water.

MY MOTHER'S BRISKET

SERVES 8. (M)

Before the middle of the nineteenth century, beef was not widely eaten. Most Jews ate chicken, goose, or, in the Middle East, lamb. Potting what beef was available was a good way to preserve it. It is no wonder, then, that every Jewish mother has her special pot roast recipe, something that can be prepared in advance of Jewish holidays. Here is my mother's, a perfect accompaniment to potato latkes and applesauce, and one of the most popular recipes in this book.

2 teaspoons salt, or to taste
1 tablespoon pepper
3 tablespoons brown sugar
1 cup chili sauce
1½ cups white vinegar
One 5-pound brisket of beef,
    shoulder roast of beef, chuck
    roast, or end of steak

1 cup chopped celery leaves
2 onions, sliced
4 carrots, sliced
2 cups water

1. Mix the salt, pepper, brown sugar, chili sauce, and vinegar together. Pour over the meat and let stand overnight in the refrigerator.
2. Preheat the oven to 325 degrees. Place the meat in an ovenproof casserole and pour the marinade over the meat. Cover with the celery leaves, onions, carrots, and the water.
3. Cover and bake for about 2 hours, basting often with the marinade. Remove the cover and bake for 1 more hour. (Allow approximately 30 minutes per pound for roasting.) When done, strain the marinade and reserve.
4. This dish is best prepared in advance so that the fat can be easily skimmed from the surface when it has cooled. When ready to serve, slice and reheat in the strained pan marinade.

Note: You can also put all the ingredients in a covered casserole and bake in a 200-degree oven overnight, for about 9 hours. This slow cooking breaks down the membranes of the meat, making a more tender roast.

Sanford Herskovitz, known as Mr. Brisket in Cleveland, says that when the brisket is roasting, the point (fatter side) should be down; when reheating, the flat (leaner side) should be down. "Use a choice, whole brisket; never use a first cut, because the butcher throws away the fat and it's drier."

BOB PRITSKER'S VEAL TONGUE WITH CARROTS, GINGER, AND TOMATO

SERVES 6–8. (M)

"My passion for food was there inside me just waiting to pop," said former law-student-turned-self-taught-chef Bob Pritsker. "I was ignited by the presence of Julia Child in Boston. Working in a corporate environment during the day and going to law school at night, I wasn't doing anything that was a physical, creative, or artistic workout. Now I am." Today Pritsker is the chef-owner of the Brive Restaurant in Manhattan. His passion is shared by other Jewish chefs who, perhaps a generation earlier, without the options open to so many of us, might have become butchers, wholesale fruit or vegetable purveyors, or wine dealers. This generation is privileged, one that can take the risk of setting up shop in a restaurant.

1 large Spanish onion, peeled and diced
3 large carrots, peeled and diced
2 tablespoons chicken fat or pareve margarine
2 ounces fresh ginger, peeled and finely chopped
20 parsley stems, tied
2 pounds tomatoes, peeled, seeded, and chopped

10 whole cloves garlic, peeled
3 cloves
2 tablespoons red wine
2 tablespoons sugar
1 bay leaf
2 cups chicken stock*
3 fresh veal tongues or 1 beef tongue
Salt and freshly ground black pepper to taste

1. Soften the onion and carrots by cooking in a heavy pot with the chicken fat or margarine. Add all the other ingredients and bring to a simmer on top of the stove.
2. Cover and bake in a 350-degree oven until the tongues do not resist when

*Canned chicken broth is a good substitute.

pierced with a roasting fork at the tip, about 1½ hours for the veal and 2½ hours for the beef tongue.

3. Remove from the oven, let cool, lift out the tongues, and peel the outer skin. Slice the tongues on the bias. Taste the braising liquid and remove the grease. Reduce by half by boiling it down if necessary. Add more salt, pepper, sugar, or wine as needed. Reheat the tongue in the sauce and serve with pot-browned noodles or spaetzle.

ROAST GOOSE WITH CHESTNUT
AND APPLE STUFFING

SERVES 8. (M)

Geese is my business . . . but you think it's as easy as all that? The first thing you got to do is this: you start buying geese right after Sukkoth, in the autumn. You throw them into a coop and keep them there all winter, until December. You feed them and take good care of them. Comes Hanukah, you start killing them, and you turn geese into cash. If you think it's so easy to buy them, feed them, kill them, and turn them into cash, you're wrong. First of all, I fry the skin and the fat and make goose fat out of it. I make Passover fat every year, for my Passover fat is considered the best and most kosher fat in the village. When I make kosher for Passover goose fat, Passover steps into the house smack in the middle of Hanukah. . . . Goose meat. You'd be in some pickle if you only depended on the goose meat. Besides that there were fried scraps and livers and gizzards and heads and feet. Then there were the gullets and wings and tongues and hearts and kidneys. Not to mention necks.

Sholem Aleichem, "Geese"

As this tale relates, the goose became the most cost-effective meat within the Jewish economy of Europe. Although one goose required four to five times as much feed per pound of meat as a chicken and used the same small plot of land, its yield to its owner was greater. First, there was the meat. Then there was all the rendered fat used for cooking. The neck could be stuffed and the skin and fat fried into *grieben*. The feathers could be sold as quills and the down stuffed into pillows. The fattened liver could be sold for pâté de foie gras.

It is no surprise that the area surrounding Strasbourg in Alsace-Lorraine, long a Jewish area of settlement, is one of the centers of the goose-liver industry. There is even a factory selling kosher pâté de foie gras. Moreover, a large percentage of the goose livers used today in that delicacy are exported by Israel to France. A side effect is that Israeli newspapers have advertisements encouraging people to eat geese.

In sixteenth-century Germany, geese were known as "the Jews' fowl." Beef and pork were the everyday meat of the poor. Wild game was that of the rich. Since Jews are not traditionally hunters, they sought out meat that conformed to their religious beliefs. Chicken and geese were the most appropriate, within easy reach of a *shohet*.

In northern countries, no pareve margarine or vegetable oil existed until the turn of this century. Olive oil, produced in the Middle East, was prohibitively expensive. For Jews, who did not use pork fat in their cooking, geese were all the more essential. The rendered goose fat was used in cooking throughout the winter. It is therefore understandable that geese would be known as the Jews' fowl.

My father still remembers eating goose as a boy in Germany. Young geese were eaten from May to September and the older ones throughout the winter. His father had his own jar of *grieben*, skin that had been deep-fried. German Christians traditionally eat goose for Christmas; Jews eat it at Hanukkah. The following is a recipe that my grandmother Lina Nathan made for goose stuffed with chestnuts and apples. The recipe appears in the cookbook she gave my aunt Lisl on her wedding day in 1921. The recipe that follows this one is for *gribenes* and is much like what my father and grandfather enjoyed.

Note: Instead of this stuffing, you can use the whole apples.

One 8–10 pound goose
2 cups cooked, peeled chestnuts, quartered
½ cup raisins
1 cup prunes

6 cups peeled, cored, and quartered Granny Smith or other flavorful apples, instead of the stuffing
Salt

1. Preheat the oven to 400 degrees.
2. Remove the excess fat from the cavity and giblets. Render the fat to use in cooking.
3. Combine the chestnuts, raisins, and prunes, and stuff the cavity about ¾ full. (Figure 1 cup of stuffing per person. Vary the ingredients to suit the size of your goose. Any leftover stuffing can be cooked in aluminum foil alongside the goose for the last hour.) After stuffing the goose, truss it and place the bird, breast side up, on a rack in a roasting pan. Rub with salt.
4. Roast for 1 hour. Prick the skin with a fork at ½-inch intervals to let the fat escape. Reduce the temperature to 350 degrees and roast for another hour. As the fat accumulates, remove it with a bulb baster. To see if the goose is done, prick the thigh with a fork. It is done if the juices are yellowish. If not, reduce the oven to 325 degrees and continue cooking.
5. Let sit 15 minutes while you make a gravy, then serve. The goose goes well with potato latkes or cabbage strudel and a light salad. Reserve the goose fat for cooking.

GRANDMOTHER'S NOTES ON ROAST GOOSE:

1. A young goose can be roasted in 1 hour. It has to be covered with salt, pepper, and onion.
2. To render as much fat as possible from a goose, use an older one. Remove the skin completely and cut into small squares. Place in an iron casserole, add salt and some water, and bring quickly to a boil. Then turn down the heat. The crispy *grieben* should be light brown when they are done, with all the fat removed from the skin. The *grieben* should be removed from the fat, and pressed to extrude remaining fat. Fresh, they taste delicious.
3. Leave the fat from the *grieben* standing until it is clear, then pour it into a stone pot, where it will keep all winter.
4. *Geschundenes* [hurt goose] is the goose without the skin. Roast it in the oven like any other roast. It takes 2–3 hours.
5. *Ganef*—stuffed goose neck or even back of the goose. You can cut around the skin where the neck starts and pull the skin off whole. This can be stuffed in various ways. Soak 3 slices of white bread in water; press as much water out as possible. Add slices of onion and parsley and fry everything together in some goose fat or margarine. Add ¼ pound ground beef, salt, pepper, and other

spices to taste, and 1 egg. Mix everything and stuff the skin of the neck, which you sew closed. Roast the neck in bouillon in the oven for 1 hour.

6. Goose Liver: Put salt and pepper on the liver and fry it in goose fat, turning it frequently. It takes 8–10 minutes. Cool in the fat and leave fat around the liver. Serve on slices of toast.

GRIBENES

Adapted from Charlie Klatskin

MAKES ABOUT 1 CUP. (M)

My grandfather would sit eating these at night, the way we eat chips while watching television today.

1 large chicken (at least 5 pounds)
1 large onion, chopped
Kosher salt

1. Remove the fat and the fatty skin from the chicken. Slice the skin in small strips, approximately 1 inch long, measuring about 1½ cups. Reserve the chicken for another use.
2. Place the skin and onion in a heavy skillet. Cook for about 20–30 minutes over a low heat, stirring occasionally with a wooden spoon, until the fat is melted. As the skin cooks, the fat separates from it, and the skin becomes crispy.
3. Once the fat has mostly melted, turn up the heat to medium-high and continue to cook until the onions and skin are golden brown to black. Sprinkle with kosher salt to taste. Using a slotted spoon remove the crispy skin and onions from the pan and place them on heavy paper to drain. Reserve the chicken fat in the pan or store in a jar. The fat can be used for cooking and is especially good for making chopped liver, potato pancakes, and matzah *brei* (matzah pancakes).

PAMPUSHKI
(Baked Dumplings)

MAKES 25. (P)

When Justice Arthur Goldberg was invited to the Soviet Union as chairman of the United Nations Association, after having stepped down from his post as U.S. ambassador to the United Nations, he had two requests: to visit Zinkov in the Ukraine, birthplace of his parents, and to taste *pampushki*, little round yeast dough balls, the size of dinner rolls, a dish he remembered from his childhood in Chicago. "I remember eating *pampushki* with my six older brothers and sisters. There was nothing like it to fill your stomach." Each time he asked if he could visit Zinkov, his Soviet hosts said no, but finally toward the end of his stay, he was asked if there was any place he would like to go. "Zinkov," he replied. He was flown to Kiev, where he and his government escort drove the 250 miles into the old Jewish Pale of Settlement to Zinkov. On the way they stopped at a small restaurant where they were served *pampushki*. "Like all childhood things, they didn't taste as good as my mother's," the judge said. As for Zinkov, nothing whatsoever remained of the Jewish presence in the city.

Having searched every Jewish cookbook in my own collection, I looked elsewhere, finding that *pampushki* were often raised doughnuts sometimes flavored with rose water. Finally, Dr. Joyce Toomre, a scholar of nineteenth-century Russian cookbooks, located a wheat flour *pampushki* recipe that is typically served with a garlic sauce.* A buckwheat alternative is served with borscht. Since Justice Goldberg remembered a meat sauce, I made it with a brisket for him, although my guess is his mother, a poor woman with many mouths to feed, used only the sauce left over from brisket.

*The recipe given here is adapted from V. V. Pokhlebkin, *Natsional'nye kukhni nashikh narodov* (The National Kitchens of Our People) (Moscow, 1980).

¾ cup water

2 scant tablespoons (2 packages) active dry yeast

2 tablespoons sugar

3–3½ cups all-purpose flour

1 teaspoon salt

6 tablespoons safflower or vegetable oil

1 egg

1. Dissolve the yeast with the sugar in ½ cup of the water. Add 1 cup of flour and the salt. Mix and then let rise, covered, until doubled in size, about 1½ hours.

2. Punch down and add the remaining water, the oil, and enough flour to make a soft dough. Form the dough into *pampushki* the size of walnuts, brush with an egg wash, and let rise 1 hour.

3. Preheat the oven to 300 degrees, and grease a cookie sheet.

4. Arrange them, touching each other, on the cookie sheet and bake for 25 minutes, or until golden. Serve immediately with borscht or a leftover meat sauce.

ROSE FAMILY POTATO KUGEL

SERVES AT LEAST 8. (M OR P)

Rochelle Rose and her sons Jason and Joel Wollin owned several Washington restaurants, including the popular Mrs. Simpson's. Although the public food was strictly nouvelle American, at home the food was traditionally Jewish.

2 pounds plain white Idaho potatoes, peeled

Salt

2 cups chopped onions

1 tablespoon chopped shallot

Chicken fat or pareve margarine (a generous ½ cup)

Dash of pepper

4 large eggs, well beaten

Nondairy sour cream or applesauce

1. Preheat the oven to 400 degrees. Grate the potatoes. Salt lightly and let drain in a colander for about 30 minutes.

2. Sauté the onions and shallot in ¼ cup of chicken fat for about 5 minutes. Remove from the heat, add the potatoes and pepper, and mix well. Don't mush. Let cool a few minutes and then add the beaten eggs.

3. Warm ¼ cup melted fat in a 10-inch iron skillet. Turn the potato mixture into the skillet and smooth the top with a rubber spatula. Bake 50 minutes, uncovered, in a 400-degree oven. Before serving, brush with a little margarine or chicken fat (if your heart can take it) and broil about 6 inches from the heat so that it is crispy.
4. Serve with nondairy sour cream or applesauce.

ROMANIAN FRIED NOODLE PUDDING

SERVES 4–6. (P)

Potato latkes may not be essential to Hanukkah, but cooking with oil is. If you want a change from potato pancakes, try this Romanian fried noodle pudding, which goes well with sauerbraten or roast goose.

8 ounces fine egg noodles	6 tablespoons vegetable oil
2 tablespoons pareve margarine	2 eggs, beaten
1 large onion, diced	Salt and pepper

1. Cook the noodles according to the directions on the package and drain. Transfer to a large bowl and add the margarine, blending well. Set aside.
2. Sauté the onion in 2 tablespoons of the oil until golden. Add the onion to the noodles. Add the eggs and salt and pepper to taste. Mix all the ingredients well.
3. Heat the remaining 4 tablespoons of oil in a large, heavy frying pan. Add the noodle mixture and let it brown on the bottom and sides, taking care not to burn it.
4. When it is browned on one side, place a large plate over the pan. Turn it over onto the plate and then slide it back into the pan to brown the other side.

FRUIT-FILLED RUSSIAN TEA BREAD

MAKES AT LEAST 2. (D OR P)

Babka, made of yeast dough with eggs and sometimes butter or shortening and sweetened with sugar and dried fruits, is a Polish sweet often eaten with tea. Each country has its version, such as the *kugelhopf* on page 196.

Until I tasted the braided version baked by Fred Loeb, the former baker-owner of De Luxe Bakery in Silver Spring, Maryland, whom I call a bootleg baker, I dismissed *babka* as dry and tasteless. Mr. Loeb, who had apprenticed in a kosher bakery in Bridgeport, Connecticut, also thought *babka* was too dry, and he increased the eggs and the butter as for a Danish pastry. By the time he had moved to Silver Spring and established himself as one of the finest bakers in the Washington area, he had perfected his *babka,* which he calls Russian tea bread. As rich as brioche, it is filled with apricot preserves, nuts, and raisins.

1½ scant tablespoons (1½ packages) active dry yeast	½ teaspoon vanilla extract
¾ cup warm water	6 large eggs
¾ cup sugar	5 cups all-purpose flour
Salt	1 cup apricot jam
10½ ounces (2 sticks plus 5 tablespoons) unsalted butter or pareve margarine, softened	½ teaspoon cinnamon
	1 cup raisins
	4 tablespoons chopped walnuts
Grated zest of 1 lemon	¼ cup cake crumbs

1. Dissolve the yeast in the warm water with 1 teaspoon of the sugar.
2. Cream together ½ cup of sugar, 2 teaspoons salt, 5 tablespoons of the butter or margarine, lemon zest, and vanilla. Add 5 of the eggs, 1 at a time, blending well. An electric mixer will be helpful for this.
3. Add the yeast to the sugar mixture and add enough flour to make a light, pliable dough. It should be sticky. Place in a greased bowl, cover, and let rest 30 minutes in the refrigerator.

4. Roll the dough out on a floured board to about ½ inch thick. Spread two-thirds of the dough with the remaining 2 sticks of butter. Fold the remaining dough over like an envelope and close with the third buttered part. Roll out again, fold again, and let rest for 30 minutes in the refrigerator.

5. Roll out again, thinner and longer, and fold the outer fourths into the center and then close like a book. Cover and let rest in the refrigerator another 30 minutes.

6. Remove from the refrigerator and fold as in step 4 two more times, resting at 30-minute intervals. Then cover with plastic wrap and refrigerate a few hours or overnight.

7. Roll out half the dough to about 12 by 10 inches. Cover two thirds with apricot jam, leaving the top, long third plain. Sprinkle very generously with half the cinnamon, raisins, 2 tablespoons of nuts, the remaining sugar, and the cake crumbs. Then roll the plain top third over, pressing down with a rolling pin, and then the bottom third over like an envelope. Pack the 3 layers down hard with your hand and the rolling pin to form a rectangle. Roll and fill the remaining dough the same way.

8. Using a knife or a pastry wheel, divide the 2 rectangles into 3 long pieces. Pack them down well because they will have jam oozing out. Braid as you would a challah. Turn over and finish braiding.

9. Preheat the oven to 350 degrees, and grease a cookie sheet.

10. Mix the remaining egg with a pinch of salt and brush over the cakes. Sprinkle with the remaining nuts. Let rise, covered, for about 1 hour on the cookie sheet, then bake for about 35 minutes, or until golden.

AUNT LISL'S BUTTER COOKIES

MAKES 48. (D OR P)

In Eastern Europe, Jewish children used Hebrew alphabet cookie cutters to learn their letters—and to make cookies. In the United States today there are all kinds of menorah and shofar cookie cutters, but no Hebrew alphabet ones as yet. While growing up, I went to my aunt Lisl's at Hanukkah time and made these butter cookies, which we decorated with blue sugar.

½ pound (2 sticks) unsalted
    butter or pareve margarine
¾ cup sugar
2 eggs
1 tablespoon brandy or water

1 teaspoon vanilla extract
⅛ teaspoon salt
3½ cups all-purpose flour
1 egg white, slightly beaten
Blue sugar (see below; optional)

1. Cream together the butter and sugar. Add the eggs, brandy, vanilla, and salt. Beat well.
2. Gradually add the flour, mixing well. Cover and chill at least 1 hour or overnight.
3. On a lightly floured surface roll half the dough ⅛ inch thick. Keep the remaining dough chilled while working. Cut with the desired cookie cutters, dipping the cutter into flour between cuts to prevent sticking. Transfer the cutouts to ungreased cookie sheets. Brush the cutouts with egg white and lightly sprinkle with blue sugar. Repeat with the remaining dough.
4. Bake in a 350-degree oven 10–12 minutes, or until the cookies are golden. Remove and cool on wire racks.

BLUE SUGAR:

In a shaker jar combine ½ cup granulated sugar and 2 or 3 drops blue food coloring. Or mix together in a shaker jar ½ teaspoon water and 2 or 3 drops blue food coloring. Add ½ cup pearl sugar and shake well.

RUGELACH

(Cream Cheese Cookies)

MAKES 64. (D)

In the Middle Ages it was traditional to eat cheesecakes at Hanukkah in commemoration of the cheesecakes or pancakes Judith gave to General Holofernes. After eating these cakes, the general became thirsty for wine, which Judith also served him. Soon he swooned, Judith slew him, and the Jews were saved. Today many people serve sour cream pancakes at Hanukkah in memory of Judith. Others serve *rugelach,* a half-moon cream cheese cookie, which may be a far cry from the original cheesecake but is nevertheless a melt-in-the-mouth delicacy perfect for the fanciest party.

Probably the most popular of American Jewish cookies, this horn-shaped treat was made in Europe with butter; cream cheese was added in this country. I *love* Ann Amernick's version: it has no sugar in the dough but a sprinkling on top of the finished cookie. She also uses this dough to make hamantashen.

THE DOUGH:

8 ounces cream cheese, at room temperature

½ pound (2 sticks) unsalted butter, at room temperature

2 cups unbleached all-purpose flour

Confectioners' sugar

APRICOT FILLING:

1 cup thick apricot preserves

¾ cup walnuts, roughly chopped

CHOCOLATE FILLING:

1 cup (about 8 ounces) shaved bittersweet chocolate, preferably imported

¼ cup sugar

CINNAMON-SUGAR FILLING:

4 tablespoons (½ stick) unsalted butter, melted

½ cup sugar

2 teaspoons cinnamon

1. To make the dough, place the cream cheese and the butter in an electric mixer fitted with the paddle. Cream at a low speed until combined, about 2 minutes. Add the flour and mix until a very soft dough is formed, about 2 more minutes. Cover with plastic wrap and refrigerate for at least 2 hours.

2. Preheat the oven to 350 degrees and line 2 cookie sheets with baking parchment.

3. Mix the ingredients for the apricot or chocolate filling and divide the dough into 4 balls. Roll the balls out into 4 circles about ⅛ inch thick and 9 inches in diameter. Spread the apricot or chocolate filling over the dough. If using the

cinnamon-sugar filling, brush the melted butter on first, then the combined cinnamon and sugar.

4. Using a dull knife, cut each circle of dough into 16 pie-shaped pieces about 2 inches wide at the circumference. Roll up from the wide side to the center. Place the *rugelach* on the parchment-lined cookie sheets. Bake in the oven on the middle and lower racks, switching after 12 minutes, also switching back to front. Continue baking about 13 more minutes, or until golden brown. Remove the *rugelach* to racks to cool. Sprinkle the apricot and chocolate rugelach with confectioners' sugar just before serving.

KUPFERLIN

(NUT HORNS)

MAKES ABOUT 30. (D OR P)

Most countries have a recipe for half-moon butter cookies with ground nuts and sugar. The Greeks have *kourambiedes* and the Viennese *kupferlin*. Crescent-shaped rolls and cookies in Budapest date from the year 1686, during the Turkish siege of the city. Bakers working at night heard the Turks digging an underground passage into the city and were able to warn the authorities. To reward the bakers who saved the city, they were permitted to make a special crescent pastry in the shape of the emblem that decorates the Ottoman flag. The following nut horn or crescent recipe—originating in Austro-Hungary, continuing to the Bronx and Belmont, Massachusetts—requires less sugar than many Hungarian and Austrian versions of *kupferlin*.

¼ cup sifted confectioners' sugar
2 cups sifted all-purpose flour
½ pound (2 sticks) cold unsalted
    butter or pareve margarine,
    cut into cubes

3 ounces pecans or unblanched
    almonds, ground

1. Preheat the oven to 350 degrees.
2. Combine the sugar, flour, and butter by cutting the butter into the dry ingredients. (This is done very simply with a food processor.)
3. Add the nuts, mixing with your hands or a food processor until the dough is smooth and no longer sticky.
4. Taking a handful of dough at a time, roll it into long 1-inch-wide cylinders. Slice into ½-inch-long pieces and shape into small crescents. Place on ungreased cookie sheets.
5. Bake 10–15 minutes. Remove to a plate and sprinkle with confectioners' sugar.

GINGERBREAD COOKIES

Jewish parents often find themselves in a quandary at Christmas. Neighbors are busily baking cookies to give as gifts and to have on hand for guests. Although baked delicacies are more of a traditional Jewish custom at Purim, there is no reason to feel left out. A satisfying way for your children to share in the Hanukkah preparations is to spend a "cookie day" making free-form designs of menorahs. Just watch their eyes light up as their hands get into the dough. Forget the cookie cutters. Four- to six-year-olds might need some assistance but the six-and-above set quickly create their own cookie world of plumed birds, alligators, and, of course, Judah Maccabees.

From a light honey and a dark molasses dough, you can create two-tone fantasy figures in your own style or in the grand tradition of Matisse cutouts. A garlic press will do nicely to make curly hair or just curlicues. Or turn this dough into an edible gingerbread dreidel.

LIGHT HONEY GINGERBREAD

MAKES TWENTY-FOUR 5-INCH COOKIES. (P)

⅓ cup vegetable shortening

⅓ cup sugar

1 egg

⅔ cup honey

1 teaspoon lemon extract

3 cups sifted flour

1 teaspoon baking soda

1 teaspoon salt

1. Blend the shortening, sugar, egg, honey, and lemon extract in a large bowl with a wooden spoon or mixer.
2. Sift together the flour, baking soda, and salt onto waxed paper. Add the dry ingredients to the wet, about 1 cup at a time, mixing well after each addition. Add more flour if necessary to make a stiff but malleable dough, and pat into a large ball. Keep in a plastic bag in the refrigerator at least 1 hour before using.
3. Preheat the oven to 350 degrees. (A toaster oven will do nicely if the cookies are being made in a school or playroom.)
4. Before working the dough, dip your hands in flour. For each cookie, take about a handful of dough. Roll it out on aluminum foil with a rolling pin or press it with your hands until the cookie is about ¼ inch thick.

There are a number of ways to use this basic dough:

Free-form: Cut into shapes with a dull knife, popsicle stick, pastry wheel, or any blunt instrument. Do not try to draw with the knife as this will produce fuzzy edges, but actually cut the contours of basic shapes with small, swift strokes. You can cut out abstract designs, animals, or human shapes of your choice. Don't add detail, because shapes spread in baking. Leave sufficient space between the cookies to allow for spreading.

Two-tone: Use this dough with the following dark one to make two-tone, free-form designs, animals, and people. Use one dough for the body and another for the head, tail, or feet. The light and dark doughs will merge when placed next to each other.

Cutouts: To make cutouts, first make a design on drawing paper, then cut out with scissors. Use a knife or other sharp instrument to outline the design in the cookie dough.

5. After the cookies are cut out, decorate with sunflower seeds, blanched almonds, pine nuts, pecans or walnuts, currants, yellow or black raisins. Use a garlic press to make hair from the dough and the tines of a fork for lines.

6. Bake 8–10 minutes or longer, according to the thickness of the cookie. Test for doneness by pressing the dough with your finger. If it springs back, the cookie is ready. Leave the cookies as they are, or decorate with icing and place candies, sprinkles, nuts, or candied fruit on top. Icing alone can make decorative mustaches, feathers, and other designs. Press long strands of licorice or soft ribbons of icing into the dough for legs and arms.

DARK MOLASSES COOKIES

MAKES 24 5-INCH COOKIES. (P)

⅓ cup vegetable shortening
1 cup light brown sugar
1½ cups molasses
⅔ cup water
6 cups sifted flour

2 teaspoons baking soda
1 teaspoon salt
½ teaspoon cinnamon
¼ teaspoon ground nutmeg
¼ teaspoon ground ginger

1. Combine the shortening, sugar, molasses, and water in a large bowl. Blend thoroughly with a wooden spoon or mixer.

2. Sift together the flour, baking soda, salt, cinnamon, nutmeg, and ginger onto waxed paper. Add the dry ingredients to the wet, 1 cup at a time, mixing well after each addition. Add more flour if necessary and pat into a large ball. Keep in a plastic bag in the refrigerator at least 1 hour, or until ready to use.

3. Preheat the oven to 350 degrees.

4. Shape and decorate as you would the light honey cookies. Bake for 15 minutes or longer, according to the thickness of the dough.

CAROB BROWNIES

MAKES 16. (D OR P)

If memory serves me, [my mother] carried mostly chalk and carob—two items with a big turnover in Kasrilevke. Chalk was needed for whitewashing the houses, and carob provided sweet snacks that were cheap and plentiful. The kheder *boys spent all their breakfast and lunch money on carob, and the groceries did a thriving business.*

Sholem Aleichem, "The Dreydl"

In Sholem Aleichem's world, children nibbled on carob chips while playing with dreidels at Hanukkah. The evergreen carob tree is indigenous to Israel. Its 6–8-inch dark pods have a dark, chewy substance with the flavor of chocolate. The ground powder is used in cakes. The tougher pods used to be food for the poor or fodder for the cattle. In traditional Jewish lore, the carob symbolizes humility.

In affluent America, carob powder has become a health-food substitute for chocolate. The following is my favorite chocolate brownie recipe—a good accompaniment to dreidel spinning!

¼ pound (1 stick) unsalted butter or pareve margarine, at room temperature
1 cup sugar
2 eggs
1 teaspoon vanilla extract

3 tablespoons carob powder, or 3 squares bittersweet chocolate, melted* and cooled
1 cup sifted all-purpose flour
½–1 cup broken walnuts or pecans

1. Preheat the oven to 350 degrees. Grease a shallow 8- by 8-inch pan.
2. Cream the butter or margarine and gradually add the sugar. Add the eggs, 1 at a time. Add the vanilla and melted chocolate or carob powder.
3. Add the flour gradually to the wet ingredients. Fold in the nuts.
4. Pour into the pan and bake 20 minutes (30 minutes if using carob powder). Test. If too moist, leave in the turned-off oven a few minutes longer. Cool and cut into squares.

*The chocolate can be melted in a microwave.

SUFGANIYOT

(Jelly Doughnuts)

MAKES TWENTY-FOUR 2-INCH-WIDE *SUFGANIYOT*. (D OR P)

Dov Noy, the dean of Israel's folklorists, tells a Bukharran fable about *sufganiyot*. The first *sufganiya,* from *sof,* "end," *gan,* "garden," *ya,* "of God's," was given to Adam and Eve after their expulsion from the Garden of Eden. This sweet dough-nut had three characteristics: it was round like the wheel of fortune, it had to be looked at not for its external qualities but for what was inside, and it could not be enjoyed the same way twice. According to Dr. Noy, this fable had to have been created at about the beginning of the twentieth century, since "*sufganiya*" is a new Hebrew word coined by the pioneers.

The *sufganiya* may be the fruit of the merger of the *pfannkuchen,* the jelly-filled pastry favored by Austrians and Germans, and the sweet, spongy cookie called *sufganne,* a fried dough popular along the Mediterranean since the time of the Maccabees.

According to Hebrew dictionaries "*sufganiyot*" comes from the Greek *sufgan,* meaning "puffed and fried." The closest Greek sweet to the Israeli jelly doughnut rolled in sugar is a doughnut called *zvingous.* In Ladino, *zvingous* are called *boumwelos.* These fried doughnuts, unlike *sufganiyot,* are dipped in a honey syrup and rolled in crushed walnuts and almonds or nuts and cinnamon. *Zvin-gous* and *sufganiyot* are descended from one of the oldest sweets known to mankind—the Greek *loukomades,* a sweet fritter dipped in honey-and-sugar syrup. *Loukomades* were originally wheatcakes fried on an iron grill, then cov-ered with grape-derived molasses and often used for feasts of the gods. The honey syrup used today as a coating on the *zvingous* was borrowed from the Turks; the cooking method has changed to deep-frying.

Every bakery in Jerusalem, no matter the ethnic origin of the baker, makes these jelly doughnuts for Hanukkah. They used to consist of two rounds of dough sandwiching some jam, and the jam always ran out during the frying. Today, with new injectors on the market, balls of dough can be deep-fried first and then injected with jam before being rolled in sugar. This is a much easier, quicker way of doing them. And no jam escapes.

2 scant tablespoons (2 packages) active dry yeast

4 tablespoons sugar, plus sugar for rolling

¾ cup lukewarm water or milk

2½ cups unbleached all-purpose flour, sifted

2 large egg yolks

Pinch of salt

1 teaspoon cinnamon

1½ tablespoons unsalted butter or pareve margarine, at room temperature

Vegetable oil for deep-frying

½ cup plum, strawberry, or apricot jam

1. Sprinkle the yeast and 2 tablespoons of the sugar into the water or milk and stir to dissolve.

2. Place the flour on a work surface and make a well in the center. Add the yeast mixture, egg yolks, salt, cinnamon, butter, and the remaining 2 tablespoons sugar. Knead well, about 5 minutes, working the butter or margarine into the dough and kneading until the dough is elastic. You can also use a food processor fitted with the steel blade to do this, processing about 2 minutes.

3. Put the dough in a greased bowl, cover with plastic wrap, and let it rise overnight in the refrigerator.

4. Sprinkle flour on the work surface. Roll out the dough to an ⅛-inch thickness. Using a 2-inch cookie cutter or floured drinking glass, cut out circles. Let the dough circles rise 15 minutes more.

5. With your hands, gently form the dough circles into balls.

6. Pour 2 inches of oil into a heavy pot and heat until very hot, about 375 degrees.

7. Slip the doughnuts into the oil, 4 or 5 at a time, using a slotted spoon. Turn them when brown, after a few minutes, to crisp on the other side. Drain on paper towels.

8. Using an injector available at cooking stores, inject a teaspoon of jam into each doughnut. Then roll all of them in granulated sugar and serve immediately. You can make larger *sufganiyot* if you like.

TWO SISTERS, TWO COOKBOOKS, TWO COUNTRIES . . .

Growing up between the wars in the Hungarian village of Subotica (pronounced *Subotitsa*) near the then-Yugoslav border, the four Span sisters and their mother were known for their baking skills. Aranka, the eldest, born in 1899, even studied at the Cordon Bleu Cooking School in Paris. In the early 1930s, as a young mother with three children, Aranka wrote the first of her three cookbooks, *Zsidono Szakacskonyve* (Jewish Woman's Cookery Book), which became the bible of Jewish cookbooks for Hungarian women until World War II. Her second cookbook about inexpensive Jewish food was written in Hungarian in 1953 and published in Israel. It was she who taught her younger sister, Elisabeth, how to cook. Elisabeth would later bring her recipes across the ocean to Mexico City.

Born in 1905, Elisabeth Span married Ignatius Rosenfeld and moved to Belgrade, where he manufactured wood-burning stoves. The couple traveled a great deal throughout Europe and the Middle East to visit their clients. But in 1939, as war looked more and more certain, the Rosenfelds took an exploratory trip across the Atlantic to see where they might want to settle. They visited Toronto, the New York World's Fair, Bogotá, and Mexico City, to see Elisabeth's brother. "After that trip my mother claimed that the most beautiful cities in the world were Barcelona, Cairo, and Mexico City," said her son Peter Span, who now lives in Los Angeles. When the Rosenfelds returned home in September 1939, it was getting more difficult to leave. The Germans invaded Yugoslavia in 1941. As a Yugoslav reserve officer, Ignatius joined the army. He was eventually taken prisoner by the Germans and spent two years in a prisoner-of-war camp. Later, his wife, his three sons, and his wife's sisters' families were put in an Austrian forced-labor concentration camp, Ulrichkirchen, twenty miles from Vienna. Miraculously, the Rosenfeld family survived the war and were reunited briefly in April 1945, but Ignatius died several months later from sickness contracted in the camp.

Back home in Belgrade, Elisabeth and her sons had to share their home with two other families, the Communists considering their house too large for one. Elisabeth decided to emigrate, and in 1947, on a tourist visa, departed with her children for Mexico City, leaving behind everything she owned and her sister Aranka as well, who had lost much of her own family at Auschwitz. "She dared to leave her home and go with three small children across the world and make something out of them," said Jelena Blumenberg, Aranka's granddaughter, who came to the United States from Belgrade in 1972.

Like many other women in similar situations, Elisabeth began giving cooking lessons in her new home. "For lunch every day we ate the whole menu," recalled Peter, now fifty-eight. "My mother let the students taste the food, but she told them that this was her children's dinner. After school we helped deliver dobos tortes, strudels, and Prince Albert cakes to restaurants. It is still strange to me today that my mother was making the cakes for a restaurant called Pastelandia, 'Cake Land' in Spanish."

Elisabeth Rosenfeld was, in fact, the cooking teacher for a whole generation of upper-class Jewish and non-Jewish Mexican women. "It was an in thing to go there," said one of her former students. "She was a thin woman who spoke five languages, but none properly."

In the 1950s she opened Restaurant Elisabeth, which served Central European cooking and pastries. There she also gave lessons and wrote a cookbook, *Tres Cursos de Cocina Húngara y Yugoslava* (Three Courses of Hungarian and Yugoslav Cooking).

"Whenever I would walk into the kitchen to say hello to my mother, there would always be dough on the counter, a mixer always going and the kitchen smelling like warm chocolate, sugar, and eggs," said Peter. "I would dip my fingers into the chocolate cream from her Prince Albert Cake, I would take a handful of walnuts and nibble on them. This is how I remember my mother. She never talked about the Holocaust, but her cooking gave us a new life."

MEXICAN BANANA CAKE

From Lisette Span

MAKES 8–10 SERVINGS. (D OR P)

My friends are always asking me for a good banana cake recipe, and this is the best I have ever tasted. It comes from Lisette Span, the French-born daughter-in-law of Elisabeth Rosenfeld, whom I met when I stayed at her pension in Zitacuaro, Mexico. This recipe came to Lisette from a visitor from the United States. She embellished it, and here it is. It has also traveled to Israel, where Elisabeth Rosenfeld's granddaughter is pastry chef at the Michael Andrew restaurant in Jerusalem.

2½ cups unbleached all-purpose
    flour
¾ cup plus 2 tablespoons sugar
1 teaspoon baking powder
1 teaspoon baking soda
½ teaspoon salt
½ cup vegetable oil
½ cup milk or water

3 large eggs, separated
1 teaspoon vanilla extract
4 large, ripe bananas, mashed
    (about 2 cups)
½ cup chopped walnuts
    (optional)
Confectioners' sugar (optional)

1. Preheat the oven to 350 degrees. Butter and flour a 10-inch Bundt pan.
2. In a large mixing bowl, put the flour, ¾ cup of the sugar, baking powder, baking soda, and salt. Add the oil, milk or water, egg yolks, vanilla, and mashed bananas and mix well. Stir in the walnuts.
3. Using an electric mixer, whip the egg whites until they form stiff peaks. Gently fold into the banana mixture.
4. Pour into the Bundt pan or other tube pan and bake for 45–50 minutes, or until a toothpick inserted in the center comes out clean.
5. Allow the cake to cool for 10 minutes before removing it from the pan. Continue cooling it on a rack. When ready to serve it, sprinkle with the remaining 2 tablespoons sugar or with confectioners' sugar.

CRANBERRY-WALNUT TART

From Andra Tunick Karnofsky

MAKES ONE 10- OR 11-INCH TART. (D OR P)

Andra Tunick Karnofsky of Heavenly Hallah makes this cranberry-walnut tart at Hanukkah because the red color of the cranberries reminds her of the flames of the menorah candles. It's a great winter dessert. At her family's Hanukkah parties, her children Holden and Daliya and their friends work at cooking stations—one for latke frying, another for cookie cutting, and a third for filling Israeli *sufganiyot* (doughnuts) with jelly and sprinkling them with sugar (see *Sufganiyot,* page 283).

THE CRUST:

1¾ cups unbleached all-purpose flour

¼ cup sugar

¼ pound (1 stick) unsalted butter or pareve margarine, chilled

3 tablespoons chilled vegetable shortening

¼ cup ice water

THE FILLING:

⅔ cup light corn syrup

⅔ cup light-brown sugar

3 large eggs

1 teaspoon vanilla extract

4 tablespoons (½ stick) unsalted butter or pareve margarine, melted

1½ cups coarsely chopped fresh cranberries

1 cup coarsely chopped walnuts, toasted lightly (see Note on toasting nuts, page 155)

1. To make the crust, put the flour, sugar, butter or margarine, and vegetable shortening in a food processor fitted with the steel blade. Pulse until crumbly. Gradually add the ice water, processing until the dough forms a ball. Wrap the dough and refrigerate for at least 1 hour.
2. Preheat the oven to 350 degrees.
3. Remove the dough from the refrigerator and, on a floured surface, roll it into a circle 13 inches wide. Line a 10- or 11-inch tart pan with a removable bottom with the dough, trimming off the excess. Prick the dough with a fork.
4. Line the dough with baking parchment. Fill the baking parchment with dried beans, just enough to cover the paper. This helps set the crust by weighing down the dough as it bakes.
5. Bake for 10–12 minutes, or until the dough just begins to brown. Remove the beans and parchment and let the crust cool. Leave the oven on at 350 degrees.
6. To make the filling, put the corn syrup and light-brown sugar in a mixing bowl and blend until smooth.
7. Beat in the eggs, 1 at a time, then the vanilla and the melted butter or margarine. Stir in the chopped cranberries and walnuts.
8. Pour the mixture into the partially baked and cooled pie crust.
9. Bake for 40–50 minutes, or until a knife inserted in the center of the pie comes out clean.

PURIM

PURIM

Therefore do the Jews of the villages, that dwell in the unwalled towns, make the fourteenth day of the month of Adar a day of gladness and feasting, and a good day, and of sending portions to one another.

Megillat Esther 9:19

The Shalachmones *that Black Nechama carried consisted of a fine slice of strudel, two big sugar cookies, a large honey* teigl, *two cushion cakes stamped with a fish on both sides and filled with tiny sweet* farfel, *and two large slabs of a poppyseed confection, black and glistening, mixed with ground nuts and glazed with honey. Besides all this, there lay on the plate, smiling up at them, a round, golden sweet-smelling orange that wafted its delicious odor right into their nostrils.*

Sholem Aleichem, "Two Shalachmones"

Purim places a greater emphasis on physical delights than does any other Jewish holiday. When Purim approaches, troubles are forgotten and festivities begin. It is a holiday of letting go, of celebrating a festival meal, and of joy.

Celebrated on Adar 14, which falls in February or March, Purim is a reminder of the Jewish people's deliverance from serious danger in the remote past. Wicked Haman, the favorite and minister of the Persian King Ahasuerus, wished to exterminate all the Jews of the Persian Empire because he thought the Jew Mordecai had failed to show him proper respect. Mordecai, helped by his cousin and foster daughter Esther, who was also the second queen of King Ahasuerus, foiled his plot. On Adar 13, the Jews were to be destroyed. Instead, on this day the Jewish population overcame those who wanted to wipe them out and then celebrated the victory the next day.

In their ecstasy, Mordecai and Esther proclaimed that the festival of Purim should be celebrated for all time by two annual recountings of the story of the Megillah (the Book of Esther) in the synagogue (on the evening and on the day of Purim), a *seudat Purim,* or festival meal in the late afternoon of Purim, charity to the poor—usually in the form of money to at least two people—and the sending of gifts (*mishloah manot*). Gifts and charity are given because the Jews were rescued from the wicked Haman through repentance. Repentance requires prayer, fasting, and charity. On Purim all three are to be fulfilled. To remind us of the three-day fast that Esther made before her dangerous approach to the king, one fast day on Adar 13—*Taanit Esther*—was introduced in the ninth century.

The origins of Purim lie shrouded in mystery. Most authorities doubt the historic validity of the Megillah and consider it an allegorical story. Throughout history, however, stories similar to that of Purim have repeated themselves, with the Jews being saved in the nick of time.

Wine plays a vital role in Purim, because the downfall of Haman was attributed to the wine and other drinks Esther served liberally at the banquet. In addition, the first queen, Vashti, was killed because the king was drunk; her death paved the way for Esther. The Talmud recommends drinking until it is impossible to distinguish (*add' lo yada*) between Haman and Mordecai. Wine is also a sign of happiness and "wine makes the heart of man happy." It also inaugurates all Jewish religious ceremonies.

At the Purim feast, kreplakh, *sambusak,* chickpeas, and turkey are typical foods. Turkey, considered to be a stupid animal, is often served in remembrance of Ahasuerus, who was a foolish king and who "reigned from India unto Ethiopia."

In the seasonal cycle of Jewish holidays, Purim's gastronomic position is quite important. As the last festival prior to Passover, it is an occasion to use up all the previous year's flour, so many delicacies with risen flour are prepared. All kinds of deep-fried and baked pastries are prepared the Jewish world over.

In the Russia of Sholem Aleichem, for example, women baked strudels, *teyglakh,* sugar cookies, and of course hamantashen. In Morocco, women bake small breads filled with hard-boiled eggs. In Iraq, they make all kinds of *sambusak,* or turnovers filled with chicken or cheese. In Tunisia, Lebanon, and Egypt, deep-fried pastries filled with nuts and oozing with honey are prepared.

The many varieties of baked goods were made into *shalah manot,* "portions sent by messenger," often a young child. The sending of *shalah manot* goes this way: At least two different kinds of food are placed on a tray. One should be of flour and one of a fruit that does not have to be cooked. Two blessings are recited, one over grain and one over fruit. Through the years it became traditional to fill sweet trays with honey cakes; gingerbread Haman's ears, pockets, or whatever the national representation of a cookie Haman might be; and dried figs, pomegranates, or oranges. One woman would send a portion to a friend. Not to be outdone, the friend would repay the gift, with at least one additional sweet added to it. A third would fill her tray with still more delicacies, and so on.

While testing hamantashen recipes for this book, I invited in several neighborhood children to help. After I explained to them the concept of *shalah manot,* the girls went to various neighbors bearing portions of cookies and fruit. Both the recipients and the donors were delighted—and molding the cookies was a perfect afternoon's entertainment.

Try making the cookie recipes in this section or those listed under Hanukkah and the Sabbath for your own *shalah manot.* And don't forget the fruit!

MENUS

PAN-SEPHARDIC

Sambusak (meat-filled)

Turkey with Persian Rice and Fruit Stuffing

Fagots de Légumes (Vegetable Bundles)

Ma'amoul (Nut-filled Cookies)

Figs Stuffed with Walnuts

AMERICAN JEWISH

Herkimer Chicken Soup with Matzah Balls

My Mother's Brisket

Kasha Varnishkes

Chickpeas for Purim

Hungarian Green Pepper and Tomato Salad

Sliced Oranges and Strawberries with Liqueur

Beigli or *Kindli*

ISRAELI

Jerusalem Hummus

Israeli Felafel

Tabbouleh

Pita

Poached Figs, Prunes, and Pecans with Wine

CENTRAL EUROPEAN
Mushroom and Barley Soup
Roast Chicken
Chestnuts and Prunes
Rice
Salade à Ma Façon
Fresh Fruit Cup
Hamantashen

DAIRY BRUNCH
Baked Whitefish
Sambusak (cheese-filled)
Bulgarian Zucchini *Fritada*
Hamantashen

CHICKPEAS FOR PURIM

MAKES ABOUT 2 CUPS. (P)

The table was more richly prepared than for any other meal in the year—foods and drinks of all kinds; twisted loaves that shone yellow, a huge baked fish touched up with saffron, golden colors that harmonized with the light of the candles stuck in the big Menorahs, or seven-branched candlesticks, that burned brilliantly, one at each end of the table. But in the center of the table, and near each Menorah, had been placed three piles of plain boiled chick peas. I asked my mother why these plebeian dishes had been permitted in the midst of this glorious company. And she explained that they were commemorative of the extreme piety of Esther the Queen. For Esther was a good Jewish daughter and, though she lived in the luxurious and profligate palace of the great king, she would touch none of the food. Haman the wicked, knowing of the laws of the Jews, had forbidden the presence of a Shohet, or ritual slaughterer, in the palace. And Esther therefore contented herself, at all the feasts, with plain peas and beans: yet, on this diet she was as well fed, and as beautiful, as those that gorged themselves on the most tempting dishes.

Schmaryahu Levin, *Childhood in Exile*

Esther was not the only one in Jewish history to restrict herself to a vegetarian diet lest she disobey the dietary laws. Daniel would eat only porridge or the edible seed of peas and beans in the court of Nebuchadnezzar.

Nahit, or chickpeas, are traditional at Purim. I first tasted this easily prepared dish at the Jerusalem home of my coauthor for *The Flavor of Jerusalem*, Judy Stacey Goldman.

One 20-ounce can chickpeas   Freshly ground pepper
Salt

1. Place the chickpeas with the liquid from the can in a saucepan. Simmer a few minutes, until heated through.
2. Drain the water. Sprinkle with salt and freshly ground pepper to taste. Serve in a dish with toothpicks, or eat the chickpeas as you would sunflower seeds or peanuts.

MADELEINE KAMMAN'S JAFFA SALAD

SERVES 6–8. (D)

In 1977, around Purim, Boston's Quincy Market became a Jerusalem souk. To honor this Jerusalem month, Madeleine Kamman, author of several French cookbooks, created a salad that she demonstrated for the public in the rotunda of Boston's original marketplace.

4 endives
1 bunch watercress, with the stems removed
3 large navel oranges, peeled and sliced in rounds

½ cup homemade mayonnaise (see page 379)
2 tablespoons Dijon mustard
½ cup heavy cream
Salt and pepper

1. In your salad bowl, layer the endives, watercress, and oranges, ending with oranges on top.
2. Just before serving, combine the mayonnaise and mustard, beating well with a whisk. Slowly add the cream, beating constantly. Season with salt and pepper to taste.
3. Add to the salad. Toss at the table.

MUSHROOM AND BARLEY SOUP

SERVES 8–10. (P)

When I was an aide to New York City's former Mayor Abe Beame, we had dinner one evening at Ratner's Dairy Restaurant on Manhattan's Lower East Side. The mayor, not known for his gourmet tendencies, whispered excitedly to his press secretary that he was going to order a favorite dish—mushroom and barley soup. Intrigued by what had caught the mayor's fancy, I followed suit. It was a heavenly combination of dried and fresh mushrooms, dill, and barley—thick, but not so heavy as many other varieties.

At home I have tried to duplicate the soup. Although the result was satisfactory, I could not of course duplicate the flavor of a Ratner specialty without the presence of one essential Ratner ingredient: Old World gentlemen waiters.

One 1-pound can tomatoes, chopped, with the juice
2 quarts water
1 onion, thinly sliced
2 ribs celery with leaves, diced
2 tablespoons chopped fresh flat-leaf parsley
½ green pepper, chopped
½ cup whole barley
½ cup small dried lima beans
1 carrot, sliced
1 pound mushrooms, sliced*
2 teaspoons salt
2 tablespoons snipped fresh dill

1. In a large saucepan combine the tomatoes, juice, water, onion, celery, parsley, green pepper, barley, and lima beans. Bring to a boil. Simmer, covered, 1½ hours.
2. Add the carrot, mushrooms, salt, and dill. Continue simmering until the carrot is tender, about 20 minutes.
3. Correct the seasonings and sprinkle on additional dill, if desired.

*In Eastern Europe, dried mushrooms are used instead of fresh. People were often afraid that fresh mushrooms were poisonous, and the dried are tastier. This soup can also be made with a meat base.

ROAST CHICKEN

SERVES 6–8. (M)

My grandmother Martha Kops Gluck had a millinery store in New York City. Because she was busy during the day, it was my great-grandmother or a maid who did the cooking in their home. Each Friday, however, my grandmother made one dish—roast chicken. Hers is low in calories, delicious, and easy to prepare. Serve it with rice, and Chestnuts and Prunes (page 303), perfect for a Purim dinner.

Two 3½-pound broiler chickens, quartered	Paprika
	2 small onions
Salt	½ cup water
Pepper	½ cup white wine
Garlic, crushed, or garlic powder	
Seasoning salt	

1. Preheat the oven to 350 degrees. Grease a large roasting pan.
2. Season the chicken with salt, pepper, crushed garlic, or garlic powder, seasoning salt, and paprika to taste. Lay each piece, skin side up, in a roasting pan.
3. Slice the onions and lay them over and around the chicken.
4. Roast 20 minutes. Turn the chicken over and roast 20 minutes more, basting occasionally. Add water if the pan becomes dry. Then turn the chicken over once more and roast 20 minutes with the skin side up. Baste with the wine.
5. If you like the skin crisp, place the chicken under the broiler before serving. Otherwise, mere basting from the drippings will add to the flavor.

SAMBUSAK

(Sephardic Stuffed Pastries)

MAKES ABOUT 36. (D OR M)

When Abe Sofaer, former legal adviser to the State Department, was a young boy in Bombay and later in New York City, he did not take sandwiches to school for lunch. His mother filled his lunchbox with *sambusak*. These pastries stuffed with cheese or meat are traditional for Iraqi, Indian, and Persian Jews. Eaten at any time, *sambusak* especially prepared for Purim are filled with dates or chicken. Who knows? Perhaps Queen Esther ate cheese-filled *sambusak* in Ahasuerus's palace. The following is the recipe of Mozelle Sofaer, Abe's mother.

DOUGH:

2 tablespoons (2 packages) active
   dry yeast
1 cup lukewarm water
Pinch of sugar
1 teaspoon salt
½ pound (2 sticks) pareve
   margarine

1 tablespoon ground anise seeds
7–8 cups sifted all-purpose flour
Vegetable oil for deep-frying meat
   sambusak

1. Dissolve the yeast in about 1 cup warm water. Add a pinch of sugar.
2. Add the salt, margarine, anise seeds, and 6 cups of the flour. Gradually add more flour to make a soft dough. Blend with your hands and knead well. (Abe Sofaer's mother insists that hands are best—and good therapy. "Don't use a machine," she insists. If you do succumb to a food processor, however, divide the dough in half and work in the remaining flour.)
3. Place in a greased bowl and let rise, covered, until doubled in size (about 1 hour or more.)
4. Punch down, knead again, and let rise again until doubled.
5. Punch down again and take a piece of dough the size of a plum and roll it into a ball. Press it down on a floured board until it flattens into a circle. Place

1 tablespoon of filling in the center. Fold over and pinch down into a half-moon shape.

6. For meat *sambusak,* heat the oil to 375 degrees. Deep-fry until golden on each side. Drain and serve.

7. For cheese *sambusak,* preheat the oven to 400 degrees. Place on a greased cookie sheet and bake about 15 minutes, or until golden.

MEAT FILLING:

1 tablespoon vegetable oil	Dash of ginger
1 bunch scallions (about 5), diced	Dash of turmeric
1 pound very lean ground beef or lamb	1 teaspoon cinnamon
	Salt
Dash of garlic powder	

1. Heat the oil. Add the scallions, ground beef or lamb, spices, and salt to taste. Keep turning the meat as it browns.

2. When it is cooked, turn the heat up so all the liquid evaporates. Let cool.

CHEESE FILLING:

2 cups feta cheese	2 eggs, separated

1. Combine the feta cheese with the yolks of the eggs.

2. Whip the egg whites until stiff peaks form. Carefully fold them into the cheese.

Note: The Sofaers serve the *sambusak* with chutney, grated coconut, and parsley. Mrs. Sofaer suggests making *sambusak* when the kitchen is warm and when you have a great deal of time and patience. She uses the formula of 2-2-2-2, up to 10-10-10-10—meaning that 2 pounds of flour go with 2 packages of yeast, 2 cups of water, and 2 sticks of margarine. She often makes 10 times everything and, after forming the pastries, freezes packages of them. She always has some *sambusak* in her home.

KASHA *VARNISHKES*

SERVES 6–8. (M OR P)

Just as *mamaliga* or polenta was the daily fare of the poorer Jews in Romania, kasha was that of the poor in Russia. Usually made from buckwheat groats or grains, it could also be made from wheat, oats, barley, millet, or any other grain. Buckwheat is the grain most indigenous to Russia. Cooked with water, milk, or broth, whole buckwheat groats make a hearty and nourishing porridge. Kasha was also a thick soup made of barley and lima beans. Grains are often browned first to produce a crunchy, nutty flavor.

Kasha and bread-and-potato or cabbage soup were the basic foods of the poor Jews in Russia and Poland. Kasha *varnishkes* was a dish for special occasions. Eaten on Purim, it is made from sautéed onions, kasha, and noodles made in squares or in the shape of bow ties or shells.

2 cups kasha	Salt and pepper
4 tablespoons chicken fat or vegetable oil	2 cups *varnishkes* (shell- or bow-tie-shaped noodles)
4 cups water	2 large onions, sliced

1. Place the kasha in a pan with 2 tablespoons chicken fat or oil. Sauté until the grains become dry and crunchy. Then add the water and salt and pepper to taste, and bring to a boil. Cover and simmer for about 20 minutes.
2. Cook the *varnishkes* according to the directions on the package. Drain.
3. Sauté the onions in the remaining chicken fat or oil until golden.
4. When the kasha is ready, combine with the onions and noodles. Adjust the seasoning and serve alone or as an accompaniment to brisket or chicken.

CHESTNUTS AND PRUNES

SERVES 6–8. (P)

Ever since I can remember, my mother has craved chestnuts. Whenever we visited museums in New York City or watched the Macy's Thanksgiving Day parade, she would buy a bag of hot roasted chestnuts and tell us about growing up in New York. So it was no surprise to me that she recalled a dish prepared by her grandmother for special occasions—chestnuts and prunes. Together we reconstructed the recipe, which has again become a family favorite at holiday festivals. It is perfect with chicken or turkey at Purim or Sukkot.

1 pound chestnuts
Water
5 tablespoons sugar
1 tablespoon pareve margarine

1 pound prunes
Juice of ½ lemon
½ teaspoon cinnamon

1. Freeze the chestnuts for 24 hours. Pour boiling water over the chestnuts and let sit for 5 minutes. Then pick the nuts out of the water. Using a sharp knife, shell and skin them.
2. Place the chestnuts in a saucepan in a single layer and add water to cover, 1 tablespoon of the sugar, and margarine. Bring to a boil, then reduce to a simmer. Cook until just tender, about 5 minutes. Cool, drain, and halve.
3. In another saucepan, place the prunes in water to cover. Bring to a boil, then reduce to a simmer. Cook 20 minutes. Add the 4 remaining tablespoons of sugar, lemon juice, and cinnamon. Add the chestnuts and cook 5 minutes more. Serve hot or cold.

FIGS STUFFED WITH WALNUTS

SERVES 6. (P)

And the eyes of them both were opened, and they knew that they were naked; and they sewed fig-leaves together, and made themselves girdles.

Genesis 3:7

The Talmud asserts that Adam and Eve sinned and ate of the same fig tree, the tree of knowledge. First they ate of the forbidden fruit, and then the leaves covered Adam and hid him after the fall.

Driving through Israel, my husband and I never fail to buy a bag of fresh figs, a rare delicacy in this country and such a refreshing snack in Israel.

12 dried figs   Grated coconut (optional)
12 walnut halves

1. Open the center of each fig.
2. Place a walnut half in the center of each fig and roll the stuffed fruit in grated coconut, if using. Place on a dish with other fruit and serve.

BEIGLI OR *KINDLI*

MAKES 6 LARGE OR 36 SMALL *KINDLI*. (D OR P)

These yeast-dough cookies, served by Hungarian and German Jews at Purim, resemble little children wrapped in blankets—thus the name *kindli*. They can also be shaped like three-cornered hats or hamantashen. The poppy-seed filling includes jam, lemon, orange, rum, and sugar, rather than the traditional Polish and Russian honey. Wine and rum are especially appropriate ingredients at Purim, since this is the one holiday in which drinking to excess is encouraged.

DOUGH:

8 cups unbleached all-purpose flour

2 large eggs, slightly beaten

3 egg yolks

½ pound (2 sticks) unsalted butter or pareve margarine, at room temperature

2 tablespoons (2 packages) active dry yeast

¼ cup warm water

1¾ cups potatoes, peeled and boiled (still warm)

1 cup sugar

Dash of salt

1 teaspoon vanilla extract

Grated zest of 1 lemon

2–3 tablespoons white wine

1. Place the flour in a large bowl and make a well in the center.
2. Put the whole eggs plus 1 egg yolk into the center and blend with your fingers.
3. Add the softened butter or margarine and knead together.
4. Dissolve the yeast in the warm water and then add to the potatoes. The warm potatoes will help to activate the yeast. Purée the potatoes and add to the flour mixture.
5. Add the sugar, salt, vanilla, lemon zest, and enough wine to bind the ingredients together. Knead well until a firm, smooth dough is achieved. (You can divide the dough and work it in the food processor.)
6. Divide into 6 round balls and let stand, covered, while you make the filling, about 45 minutes. Preheat the oven to 325 degrees.
7. When the filling (see below) is ready, punch the dough and divide each ball of dough again into 6 or 7 round balls. Or proceed, if you prefer, with the large rolls, which can be sliced into small individual pieces.
8. If you are making small cookies, roll the dough out and cut circles 3 inches in diameter. Then put 1½ tablespoons of filling in a line down the center, leaving a ½-inch border.
9. Fold the top and bottom of the circle over to cover the ends of the filling. Then take the left side and fold over ⅔ of the dough to cover the line of filling. Fold the right side over to the left edge. Press the sides together at the

center and edges, as if you were tucking a baby into a blanket. Place on an ungreased cookie sheet. Lightly beat the remaining 2 egg yolks. Brush the cookies with the yolks.

10. To make a large *kindli,* take one of the original 6 balls and roll out the dough into a circle about 7 inches in diameter. Smear with tablespoons of the filling. Fold the top and bottom over into 1-inch flaps. Then roll from one side like a jelly roll. Pinch down the edges. Brush with the egg yolks and place on an ungreased cookie sheet.

11. Bake about 30–45 minutes, until golden brown. Halfway through cooking, it is a good idea to brush more egg yolk on the kindli to achieve a lovely glazed effect.

The following two fillings will each make enough for the entire dough recipe. A quarter of each will fill the hamantashen dough (page 308).

POPPY-SEED FILLING:

MAKES ABOUT 2¼ CUPS, ENOUGH FOR ABOUT 36 HAMANTASHEN. (D OR P)

2 cups sugar	2 tablespoons rum
½ cup water	4 ounces raisins
2 cups poppy seeds	2 ounces dried figs, chopped
2 egg whites	1 teaspoon cinnamon
1 teaspoon vanilla extract	2 cups apricot or raspberry jam
Grated zest and juice of 1 lemon	¼ pound (1 stick) unsalted butter
Grated zest and juice of 1 orange	or pareve margarine

1. Combine the sugar and water and simmer while stirring over low heat.

2. Grind the poppy seeds in a food processor or blender. Add to the sugar mixture.

3. Add the egg whites, vanilla, lemon and orange zests and juices, rum, raisins, figs, and cinnamon. Simmer over low heat for about 5 minutes. Add the jam and butter, and continue simmering until the butter is melted and all the ingredients are combined. Use as is, or put in the refrigerator for a few minutes until the filling becomes a bit firmer.

NUT FILLING:

MAKES ABOUT 2¼ CUPS, ENOUGH FOR ABOUT 36 HAMANTASHEN. (D OR P)

2 cups walnuts, ground
1¾ cups sugar
1 teaspoon vanilla extract
Grated zest and juice of 1 lemon
Grated zest and juice of 1 orange
2 tablespoons rum

½ cup raisins
4 figs, chopped
1 teaspoon cinnamon, or to taste
1 cup orange marmalade or
  apricot jam
2 large egg whites

Combine all the above ingredients and mix well. Refrigerate.

HAMANTASHEN

Hamantashen have through the centuries become known as the Purim sweet. As in so many questions Jewish, there are disputes as to the origin of the word "hamantash." Some say it comes from *Haman tash kocho,* meaning, "May Haman's strength become weak." Others say it was merely Haman's hat. And then there is the theory that *mun-tasche* (bag of poppy seeds) is the correct name, and "hamantash" is merely a corruption of it. The three corners of the cookie are even said to represent the three patriarchs, Abraham, Isaac, and Jacob, whose merit saved the Jews.

Not everyone eats hamantashen at Purim. German Jews make gingerbread men and eat smoked meat. Egyptians eat *ozneï Haman,* or deep-fried sweets shaped like Haman's ears. In fact, everyone has some part of Haman to be eaten at Purim.

HAMANTASHEN YEAST DOUGH

MAKES 36. (M)

Whenever I make a speech about Jewish food, invariably someone asks for a hamantashen yeast dough. Here is a great one from Alex Lichtman.

3 scant tablespoons (3 envelopes) active dry yeast
4½ tablespoons warm milk
1 cup plus ½ teaspoon sugar
1 pound (4 sticks) unsalted butter, cold
¾ teaspoon salt

1 teaspoon vanilla extract
1 teaspoon grated lemon zest
7 cups unbleached all-purpose flour, plus ½ cup for dusting
1 cup sour cream
3 large eggs
Filling of choice (see below)

1. To make the dough, in a small bowl, dissolve the yeast in the milk, sprinkled with ½ teaspoon of the sugar.
2. In an electric mixer fitted with the paddle, combine the butter, salt, vanilla, lemon zest, and remaining sugar. Beat at low speed for 3 minutes.
3. Add 7 cups of the flour. Beat at low speed for 4 minutes more.
4. Add the sour cream, 2 of the eggs, and the yeast mixture. Beat at medium speed for 4–5 minutes, until the dough separates easily from the sides of the bowl.
5. Divide the dough into 4 pieces, and then each piece into 9. You will have 36 equal pieces. Shape them into balls and put them in a large bowl. Cover and refrigerate for 15 minutes.
6. Dust a work surface very lightly with some of the remaining ½ cup flour. Roll the balls out into ovals about 2¼ inches long by 2 inches wide (or, if you want larger ones, 3 inches long by 2½ inches wide).
7. Place 1 heaping teaspoon of the filling in the center of each oval. Make 12 at a time, setting them side by side. To make the three-cornered-hat shape, lift the 2 longer sides of the oval over the filling, making a point at the top. Then fold the remaining short edge up to meet the folded long sides, making a triangle. Gently shape the 3 closed edges and smooth out the surface. There should be no filling visible.

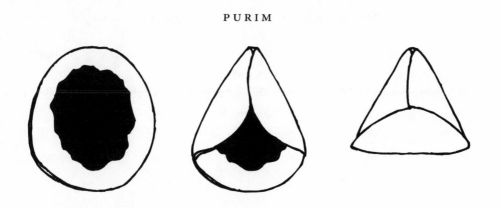

8. In a small bowl, beat the remaining egg.
9. Lightly grease 2 large cookie sheets. Place the hamantashen on the sheets 1½ inches apart and preheat the oven to 375 degrees.
10. Lightly brush the tops of the hamantashen with the beaten egg and allow to dry. Let them rise for 30–35 minutes and brush again with the beaten egg. At the center of each top, put a pinch of plain ground walnuts for the hamantashen filled with nut filling and a pinch of plain poppy seeds for those with the poppy-seed filling. Allow to dry for 20–25 more minutes.
11. Bake the hamantashen on the middle rack for 16–20 minutes, or until golden.

POPPY-SEED FILLING:

MAKES 2¼ CUPS, ENOUGH FOR ABOUT 36 HAMANTASHEN. (P)

This filling is best made 1–2 days before use.

⅔ cup water
¼ teaspoon cinnamon
¾ cup sugar
¼ cup raisins
2½–3 teaspoons grated orange zest

½ teaspoon grated lemon zest
2 tablespoons honey
2 cups poppy seeds*
3 tablespoons cake crumbs (from pound cake or other leftover cake)

*Available at health-food stores, where they are sold in bulk and are much cheaper than the commercial varieties sold elsewhere.

1. Bring the water to a boil in a medium saucepan. Whisk in the cinnamon.
2. Add the sugar, raisins, orange zest, lemon zest, and honey, and return to a boil.
3. Lower the heat, add the poppy seeds and the cake crumbs, and stir well with a wooden spoon. Simmer on low heat for 5–6 minutes.
4. Pour into a bowl, cover tightly with plastic wrap, and refrigerate. It will keep for up to 2 weeks.

NUT FILLING:

MAKES 2¼ CUPS, ENOUGH FOR ABOUT 36 HAMANTASHEN. (P)

This filling is best made 1–2 days before use.

½ cup plus 1 tablespoon cold water

¼ teaspoon cinnamon

¾ cup sugar

2 tablespoons raisins

1½ tablespoons grated orange zest

½ teaspoon grated lemon zest

2 tablespoons honey

2¼ cups coarsely ground pecans or walnuts

2 tablespoons cake crumbs (from pound cake or other leftover cake)

1. Bring the water to a boil in a medium saucepan. Whisk in the cinnamon.
2. Add the sugar, raisins, orange zest, lemon zest, and honey, and return to a boil.
3. Add the nuts and the cake crumbs and stir well with a wooden spoon. Simmer on low heat for 3–4 minutes.
4. Pour into a bowl, cover tightly with plastic wrap, and refrigerate. It will keep for up to 2 weeks.

HEAVENLY HAMANTASHEN

MAKES 48 HAMANTASHEN. (D OR P)

At Purim, Andra of Heavenly Hallah makes a meal with all foods shaped like triangles—potatoes, carrots, spinach phyllo, gefilte-fish patties, even peanut butter–chocolate mousse, and, of course, hamantashen stuffed with apricot, strawberry, or prune *lekvar* or jam, or chocolate chips. If you can find *lekvar*, often made from dried apricots or prunes, use that rather than regular fruit preserves because it holds together much better in baking. This dough is the more common cookie dough used in the United States.

¼ pound (1 stick) unsalted butter
    or pareve margarine, at room
    temperature
1 cup sugar
1 large egg, beaten
2 tablespoons orange juice
½ teaspoon vanilla extract

2 teaspoons baking powder
½ teaspoon salt
2 tablespoons wheat germ
2 cups unbleached all-purpose
    flour
Filling of choice

1. In a food processor fitted with the steel blade, cream together the butter or margarine and sugar. Pulse just a few seconds. Or use your fingers or 2 forks to crumble the butter together with the sugar in a large mixing bowl.
2. Add the beaten egg, orange juice, vanilla, baking powder, and salt and mix well, again just a few seconds in the processor. Add the wheat germ and the flour, ½ cup at a time. If you use a food processor, the mixture will come together in a ball. Or you may use your fingers to mix the ingredients and shape the dough into a ball. Wrap and refrigerate the dough for 2 hours.
3. Preheat the oven to 375 degrees and grease 2 cookie sheets.
4. On a lightly floured work surface, roll out the dough to a ⅛-inch thickness. Cut in circles with a 2-inch cookie cutter or the floured rim of a 2-inch glass. Place 1 tablespoon of the filling of your choice (see previous pages) in the center of the circle. Pinch together 3 corners evenly spaced along the

edge of the circle to form a triangular hamantashen shape. Some of the filling will show in the center. Arrange the cookies on the cookie sheets 1 inch apart.

5. Bake 1 sheet at a time on the middle rack of the oven for 10–12 minutes, until the hamantashen are light golden brown.

HAMANTASHEN COOKIE DOUGH

MAKES 36. (D OR P)

Just as there is great controversy over light versus heavy matzah balls, there seems to be discussion about which are better—yeast- or cookie-dough hamantashen. This is the tastiest cookie-dough base I have ever tried. Use one-quarter of either of the fillings on pages 309–10.

⅓ pound (10⅔ tablespoons) butter or pareve margarine, softened
½ cup sugar
1 egg

½ teaspoon vanilla extract
2½–3 cups sifted unbleached all-purpose flour
1 teaspoon baking powder
Dash of salt

1. Cream the butter or margarine with the sugar. Add the egg and continue creaming until smooth.
2. Add the vanilla. Sift together the flour, baking powder, and salt. Add to the butter mixture and mix until a ball of dough is formed. (A food processor is excellent for this.)
3. Cover with plastic wrap. Chill for 2–3 hours, or overnight.
4. Preheat the oven to 375 degrees.
5. Taking ¼ of the dough, roll out on a lightly floured board to a thickness of ⅛ inch. Cut into 2-inch circles. With your finger put water around the rim of each circle. Fill with 1 teaspoon of poppy-seed or nut filling and fold into

three-cornered cookies. (Press 2 sides together, and then fold the third side over and press the ends together.)

6. Bake on a well-greased cookie sheet 10–16 minutes, until the tops are golden.

NANA'S PRUNE AND NUT ROLL

MAKES 3 ROLLS OR 45 COOKIES. (D OR P)

Michael London's grandmother's cookie roll, similar to my great-aunt Eva's cookies, is a perfect alternative to prune hamantashen at Purim and a delicious dessert any time of year. His grandmother Betty Seltzer, known to Michael as Nana Banana or Betty Baby, was famous in Brooklyn for her gefilte fish and her baked goods. Born in New York, she learned this recipe from her mother, who came from Austria-Hungary. Although Michael remembers his grandmother making the *lekvar* from prunes, his great-grandmother probably dried freestone plums herself and then made the jam. You can substitute prepared apricot or prune *levkar* or good preserves, allowing 1 cup per roll.

THE CRUST:

½ pound (2 sticks) unsalted
   butter or pareve margarine,*
   at room temperature
1 cup sugar
¼ teaspoon salt
3–3½ cups unbleached all-
   purpose flour

2½ teaspoons baking powder
3 large eggs
1 teaspoon vanilla extract
Grated zest and juice of 1 orange

THE FILLING:

3 cups pitted prunes
2 cups water
½ teaspoon cinnamon

1 tablespoon sugar
1 cup chopped walnuts

*Although I have included pareve margarine, the Londons would never use a substitute for butter.

1. Prepare the crust: Blend the butter, sugar, and salt in the bowl of an electric mixer fitted with the dough hook or a food processor fitted with the steel blade.

2. In a separate bowl, mix together 3 cups of the flour and the baking powder.

3. Add 2 of the eggs, the vanilla, orange zest, and orange juice to the sugar-butter mixture. Blend for a few minutes or process a few seconds. Then add the flour mixture and mix again just until incorporated. Depending on the juiciness of the orange, you may have to add more flour.

4. Divide the dough into 3 pieces and pat into 3 rectangles about 3½ by 6 inches. Cover each with plastic wrap and refrigerate a few hours or overnight.

5. Prepare the filling: Put the prunes and water in a saucepan and simmer, uncovered, for 45 minutes, or until the prunes are soft enough to break apart with the back of a fork and most of the water has evaporated. Be sure to watch the prunes so that they don't burn. Add more water if needed. Once the prunes are done, remove them from the pan and mash them.

6. Preheat the oven to 325 degrees and mix the cinnamon and sugar in a small bowl. Cover a cookie sheet with baking parchment.

7. Dust a work surface with flour and roll out 1 rectangle of the dough, turning and flipping it occasionally, until it measures about 8 by 11 inches. Sprinkle it with a little cinnamon-sugar.

8. Using a plastic spatula, spread one third of the prune filling lengthwise along one side in a 4-inch-wide strip, leaving a 1-inch border. Then sprinkle one-third of the walnuts over the prunes. You should still have a 3-inch-wide strip of bare dough.

9. Beat the remaining egg and brush it in another 2-inch stripe on the bare part of the dough, alongside the filling, leaving 1 inch bare at the edge.

10. Starting from the long edge with the fillings, roll up the dough like a jelly roll. Pinch the ends under and place this roll seam side down on the parchment-lined cookie sheet. Sprinkle with more cinnamon-sugar. Repeat the process with the other 2 pieces of dough.

11. Bake the rolls on the middle oven rack for 45–60 minutes, or until lightly browned. Cool and cut with a sharp knife into ½-inch slices.

TRAVADOS

(Jerusalem Cinnamon-Nut Cookies)

MAKES 48 *TRAVADOS*. (D OR P)

Zohar Cohen-Nehemia Halleen remembers these sweet walnut-stuffed cookies as *burekas,* called that because of their crescent shape. They are an old Jerusalem Sephardic treat, similar to *mahmoul,* a nut-filled cookie often pressed into a wooden mold that prints a design on top. *Travados* are traditionally served on all holidays, but particularly at Purim. They taste even better the second day.

10 ounces (2½ sticks) unsalted butter or pareve margarine, at room temperature
1¼ cups plus 2 tablespoons sugar
1 teaspoon vanilla extract
Dash of salt
4 cups unbleached all-purpose flour

2 cups plus 1 teaspoon ice water
1½ cups walnuts
¾ teaspoon cinnamon
1 large egg yolk
Juice of ½ lemon

1. Place the butter or margarine and 2 tablespoons of the sugar in a food processor fitted with the steel blade and process a few seconds. Add the vanilla, salt, and flour. Pulse to combine, then gradually add ½ cup of the water as you pulse until a soft dough is formed. Set aside.
2. Using a food processor fitted with the steel blade, grind 1 cup of the walnuts with the cinnamon and ¼ cup of the sugar. Then add the remaining ½ cup of nuts and roughly chop.
3. Divide the dough into 4 pieces. On a work surface lightly dusted with flour, roll each piece of dough out into a circle ⅛ inch thick. Using a 3-inch round cookie cutter or floured rim of a glass, cut out circles. Place 1 heaping teaspoon of the walnut mixture in the center of each circle. Fold over, crimp the edges to seal, and shape into a crescent. Repeat until the dough is used up.
4. Beat the egg yolk and 1 teaspoon of the ice water and brush onto the cookies.

5. Preheat the oven to 350 degrees and grease 2 cookie sheets.

6. Place the cookies about 1 inch apart on the sheets, and bake 1 sheet at a time on the bottom rack of the oven for 15–20 minutes. Slightly cool the *travados* on a rack.

7. While the *travados* are baking, bring the remaining 1 cup sugar and the remaining 1½ cups water to a boil and simmer about 15 minutes. Add the lemon juice and return to a boil. Remove from the heat.

8. Using a slotted spoon, submerge the warm cookies in the warm syrup. Remove the cookies and place on a cooling rack. Alternatively, you can simply roll the cookies in confectioners' sugar.

ERASS B'ADJWAH

(Syrian Date-filled Crescents)

MAKES 36 *ADJWAH*. (D OR P)

For Syrian Jews, dates are not only a sign of welcome throughout the year but also a symbol of sweetness for the new year. "In the Syrian community, we eat *adjwah* at every holiday except for Passover," said Josiane Mansoura of Mansoura Middle Eastern Pastries. The Mansouras pat out the dough with the palms of their hands, while other bakers such as Sarina Roffe, also from this community, use a tortilla press to flatten the dough. Although the Mansouras make their *adjwah* without walnuts, I've included them as an option.

THE DOUGH:

1 cup *smead* (semolina, not semolina flour)*

2 cups unbleached all-purpose flour

Dash of salt

1 tablespoon vegetable oil

½ pound (2 sticks) unsalted butter or pareve margarine, at room temperature

½–¾ cup cold water

*Available at Middle Eastern markets.

THE FILLING:

1 pound pitted dates   2 tablespoons grated orange zest
1–2 cups water   ½ cup confectioners' sugar
½ cup chopped walnuts
    (optional)

1. Place the semolina, flour, salt, oil, and butter or margarine in a food processor fitted with the steel blade. Process, adding the water a little at a time, until the dough forms a ball. You can also make it by hand as the older Syrians do: Pour the semolina, flour, and salt in a bowl. With a fork or your fingers, mix in the oil and butter until the dough is lumpy. Do not overmix. Add the water, a little at a time, until the dough comes together and is smooth and pliable.

2. Remove the dough from the food processor, cover, and let it rest. At this point you can refrigerate the dough to continue at a later time, bringing it to room temperature before working it.

3. Grind the dates in the food processor fitted with the steel blade. Then scoop them into a saucepan, add water barely to cover (about 2 cups), and cook the dates over low heat, stirring occasionally, for about 15 minutes, or until the water is mostly absorbed and a thick date paste is formed. Stir in the nuts and orange zest. Let the filling cool.

4. Preheat the oven to 350 degrees.

5. Separate the dough into 4 equal parts and divide each part into nine 2-inch balls. Flatten each ball with a rolling pin, the palm of your hand, or a tortilla press to a 4-inch diameter. If using a tortilla press, flour it or cover it with plastic wrap so the dough doesn't stick to the press. Place 1 tablespoon of the date mixture in the middle of the circle of dough, pressing the dates down on the circle. Fold into a half-moon shape to enclose, gently pinch the edges along the round side to seal in the date mixture, and then shape into a crescent. Repeat with the remaining dough and filling. You may have about 3 tablespoons of filling left; this makes a great hamantashen filling.

6. Bake on the middle rack of the oven on an ungreased cookie sheet for 20–25 minutes, or until slightly golden. The *adjwah* can be frozen after they cool. Sprinkle with confectioners' sugar when ready to serve.

MA'AMOUL

(Nut-filled Cookies)

MAKES 35–40. (P OR D)

Have you ever visited the marketplace of Jerusalem and noticed small wooden imprinted molds with handles? To be sure, the merchant is hard put to explain their significance. They are *ma'amoul* molds. *Ma'amoul* means "filled" in Arabic, and these molds make filled cookies eaten by Jews and Arabs throughout the Middle East, especially in Syria, Lebanon, and Egypt.

A piece of short-pastry dough the size of a walnut is pressed into the crevices of the *ma'amoul* mold. A tablespoon of date or nut filling is inserted, and you close the pastry with your fingers. Holding the handle of the wooden mold, you slam it on the table, letting the enclosed dough fall out. On the top of the cookie is a lovely design. After baking and rolling in confectioners' sugar, the design stands out even more. Of course, the *ma'amoul* mold is not necessary to the preparation of these sweets, though it certainly adds to their beauty. The tines of a fork, tweezers with a serrated edge, or a tool of your own devising will do quite well.

The following *ma'amoul* recipe came from Aleppo to the Syrian Jewish community on Ocean Parkway, Brooklyn. These cookies are served at Purim. A similar cookie, called *karabij* here (*nataife* in Syria), topped with marshmallow fluff, is also served at Purim. *Arasibajweh*—rolled cookies from the same dough and stuffed with dates—are served at the New Year or Hanukkah.

DOUGH:

2½ cups unbleached all-purpose flour

½ cup semolina flour

10 ounces (2½ sticks) pareve margarine or 1 pound (2 sticks) butter

2 teaspoons vegetable oil

¼–½ cup water

Confectioners' sugar

FILLING:

1½ cups roughly ground walnuts   ½ cup sugar
1 teaspoon cinnamon

1. For the dough, place the flour, semolina, margarine, and oil in a food processor equipped with a steel blade. Add the water gradually, pulsing until a soft dough is formed. Cover and set aside for 10–15 minutes in the refrigerator.
2. For the filling, combine the walnuts with the cinnamon and sugar.
3. Preheat the oven to 350 degrees.
4. Either use the *ma'amoul* mold described above or take a piece of dough about the size of a walnut. Roll it into a ball and hollow out the center. Inside, place a heaping teaspoon of walnut filling. With your hands, mold the dough closed. Continue with the rest of the dough.
5. Place the cookies on an ungreased cookie sheet. With the tines of a fork or tweezers with a serrated edge, make designs on the top of each cookie, being sure not to penetrate the crust.
6. Bake in the oven for about 30 minutes. Do not brown; the cookies should look white. Cool. When hard, roll in confectioners' sugar.

GHOURIBI

(Moroccan Sugar Cookies)

MAKES ABOUT 30. (P OR D)

On the morning of Purim, Moroccan Jews decorate the table with flowers and sweets. Marzipan-stuffed prunes with walnuts and cookies such as *ghouribi* are a few of the delicacies. *Ghouribi* are easily prepared walnut cookies that children enjoy rolling with their hands.

1 cup vegetable oil or ½ pound (2 sticks) unsalted butter, melted	3 cups unbleached all-purpose flour
1 cup sugar	⅓ cup finely ground walnuts or almonds
Dash of salt	Cinnamon

1. Preheat the oven to 350 degrees. Lightly flour an ungreased cookie sheet. You can use a sifter for this.
2. Place the oil or melted butter and sugar in a large bowl and mix well. Gradually add the salt and the flour, 1 cup at a time, and knead well. Blend in the nuts.
3. When the dough feels smooth, use the palm of your hand to roll it into balls the size of an egg. Pat into a round cookie about 2 inches in diameter. The cookie should not be flat.
4. Place on the cookie sheet and sprinkle the center of each cookie with cinnamon. Bake for 25–30 minutes. Do not let the cookies become even slightly brown; they must remain off-white.

A Turkish variation uses cocoa powder instead of cinnamon and is sprinkled with confectioners' sugar. These cookies can also be shaped into crescents. Made with butter, they are similar to the Austro-Hungarian *Kupferlin* (page 278).

PURIM PUFFS

SERVES 6. (D)

Gershom Mendes Seixas was a famous American-Jewish Revolutionary figure. The minister of the Shearith Israel Synagogue in New York, he led his co-congregants out of the city when the British invaded, carrying the Torah scrolls in his arms. He later resettled in Philadelphia, the seat of the Revolution, and headed another synagogue.

A religious man, Seixas described Purim in a letter of 1813, three years before his death: "With all the merriment and festivity usually practiced in my family, the children seated at our large Table, in the Parlour, with two lighted Candles, and a great display of fiar Tea (no water and milk for a mockery), a sweet loaf, gingerbread, and some few nic-nacs from our friend L in Broad St.—sent in the morning for Shalah Monot."

The sweets mentioned show how, early on, Jews became assimilated in the United States. A loaf and gingerbread sound vastly more American than they do Sephardic. The Seixas family may well have also eaten Purim puffs, which I found in the *Twentieth Century Cookbook* of 1897. The clue to the Jewishness of the doughnuts is in the title and in the fact that here goose grease or butter is used as opposed to the lard of other recipes.

½ tablespoon (½ package) active dry yeast	1 teaspoon plus a pinch of salt
1 cup lukewarm milk	¼ pound (1 stick) unsalted butter
6½ cups sifted all-purpose flour	2 eggs, beaten
1 cup plus 1 teaspoon sugar	Oil for frying
	Confectioners' sugar

1. Dissolve the yeast in the warm milk. Gradually add 1½ cups of the flour, 1 teaspoon sugar, and a pinch of salt to form a soft dough. Knead well, cover, and set aside to rise in a warm, draft-free spot for at least 1 hour.
2. When the dough has risen, cream together the butter and the remaining 1 cup sugar. Gradually add the eggs, the dough, and 1 teaspoon salt. Work in 5 cups

of flour, kneading until the dough leaves the sides of the bowl. Set aside to rise again, covered, for another hour.

3. When the dough is well risen, punch down and roll out on a floured board to a thickness of ½ inch. Cut in triangles and lay on a floured board to rise.

4. Add at least 2 inches of oil to a heavy pan (I use a wok for this). Heat the oil to 375 degrees.

5. When well risen, drop the risen dough triangles into the oil a few at a time. Brown a few minutes, turning to cook the other side. Remove with a perforated skimmer and sprinkle with confectioners' sugar. Serve immediately.

PASSOVER

PASSOVER

Seven days shall ye eat unleavened bread; howbeit the first day ye shall put away leaven out of your houses; for whosoever eateth leavened bread from the first day until the seventh day, that soul shall be cut off from Israel.

Exodus 12:15

I peeked into our own courtyard and saw all the neighbors washing and scrubbing, scraping and rubbing, making the tables and benches kosher-for-Passover. They carried huge pots of boiling water, heated irons and red-hot bricks, all of which gave off a white vapor. . . . We had bought our matzohs a long time ago and had them locked in the cupboard over which a white sheet had been hung. In addition, we had a basketful of eggs, a jar of Passover chicken-fat, two ropes of onions on the wall, and many other delicacies for the holiday.

Sholem Aleichem, "The Passover Eve Vagabonds"

Passover is probably the Jewish holiday that occasions more joyful anticipation than any other. It is one of the world's oldest continually observed festivals and, despite intrusions of modernity, still retains its ancient charm.

It is celebrated in commemoration of the Exodus of the Jews from Egypt. For eight days we do not partake of any leavening agent in our food. A reading of the Haggadah—a narration of the Exodus—is a central part of the first (and second) night of Passover.

For weeks prior to the festival, houses are thoroughly cleaned to remove any trace of leavening, and the day before the Seder feast, the head of the household searches for leavening (*hametz*). Before the search (*bedikat hametz*), someone, often a child, places bread crumbs on napkins and hides them in various rooms of the house. The head of the household then recites a blessing on the search for and destruction of *hametz* (which is actually burned the following morning) and proceeds to search the house for any crumbs overlooked during the cleaning. One hopes no *hametz* is found, except the crumbs intentionally hidden. The crumbs serve the purpose of not allowing the head of the household to make the blessing on the burning of the *hametz* in vain.

No products made from regular flour and no leavening agents can be eaten at Passover. Although the Sephardim eat all vegetables and some even eat rice, Ashkenazim eschew all grain-like vegetables such as corn, string beans, and peas. They also refrain from lentils, chickpeas, and other dried beans.

Observant families who can afford it have separate sets of dishes, cutlery, and cooking utensils for Passover, which are kept carefully packed away the rest of the year. The less well-to-do convert dishes, pots, and silverware for Passover use by scalding them in boiling water. Metal pans can be passed through fire and broilers heated red hot.

The observance was originally a spring festival celebrated by nomadic desert Jews, with a roasted sheep or goat as the central food. Centuries later, the peasants of Israel had a spring grain observance, the Festival of Unleavened Bread.

Later still, the seasonal aspect of the festival was transformed into a freedom holiday representing more closely the history and social and spiritual strivings of the Jewish people.

The meal of the first two nights has been formalized into a Seder (order), imbuing the original lamb, bitter herbs, and matzah with new symbolism. Additional foods recall the historical trials of the Jewish people. The Seder is a family meal, and those sitting at it are reminded, both by narration and by the foods to be eaten, of the rich heritage of thousands of years and the suffering through those millennia.

Pesah means "passing by" or "passing over," and the holiday was called Passover because God passed over the Jewish houses when He slew the firstborn

of Egypt. Matzah, unleavened and quickly baked, now recalls that the Jews flee-
ing Egypt had no time to leaven their bread and to bake it properly. Usually two
challahs are served at ceremonial meals; but on Passover, three matzot are placed
on the table instead.

Originally *maror,* bitter herbs, are served as reminders of the bitterness of
enslavement in Egypt. *Haroset,* a blend of sweet fruits and nuts, represents the
mortar used by Jewish slaves in building for their masters. A roasted egg (*betzah*)
represents the festival sacrifice brought to the Temple and is thus a symbol of
mourning for the destroyed Temple. *Karpas*—parsley or other available greens
such as celery—recalls the "sixty myriads" of Israelites oppressed with difficult
labor.

Four cups of wine are poured during the service; a fifth cup is left for the
Prophet Elijah, a harbinger of freedom and the Messiah. The wine symbolizes
the four divine promises of redemption found in the Scripture in connection
with Israel's liberation from Egypt: "I will bring you out. . . . I will deliver
you. . . . I will redeem you. . . . I will take you to Me" (Exodus 6:6–7).

Since the destruction of the Second Temple in 70 C.E., there have been no sacrifices at Passover. Therefore, for some it is forbidden to eat roast lamb at the
Seder meal until the Temple is rebuilt. Jews usually substitute turkey or chicken
as a main Seder dish and lift *zeroa,* a roasted lamb shank bone, as a reminder of
the pascal sacrifice at the Temple.

Each civilization has left its mark on the customs and foods of the Seder. Wine
and soft sofas upon which to recline were added in Graeco-Roman times, as
these were part of a feast. Eastern European Jews may eat parsley, while Sephardic Jews choose romaine lettuce. The *haroset* varies, too, depending on the availability of ingredients.

Today, despite the dispersal of Jews throughout the world, the eight-day
festival maintains its family character and begins with the traditional Seder meal.
The central object of every table is the Seder plate arranged with the symbolic
foods. There is no rule for menus for the meal, although there are traditions, as
shown in several of the menus that follow. Some families repeat the same menu
both nights; others have two different ones. From what I have ascertained, what
once had to do with the wealth of the family became a nostalgic custom. Some
families with no servants repeated the menu, making it easier for the housewife.
Wealthier families had no problem in varying the food for large gatherings.

Besides the traditional Seder dish with symbolic foods, Passover recipes themselves have evolved throughout the years, according to the country to which Jews immigrated. To compensate for the absence of flour demanded by this ancient rule, Jews the world over have created all kinds of baked goods from soaked matzah and, later, matzah cake meal (almost the consistency of regular flour but without the name). Flourless tortes using ground nuts, sponge cakes made from matzah meal or potato flour, macaroons, *krimsel,* and other Passover fritters are all favorites during this eight-day holiday.

FLOUR SUBSTITUTIONS FOR PASSOVER

1 cup of flour = ¾ cup matzah cake meal or ¾ cup potato starch

For bread crumbs, use matzah meal

For graham cracker crumbs substitute Passover cookie crumbs

1 tablespoon flour for thickening: use ½ tablespoon potato starch

1 teaspoon baking powder = ½ teaspoon baking soda plus ½ teaspoon cream of tartar

Cornstarch = Potato starch

1 cup confectioners' sugar = 1 cup granulated sugar minus 1½ teaspoons sugar blended with 1½ teaspoons potato starch

SEDER MENUS

TRADITIONAL AMERICAN
(**BASED ON** *THE* "*SETTLEMENT*" *COOK BOOK*)
Chicken Soup with Matzah Balls
Honey-Orange Chicken
New Potatoes with Chopped Parsley
Fresh Asparagus
Honey-Glazed Carrots
Salade à Ma Façon
Matzah Almond Torte
Syrian Stuffed Prunes

RUSSIAN
Zamosc Gefilte Fish
Chicken Soup with Matzah Balls
Passover *Tsimmes*
Potatoes
Green Salad
Passover Popovers
Passover Apple Blintzes
Passover Lemon Sponge Cake

MIXED SEPHARDIC
Egg-Lemon Soup
Veal with Artichokes
Asparagus
Syrian Stuffed Prunes
Rice
Fresh Fruit
Almond Macaroons

MIXED ASHKENAZIC

Gefilte Fishballs

Chicken Soup with Matzah Balls

Roast Turkey with Matzah Stuffing

Mrs. Feinberg's Vegetable Kugel

Tossed Green Salad

Krimsel with Stewed Prunes

Chocolate Soufflé Roll

SAN FRANCISCO CHEF

Pickled Salmon

Patty Unterman's Potato Kugelettes

Cornish Hens with Apricots, Tomatoes, and Spices

Stir-fried Greens

Barbara Tropp's Pecan-Ginger Torte

MY SEDER

Zamosc Gefilte Fish

Hard-boiled Eggs

Chicken Soup with Matzah Balls

Brisket

Asparagus

Passover Chocolate Cake

Krimsel

Strawberries

HAROSET

Haroset, the blend of fruits and nuts symbolizing the mortar which our forefathers used to build pyramids in Egypt, is one of the most popular and discussed ritual foods served at the Seder. The fruit and nuts found in almost all *haroset* recipes refer to two verses in the Song of Songs closely linked with the spring season: "Under the apple-tree I awakened thee" (8:5) and "I went down into the garden of nuts" (6:11). The red wine recalls the Red Sea, which parted its waters for the Jews.

The real purpose of the *haroset* is to allay the bitterness of the *maror* (bitter herbs) required at the Seder. And from this combination of *haroset* and *maror* between two matzot, the sandwich may have been invented by Rabbi Hillel, the great Jewish teacher who lived between 90 B.C.E. and 70 C.E. *Haroset* also shows how Jewish cookery was developed by the emigration from Mediterranean countries to Eastern Europe and by local ingredients supplemented or discarded depending on their availability.

Although most American Jews are familiar with the mixture of apples, almonds, cinnamon, wine, and ginger, this is by no means the only combination possible. Walnuts, pine nuts, peanuts, or chestnuts can be mixed with apricots, coconuts, raisins, dates, figs, and even bananas.

Whereas Ashkenazic *haroset* is quite universal, differing only texturally, that of the Sephardic Jews changes according to the country and sometimes even the city of origin. On the island of Rhodes, for example, dates, walnuts, ginger, and sweet wine are used. The Greek city of Salonika adds raisins to this basic recipe; Turkish Jews, not far away, include an orange. Egyptians eat dates, nuts, raisins, and sugar, without the ginger and wine. Yemenites use chopped dates and figs, coriander, and chili pepper. An interesting *haroset* from Venice has chestnut paste and apricots, while one from Surinam, Dutch Guiana, calls for seven fruits including coconut. Each Israeli uses the Diaspora *haroset* recipe of his ancestors or an Israeli version that might include pine nuts, peanuts, bananas, apples, dates, sesame seeds, matzah meal, and red wine.

Most people like their *haroset* recipe so well that it is not only spread on matzah and dipped in horseradish at the Seder table but also is eaten for breakfast, lunch, and snacks throughout Passover. I always serve at least five different *haroset* at my table to illustrate how Jewish recipes have wandered throughout the Diaspora.

EGYPTIAN *HAROSET*

MAKES 4 CUPS. (P)

1 pound raisins	¼ cup sugar
8 ounces pitted dates	¼ cup chopped walnuts or pecans

1. Place the raisins and dates in a bowl with enough water to cover. Let stand for 1 hour.
2. Add the sugar. Whirl the mixture in a blender, a few spoonfuls at a time. Or divide the mixture in thirds and place in a food processor.
3. Transfer the chopped fruits to a heavy saucepan and let simmer over low heat until the fruits are cooked and the liquid absorbed. It should take about 20 minutes.
4. Remove from the heat and place in a jar. When cool, sprinkle with chopped nuts.

VENETIAN *HAROSET*

MAKES ABOUT 4 CUPS. (P)

This delicious *haroset* recipe comes from the famous Luzzatto family of Venice. Members of the family have lived in Italy since 1541 and probably before. Names like Benedetto Luzzatto, Simone Luzzatto, Moses Haim Luzzatto, and Samuel David Luzzatto were well known to Italians from the Renaissance to the Enlightenment as authors, professors, and rabbis. The late Francis Luzzatto was a keeper of family traditions; the following is his family's recipe.

1½ cups chestnut paste

10 ounces dates, chopped

12 ounces figs, chopped

2 tablespoons poppy seeds

½ cup chopped walnuts

½ cup chopped almonds

½ cup pine nuts

Grated zest of one orange

½ cup golden raisins

¼ cup chopped dried apricots

½ cup brandy

Honey to bind

Combine all the ingredients, gradually adding just enough brandy and honey to make the mixture bind.

Other Italian *haroset* recipes include mashed-up bananas, apples, hard-boiled eggs, crushed matzah, pears, and lemon.

SEVEN-FRUIT *HAROSET* FROM SURINAM

MAKES ABOUT 5 CUPS. (P)

Many Sephardic Jews went to Holland at the time of the Inquisition. From there some went to Dutch colonies, often engaging in the sugar and spice trade. Mrs. Abraham Lopes Cardozo (née Robles) is a fine cook who makes an effort to preserve for her family and friends her Surinam culinary heritage. She is the wife of the former *hazan* of Shearith Israel Synagogue in New York City, the former minister of the Sephardic Congregation in Surinam.

At Passover, Surinam customs are quite unusual. Mrs. Cardozo explained to me, for example, that matzot were a rarity in Surinam. Because they had to be imported from Holland and later on from the United States, cassava (a kind of potato) meal was often used instead to bake sweet breads for Passover. The potato was first grated and washed, then dried in the sun for weeks. Once dried, it was ready to be mixed with other ingredients, as we use matzah flour for sweet desserts.

Easier for us to make is Mrs. Cardozo's *haroset* recipe, which I tasted for breakfast one morning at the Cardozo home.

8 ounces unsweetened coconut
8 ounces walnuts, chopped, or
    almonds, grated
¼ cup sugar
1 tablespoon cinnamon
8 ounces raisins
8 ounces dried apples

8 ounces prunes
8 ounces dried apricots
8 ounces dried pears
4 ounces cherry jam
Sweet red wine, such as
    Manischewitz

1. Combine everything except the jam and wine in a large, heavy pot. Add water to cover. Simmer over low heat, stirring occasionally with a wooden spoon. Add small amounts of water periodically, so that the mixture does not stick to the pot. Continue stirring.
2. Cook for at least 60 minutes. When all the ingredients have come together, stir in the cherry jam. Let stand until cool.
3. Add enough sweet wine to be absorbed by the *haroset* mixture. Refrigerate.

ASHKENAZIC APPLE-NUT *HAROSET*

MAKES ABOUT 3 CUPS. (P)

6 McIntosh or Gala apples
    (2 pounds), peeled, cored,
    seeded, and coarsely chopped
⅔ cup chopped almonds

3 tablespoons sugar, or to taste
½ teaspoon cinnamon
Grated zest of 1 lemon
4 tablespoons sweet red wine

1. Combine all the ingredients, mixing together thoroughly. Add a little more wine as needed.
2. Blend (you can use a food processor) until it reaches the desired consistency. (I like my *haroset* in large pieces, with a crunchy texture, but my husband's Polish family prefers theirs ground to a paste.) Chill.

PERSIAN *HAROSET*

MAKES ABOUT 5 CUPS. (P)

Herbs for Passover must be separated from those used during the year. So, two months prior to the holiday, Persian-born Mohtaran Shirazi buys whole spices and herbs such as turmeric, rock salt, cinnamon, and cardamom and methodically washes and sun-dries them before pounding them with a mortar and pestle. The same procedure is used for watermelon and sunflower seeds, as well as pistachio nuts; after being washed and dried, they are baked in the oven. Some of these spices are used in her tempting *haroset* with pistachio nuts and pomegranate.

25 dates, pitted and chopped	1 banana, sliced
½ cup unsalted pistachio nuts	½–1 cup sweet red wine
½ cup almonds	¼ cup cider vinegar
½ cup yellow raisins	½ tablespoon cayenne pepper
1½ apples, peeled, cored, and diced	1 tablespoon ground cloves
	1 tablespoon ground cardamom
1 pomegranate, peeled and seeds removed	1 teaspoon cinnamon
	1 tablespoon freshly ground black pepper
1 orange, peeled and diced	

1. Combine all the fruits and nuts in a food processor fitted with a metal blade.
2. Add the wine and vinegar. Pulse until a pasty consistency is reached.
3. Add the spices and blend well. Adjust the seasonings.

YEMENITE *HAROSET*

MAKES ABOUT 7 CUPS. (P)

Probably closest to the way the Jews originally ate is the Seder of the Yemenites. According to Hava Nathan, an Israeli cookbook writer (see *Carciofi alla Giudia,* page 380), the Yemenites transform the entire dining room table into a Seder plate, with the guests sitting on the floor around it. While the men set the table with greens, radishes, and parsley which they bring in picked straight from the garden, the women prepare the meal. The men set the table in gratitude for the women who prepare the food. This comes from Nathan's *Passover Seder Cookbook,* published by Zmora Bitan Publishers in Tel Aviv.

1 pound fresh dates

1 pound raisins

3 whole pomegranates, peeled and
    seeds removed

¾ pound almonds

½ pound walnuts

1 tablespoon mixed ground
    spices: cinnamon, pepper,
    cumin, cardamom, cloves, and
    ginger

In a food processor or with a chopper in a wooden bowl, chop all the fruits, including the pomegranate seeds and juice, and the nuts. Add the spices, adjusting the amounts of each to your family's taste.

LARRY BAIN'S BUBIE'S *HAROSET*

MAKES 6 CUPS. (P)

For many years five San Francisco–based chefs have sat down to their Passover Seder together. The tradition started when restaurateur Larry Bain and his wife, chef Catherine Pantsios, found themselves new in town just before Passover. Their first Seder became an excuse for them to invite their closest friends, other Jewish chef-owners, to Zola, their newly opened restaurant: cookbook author and chef Joyce Goldstein of Square One, Patty Unterman of the Hayes Street Grill, and the late Barbara Tropp of the China Moon Café.

Since that first Seder at Zola's, the Seder has grown to include expanded families and other close friends of the chefs. It has settled down to about twelve or fourteen at Patty and her lawyer husband Tim Savinar's small palazzo on Telegraph Hill overlooking San Francisco Bay.

The Bains, who prepare the Seder plate, bring Larry's Polish Bubie's *Haroset.* See page 357 for Justina Hendricks Henry's Pickled Salmon; page 365 for Joyce Goldstein's Cornish Hens with Apricots, Tomatoes, and Spices; page 374 for

Patty Unterman's Potato Kugelettes; and page 402 for Barbara Tropp's Pecan-Ginger Torte.

½ pound walnut meats	½ cup sweet Passover wine
¼ pound dried apricots	⅛ cup kosher-for-Passover brandy
¼ pound pitted prunes	½ teaspoon cinnamon
¼ pound pitted dates	⅛ teaspoon ground cloves
3 whole apples, peeled, cored, and quartered	⅛ teaspoon ground nutmeg
1 large unpeeled seedless orange, quartered	1 tablespoon lime juice
	2 tablespoons matzah meal, or as needed

1. In a food processor with a steel blade or using another chopper, chop very fine but not to a paste the walnuts, apricots, prunes, dates, apples, and orange.
2. Add the wine, brandy, cinnamon, cloves, nutmeg, and lime juice. If necessary, add enough matzah meal to make a paste.

Note: Any leftover *haroset* makes a wonderful chicken stuffing or a marvelous fruit topping for pot roast.

HORSERADISH AND BEET SAUCE

MAKES ABOUT 3 CUPS. (P)

And fresh matzo *with strongly seasoned fish and fresh horseradish that tore your nostrils apart, and Passover borsht that tasted like something in Paradise, and other good things that man's evil spirit can summon.*
                           Sholem Aleichem, "Home for Passover"

Although horseradish per se is not mentioned in the Bible and was not native to the Middle East, *maror,* or bitter herbs, are cited in the book of Exodus, with the pascal lamb and unleavened bread, as prescribed foods for the Passover feast. In the second century horseradish became—along with coriander, nettle, horehound, and romaine lettuce—one of the bitter herbs of the Passover.

Seventy-five percent of all horseradish production in the United States is done at Tulkoff's, located on Horseradish Lane in Baltimore. Harry and Lena Tulkoff, immigrants from Russia, started a fruit-and-produce market on Lombard Street, across from the present factory. So often would people ask the Tulkoffs to grate their horseradish that they decided it would be more profitable to produce packaged horseradish sauce. With the amount of corned beef consumed in Baltimore, it was a wise decision.

1 medium horseradish root (about ½ cup)	¼ teaspoon pepper
	2 tablespoons sugar
One 16-ounce can beets, drained	¾ cup white vinegar
1 teaspoon salt	

1. Peel the horseradish and grate it by hand or with a food processor.
2. Grate the beets, adding them to the horseradish. Combine well.
3. Add the salt, pepper, and sugar gradually. Since the strength of the horseradish will vary according to age and the individual root, you should test as you add each ingredient.
4. Add all the vinegar the horseradish and beets will absorb. Adjust to taste. Mix well.
5. Store in the refrigerator in a tightly covered jar. Serve with gefilte fish or boiled beef.

MATZAH

This is the bread of affliction, the poor bread which our ancestors ate in the land of Egypt. Let all who are hungry come and eat. Let all who are in want share the hope of Passover. This year we celebrate here. Next year in the land of Israel. Now we are all still servants. Next year may all be free.

The Passover Haggadah

THE BREAD OF AFFLICTION AND FREEDOM

The eating and baking of matzah, besides being central to the history of Jewish food, have always reflected the times and spirit of the Jews themselves. In Exodus, unleavened bread symbolizes both affliction and the journey to freedom. It is what the Hebrews ate, with the bitter herbs, as they fled Egypt (Exodus 12:31–39); it was made part of their ensuing celebrations of Passover (Exodus 12:15–20); and it became a sacrament in their priestly rituals (Exodus 29:2).

The earliest matzah was probably made of barley, the word *"matzah"* coming from the Old Babylonian *maassaartum,* which means "barley." It was the first grain harvested in the Middle East, used for many centuries before wheat appeared, about 4000 B.C.E. Later, however, only wheat came to be used, a practice that continues today.

Each year in the spring, long before the Exodus, the Hebrews celebrated a Festival of Unleavened Bread in thanks for the new grains after the barley planting. When they went to Egypt they learned about yeast, and in their flight from Egypt the original spring festival became a patriotic one devoted to freedom. Matzah represents the Jews' flight from Egypt, when they had no time to let their bread rise, or bake properly. In Exodus, God describes this feast: "They are to eat the flesh on that night, roasted in fire, and matzot, with bitter herbs they are to eat it" (Exodus 12:8). At the Seder the first food eaten is parsley or potatoes, followed by a piece of matzah. Later, one eats a symbolic "sandwich" of matzah and bitter herbs, which have been dipped in the *haroset.*

Until the advent of machine-made matzah at the end of the nineteenth century, Jews made their own, or bought it directly from their synagogues, where special committees shaped matzah by hand into round or rectangular forms. "When I lived in Germany," said the late Paula Stern Kissinger, "we bought matzah flour from our shul and brought it to a communal oven to be baked. Together we baked enough matzahs for our entire family."

For centuries before this, leftover matzah had been made into crumbs with a large wooden mortar and pestle. Early American immigrant recipes, for example, call for broken-up matzah to be made into matzah balls or *krimsel.* In addition to manufacturing matzah, companies like Manischewitz made matzah meal from broken pieces and packaged it so cooks could make dishes such as "airy matzah balls."

Purists today use handmade, or *shmurah,* matzah. Prepared in bakeries like D. and T. Matzah Bakery in Crown Heights, Brooklyn, this matzah is served to a dedicated and ever-increasing clientele. D. and T. produces about 12,000–15,000 pounds of *shmurah* matzah each year. "*Shmurah* matzah means it is watched or supervised from when the wheat is cut until after it is baked," says Isaac Tenenbaum, the owner. The wheat comes from small farms in New Jersey, Pennsylvania, and upstate New York and is ground in local mills kashered for Passover runs. Despite the commercialism now attached to matzah, it still remains the ancient unleavened bread of affliction. The original matzah, manually molded in circles and roughly hewn, was thicker than the crispy machine-made brands available today.

In a tiny bakery, with walls and tables protected with brown paper, the carefully watched flour is mixed with pure spring water from wells in Brooklyn, rolled with a long, narrow wooden rolling pin, pricked (to reduce air bubbles, which may enhance the forbidden fermentation), baked, and stacked, all within the stipulated eighteen minutes. The men and women working do it very quickly, yelling, "Matzah, matzah!" when their rolled-out dough is ready for the oven. "The law is that only eighteen minutes can elapse from when the water touches the flour until when it goes in the oven," said Rabbi Tenenbaum. After eighteen minutes it expands, and is no longer kosher for Passover.

As Reuven Sirota shoveled the hand-formed matzah into the brick oven, he recalled his native Uzbekistan, which he left in the 1970s. "Making matzah is a mitzvah," he said. "In Uzbekistan, I had to make it in secret at four o'clock in the morning. It was forbidden for Jews to celebrate Passover. For me, making matzah openly represents the freedom of living in America."

Matzah must be prepared without any yeast. The unbleached flour is watched from the time the wheat is reaped (for *shmurah,* or hand-made, watched matzah allowing no water to brush the stalks of wheat) or from when it is brought to the mill (for regular Passover matzah). Even today the water used in baking must sit for twenty-four hours, with no foreign elements allowed to contaminate it.

Mills are reserved to grind the Passover flour. The factories are carefully cleaned. Workers, versed in the traditional rules, watch over the machines reciting "for the sake of the mitzvah" (religious obligation) of making matzah. The flour is then set aside until the time comes to make Passover products.

The matzah of the Seder table consists of three sheets placed one above the other, which came to symbolize the three groups of Jews: Kohanim (priests), Levites, and Israelites. At the beginning of the Seder, the central matzah is divided. The larger part, or *afikomen* (meaning "dessert" in Greek), is put aside and hidden. It should be the last item of food eaten at the Seder.

At the beginning of the reading of the Haggadah, the leader holds up the remaining half of the *afikomen* and recites the passage given above.

Although the great majority of people use commercial matzah throughout the Seder, it is considered a mitzvah to use *shmurah* matzah at least for the three central matzot. If you cannot find them easily in your community, ask at your synagogue.

The *afikomen*—that hidden piece of matzah which keeps the children's attention throughout the long Seder meal—was once a good-luck omen. Even today the lucky person who finds the *afikomen* wins a prize. In ancient times, a woman in childbirth would often bite into this matzah for good luck. By the Middle Ages, Jews used it as an amulet, hanging in the house throughout the year or carried in the pouch or wallet. Venetian Jews do so even today. Some Jews save the remains to use for the *bedikat hametz* the following year.

Matzah is not only central to the Seder meal, it is central to all Passover cuisine. As a substitute for bread, it is best spread with whipped butter or salt or honey; the *haroset* from the Seder also makes an excellent topping.

Because of the stringent laws concerning the baking of matzah, one should not try to make it at home for Passover. The specially processed flour required is not available commercially. But this recipe is good for use at other times, and to show how it is done.

Edda Servi Machlin, author of *The Classic Cuisine of the Italian Jews,* also felt the importance of the mitzvah of making matzah. "While we were hiding in Italy, every night as Easter approached during that spring of '44, we carefully watched the moon. We knew that when it was as round as a wheel of cheese, it would be the fourteenth of Nissan, the first night of Passover. We began to make a few matzot with the flour that the farmer who was sheltering us allotted to us, and baked them in the rustic stone oven that was built outside. The farmers had never seen unleavened bread before and gathered around to watch us make these round and oval cakes, about a quarter inch thick and cut and trimmed like doilies. But for us, not only did they symbolize the festival of remembrance and freedom, they also represented home. By being able to make and bake our own matzah, something we used to do with our parents as little children, we nourished our souls even more than our stomachs."

In the Middle Ages, matzah often had decorations on it, and in some countries, such as Italy, it was almost an inch thick and did not crumble.

Today Edda, in her home outside New York City, still makes the elaborate matzah of her childhood, in honor of the past. "The trick," she said, "is to use flour with absolutely no bran in it, so that no fermentation takes place."

ITALIAN MATZAH

(Assima Semplice Pitiglianese)

From Edda Servi Machlin

MAKES 12 MATZAHS. (P)

Try this recipe with children. The decorative matzah will be a hands-on introduction to the traditions of the Italian Jews. Of course, to be truly correct for Passover, matzah making must be rabbinically supervised.

3½ cups cold spring water	7 cups matzah cake meal

1. Preheat the oven to 550 degrees.
2. In a large bowl, quickly mix the water with enough of the matzah cake meal to form a very stiff dough. Spread the remaining cake meal on a smooth working surface (preferably marble or glass) and turn the dough out over it. Knead with force for 3 minutes. During the first phase of kneading, make a few cuts in the dough with a sharp knife, which will enable you to incorporate more cake meal into it. Continue to knead quickly until the dough is perfectly smooth.
3. Divide the dough into 12 equal parts (at this point, the more people helping, the better). Have each of your helpers knead the little pieces of dough until

elastic. With rolling pins, roll into 9- by 5-inch ovals or into circles 6½ inches in diameter.

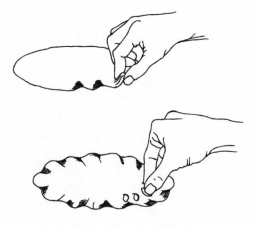

4. To finish the edges and make rings of holes, place your thumb at an angle to the edge of the circle of dough and then pinch with your thumb and index finger to create a small bump. Repeat this motion at the same angle all around so that the bumps are the same distance apart. Now for the holes: A quarter inch from the pinched border, pinch a piece of dough with your thumb and index finger, creating 1 small tear on each side of the pinch. Move the thumb into the hole made by the index finger and pinch the dough again with the 2 fingers, following the shape of the dough and repeating the process above. Continue all around until an outer ring of holes is completed. About a quarter inch in from the outer ring, pinch the dough and make another ring of holes to make a decorative circle. Repeat until you have 3 concentric rings of holes. At this point, your matzah will look like a doily and be almost ready to bake. Repeat this process with all the circles of dough.

5. Place the matzahs on an ungreased cookie sheet. With a metal comb or fork, prick tiny holes all over the matzahs to prevent swelling and blistering during baking.

6. Bake in the oven on the middle rack for 6–7 minutes, or until the matzahs are pale brown.

PASSOVER POPOVERS

MAKES ABOUT 12. (P)

Since Jews were forbidden to eat anything leavened during the eight days of Passover in the memory of Exodus, they substituted soaked matzah, and later matzah meal, for regular flour and soaked bread.

Ultra-Orthodox Jews still refuse to eat matzah in other than a pure form during Passover. "The scrupulously observant refrain from any contact between matzah and water," said Rabbi Yehuda Krinsky, speaking for the Lubavitch Hasidic movement. He explained that if matzah or matzah meal touches water it will rise, going against the biblical injunction against eating leavened food. "We eat noodles made from potato starch and eggs instead," he said.

Although the Ultra-Orthodox shy away from the use of commercially prepared products, including packaged matzah and matzah meal, the great majority of Jews have come to rely on these twentieth-century innovations as a way to enjoy some of their favorite foods during Passover. One extremely popular example is the following recipe for popovers.

½ cup vegetable oil	1 cup matzah meal
1 cup water	1 tablespoon sugar, or to taste
½ teaspoon salt	4 eggs

1. Preheat the oven to 375 degrees. Grease a cookie sheet.
2. Bring the oil, water, and salt to a boil. Add the matzah meal and stir with a spoon. When the mixture becomes sticky, let it cool completely.
3. Add the sugar to the mixture and the eggs, 1 at a time, beating well after each addition.
4. Dipping your hands in cold water first, take dough about the size of a tennis ball and mold it into a ball. Place on the cookie sheet. Repeat until all the dough is used up, dipping your hands in water before forming each popover.
5. Bake in the oven 15–20 minutes, until the popovers are puffy. Then turn down the oven to 325 degrees and bake another 30 minutes, until golden brown.

MATZAH BALLS

(Kneydlakh)

MAKES 20. (M)

Pesakh essen mir
Matzo kneydlakh
Vayl arum dem tish
Zitsn file meydlakh

At Passover we eat
Matzah balls
While around the table
Sit many young maidens

While doing research for this book, I visited the Hebrew Home for the Aged in Rockville, Maryland. There I conducted a culinary exchange session with the elderly. Each food I mentioned triggered a memory, which these people—mostly Russian immigrants—shared with me. All of a sudden, a woman in her eighties who did not seem to be listening chanted the above verse from her childhood in Vilna.

Others had their own opinions of *kneydlakh*, or matzah balls. To some, the eggs should be separated; others added a speck of ginger or a few ground almonds. Some attributed success to sufficient chicken fat to make the matzah balls firm and tender at the same time.

When I spoke before groups about my first book, *The Flavor of Jerusalem*, no food caused so much discussion as the late Golda Meir's matzah ball recipe. Hers—the heavy variety—invites women to give me their own opinion about separating eggs, not separating eggs, adding onion, and so on. Even Haim Shapiro of the *Jerusalem Post* contrasted Golda's recipe with that of his mother, whose matzah balls are "the lightest and fluffiest imaginable." According to Shapiro, they are the only ones that "quiver" when breathed upon.

At every Jewish Seder I am reminded of Italian families in which the mother brings a thread of pasta to the father to taste. When he says "al dente," everyone breathes a sigh of relief. So it is when guests comment on the lightness of the host's matzah balls, whether they are light or not!

There is a light-and-fluffy school of matzah balls, and there are those of cannonball persuasion, who hold that matzah balls should plummet to the floor. After much experimentation in both categories, I have concluded that heavier matzah balls take a higher proportion of matzah meal to eggs and fat and should cook for 20 minutes or less. You need some fat, but I have reduced mine by half. Contrary to popular opinion, the substitution of soda water for water does not lighten matzah balls. To prepare light matzah balls, you can increase the number of eggs and simmer the matzah balls 30 minutes or longer. Never take the lid off until you have finished cooking them. Patty Unterman, chef of the Hayes Street Grill in San Francisco, insists that the secret of perfect matzah balls is simmering them in a huge quantity of chicken soup for at least an hour. The lightest versions usually call for stiffly beaten egg whites folded into the mixture.

Matzah balls can be made ahead of time, drained, and then placed in the broth. Freeze the entire pot full of soup; when ready to serve, defrost and reheat. Another trick is to make the matzah balls, squeeze them out, freeze them on a cookie tray, and then throw them into a plastic freezer bag for your next occasion.

Extra matzah balls can be served the next day, although the texture will be a little denser. They are also good as a starch when browned in margarine or chicken fat. Refrigerate them thoroughly before frying or they will fall apart.

4 eggs, slightly beaten	2 teaspoons salt
2 tablespoons chicken fat, skimmed from the top of the soup	2 tablespoons chopped fresh flat-leaf parsley
1 cup matzah meal	6 tablespoons chicken soup or water

1. In a medium bowl, beat the eggs and the fat together. Stir in the matzah meal, salt, and parsley. Add the chicken soup or water. Refrigerate 1 hour or more, to permit the meal to absorb the liquids.
2. In a 6-quart pot with a lid, bring 4 quarts of salted water to a boil. Reduce the water to a simmer and drop in balls of the matzah mixture about 1½ inches in

diameter. Cover the pot and cook just at a simmer for 20–40 minutes. The longer you cook them, the softer the matzah balls will be. When they are ready, they may be placed in chicken soup to serve.

CHARLESTONIAN CHICKEN OR BEEF BROTH WITH "SOUP BUNCH" AND MATZAH BALLS

MAKES ABOUT 10 CUPS. (M)

Ever since the first Jews settled in the bustling port of Charleston, South Carolina, in 1694, Jewish life there has reflected both assimilation and cultural stick-to-itiveness. Nothing points this out better than *Historically Cooking: 200 Years of Good Eating,* the cookbook of Charleston Reform Congregation Kahal Kadosh Beth Elohim.

The more unusual hand-me-down recipes in the synagogue cookbook unveil the diverse cultural and culinary history of this Southern Jewish community, which by 1750, the year the synagogue was founded, was the largest in the Colonies. Early immigrants were Sephardic Jews, most of whom came from the West Indies, where their ancestors had fled during the Spanish Inquisition. A number of German and Alsatian Jews arrived in the early and middle nineteenth century. Eastern European Jews came with the wave of immigration that began in 1880.

Recipes that the immigrants brought from Germany and Alsace-Lorraine now have a Southern flavor. Sweet-and-sour carp has become sweet-and-sour shad, a popular Charleston fish in the spring.

Every Jewish cookbook has a chicken soup recipe, but the one in *Historically Cooking* is unique. In addition to the chicken, once slaughtered by the ritual slaughterer employed by the synagogue at least until the Civil War, the recipe included a "soup bunch." This was made up of fresh collards, parsnips, rutabagas, turnips, red and white cabbage, onions, thyme, carrots, celery with greens, and fresh tomatoes that were sold together in bunches at the marketplace. The "soup bunch" was added to a broth made from chicken or to a beef base made from a shank bone with meat. The clear, sieved broth was then served with matzah balls. The matzah balls, prepared in the nineteenth-century German tradition with parsley, onion, nutmeg, and ginger, are poached in salted water, drained, and then floated, ever so lightly, in the soup.

One 5–6-pound chicken or 3 large shank bones with meat (about 3 pounds)
1 sliced parsnip
1 sliced white turnip
¼ green cabbage, shredded
¼ red cabbage, shredded
½ sliced rutabaga
4 large carrots, cut in chunks

2 large onions, quartered
One 28-ounce can tomatoes
1 handful collard greens
1 stalk celery, cut in chunks
2 teaspoons dried thyme or 2 tablespoons fresh
Salt and freshly ground pepper to taste

Cover the shank bones or chicken with cold water plus 2 inches and simmer, covered, about 2 hours, or until tender. Add the remaining ingredients and simmer, covered, at least 30 minutes, until the vegetables are very tender. Remove the meat and strain the soup. Adjust the seasoning. Serve with matzah balls.

MATZAH BALLS WITH GINGER AND NUTMEG

MAKES ABOUT 20. (M)

¼ cup chicken soup
4 tablespoons *schmaltz* (rendered chicken fat) or melted pareve margarine
2 teaspoons salt, or to taste
¼ teaspoon grated nutmeg
¼ teaspoon ginger

2 tablespoons grated onion
2 tablespoons chopped fresh flat-leaf parsley
2 shakes paprika
1 cup matzah meal
4 large eggs

1. In a large bowl, combine all the ingredients except the eggs. Stir in 1 egg at a time with a wooden spoon until all 4 eggs are incorporated. Refrigerate a few hours or overnight.
2. Bring an 8–10-quart pot of water to a boil. Add a tablespoon of salt. Wet your hands with warm water and form the mixture into balls the size of walnuts. Drop into boiling water, cover, and let simmer 30 minutes, or until the matzah balls are fluffy and floating at the top. Remove with a slotted spoon to bowls of hot chicken soup.

Note: For a modern twist on this German-Jewish recipe, reduce the fat to 2 tablespoons and add 2 more tablespoons chicken soup. Substitute 1 teaspoon freshly grated ginger for the dry, and omit the onion and paprika.

SYLVIA SHELL BUB'S SOUTH AFRICAN-LITHUANIAN STUFFED *KNEYDLAKH*

(Matzah Balls)

MAKES 8–10. (M)

In the eighteenth and nineteenth centuries, recipes for matzah balls began to vary by region. Called "*kleis*" in German and "*kneydlakh*" in Yiddish, they were spiced with mace, ginger, nutmeg, and cinnamon. As seen in Esther Levy's 1871 *Jewish Cookery Book,* by the late nineteenth century American matzah *kleis* included soaked and drained matzah, onions sautéed in chicken fat, eggs, salt, dried ginger, nutmeg, parsley, and pepper.

Stuffed *kneydlakh* seems to be a Litvak dish, dumplings made with a filling of liver, potato, carrot, and even ground almonds, and served with chicken or beef broth or a milk soup where appropriate. One version from Anne Sinai of Santa Monica, California, calls itself "the *kneydlakh* with a heart" because it is filled with a cinnamon-matzah stuffing.

According to Mrs. Bub, whose family emigrated to South Africa from Lithuania, and now lives in Allentown, Pennsylvania, the cinnamon provides a dark color. Dr. Dov Noy, professor of folklore at the Hebrew University in Jerusalem, believes that the use of cinnamon in the stuffing is not accidental. "It is like the secret sweetness within the spice box at the Havdalah service ending Sabbath. The cinnamon stuffing represents a wish to stretch the sweetness of the Seder meal as long as possible."

MEAT FILLING:

¼ pound ground beef

1 tablespoon vegetable oil, kosher
    for Passover

2 large egg yolks

2 tablespoons softened chicken fat

2 tablespoons matzah meal
    (approximately)

Pinch of salt

¼ teaspoon cinnamon

MATZAH BALLS:

2 large eggs

2 cups water

10 teaspoons chicken fat plus fat
    for greasing pan

1¼ cups matzah meal
    (approximately)

1 teaspoon salt, or to taste

3 quarts rapidly boiling salted
    water

2 teaspoons cinnamon

1. To prepare the filling, sauté the meat in the oil in a skillet until brown. Drain and cool and combine with the egg yolks, chicken fat, matzah meal, salt, and cinnamon. Refrigerate at least 1 hour.

2. Meanwhile, to prepare the matzah balls, begin by beating the eggs well in a bowl. Add the 2 cups water and 6 teaspoons of chicken fat and mix well. Add enough matzah meal and salt to make a soft mass. Refrigerate for at least 1 hour.

3. Divide the matzah meal mixture into 8–10 balls of equal size. Flatten them and place 1 teaspoon of meat filling in the center of each. Enclose the filling, pinch the edges together, and form into balls.

4. Place the matzah balls into the 3 quarts of rapidly boiling salted water. Cover and simmer 20 minutes.

5. Preheat the oven to 400 degrees. Drain the matzah balls and place in a pan greased with chicken fat, cover with the remaining 4 teaspoons of chicken fat,

and sprinkle with the cinnamon. Bake for 15–20 minutes, or until slightly browned. Serve each matzah ball in a soup bowl with chicken soup ladled over it.

MATZAH *BREI*

My husband considers matzah *brei* a real treat. It is one of those holiday recipes that has nothing whatsoever to do with religion—just gastronomy.

A simple dish, matzah *brei* cannot be made with milk. With milk, it is like pastrami on white bread or chicken livers with mayonnaise. How could Eastern European Jews, with only goose fat available for frying, include milk in matzah *brei*?

Perhaps the fascination with matzah *brei* is the ease of preparation. It consists of soaking matzah in water, squeezing very hard, and then frying in grease with or without an egg. It is served with sugar, honey, cinnamon, cinnamon-sugar, and even—by some iconoclasts—with catsup!

The late Jacob Licht, father of Rhode Island's late governor, Frank Licht, was a master matzah *brei* maker all his life. This is his recipe.

3 matzahs
2 large eggs, beaten
Salt and freshly ground pepper
2 tablespoons chicken fat, pareve
    margarine, or butter for frying

Cinnamon, cinnamon-sugar,
    honey, or maple syrup

1. Break the matzahs and soak in warm water for a few minutes. Drain and squeeze dry.
2. Add the eggs and mix well. Add salt and pepper to taste.
3. Taking tablespoonfuls of batter at a time, fry in the chicken fat, margarine, or butter, patting the center down a bit. (You may want larger matzah pancakes, in which case just add more batter each time.) When brown on one side, turn

and fry on the other. Serve with cinnamon, cinnamon-sugar, honey, maple syrup, or even catsup!

MATZAH STUFFING

MAKES 4 CUPS. (M OR P)

What Jewish holiday cookbook would be complete without a good recipe for Passover stuffing?

2 matzahs
1 large onion
1 large potato
2 stalks celery, finely diced
2 tablespoons chicken fat or
    pareve margarine

2 eggs
3 tablespoons matzah meal
1 tablespoon chopped flat-leaf
    parsley
Salt and pepper
Paprika

1. Break the matzahs in small pieces and soak in hot water for 15 minutes. Drain thoroughly and squeeze well.
2. Grate the onion and potato. Drain off the excess water. Combine with the celery. Sauté in chicken fat or margarine. Add the parsley and salt, pepper, and paprika to taste, mixing well.

FEZ-INSPIRED SPINACH OR BEET TOP SALAD

Adapted from Nicole Amsellem

SERVES 6 TO 8. (P)

About thirty Amsellems attend the Moroccan-inspired Seder at Jean-Paul Amsellem's northwest Washington home. Jean-Paul is the godfather of Washington hairdressers and owner of the Bistro Français Restaurant in Georgetown. He commences the meal by passing the Seder plate over the heads of all those attending. The meal itself, prepared by his wife, Nicole, starts with about ten salads including roasted green pepper with tomatoes, eggplant, and spinach or beet top salad. The menu goes on to shad with fava beans, brisket, veal or lamb with green beans and carrots. Raisins and toasted almonds cleanse the palate before the fruit salad, strawberries, and bananas with nougat of sesame and almonds for dessert.

2 large bags fresh spinach, washed and cut in small pieces, or 4 packages frozen leaf spinach, or the tops of 2 big bunches of fresh beets, washed and cut in small pieces	2 cloves garlic, diced ¼ cup vegetable oil 1 teaspoon ground cumin 1 teaspoon paprika Salt Juice of 1 lemon, or to taste

1. Cook the spinach or beet tops in salted water just until wilted. Beet tops need to soak a long time. Drain and squeeze out as much water as possible. This is very important.
2. In a skillet, sauté the garlic in the oil until golden. Then add the spinach or beet tops, cumin, paprika, and salt to taste. Stir until the spinach or beet tops absorb all the oil, adding more oil if necessary. Add the lemon juice.

NICOLE'S EGGPLANT SALAD

SERVES 8. (P)

2 large unpeeled eggplants, sliced
   ¼ inch thick
2 tablespoons salt
Peanut oil for frying
½ cup chopped fresh flat-leaf
   parsley

2–3 large cloves garlic, depending
   on taste, minced
Juice of 1 lemon

1. Sprinkle the eggplant slices with salt, place in a 9- by 13-inch dish, and weigh down with another 9- by 13-inch dish overnight to allow the bitter juice to run off. Drain and then dry the eggplant with paper towels.
2. Fry the slices in the oil, 1 inch deep, adding oil as necessary. When finished, place on a serving platter. Layer the eggplant with parsley and garlic. Add the lemon juice. Serve cold.

YOGURT

Abraham drank it. Some authorities attribute Sarah's long reproductive cycle to it. Solomon's wisdom came from his consumption of it. Yogurt, of course!

Legend has it that yogurt was discovered some six thousand years ago. A camel merchant, traveling with his herd, concubines, and servants from Ur to Eridu, filled a leather bag made from the stomach of a sheep with milk. When the sun went down at the end of the day, he settled his herd and prepared to enjoy a cool drink. To his surprise, he found instead a custardy, slightly acid milk product. He further discovered that this drink, mixed with water, quenched his thirst.

Bacteria contained in the bags had combined with the milk as a result of the body warmth of the camel he was riding and the heat of the sun. At nightfall, when the desert temperature dropped dramatically, it cooled the milk and stopped the action of the bacteria. Whether or not this particular story is true is not important. This is more or less the way yogurt was discovered somewhere in the Middle East or the Balkans. Soon the nomads learned that they could make yogurt by inoculating fresh milk with a small amount of already prepared yogurt.

To make your own yogurt, boil milk, remove from the heat at the boiling point, let sit 15 minutes, add 1 teaspoon of yogurt culture per cup of milk, stir, pour into cup containers, cover, place in a warm oven, turn the oven off, and let sit overnight. That is all there is to it!

To Persians, yogurt is an essential food. But with no kosher dairies in the country, even the less observant Jews would abstain from milk, cheese, butter, and yogurt products during Passover. Thus, on the evening of the last night of Passover, yogurt would be served again, in the form of a special yogurt dish, more like a thick soup, to break the abstention from bread.

Yashar Shirazi remembers how on this last night his father would place silver coins in a bowl of water. Whoever could put his thumb in the water and raise up the coin without touching the wall of the bowl would have good luck through the year. Flowers and green branches would adorn the table on this evening, as a wish for a green and fruitful life until next Passover.

PERSIAN CUCUMBER-YOGURT SALAD

(Mastva Khiar)

SERVES 4–6. (D)

2 cups plain yogurt
1 cup cold water
3 ice cubes
2 small cucumbers or 1 large, peeled and diced
1 small onion or the white part of 2 scallions, diced

2 radishes, sliced thin
¼ cup golden raisins
¼ cup chopped walnuts
1 tablespoon crushed dried mint or 3 tablespoons chopped fresh mint
Salt and freshly ground pepper

Combine all the ingredients. Adjust the mint, salt, and pepper to taste. If possible, let sit overnight.

MEXICAN FISH WITH GREEN SAUCE

SERVES 6. (P)

The late Minerva Etzioni, an extraordinary Mexican cook who, at the time of her death, was writing a book on Mexican cuisine, shared the following southern Mexican recipe for fish with green sauce with me. She found it a challenge to adapt Mexican cuisines to a Passover Seder menu, serving this light fish dish instead of the standard gefilte fish appetizer.

1 tablespoon kosher-for-Passover vegetable oil

5–6 pounds red snapper, bass, or striped bass, cleaned and boned, fins removed, and head and part of tail preserved

Juice of ½ lime

Salt and white pepper

25 large romaine lettuce leaves, center white part trimmed and removed

1 green pepper, cored, seeded, and cut into large chunks

1 small white onion, cut in chunks

3 cloves garlic

5–6 radish leaves (optional)

6 scallions, green part only

Juice of 5½ limes

6–8 small, firm, ripe Italian plum tomatoes, sliced in half lengthwise

6–8 large stuffed Spanish olives, sliced in half lengthwise

1. Coat a large, deep roasting pan with oil and place the fish in the center. Rub it inside and out with the juice of half a lime and sprinkle it with salt and white pepper. Refrigerate while preparing the sauce.
2. Using a blender or food processor, purée the lettuce leaves, green pepper, onion, garlic, radish leaves, if using, scallions, lime juice, and salt and white pepper to taste. Pour the sauce over the fish and cover the pan with aluminum foil. Marinate the fish in the sauce for at least 2 hours in the refrigerator.
3. Bake in the middle of a 350-degree oven, uncovered, 20–25 minutes, basting every 5 minutes. The fish is done when the flesh is opaque and moist.

4. Carefully transfer the fish to a warm serving platter. Pour the sauce over the fish and decorate with the tomatoes and olives. Serve warm or cold.

PICKLED SALMON

Adapted from Justina Hendricks Henry

SERVES 6–8. (P)

2 cups white vinegar	1 inch fresh ginger, peeled and
6 tablespoons sugar	sliced
2 tablespoons kosher salt	1 cinnamon stick
½ teaspoon mustard seed	6 bay leaves
½ teaspoon cardamom pods	3 pounds salmon fillet, skin
½ teaspoon mace blades	removed
½ teaspoon coriander seeds	1 large red onion, peeled and
½ teaspoon black pepper	sliced thin
½ teaspoon whole cloves	1 red hot pepper (like a pequin)

1. Bring 2 cups of water, the vinegar, sugar, and salt to a boil. Add the mustard seed, cardamon, mace, coriander, black pepper, cloves, ginger, cinnamon stick, hot pepper, and bay leaves. Simmer for a few minutes. Add the salmon and cook for 5 minutes. Remove from the heat and let cool completely.
2. Remove the salmon fillet from the pot and reserve the marinade. Cut the salmon into 2-inch slices. Place the salmon in a glass bowl and cover with the reserved marinade. Top with the onion. Cover the container and refrigerate for 3 days, making sure that the salmon is submerged in the marinade.
3. Remove the salmon and the onions, straining and discarding the spices but reserving the marinade. Serve the salmon as an appetizer with the onions and a little bit of marinade. If you like, you can also serve the salmon with sour cream.

MEAT BORSCHT

SERVES 8. (M)

At one time fresh milk products and coffee were not made commercially for Passover. Other means had to be devised to make tasty meals for a people accustomed to the wide use of milk, cheese, sour cream, and farmer cheese. Passover borscht, for example, was thickened by being slowly poured over the beaten yolk of an egg.

Eva Lubetkin Kantor, who lived to be 102, recalled how Passover borscht was made at her home in New York City at the turn of the century: "Then there was the brewing of the *russell* which was genuine borscht, only it was beet brew. The beets were put in a large barrel covered with warm water and salt. It took three or four weeks to ferment and turn sour. Every day or so the fermentation and crust were skimmed off with a slotted ladle. When it didn't form any sediment on top, it was ready. Most delicious, clear beet juice. It was the basic ingredient for borscht. We just added to it water, sugar, eggs, sour cream, and for *fleishig*, meatballs and hot plain boiled potatoes."

Originally a Ukrainian dish made with a pork base, this economical staple was varied by the Jews with a beef base.

2 pounds lean beef, cubed	1–2 cloves garlic
1 cracked soup bone	1 teaspoon salt
2½ quarts cold water	2 tablespoons brown sugar
8 beets, grated	⅓ cup lemon juice, or to taste
2 onions, diced	2 eggs

1. In a large, heavy pot, cover the meat and bone with the cold water. Bring to a boil, reduce the heat, and simmer for 1 hour.
2. Add the beets, onions, garlic, and salt. Simmer, covered, for another 1½ hours.
3. Add the brown sugar and lemon juice and correct the seasonings.
4. In a separate bowl, beat the eggs. Gradually add a little hot soup to them, beating continuously to prevent curdling. Add the eggs to the large pot and blend in.

MATZAH-STUFFED BREAST OF VEAL

SERVES 8. (M)

Every Passover people ask me for an unusual stuffing recipe for turkey or veal to replace the year-round bread stuffings that we all enjoy so much. I have fiddled around and finally created this tasty solution. You may have to pre-order the veal. Canned chestnuts are fine in this dish.

One 5-pound breast or shoulder
    of veal with pocket
2 cloves garlic, peeled
½ teaspoon ground ginger
1 carrot, sliced
2 onions, diced
2 matzahs
2 stalks celery, finely diced
4 tablespoons rendered chicken
    fat or pareve margarine

2 eggs, beaten
1 tablespoon chopped fresh
    flat-leaf parsley
1 cup cooked and diced chestnuts
1 cup sliced porcini or other
    mushrooms
Salt and freshly ground pepper
Paprika
Water or white wine for basting

1. Preheat the oven to 450 degrees. Rub the breast or shoulder with garlic or insert slivers of garlic into slits in the meat. Sprinkle the ginger in the veal pocket. Place the veal, carrot, and half of the diced onions in a greased roasting pan. Set aside.

2. Soak the matzahs in warm water. Squeeze dry when soft. Sauté the remaining onions and celery in 2 tablespoons chicken fat or margarine. When the onions are golden, combine with the broken pieces of matzah. Allow to cool and then combine with the beaten eggs, parsley, chestnuts, mushrooms, salt, pepper, and paprika to taste.

3. Stuff the veal. Place any remaining stuffing under the veal in the roasting pan. Sew up the pocket of the veal or truss it closed. Rub the veal with the remaining chicken fat or margarine if the meat is not very fatty.

4. Roast the veal for 10 minutes at 450 degrees, then reduce the heat to 300

degrees, roasting 30 minutes to the pound. Baste occasionally with the pan juices and add water or white wine if necessary.

MEXICAN SPINACH AND CHEESE PIE

SERVES 8. (D)

The late Minerva Etzioni improvised the following Passover recipe from a spinach and tortilla dish her mother served her as a child in Mexico.

4–5 matzahs
½ cup peanut oil
7 bags fresh washed spinach or six
    10-ounce packages frozen
    chopped spinach
2 onions, chopped

3 cloves garlic, peeled and minced
2 serrano peppers, chopped
Salt and freshly ground pepper
4 eggs, well beaten
2 cups shredded mozzarella cheese

1. Soak and squeeze the matzot. Preheat the oven to 350 degrees and grease a 9- by 12-inch baking pan and cover the bottom with matzahs.
2. If using fresh spinach, wash and briefly cook the spinach in boiling water. If using frozen spinach, cook according to package directions. Squeeze out the water. Chop fine.
3. In a frying pan, sauté the onions and garlic lightly in the oil. Add the peppers, spinach, and salt and pepper to taste. Cook until the flavors meld. Cool and pour into the prepared pan.
4. Combine the eggs and 1 cup of the cheese. Mix well. Pour over the spinach and sprinkle the remaining cheese on top. Bake for 15–20 minutes.

TURKISH *MINA DE ESPINACA CON CARNE*
(Matzah, Spinach, and Meat Pie)

SERVES 4–6. (M)

Mina, the classic vegetable or meat matzah pie, is a Sephardic favorite. Basically, it is a substantial matzah *brei* with spinach filling. Often prepared for brunch during Passover, when the men return from Sabbath morning services, it is served with brown hard-boiled eggs, fruit, and coffee. A meat *mina* is also used as one of the dishes for a Sephardic Seder or main-meal dish during Passover. This Turkish rendition is especially tasty.

6 tablespoons vegetable oil	2 tablespoons pine nuts (optional)
4 whole matzahs	1 teaspoon salt, or to taste
1 pound fresh spinach	Pinch of allspice
1 medium onion, chopped	1 cup mashed potatoes
1 pound chopped beef	3 eggs

1. Preheat the oven to 400 degrees. Grease a pie plate or square baking pan with 2 tablespoons of the oil.
2. Soak the unbroken matzahs in warm water until soft, about 2 minutes. Drain very well on a cloth or paper towel. Carefully press out any excess water. This step is important; otherwise, the *mina* will be too soggy and not crunchy.
3. Wash the spinach, drain thoroughly, and dry. Then chop lightly.
4. Sauté the onion in 2 tablespoons of oil. Add the meat and cook until the meat is brown. Just before it is done, add the pine nuts, if using. Season with salt and allspice. Degrease.
5. Cook the spinach briefly in a little water, until it just wilts. Drain and mix with the meat. Stir in potatoes. Allow to cool.
6. Beat 2 of the eggs very well. Pour over the spinach-meat mixture and mix well.
7. Cover the bottom of the pan with 2 of the whole matzahs. If they break up, you can patch them.
8. Spread the spinach-meat mixture on top. Cover with the remaining 2 matzahs.

Brush the top with the remaining 2 tablespoons oil. Beat the remaining egg and spread over all.

9. Bake 50 minutes, or until the top is lightly browned.

LAMB

And they shall eat the flesh in that night, roast with fire, and unleavened bread; with bitter herbs they shall eat it.

Exodus 12:8

American Jews are often confused about the use of lamb on Passover. Spring is the time of year when young lambs are most plentiful, and a time of thanksgiving to celebrate the herd's survival through the long winter. It was and still is logical that lambs be slaughtered to eat at springtime feasts. Indeed, roast lamb is the traditional spring food throughout the Middle East.

Until the destruction of the Second Temple, a one-year-old lamb was always sacrificed on the eve of Passover and eaten that same night, inaugurating the festival. It was eaten with bitter herbs and matzah. To this day, Samaritans roast lambs on Passover.

Traditional Ashkenazic Jews, however, will not eat roast lamb or any roasted meat at Passover because of the bitter memory that the Temple sacrifices are no longer possible. Middle Eastern Jews will eat lamb, but never roasted. For many Reform Jews, exactly the reverse is true: roasted lamb or other roasted food is served to commemorate the ancient sacrifices.

The following is my mother's roast lamb recipe.

PASSOVER ROAST LAMB

SERVES 6–8. (M)

One 7-pound shoulder of lamb*
Salt and pepper
1 clove garlic, cut in slivers
½ cup shredded celery leaves

⅓ cup cubed green pepper
2 tablespoons tomato sauce, or to
 taste

1. Preheat the oven to 325 degrees.
2. Rub the meat all over with salt and pepper. Place slivers of garlic in between the bone and the flesh. Place the meat on a rack in a roasting pan, surrounded by celery leaves and green pepper.
3. Allowing 20 minutes per pound, roast in the oven. About 1 hour before it is done, smooth tomato sauce over the top of the lamb. This will make a crusty skin and add to the flavor of the gravy.
4. To make the gravy, first remove the lamb to a warm place and drain off all the fat. Add a little water to the juices in the pan, leaving in the celery leaves and green pepper, and boil down on the top of the stove. Serve with asparagus, roasted new potatoes, and mint jelly.

LAMB SHANKS IN LEMON SAUCE

SERVES 4. (M)

The stewed lamb that follows is a standard main dish for a Sephardic Seder.

4 lamb shanks (about 3 pounds)
1 large onion, chopped fine
1 clove garlic, minced
1¼ cups water

1 tablespoon lemon juice
1 teaspoon salt
1 bay leaf
1 tablespoon potato starch

*A leg of lamb is basically a kosher cut of meat, but it would be extremely laborious and costly for a butcher to cut the many veins in the hind legs of the animal for the blood to run out. For this reason, kosher butchers prefer to sell the shoulder cut.

1. Brown the lamb in a heavy casserole on the stove top. Push to one side of the casserole. Add the onion and garlic, and sauté until soft. Stir in 1 cup of the water, lemon juice, salt, and the bay leaf. Cover.
2. Simmer 3 hours, or until very tender. Remove the meat and keep hot.
3. Blend the potato starch with the remaining ¼ cup water. Stir into the liquid in the pan. Cook, stirring constantly, until the gravy thickens and boils for 1 minute. Remove the bay leaf and serve.

GREEK EGG-LEMON CHICKEN

(Agrastada)

SERVES 4–6. (M)

This is a favorite Greek Passover dish.

One 2½-pound chicken
Salted water
5 eggs
Juice of 1 lemon

Salt and pepper
4 tablespoons (½ stick) pareve
    margarine, melted

1. Place the chicken in a heavy pot. Cover with cold salted water and bring to a boil. Reduce the heat, cover, and simmer 30 minutes, or until the chicken is cooked. Remove the chicken to a separate plate and let cool. Reserve ⅔ cup of cooking liquid.
2. Preheat the oven to 350 degrees.
3. Bone the chicken and place all the meat and skin in a shallow ovenproof casserole.
4. Pour the reserved liquid into a small bowl. Gradually beat in the eggs, lemon juice, salt and pepper to taste, and margarine. Pour this sauce over the chicken.
5. Bake about 25 minutes, or until golden brown.

CORNISH HENS WITH APRICOTS, TOMATOES, AND SPICES

Adapted from Joyce Goldstein

MAKES 12 SERVINGS. (M)

Joyce Goldstein, who was the chef at her Square One Restaurant in San Francisco, always prepares the main course for the San Francisco chefs' Seder. "I am interested in seeing Jewish food from other countries," says Joyce. "Each year I make a chicken recipe from a different Mediterranean culture." This Cornish hen recipe is her rendition of a traditional Moroccan dish.

12 tablespoons *schmaltz* (rendered chicken fat) or peanut oil
6 Cornish (game) hens, halved, or 2 large chickens, cut up
Salt
Freshly ground pepper
4 teaspoons cinnamon
4 cups chopped yellow onions
1 teaspoon ground cloves
3 cups canned plum tomatoes, diced, drained (reserve juices)
3½ cups dried apricots, soaked in hot water for 1 hour and drained
2 cups chicken stock or water
⅓ cup brown sugar

1. Heat 6 tablespoons of the fat or oil in a large saucepan. Sprinkle the hens or chicken parts with salt, pepper, and 1 teaspoon of the cinnamon, and brown.
2. In another saucepan heat the remaining fat or oil, add the onions, and cook over low heat 5 minutes, or until the onions are transparent. Add the remaining 3 teaspoons cinnamon and the cloves and cook about 3 more minutes, stirring occasionally. Add about ½ cup of reserved tomato juices.
3. Purée half the soaked apricots in a food processor or blender with a little water, and coarsely chop the rest. Add the puréed apricots, the diced tomatoes, and 1 cup chicken stock to the onion mixture. Simmer, uncovered, 5 minutes.
4. Purée 2 cups of the onion mixture. Return to the pan, add the chopped apri-

cots, remaining chicken stock, and brown sugar, and add enough liquid to make a medium-thick sauce.

5. Preheat the oven to 350 degrees.

6. Place half of the sauce in a large casserole. Add the hens or chicken parts and cover with the remaining sauce. Bake, covered, in the oven until done, about 30–40 minutes.

VEAL WITH ARTICHOKES

SERVES 6–8. (M)

Veal with artichokes, a delicious dish, is served in Egyptian-Jewish homes, often for the second night of Passover. I first tasted this dish at the home of the Egyptian-born, Israeli-raised Harvard University Professor Nadav Safran.

9–12 artichokes, depending on
size, or two 14-ounce cans
artichoke hearts
2 lemons
3 pounds veal shanks with bones
removed, cut in chunks
⅓ cup vegetable oil

Salt and pepper
½ teaspoon turmeric
½ teaspoon ground cumin
2 tablespoons fresh flat-leaf
parsley, chopped
1–2 cloves garlic, peeled

1. Peel off the outer leaves of the artichokes and pull out the hairy center. Cut out the heart. Divide each heart in quarters and drop into water to cover with 1 quartered lemon. If using canned artichoke hearts, merely quarter and place in water with 1 quartered lemon.

2. Sauté the meat in oil, leaving 3 tablespoons of oil for later use with the artichokes. Add salt and pepper to taste, turmeric, cumin, and parsley. When the meat is brown, lower the flame and add ⅓ cup water. Cover and simmer over a low flame for 1 hour.

3. Meanwhile, place the artichoke hearts in ½ cup water with the remaining 3 tablespoons oil, garlic, salt, and the remaining lemon, quartered. Bring to a

boil and lower the flame. Simmer, covered, about 10–15 minutes, until tender but not soft.

4. Add the artichokes and the sauce to the meat. Cover and let stew for another 30 minutes. Serve with Syrian Stuffed Prunes and rice.

BARRY WINE'S STRINGED BEEF BRISKET

SERVES 10–12. (M)

Barry Wine, once chef-owner of New York's four-star Quilted Giraffe restaurant, suggests serving this dish with the Israeli Gamla Cabernet Sauvignon.

Kosher salt and freshly ground pepper
One 6-pound beef brisket, cut in 1½-inch squares
¾ cup peanut oil
1 carrot, peeled and chopped
1 whole leek, trimmed, washed, and diced
1 celery stalk, diced
2 tablespoons puréed garlic
1 onion, chopped
2 cups Cabernet Sauvignon
12 cups good veal or chicken stock
1 bay leaf
2 tablespoons dried thyme
½ cup Cognac

1. Salt and pepper the meat. Brown the meat in batches in half the hot oil in a sauté pan. Remove the meat and set aside.
2. Brown the carrot, leek, celery, garlic, and onion in the remaining oil in the same sauté pan. Remove the vegetables and deglaze the pan with ⅓ cup of wine.
3. Place the meat, vegetables, and deglazed juices in a stockpot. Add the remaining wine, stock, bay leaf, and thyme, and ¼ cup of the Cognac. Add salt and pepper to taste. Cover and cook until the meat is tender, about 2 hours.
4. Remove the meat and, using a fork, split apart to shreds. While doing this, allow the sauce to reduce over low heat, uncovered, until thick enough to coat a spoon. Adjust the seasoning and return the meat to the sauce. You can do this much a day or so ahead.

5. Add the remaining Cognac and serve the meat mounded on a platter, surrounded by the Matzah Salad (see below). Serve with Spicy Tomato Sauce (below).

SPICY TOMATO SAUCE FOR BRISKET

MAKES ABOUT 2 CUPS. (P OR M)

⅔ cup olive oil
4 pounds plum tomatoes, sliced
   ⅓ inch thick
Kosher salt and freshly ground
   black pepper

3 sprigs fresh or 1 teaspoon dried
   thyme
3 fresh jalapeños or other hot
   peppers, thinly sliced

1. Drizzle a little oil on a cookie sheet and place the sliced tomatoes on top. Sprinkle with salt and pepper to taste and lay the thyme and half the sliced peppers evenly over the tomatoes.
2. Bake in a 300-degree oven for 40 minutes, until the tomatoes are concentrated, dryish, and wrinkled.
3. Purée the tomatoes with the thyme and the cooked pepper in a food processor, adding the remaining oil slowly. Strain this mixture through a fine strainer.
4. Add as much of the remaining peppers as needed to suit your taste. Purée and serve at room temperature as a sauce.

MATZAH "SALAD"

SERVES 10–12. (M OR P)

This recipe, created by Barry Wine, is so simple and so delicious that I can't figure out why I have never tasted it before. Similar to *fettoosh*, the Lebanese fried pita salad, it goes beautifully with his brisket but would be equally delicious with any other version, including My Mother's Brisket. It also does not have to be restricted to Passover use.

10 matzahs	1 cucumber, finely diced
4 tablespoons chicken fat or	2–3 teaspoons capers (optional)
pareve margarine (½ stick)	1 bunch of chives, finely chopped
1 red pepper, finely diced	Salt and pepper

1. Run a rolling pin over the matzahs to break them up unto small pieces no larger than ¼ inch, about the size of matzah farfel.
2. Cook the matzah pieces over medium-high heat in a dry sauté pan or toast them in a 300-degree oven for 10 minutes, stirring occasionally. Transfer to a bowl.
3. Heat the fat or margarine in a saucepan and add the pepper and cucumber. Cook 1 minute over medium heat.
4. Turn off the heat and add the capers, if using, and chives.
5. Toss in a mixing bowl with the toasted matzah. Add salt and pepper to taste. Serve at room temperature or slightly warm, surrounding the brisket.

PASSOVER *TSIMMES*

SERVES 6–8. (M)

The late Rose Siegel was born in a shtetl near Minsk, Russia, in 1900 and came to the United States in 1922. Her husband died and left her with three small children and little money. She ran a rooming house to make ends meet and later became a kosher caterer. Adhering to the Jewish dietary laws and preparing traditional fare, she was in demand for Orthodox bar mitzvahs, weddings, and other social occasions. A memorable event for her was the preparation of a kosher luncheon at the Supreme Court when an Orthodox group honored the late Chief Justice Earl Warren. "What a country America is to have a kosher caterer at the highest court in the land," commented Mrs. Siegel to the Chief Justice.

When Mrs. Siegel learned to cook as a child, there were no manufacturers of Passover products. In Russia, everything was cooked from scratch after the regular dishes were exchanged for those used at Passover and the entire house cleaned of all leavening agents. Flour—watched over after milling lest it come in contact with water—was mixed at a communal bakery with water to make the matzah. From that matzah, meal was ground by hand, to be used in such recipes as Mrs. Siegel's matzah meal dumplings, *tsimmes,* or popovers. Fine matzah meal cake flour was not available. Potato starch was made from the sediment collected after the potatoes were grated for potato pancakes. From the starch Mrs. Siegel made, among other dishes, outstanding apple blintzes.

5 cups diced carrots	½ pound pitted prunes
1 pound top rib or flanken, cut into stewing pieces	4 medium white potatoes
	1 medium onion
2 sweet potatoes, peeled and quartered	2 eggs
	½ cup matzah meal
½ cup brown sugar	Salt and pepper

1. Boil the carrots in water to cover in a 3-quart covered pot until the carrots are soft, about 30 minutes. Add the meat, sweet potatoes, brown sugar, and pitted prunes. Simmer, covered, until the potatoes are done, about 45 minutes.
2. Grate the white potatoes, squeezing out the potato starch, and the onion on the small holes of a grater or in a food processor. Stir in the eggs and matzah meal. Season with salt and pepper to taste.
3. Preheat the oven to 350 degrees.
4. Shape the potato mixture into a flat disc in the center of an ovenproof oblong casserole. Strain and reserve the liquid. Place the carrot and meat mixture on each side and on top of the potato mixture. Cover with the liquid and bake for 30 minutes. Serve immediately from the casserole.

TSIMMES TERRINE

MAKES 2 TERRINES. (M OR P)

Because Barry Wine had lost the favorite carrot-ring recipe he remembers from his childhood Seders in Milwaukee, he composed a lovely terrine including all the components of *tsimmes*—sweet potatoes, carrots, prunes, and potatoes with springtime dots of pencil-thin asparagus.

This recipe first appeared in an article I wrote for the *New York Times*. People have been requesting it ever since.

4 whole leeks

3 carrots, coarsely chopped

2 medium-size peeled sweet potatoes, in large chunks

¼ pound rendered chicken fat or 1 stick pareve margarine

¼ cup brown sugar

¼ cup cider

Kosher salt and freshly ground pepper

Juice of ½ lemon

½ teaspoon cinnamon

3 large onions

3 tablespoons kosher-for-Passover vegetable oil

1½ cups water

6 large eggs

3 large baking potatoes, peeled

12 ounces pitted prunes

16–20 pencil-thin asparagus spears*

1. Up to 2 days before serving, cut the leeks open down the center and clean the grit from them. Then blanch and immerse in ice water. Dry very well.
2. Preheat the oven to 375 degrees. In a baking dish, combine the fat or margarine, brown sugar, cider, salt and pepper to taste, lemon juice, and cinnamon with the carrots and sweet potatoes and bake until the vegetables are soft, about 1 hour. Purée the mixture.
3. Dice the onions and sweat them slowly in a covered heavy pan with the oil, cooking until the onions are translucent, about 20 minutes, stirring occa-

*If asparagus is not in season, substitute 20 additional prunes for the asparagus.

sionally. Purée and adjust the consistency by adding up to 1 cup of water until the mixture has reached the texture of heavy cream.

4. When the carrot and sweet potato mixture is cool, beat and add 3 of the eggs and 1 cup of the onion purée. Set aside.

5. Boil the potatoes and mash until smooth, combining with the remaining onion mixture. Add salt and pepper to taste. When cool, beat and add the remaining 3 eggs and fold in well.

6. Heat the prunes in about 1 inch of water for about 5 minutes, drain, and purée.

7. Cook the asparagus in boiling water for about 2 minutes and then plunge into ice water. Dry.

8. For each terrine—this recipe makes 2—grease a loaf pan. Lay 2 dry leeks across the pan to line it, alternating tops and bottoms from one side to the other so that the ends overlap the top by about 2 inches.

9. Put in ¼ of the sweet potato–carrot mixture. Bury 3–5 asparagus spears in the sweet potato–carrot mixture. Spread a thin layer of prunes on top of the layer of sweet potato mixture. Atop that, put half of the white potato mixture. Cover with ¼ of the sweet potato–carrot mixture, again pushing in 3–5 asparagus spears. Repeat for the second terrine.

10. Seal the terrine by folding the leeks over the top. Cover with aluminum foil. Place in a larger pan and create a water bath by filling the larger pan with enough water to come halfway up the sides of the loaf pans. Bake in the oven for 1 hour.

11. Cool completely in the water bath outside the oven. Weigh down each loaf with heavy cans or a brick and place in the refrigerator for 1 day. Slice while chilled with a very sharp slicing knife, making sure to wipe the knife after each slice. Warm slightly in the oven before serving.

LITVAK MATZAH KUGEL

SERVES 6–8. (M)

Kugels were described as casually as bread in writings from over eight hundred years ago in Germany. From there, the Sabbath pudding spread eastward. In 1500, for example, Polish writings describe farfel kugels.

This unusual Litvak matzah meal kugel, also called *myeena,* comes from Helen Harrison of Baltimore through her son, Steve, our next-door neighbor when we lived in Cambridge. Steve looks forward to Passover to taste this kugel, which is made with leftover chicken or brisket.

9 eggs
½ teaspoon salt
2 tablespoons chicken fat or
    pareve margarine
3 cups matzah meal

2 cups water (approximately)
2 cups cooked and ground
    chicken or brisket
Grieben or onions left over from
    rendering chicken fat

1. Beat the eggs until frothy.
2. Stir in the salt and fat or margarine. Add the matzah meal slowly, alternating with the water. Use enough water to make a medium, pastelike consistency.
3. Let stand in the refrigerator at least 1 hour to let the matzah meal expand.
4. Preheat the oven to 350 degrees and grease a round 10-inch soufflé dish.
5. Combine the ground meat and the *grieben* or onions.
6. Alternating layers, place a layer of matzah meal batter, half the meat, more batter, the rest of the meat, and a final layer of batter.
7. Bake 1 hour, or until puffy, brown, and firm. Cut into wedges and serve as a side dish with meat or chicken soup.

PATTY UNTERMAN'S POTATO KUGELETTES

MAKES 24 POTATO KUGELETTES FOR 6 SERVINGS. (P OR M)

Patty Unterman, chef-owner of the Hayes Street Grill in San Francisco, created this potato kugelette recipe for her son Harry when he was a child: "He could hold one of these in his fingers." Although Patty does not like the taste of margarine in this recipe, you can use it instead of chicken fat, if you wish.

1 cup grated and drained
    Kennebec or Idaho potatoes,
    squeezed dry
¼ cup grated onion
2 eggs, well beaten
1 teaspoon coarse kosher salt

Freshly ground pepper to taste
2 tablespoons rendered chicken
    fat, or melted pareve
    margarine plus extra for
    greasing the pans
Matzah meal

1. Preheat the oven to 375 degrees.
2. Combine the potatoes, onion, eggs, salt, pepper, and chicken fat.
3. Grease 24 mini muffin cups and dust with matzah meal. Place 1 tablespoon of filling in each muffin cup and bake 25 minutes, until golden. Serve 4 per person.

FARFEL AND CHEESE

Adapted from Hedy Pearlman

SERVES 8. (D)

My daughter Daniela remarked about four days into Passover one year, "We look forward to the Seder for so long that we forget that after a few days matzah gets boring." That is why this farfel and cheese dish went over very well in our family when my children were young, the closest thing to macaroni and cheese my children ate during Passover.

4 large eggs

3 cups matzah farfel

½ pound cheddar cheese

1½ cups sour cream

6 tablespoons butter or pareve margarine

2 cups milk

1 teaspoon salt

¼ teaspoon pepper

1. Beat 3 of the eggs and pour over the farfel. Mix well.
2. Preheat the oven to 350 degrees and grease a casserole. Pour the farfel mixture into the casserole.
3. Cut the cheddar cheese into a small dice. Add the cheese to the farfel. Using a spoon, add the sour cream in dollops and dot with butter or margarine. Mix together the milk, remaining egg, salt, and pepper, and pour it over the casserole.
4. Bake covered, for 30 minutes. Uncover and let brown for 10 to 15 minutes more. Scoop out onto plates.

GNOCCHI *DI SPINACI*

MAKES ABOUT 24 LARGE OR 40–50 SMALL GNOCCHI. (D)

In an Italian Jewish cookbook, *La Cucina nella Tradizione Ebraica*, published in 1970 in Padua, each holiday includes a menu in either the Ashkenazic, Sephardic, or Italian tradition. The following Venetian gnocchi *di spinaci*, from the Luzzatto family, comes from the Italian tradition. It is very important to squeeze out all the water from the spinach.

2 cups cooked and squeezed spinach (four bags washed fresh spinach or four 10-ounce packages frozen chopped spinach)
1 cup ricotta or farmer cheese*
¾ cup freshly grated Parmesan cheese* plus more for sprinkling (optional)

1 egg
3 tablespoons potato starch
Pinch of nutmeg
Salt
3 quarts water
2 tablespoons butter
Light béchamel sauce for drizzling (optional)

1. Combine the spinach, ricotta and Parmesan cheeses, egg, potato starch, and nutmeg and salt to taste.
2. Bring the water to a rolling boil in a large pot. Add salt to taste.
3. Wetting your hands first, form the spinach mixture into dumplings the size of walnuts and drop them, 1 by 1, into the boiling water. They will drop to the bottom. When they rise to the surface, remove and drain.
4. Just before serving, preheat the oven to 350 degrees and butter a flat casserole.
5. Place the gnocchi in the casserole. Drizzle with Parmesan cheese or a light béchamel sauce. Heat for a few minutes in the oven. This is a delicious vegetable dish at Passover or any time during the year.

*If these cheeses are not found in your area or are not kosher for Passover, substitute the closest ones available.

MRS. FEINBERG'S VEGETABLE KUGEL

MAKES 24 MUFFINS; SERVES 6–8. (P)

Try this Cincinnati vegetable kugel, one of the most popular recipes in the original edition of *The Jewish Holiday Kitchen*. It came from the late Rosa Feinberg, wife of Rabbi Louis Feinberg. Each year, my friend Arthur Schwartz tells me the recipe cannot work because it has no eggs. Each year, I call Mrs. Feinberg's daughter-in-law Micky, host of WOR radio's *Food Talk with Arthur Schwartz,* in a panic before I make it. It has no eggs, and it is a great recipe.

1 cup grated apple
1 cup grated peeled sweet potato
1 cup grated carrot
1 cup matzah meal
¼ pound (1 stick) pareve
    margarine, melted

1 teaspoon salt
1 teaspoon baking soda
1 teaspoon cinnamon
1 teaspoon ground nutmeg
½ cup sugar

1. Preheat the oven to 325 degrees and grease a 10-inch casserole or two 12-cup muffin tins.
2. Mix all the ingredients together well.
3. Pour into the baking dish. Cover with aluminum foil and bake 45 minutes. If you are using muffin tins, bake 30 minutes.
4. Raise the heat to 350 degrees, remove the cover, and bake an additional 15 minutes. Slice and serve hot as a vegetable with meat.

Note: A food processor makes this recipe effortless. Yes, baking *soda,* a pure product and not a leavening agent, can be used at Passover.

VEGETABLES, FRENCH STYLE

Michel Fitoussi, once chef of the lavishly expensive Palace Restaurant in New York, hails from Tunisia via France.

Most Jewish holiday food does not and cannot include the last-minute, rich sauces that make the preparation of French food such an art. Although Michel is familiar with traditional recipes at home and serves them for Passover, he would not give those recipes to me. He chose rather to give me two of his own creations: carrot, asparagus, and turnip bundles, and a salad with leeks, particularly appropriate for the first Seder.

FAGOTS DE LÉGUMES

(Vegetable Bundles)

(D OR P)

Quantities have been deliberately omitted for these colorful and engaging vegetable "bundles." Let your needs be your guide.

Carrots	White turnips
Trimmed green tops from very fresh scallions	Clarified butter or pareve margarine
Asparagus	Salt

1. Peel the carrots and cut them crosswise into 2–2½-inch sections. Cut the sections lengthwise into ⅛-inch slices. Stack the slices and cut them downward at ⅛-inch intervals to make "matchsticks." Briefly blanch in a large quantity of boiling water (they should remain firm and crisp) and refresh under cold running water.

2. Cut the scallion greens into strips 10 inches long and ¼ inch wide. Blanch in boiling water for 5 seconds and immediately plunge into cold water.

3. Across the centers of the scallion greens, stack the carrot sticks, 2 high and 3 across. Bring the ends of the scallion greens up over the carrot stacks, tie in simple bows, and trim as you would the ribbon of a gift package.

4. Repeat the procedure with the asparagus and turnips, leaving the asparagus whole.

5. Place the vegetable bundles in a small pan with the butter or margarine and salt to taste. Cook, covered, over low heat just until tender. Remove carefully from the butter or margarine and serve 1 bundle of each vegetable per person.

SALADE À MA FAÇON

SERVES 8. (P)

Ashkenazic Jews traditionally don't use mustard on Passover, but Sephardic Jews, including Tunisians, do, enabling Michel to serve this wonderful salad at his Seder. I love this salad and serve it all year long.

3 bunches arugula, washed and trimmed, or enough of any hearty lettuce to serve 8 people

1 bunch watercress, washed and trimmed

White part of 1 leek, julienned

MAYONNAISE:

2 egg yolks

2 teaspoons Dijon mustard

Juice of 1 large lemon

1 cup olive oil or good vegetable oil

Salt and pepper

1. In a large salad bowl, mix the greens and leek.

2. In a blender or food processor, whip the egg yolks, mustard, and lemon juice.

3. Gradually add the oil in a thin, steady stream, beating until thick. Season with salt and pepper to taste. Add the mayonnaise to the greens and toss.

CARCIOFI ALLA GIUDIA

(Artichokes Jewish Style)

SERVES 6. (P)

This famous dish was served in the ghetto of Rome in the springtime, especially around Passover. There are many variations, and to this day Italians call it "artichokes Jewish style." This particular version comes from *The Passover Seder Cookbook* by Hava Nathan, published by Zmora Bitan Publishers in Tel Aviv. In trying to discover authentic Passover Seder customs, Nathan interviewed the wives of chief rabbis in Israel and in Rome.

12 small artichokes	½ cup chopped fresh basil leaves
2 lemons	2 teaspoons salt
Olive oil	½ teaspoon freshly ground pepper
1 cup chopped fresh flat-leaf parsley	10 cloves garlic, crushed
	Matzah meal

1. Trim the tops off the artichokes, working around and around to retain the shape. Halve the lemons, juice them, and cover with cold water. Soak the artichokes in this lemon water until ready to use, then drain dry.

2. Hold the artichokes by the stems and bang them a little against the countertop to open the leaves.

3. Combine ½ cup of oil, parsley, basil, salt, pepper, and garlic and sprinkle the mixture between the leaves. Roll each artichoke in the matzah meal.

4. In a Dutch oven or other heavy frying pan with a cover pour about ⅛ inch of oil. Place the artichokes, trimmed edges down, and simmer slowly, covered, 20–25 minutes.

TURKISH BAKED EGGPLANT WITH CHEESE

SERVES 4–6. (D)

In the poor shtetls of Eastern Europe, a meat meal did not necessarily mean that meat was served. Goose or chicken fat or meat suet was all that was needed. It could be used for frying or spread on bread and served with potato soup or kasha as the main course. Thus, without bread at Passover, much frying was done and many meatless meat meals were eaten. The foods included potato latkes, matzah meal pancakes, matzah *brei,* potato starch blintzes, and so forth.

Sephardic Jews did not have this problem, however. Vegetable and olive oils were, for the most part, locally made and thus available even to the very poor. They, too, have fried meat dishes at Passover; they also have fried milk ones.

6 tablespoons vegetable oil
1 large eggplant
4 eggs
1 cup grated Parmesan, cheddar, or other sharp cheese
1 cup cooked rice or 1 mashed potato (about 1 cup)
2 tablespoons chopped fresh flat-leaf parsley
1 tablespoon chopped fresh or 1 teaspoon dried rosemary
1 tablespoon chopped fresh or 1 teaspoon dried basil
2 tomatoes, sliced
Salt

1. Preheat the oven to 350 degrees and grease a 9- by 6-inch baking dish with vegetable oil.
2. Wash and slice eggplant into ¼-inch slices. Sauté in 4 tablespoons of the oil.
3. Place half of the eggplant slices in the baking dish.
4. Beat 2 eggs well; add the cheese and rice or potato. Mix well and cover the eggplant slices with the mixture.
5. Place another layer of eggplant on top.
6. Cover with the chopped mixed herbs and tomatoes. Beat the remaining 2 eggs and pour on top of the tomato layer. Season with salt to taste and the remaining 2 tablespoons of oil.
7. Bake in the oven for 45 minutes to 1 hour, until a custardlike crust forms.

SYRIAN STUFFED PRUNES

SERVES 6–8 AS A SIDE DISH. (D OR P)

In Jerusalem there used to be a tiny restaurant called Cohen's, where only ten to fifteen people could eat comfortably at one time. If you asked Michel (Moussa) Cohen, the proprietor, to order for you, he would (depending on his mood) serve you an elegant array of *memulaim,* stuffed vegetables such as onions, carrots, eggplants, zucchini, tomatoes, and peppers. The grand finale might include stuffed prunes.

Although pomegranate syrup is extremely expensive in this country, it is the walnuts that make this a festive delicacy in Cohen's native Damascus.

12 ounces pitted prunes
½ cup walnut halves
2 tablespoons butter or pareve
  margarine

1 cup sweet red wine
1 tablespoon pomegranate syrup*
Juice of ½ lemon

1. Stuff the prunes with the walnut halves.
2. Sauté in butter or margarine for about 5 minutes, until tender.
3. Add the wine, pomegranate syrup, and lemon juice. Simmer, uncovered, over low heat for about 20 minutes. Serve as an accompaniment to turkey, lamb, or Veal with Artichokes (page 366), using the juice as a sauce.

*Available at Greek and Middle Eastern food stores.

GREEK LEEK PATTIES

(Kofta)

MAKES ABOUT 12. (D)

Leek patties, or *kofta*, are eaten at Passover by Greek Jews. According to Theonie Mark, author of *Greek Islands Cooking,* Greeks eat only braised leeks, and thus we can surmise that the Greek Jews brought this recipe with them from Spain. This Greek recipe from Rhodes via Boston includes potatoes. We can see from the potatoes that it is a late version. Leek patties with matzah crumbs and feta cheese or meat is an extremely old Sephardic holiday recipe. How far back leek patties go is anybody's guess—perhaps to Egypt: "We remember the fish, which we were wont to eat in Egypt for nought; the cucumbers, and the melons, and the leeks, and the onions, and the garlic," we read in Numbers 11:5.

2 pounds leeks	Salt and pepper
2 large boiling potatoes, peeled	½ cup grated Romano cheese
3 large eggs	Vegetable oil for frying

1. Wash the leeks carefully, slicing them vertically to remove all of the grit. Dice the white base and part of the green leaves. Parboil in salted water for 5 minutes. Drain.
2. Boil the potatoes until they are soft. Drain and cool.
3. Using a potato masher or food processor, mash the potatoes. Add the leeks, blending them in well.
4. Add the eggs, salt and pepper to taste, and Romano cheese. Blend well. Form the mixture into 12 patties.
5. Heat some oil in a heavy frying pan. When the oil is sizzling (375 degrees), drop the leek patties in and fry until golden brown on each side. Drain on paper towels.

SPINACH SOUFFLÉ

(Fritada de Espinaca)

SERVES 4–6. (D)

At Passover, some vegetables—such as corn, string beans, and peas—are not eaten by Ashkenazim but are eaten by most Sephardim. Asparagus, artichokes, and spinach are the major seasonal substitutes. For daily fare, spinach is one of the most popular vegetables at Passover, especially in Sephardic cultures. This Passover soufflé, in a less Americanized version, is served by Turkish Jews on Saturday morning after synagogue with coffee and *burekas*. Other versions include mashed potatoes and Romano cheese, rather than cream and cottage cheese.

10 ounces fresh spinach or one 10-ounce package frozen spinach, defrosted	1 pound cottage cheese
	½ cup matzah meal
	3 eggs, well beaten
8 ounces cream cheese	Salt and pepper

1. Preheat the oven to 350 degrees and grease a 1-quart soufflé dish.
2. Cook the spinach thoroughly and drain well. Melt the cream cheese over boiling water and add to the hot spinach. Add the cottage cheese and matzah meal and mix well.
3. Stir in the eggs and salt and pepper to taste.
4. Pour into the soufflé dish and bake 40 minutes, or until light golden on top.

PASSOVER APPLE BLINTZES

MAKES 20–22. (P OR D)

This is a great breakfast alternative during Passover.

PANCAKE BATTER:

6 eggs	2 cups water
1 cup potato starch	Oil for frying and for brushing

APPLE FILLING:

2 pounds apples, peeled, cored, and diced	½ teaspoon grated lemon zest
¼ cup sugar	¼ cup chopped walnuts (optional)
1 teaspoon cinnamon	½ cup raisins (optional)

1. Beat the eggs well. Slowly add the potato starch and water, beating well until the batter is pale yellow and foamy.
2. Lightly oil a 6-inch skillet or crêpe pan and place over a medium-high flame (about 350 degrees). (A nonstick pan is especially good for this.)
3. Using a ladle, pour in just enough batter to coat the pan; drain off any excess batter. When the batter seems dry, shake the pancake out onto a cloth placed on a flat surface. Let cool. Continue making blintzes until all the batter is used up, greasing the pan if the blintzes stick. When the blintzes are dry, you can pile them on top of one another.
4. Preheat the oven to 400 degrees and grease a large low casserole.
5. To the chopped apples add the sugar, cinnamon, lemon zest, and walnuts and raisins, if using. Mix well.
6. Taking 1 blintz, place a heaping tablespoon of apple filling in the center. Fold over each side and then roll up, jelly-roll fashion. Place, seam side down, on a greased cookie sheet. Continue until all the blintzes are filled.
7. Brush the top of each blintz with oil and heat in the casserole in the oven about 20 minutes, or until golden brown. Serve as is or with sour cream.

If you wish to use a cheese filling, see pages 429–30.

BISCOTTI DI PESACH DELLA MAMMA

(Mother's Passover Biscotti)

From Edda Servi Machlin

MAKES ABOUT 60 BISCOTTI. (P)

"*Mandelbrot* is almost the same thing as biscotti," said Edda Servi Machlin. "We made ours for Pesach with no leavening." According to Edda, the word "biscotti" in Italy has come to designate all sorts of hard cookies, but in the United States it has retained the original meaning—*bis* derives from Latin and means "once more, twice," and *cotti* is Italian for "cooked." Biscotti are just that—cooked twice; so are *mandelbrot* (in Yiddish), which comes from *mandel* (almond) and *brot* (bread). Which came first? Ah, there is the question, but certainly they are linked. This particular recipe came from Edda's mother, Sara Di Capua, who was born in Rome. Serve them à la Machlin, dunked in sweet vermouth or tea. During the year, substitute all-purpose flour for the matzah cake meal.

1⅓ cups sugar	1 teaspoon almond extract
½ teaspoon salt	3 large eggs
⅓ cup olive oil	3 cups matzah cake meal
1 teaspoon vanilla extract	1 cup whole almonds

1. In an electric mixer fitted with the paddle or by hand, cream together the sugar, salt, oil, vanilla, and almond extract. Add the eggs, 1 at a time, beating after each addition.
2. Add enough matzah cake meal to make a soft but manageable dough. Fold in the whole almonds.
3. Preheat the oven to 350 degrees and grease a cookie sheet.
4. Spoon the dough onto an oiled work surface and divide into 3 parts. Oil your hands and shape the dough into 3 cylinders, each 15 inches long. Place on the cookie sheet and bake on the middle rack for 25 minutes.
5. Remove from the oven. Raise the temperature to 450 degrees. Slice through

each cylinder diagonally, making approximately 20 slices per cylinder. Lay the slices flat on a greased baking sheet and bake on the middle rack of the oven for 10 more minutes.

6. Cool the biscotti thoroughly before storing.

ALMOND MACAROONS

(Maranchinos)

MAKES ABOUT 24. (P)

There are dry macaroons, chewy macaroons, tasty ones, and bland ones. Until I tasted the following crunchy-on-the-outside, chewy-on-the-inside *maranchinos* at the home of Greek Jews in Boston, my favorites had been those served in the dairy bar of the King David Hotel in Jerusalem, half-coated with rich chocolate. Since most Jews make a coconut or almond version of macaroons, these cookies are probably an ancient Jewish pareve Passover sweet, which need no grease to cook. They are also a marvelous means of disposing of extra egg whites. If you have leftover yolks, use them in the dressing for French salad on page 379. (The Greek style of separating eggs is to pierce a tiny hole in one end and then slowly let the white ooze out, preserving the yolk within the shell for later use.)

2½ cups blanched almonds
2¼ cups sugar
4 egg whites
¼ teaspoon almond extract

Sifted matzah cake meal for dusting
¼ cup blanched toasted almonds, split, for topping

1. Preheat the oven to 350 degrees.
2. Grind the almonds very fine with 1 cup of sugar in a food processor or other grinder.

3. Place the almonds in a bowl. Add the remaining sugar and the egg whites, 1 at a time, blending by hand or with a food processor until a paste is formed that can be manipulated with the hand. Add the almond extract. Refrigerate for 10 minutes.

4. Dust a large cookie sheet with matzah cake meal.

5. Take a piece of dough the size of a plum. Roll between the palms to make a ball and pinch the top to shape like a pear. Place, wide side down, on the cookie sheet. Place half a blanched toasted almond on top.

6. Bake 20–25 minutes, until the cookies rise and brown a little. Cool slightly and separate with a spatula, taking care not to break them.

AUNT FREDA'S COCONUT MACAROONS

MAKES 24 MACAROONS. (P)

While living in Japan, Gloria Goldman of Columbia, Maryland, taught Passover cooking to the Japanese. Although they weren't wild about gefilte tuna, they loved her aunt's cookie recipe.

4 cups fresh or packaged unsweetened grated coconut	6 large egg whites
2 cups sugar	¼ cup chopped walnuts
	Matzah cake meal

1. Cover the coconut with 1 cup sugar. Let sit overnight to dry.

2. Next day, whip the egg whites until foamy. Gradually add the remaining 1 cup sugar and beat until stiff and shiny. Combine with the coconut and nuts. Drop by tablespoonfuls on greased aluminum foil on a cookie sheet. Let stand for 5–10 minutes. Sprinkle with matzah cake meal and bake in a 350-degree oven 20 minutes. Let cool 5 minutes. Peel off the foil.

MACARONES

(Passover Macaroons)

From Elisabeth Rosenfeld

MAKES 30 LARGE MACAROONS. (P)

These macaroons, made from almonds or hazelnuts and egg whites, are very elegant. I recommend using baking parchment when making them.

2 cups blanched almonds or
    peeled hazelnuts, plus 15
    whole blanched almonds or
    peeled hazelnuts for garnish
1 cup sugar

3 large egg whites, unbeaten
½ tablespoon lemon juice
    (see Note)
Dash of salt

1. In a food processor fitted with the steel blade, grind the 2 cups of almonds or peeled hazelnuts with the sugar until the nuts are finely chopped but not pulverized. You could also use a metate, or grinding stone, as Elisabeth Rosenfeld did in Mexico. Put the ground nuts in a bowl.
2. Stir in the unbeaten egg whites, lemon juice, and salt.
3. Preheat the oven to 350 degrees and line a cookie sheet with baking parchment.
4. Roll a heaping teaspoon of dough between your palms to make a ball. Place on the cookie sheet and compress it slightly. Insert half a blanched almond or hazelnut into the top. Repeat with the rest of the dough, leaving 4 inches between the cookies.
5. Bake on the middle oven rack for 18–20 minutes, or until the cookies spread and brown a little. Remove them from the oven, cool, and separate with a spatula, taking care not to break them.

Note: A half teaspoon of almond extract may be used instead of lemon juice.

KRIMSEL

MAKES 34 AND SERVES 6–8. (P)

On the table, the fresh crisp matzos *were also waiting, and in the oven a delicious Passover borsht was simmering, and hot* kneidlach *with chicken fat, and maybe even a potato pudding! . . . Such wonderful* chremzlach *that it would have been hard even for an epicure to tell if there was more honey in them or more chicken fat, because they were so sugary and so rich that they stuck to the gums and ran down his beard.*

Sholem Aleichem, "The Lottery Ticket"

When my parents married, my German father asked my American mother to learn how to make one dish—*krimsel.* Here is her American variation on a German theme. With leaven forbidden at Passover, *krimsels* are easy-to-make fritters with fruit. They can be made of matzah meal and filled with nuts and preserves; or, as in my family recipe, they can be made from soaked matzah and nuts, with no jam filling. Either way, they are crispy and delicious!

3 matzahs, soaked in water and squeezed very dry	3–4 tablespoons matzah meal
2 tablespoons seeded and chopped raisins	½ cup sugar
	Grated zest of 1 lemon
2 tablespoons chopped almonds	1 tablespoon lemon juice
3 eggs, separated	Vegetable oil for deep-frying

1. Mix the matzahs, raisins, almonds, egg yolks, matzah meal, sugar, lemon zest, and lemon juice.
2. Beat the egg whites until stiff. Fold into the matzah mixture, adding more matzah meal if necessary for the dough to hold together in frying.
3. Fill a wok or heavy pot with about 3 inches of oil. Heat the oil to 375 degrees on a deep-frying or candy thermometer. Drop the mixture into the oil by

tablespoons, a few at a time, and brown on both sides. Drain well. Serve warm, with stewed prunes flavored with orange juice.

GEFULLTE MAZEKNODEL
*(Austrian Stuffed Matzah Dumplings)**

MAKES 12 DUMPLINGS. (P)

In Germany and Austria, Jews developed a dessert matzah dumpling stuffed with apples and raisins, which was fried and then rolled in cinnamon and sugar. Hungarian Jews had a potato version filled with plum jam. Lithuanian Jews served savory matzah balls stuffed with meat or sometimes with crushed matzah; both versions were spiked with cinnamon.

FILLING:

1 medium-size apple, peeled, cored, and grated
3 tablespoons coarsely chopped almonds
2 tablespoons sugar
½ teaspoon cinnamon
½ teaspoon grated lemon zest

MATZAH BALLS:

3 squares of water matzah
3 large eggs
¼ cup plus 2 tablespoons sugar
¼ cup finely chopped almonds
Grated zest of 1 lemon
Salt
1 tablespoon softened rendered chicken fat, butter, or pareve margarine
3–4 tablespoons matzah meal
Vegetable oil for deep frying
¼ teaspoon cinnamon

*A variation of this recipe appears in the unpublished manuscript called "Jenny's Cookbook," translated from the German by Elisabeth Schiff Hirsch.

1. To prepare the filling, combine the apple, almonds, sugar, cinnamon, and lemon zest in a bowl and refrigerate for 30 minutes.
2. Meanwhile, to prepare the matzah balls, crumble the matzah and soak in warm water to cover until soft. Drain well and squeeze out as much water as possible.
3. Combine the matzah with the eggs, ¼ cup of the sugar, the almonds, lemon zest, salt to taste, fat, and matzah meal in a bowl. Refrigerate for at least 30 minutes.
4. Form the matzah mixture into dumplings the size of large walnuts. Flatten the dumplings and place 1 teaspoon of filling in the center of each. Enclose the filling, pinch the edges, and re-form into balls.
5. In a heavy frying pan, add oil to a depth of 2 inches and heat to about 375 degrees on a deep-frying or candy thermometer. Fry the dumplings a few at a time, turning after a minute or so when they are golden brown. Drain thoroughly on paper towels.
6. Combine the remaining 2 tablespoons sugar and the cinnamon. Roll the dumplings in this cinnamon-sugar combination and serve immediately.

PASSOVER LEMON SPONGE CAKE

SERVES 8. (P)

This Russian Passover lemon sponge cake comes from the late Sara Garfunkle, the grandmother of my friend Ruth Nathan. One of fourteen siblings and the mother of six, Mrs. Garfunkle always had her dining room in New York open during Passover for a *pesachdik* meal, which is almost identical to the Greek *pan de España de Pesah*. According to Theonie Mark, author of *Greek Islands Cooking*, the *pan de España* was brought into Greece by Sephardic Jews at the time of the Inquisition.

The classic sponge cake includes neither butter nor leavening agents. For Jews, it is the perfect sweet pareve dish for any meal.

The trick to making a good sponge cake is to beat as much air as possible into the separated eggs before steaming the cake mixture in the oven. Given the fact that Jews checked eggs closely for blood and needed ways to experiment with rising agents acceptable at Passover, it may have been a pre-Inquisition Spanish or Portuguese Jew who discovered how to beat yolks until they are lemony and whites until stiff peaks form.

12 large eggs, separated	½ cup chopped walnuts
1½ cups sugar	(optional)
½ cup orange juice	¼ cup potato flour
Grated zest of 1 lemon	1 cup matzah cake meal
Grated zest of 1 orange	Pinch of salt

1. Preheat the oven to 325 degrees.
2. Using an electric mixer or food processor, beat the egg yolks until frothy and lemon colored. Gradually add 1 cup of the sugar. Add the orange juice and the grated lemon and orange zest. Add the nuts if desired.
3. Sift together the potato flour and the matzah cake meal. Add to the mixture.
4. Whip the egg whites until frothy. Add the remaining ½ cup of sugar and a pinch of salt and beat until stiff and shiny but not dry. (A good sponge cake needs a great deal of air beaten into the eggs.) Fold into the other ingredients.
5. Bake in an ungreased 10-inch angel-food pan for 1 hour. Remove from the oven. Invert the pan and cool thoroughly before removing the cake. Use a cake divider to cut.

MATZAH ALMOND TORTE

SERVES 8. (P OR D)

In browsing temple cookbooks, I saw frequent references to *The Twentieth Century Cookbook,* by C. F. Moritz and Adelle Kahn, published in Montgomery, Alabama, in 1897. I tracked it down and found that Passover recipes often call for a combination of matzah meal and baking powder. At the Library of Congress, I discovered that in 1926 Miss Moritz wrote a second work, *Every Woman's Cook-*

book. In both books, there are recipes for matzah almond tortes, and both include baking powder. According to most traditions, secondary leavening is permissible, so baking soda or powder can be used to leaven matzah products. Certainly, it can be used to cause non-grain–based flours—potato starch or nut flour—to rise. Kosher for Passover baking powder, which uses potato starch instead of cornstarch, is widely available. But in case you can't find it, here is a moist Passover variation of her torte recipes—without the baking powder!

8 large eggs, separated	¼ teaspoon salt
1½ cups sugar	1 tablespoon cold water
¼ cup sifted matzah meal	½ cup pecans, ground
½ tablespoon fresh lemon juice	½ cup almonds, ground
Grated zest of ½ lemon	

1. Beat the egg yolks until light. Gradually add the sugar and continue beating until the eggs are pale lemon colored.
2. Preheat the oven to 325 degrees. Grease and flour with matzah cake meal a 9-inch springform pan.
3. Add the matzah meal to the yolks.
4. Add the lemon juice and zest, salt, and water. Fold in the nuts.
5. Whip the egg whites until stiff. Fold into the yolk mixture.
6. Transfer the batter to the springform pan and bake 45–60 minutes, or until a toothpick comes out clean. Serve as is or with the following glaze.

GLAZE:

1 egg yolk	Grated zest of ½ lemon
½ cup lemon juice	1 teaspoon butter or pareve
½ cup sugar	margarine

1. While the torte is still in the oven, beat together the egg yolk, lemon juice, sugar, and lemon zest. Place the mixture in a saucepan and boil it, stirring constantly for a few minutes, until it thickens slightly. Remove from the heat and stir in the butter or margarine.
2. With a toothpick, poke holes in the top of the cake at 1-inch intervals. When the cake has cooled slightly, still in the pan, pour the glaze over it. Let stand a few minutes so the glaze sinks in and then remove from the pan.

CHOCOLATE SOUFFLÉ ROLL

SERVES 8–10. (D OR P)

When this recipe appeared in my column years ago in the *Boston Globe* magazine, the newspaper received several calls from indignant readers: How could there be such a thing as a flourless chocolate soufflé roll? Well, there is! This particular recipe came from the old Window Shop bakery on Brattle Street in Cambridge, started by Bostonians to help immigrant German refugees during World War II, and now called the Blacksmith House.

A similar soufflé roll was served at the Jewish Bake Shop in Cincinnati, also started by that city's German Jewish community for the new German refugees. The late political filmmaker Charles Guggenheim loved the chocolate roll recipe prepared by his grandmother, Grace Stix, one of the prime movers behind the Cincinnati-based shop. The Cincinnati version was made by adding flour, filling with whipped cream, and covering with a chocolate icing. The following Boston version, which even Charles approved, can be served at Passover—and will be the hit of your Seder or any dinner party.

7 ounces good-quality semisweet chocolate	7 eggs, separated
	¾ cup sugar
¼ cup strong brewed coffee	2 tablespoons cocoa powder

1. Preheat the oven to 350 degrees. Grease a 10- by 15-inch jelly-roll pan. Line with greased waxed paper.
2. Melt the chocolate in the coffee over hot water in a double boiler and stir until the chocolate is melted. Cool slightly.
3. Whip the egg yolks with ½ cup of sugar until fluffy and pale yellow.
4. Add the chocolate and coffee to the yolks.
5. Beat the egg whites until soft peaks form. Add the remaining ¼ cup sugar and beat until stiff peaks form.
6. Fold the egg whites into the chocolate mixture. Place the batter in the pan and bake 15–20 minutes, or until the cake is firm.
7. Remove from the oven and and cool for 5 minutes. Then place a damp towel

over the cake, still in its pan, and cool completely at room temperature (this prevents the cake from drying out). Store in a cool place.

8. When ready to assemble the cake (several hours before serving), remove the towel and sprinkle the cake with cocoa. Place an ungreased sheet of waxed paper over the cake and turn the pan upside down. Remove the pan and the first piece of waxed paper.

9. Spread ¾ of either the mocha or whipped cream filling over the flattened cake and roll up very carefully and quickly. Spread the remining filling on top of the cake as icing. Store in the refrigerator.

MOCHA CREAM FILLING:

9 tablespoons unsalted butter or pareve margarine
¾ cup very fine sugar
3 ounces semisweet chocolate
2 tablespoons strong brewed coffee
2 eggs
2 tablespoons shaved chocolate for garnish

1. Cream the butter or margarine and sugar very well.

2. Melt the chocolate in the coffee over hot water in a double boiler, stirring constantly. Cool slightly. Add to the butter or margarine mixture and blend well. Add the eggs and continue beating until very smooth and light. Set aside in a cool place.

3. After filling, sprinkle the top of the cake with the shaved chocolate. Since the chocolate roll usually cracks a bit in rolling, the decoration will cover this.

WHIPPED CREAM FILLING:

1½ cups heavy cream
2 tablespoons sugar
1 teaspoon vanilla or rum extract
2 tablespoons shaved chocolate for garnish

1. Just before serving, whip the cream with the sugar and vanilla or rum.

2. You may wish to reserve some of the whipped cream and decorate the outside of the cake, using a pastry bag or a spatula. Sprinkle the top with shaved chocolate.

PASSOVER CHOCOLATE CAKE

From Ann Amernick

SERVES 10–12. (D OR P)

"I created this cake because people are always asking me for a good chocolate Passover dessert," said pastry chef Ann Amernick. "Most recipes call for cocoa and potato starch. Here I use real chocolate, which gives the cake a wonderfully dense texture. The key is to use imported bittersweet chocolate, the only true chocolate, and not to mask it with too much sugar."

10 ounces good imported bittersweet chocolate, broken into pieces

¼ pound (1 stick) unsalted butter or pareve margarine,* at room temperature

½ cup sugar, plus more for sprinkling

5 large eggs, separated

⅓ cup finely ground almonds (done in a food processor)

2 tablespoons kosher-for-Passover brandy

Whipped cream (optional)

Fresh raspberries (optional)

1. Preheat the oven to 300 degrees and grease well a 9-inch springform pan; line the bottom with baking parchment.
2. Melt the chocolate in a double boiler over barely simmering water. When the chocolate has melted, turn off the heat and leave it over the hot water to cool slowly.
3. Meanwhile, in a large mixing bowl, beat the butter or margarine with ¼ cup of the sugar until the mixture is fluffy and almost white. Add the egg yolks and beat for 1 minute. Add the almonds and brandy and beat for 2 minutes more.
4. In a separate bowl, beat the egg whites until light and foamy while gradually adding the remaining ¼ cup sugar. Continue beating the whites until they are stiff and shiny.

*You can use pareve margarine, but Ann would not.

5. Add the cooled melted chocolate to the egg yolk mixture and mix with a rubber spatula until well combined. Fold one quarter of this chocolate mixture into the egg whites; then gently fold this egg white mixture back into the rest of the chocolate mixture, taking care not to deflate the batter.

6. Pour the batter into the prepared pan. Bake on the bottom rack of the oven for 25–30 minutes, or until a tester comes out covered with a thick, moist (not wet), and crumby coating.

7. Allow the cake to cool for 30 minutes in the pan. Loosen the edges with a knife, remove the sides, and carefully turn the cake upside down onto a plate. Remove the baking parchment. Sprinkle with the sugar.

8. Serve warm, at room temperature, or chilled, with whipped cream and raspberries on the side, if desired.

MERINGUE BASKETS WITH LIME CREAM JEAN-LOUIS

From Ann Amernick

MAKES 18 MERINGUES AND 3 CUPS OF LIME CREAM. (D OR P)

When I was growing up, my mother served a *schaum* (German for "foam") *torte* at our Seder, straight from *The "Settlement" Cook Book*. This was a large meringue layered with strawberries. Ann Amernick's piquant lime cream scooped into individual meringue baskets makes a very unusual Passover offering. The lime cream recipe was adapted from that of the late Jean-Louis Palladin, the great chef at Restaurant Jean-Louis at the Watergate, Washington, D.C. Ann worked there as pastry chef for several years; unfortunately, the restaurant is now closed.

THE LIME CREAM:

Grated zest of 5 large limes

1 cup fresh lime juice

¼ pound (1 stick) unsalted butter or pareve margarine

3 large eggs

3 large egg yolks

¾ cup sugar

THE MERINGUE BASKETS:

   8 large egg whites   1½ cups sugar

THE LIME CREAM:

1. Place the grated lime zest, the lime juice, and the butter or margarine in a 4-quart heavy-bottomed stainless-steel or enamel saucepan. Bring to a boil over medium heat, then remove from the heat.

2. In a medium bowl, mix the eggs, egg yolks, and sugar together until just combined. Do not beat.

3. Add 1 cup of the hot lime-and-butter mixture to the eggs to warm them. Stir and then add the egg mixture to the remaining lime-and-butter mixture in the pan.

4. Stir the mixture with a whisk over medium-high heat until thick and smooth, 5–8 minutes. Be sure to beat vigorously and touch all points of the bottom of the pan so you don't burn the mixture.

5. Strain the lime cream into a stainless-steel or glass bowl and quickly place a piece of plastic wrap over the cream to prevent a skin from forming. Cool to room temperature, then refrigerate until ready to use—it will keep for up to 2 weeks.

THE MERINGUE BASKETS:

6. In the bowl of an electric mixer, beat the egg whites with the whisk until light and foamy. Slowly add the sugar, 1 tablespoon at a time, until it has all been incorporated. Beat the meringue at medium speed for 8–10 minutes, until stiff and very glossy.

7. Preheat the oven to 200 degrees and cover 2 cookie sheets with greased baking parchment.

8. With an ice cream scoop or 2 large spoons, drop 18 mounds of the meringue on the cookie sheets, keeping each ball smooth. Make a deep pocket in each meringue by pushing the back of a spoon into the center and using a blunt knife or the back of the spoon to push the meringue away from the center.

9. Bake the meringues on the middle rack of the oven for 1 hour. Turn off the oven and leave the meringues inside for 30 minutes more, or until dry. Cool them and, when ready to serve, fill each with 2 heaping tablespoons of the lime cream.

MOROCCAN COCONUT-SABRA TORTE

SERVES 8–10. (P)

This is a variation on a recipe from my first cookbook, *The Flavor of Jerusalem*. I first tasted it at one of those typical Friday evening political discussion gatherings in Jerusalem. It is a great dessert, good at Passover or anytime, and takes about 10 minutes to prepare.

6 eggs, separated	½ cup orange juice
1 cup sugar*	¼ cup chocolate liqueur, Sabra or
1 cup walnuts, coarsely chopped	Kahlúa
2 cups unsweetened shredded	1 pint strawberries (optional)
coconut*	

1. Preheat the oven to 325 degrees and grease a 9-inch springform pan.
2. In a large bowl, whip the egg whites until soft peaks form. Add ½ cup of the sugar and beat until the mixture holds stiff peaks.
3. In a smaller bowl, beat the egg yolks with the remaining sugar until the eggs are light and fluffy. Add the nuts and coconut to the egg yolks, combining gently. Fold in the egg whites.
4. Place the cake batter in the pan and bake in the oven for 45 minutes, or until the crust is light brown on top. Remove from the oven and let sit in the pan a few minutes.
5. Combine the orange juice and liqueur and pour over the torte while it is still in the pan. When the torte is thoroughly cool, place in the refrigerator until ready to serve.
6. Decorate with the fresh strawberries, if using.

*If using sweetened coconut, reduce the sugar to ½ cup, adding ¼ cup to the whites and ¼ cup to the yolks.

BARRY WINE'S APRICOT SPONGE ROLL CAKE

SERVES 10–12. (D OR P)

While nibbling on pecan squares, bread pudding with whiskey sauce, and brioche coated with cashew butter at Barry Wine's long gone New York emporium of nouvelle cuisine, the Quilted Giraffe, we once discussed the ubiquitous fruit compote and sponge cakes. Barry's choice for a Passover dessert is apricot sponge roll cake, decorated with stripes of cocoa and confectioners' sugar, reminiscent of a *tallit,* or prayer shawl.

12 ounces dried apricots	¼ teaspoon ground ginger
2 cups apricot liqueur	¼ teaspoon ground cardamom
Juice of 1 orange	½ cup matzah cake meal
Softened butter or pareve	¼ cup potato starch
margarine	⅛ teaspoon salt
6 eggs, separated	¾ cup ground hazelnuts
1 cup sugar	Cocoa powder and confectioners'
⅓ cup apricot nectar or juice	sugar for decorating

1. The day before baking, combine the apricots and apricot liqueur in a saucepan. Bring to a boil. Transfer to another container and soak overnight. Drain, reserving the liquid.
2. Preheat the oven to 350 degrees. Grease with margarine and dust with matzah cake meal the sides and bottom of a 17- by 12- by 1-inch jelly-roll pan; line with parchment paper, also greased and dusted.
3. Purée the apricots, adjusting the consistency with the juice of an orange and the reserved liquid. Set aside.
4. In a mixing bowl combine the egg yolks, ¾ cup of the sugar, apricot nectar, ginger, and cardamom. Beat at high speed until the mixture forms a ribbon.
5. Fold in the matzah cake meal and potato starch.
6. Whip the egg whites and the remaining ¼ cup of sugar and salt until they form stiff peaks. Fold the whites into the batter.

7. Pour into the jelly-roll pan and cover with greased aluminum foil. Bake for 15 minutes.

8. Remove the cake from the oven. Unmold onto a piece of parchment placed on a moist towel or apron. Roll and cool at least 1 hour.

9. Unroll the cake and moisten with the reserved apricot liqueur. Evenly spread the apricot purée over the cake. Sprinkle the ground hazelnuts over the purée. Roll the cake back up.

10. Slice the ends to make them even. Decorate with stripes of cocoa and confectioners' sugar.

BARBARA TROPP'S PECAN-GINGER TORTE

MAKES 2 TORTES. (P)

The only cook at the San Francisco chefs' Seder to depart from tradition was the late Barbara Tropp, chef-owner of the China Moon Café and author of *The Modern Art of Chinese Cooking* (Morrow). Barbara's pecan-ginger torte is reminiscent of the tortes our grandmothers made. "All I did was lower the sugar content and give it some acidic interest with ginger and lemon juice."

4 ounces raw pecans plus 18 perfect pecan halves

6 large eggs, separated

1 cup minus 2 tablespoons sugar

1 tablespoon fresh lemon juice

2 tablespoons fresh ginger juice squeezed from very finely minced or food processor–puréed fresh ginger (about ½ cup, depending on the season and moistness of the ginger)

Several twists white pepper (optional)

½ cup matzah meal

½ teaspoon coarse kosher salt

1½–2 tablespoons finely minced crystallized ginger, finely minced glacéed apricots, or thin rings of candied kumquats

1. Preheat the oven to 350 degrees. Line the bottoms of 2 pans (two 8–9-inch springforms or two 9–10-inch removable-bottom tart pans at least 1½ inches deep) with greased waxed paper.
2. Toast the 4 ounces of pecans for 15 minutes in the oven, rotating the tray once midway. Let cool.
3. Chop the toasted pecans with a sharp knife or pulse in a food processor until fine but still dry.
4. Beat the egg yolks until light. Add the sugar gradually until the yolks turn very creamy and form ribbons when the beaters are lifted.
5. Add the lemon juice, ginger juice, and pepper, if using. Beat to mix.
6. Add the ground pecans and matzah meal. Beat until blended.
7. In a large bowl, whip the egg whites until blended. Add the salt and continue whipping until the whites form firm peaks but are not dry.
8. Lightly fold the whites into the nut mixture until well blended.
9. Divide the mixture between the 2 prepared pans.
10. Sprinkle the crystallized ginger, apricots, or kumquats evenly over the top of both cakes. Space 8 pecan halves around the edges, putting the ninth in the center.
11. Bake in the middle of the bottom third of the oven 40–45 minutes, until a toothpick or cake tester inserted in the center of the cake comes out clean.
12. Let cool completely in the pan. Wrap airtight overnight. Serve with a selection of seasonal berries. Or, if having a vegetarian Seder, serve with crème chantilly or fresh ginger ice cream.

Note: This torte tastes best if eaten 1 day after baking.

MATZAH APPLE *SCHALET*

SERVES 6–8. (P)

In writing a cookbook like this, an author follows up on many leads. Perhaps one of the most fascinating for me was a visit to the late Bruno Stern of New York's Washington Heights. From Württemberg, he was truly a keeper of tradition. In the 1930s Bruno had the foresight to take photographs of the everyday life of German Jews in his hometown of Niederstetten. The result was his audiovisual presentation, "Of Times Gone By—My Town, My House, My Family." In the slide show and in a book published in Stuttgart, *Memories of My Youth in a Small Town in Württemberg and of Its Jewish Congregation*, he described Passover in a southern German town. Side by side with old photographs are pictures of the traditional holiday foods that his wife, Lisl, prepares so well.

Holiday foods were served on "Jews' porcelain." When a Jew married in the eighteenth century, he was obliged to buy a set of porcelain from the king's factory—thus the name!

Stern also had a collection of old cookbooks from the nineteenth and early twentieth centuries. The most interesting to me was the 1874 *Kochbuch* written in beautiful script by his grandmother, Rosa Muhlfelder Stern. Here is her matzah apple *schalet* recipe.

4 matzahs
2 large eggs, separated
¼ cup sugar
½ teaspoon cinnamon
Zest and juice of 1 lemon

½ cup raisins
2–3 McIntosh apples, peeled, cored, and diced
½ cup hazelnuts or almonds, coarsely ground

1. Soak the matzahs in cold water until soft, then squeeze dry.
2. Preheat the oven to 350 degrees and grease a 9-inch springform pan.
3. In a large bowl, mix the egg yolks, sugar, cinnamon, and lemon zest and juice. Add the raisins, apples, and nuts. Mix well. Combine with the matzot.
4. Whip the egg whites until stiff peaks form. Fold into the mixture and transfer to the springform pan.
5. Bake for 1 hour, or until golden. Cool, and serve at room temperature.

PASSOVER WINE CAKE

SERVES 8. (P)

This is one of those Passover nut cakes that originated in Russia and, because of its moist texture, has had great success in this country.

9 large eggs, separated
1½ cups sugar
⅔ cup matzah cake meal plus
   more to flour the cake pan
⅓ cup potato starch
1 teaspoon cinnamon

½ teaspoon ground ginger
Pinch of salt
¾ cup ground walnuts
¼ cup sweet red wine
   (approximately)

1. Preheat the oven to 350 degrees. Grease a 10-inch tube pan and dust with the cake meal.
2. Beat the egg yolks until they are foamy, gradually adding the sugar.
3. Sift together the matzah cake meal, potato starch, cinnamon, ginger, and salt. Add gradually to the egg yolks.
4. Place the ground walnuts in a cup and add enough sweet wine to fill the cup. Fold into the cake mixture.
5. Whip the egg whites until they form stiff peaks but are not dry.
6. Fold the egg whites into the yolk mixture and carefully transfer to the tube pan.
7. Bake for 50–60 minutes, or until a toothpick comes out clean. Cool slightly, then run a knife around the cake. Flip out onto a plate and serve.

ORANGE-CHOCOLATE PASSOVER CAKE

SERVES 10. (P)

Once in a while, someone writes me about a favorite recipe. Gary Stotsky, a speech therapist in York, Pennsylvania, wrote because he liked the wine cake recipe for Passover. He then shared his favorite Passover dessert recipe. The cake is delicious, and leftovers can be diced, soaked in Sabra liqueur, and served with whipped cream and orange slices for a divine Passover trifle.

9 eggs, separated
1 cup sugar
1 cup ground almonds or walnuts
½ cup chopped almonds or walnuts
1 tablespoon potato starch
3 tablespoons sifted matzah cake meal plus more to flour the cake pan

1 tablespoon powdered instant coffee
4 ounces bittersweet chocolate, coarsely grated
Grated zest of 1 large orange

1. Preheat the oven to 350 degrees. Grease a 9–10-inch tube pan with pareve shortening or oil and dust with cake meal.
2. Whip the egg whites until foamy. Slowly add ½ cup of sugar while beating until stiff but not dry. Set aside.
3. Beat the egg yolks with the remaining ½ cup sugar. Fold the yolks into the whites. Gently fold the remaining ingredients into the egg mixture.
4. Pour the batter into the tube pan.
5. Bake for 45 minutes. Cool slightly, then run a knife around the cake. Flip out onto a plate and serve.

BEET *EINGEMACHTS*

(Beet Preserves)

MAKES ABOUT 2 PINTS. (P)

Eva Lubetkin Kantor was the youngest of thirteen children growing up in New York City at the turn of the century. Her father, who was born in Lithuania, was the first to introduce machine-made matzahs; he later went into the wholesale flour business.

In a family oral history, Eva, who died in 2000 at the age of 102, recaptured the past. Passover was "like preparing for a wedding," she said. "My mother prepared gallons of beet *eingemachts*." These beet preserves were eaten with a spoon and used as a condiment with meat or poultry or spread on matzah. *Eingemachts* could also be made from radishes and carrots. "I can still see the maids scraping the beets and getting their faces and arms all speckled with red dots. We kids used to get a bang out of that. When it was time to prepare the almonds, they had to be shelled. The most fun was when my mother poured boiling water over the nuts and we had to get the brown covering off. They were slippery, and we would shoot them at each other. When the preserves were finished, they were put into ten-gallon crocks."

Eva, until the age of ninety-nine, made and sent containers of *eingemachts* to family members around the country. Today, her daughter and one of her nieces continue the tradition.

¾ cup water
2 cups sugar
2 pounds beets

2 medium lemons
1 tablespoon ground ginger
1 cup sliced blanched almonds

1. Pour the water over the sugar. Mix well in a large enamel saucepan. Bring to a boil slowly and let simmer, uncovered, while you prepare the beets.
2. Peel and cut the beets in half, then into thin strips. Cut the unpeeled lemons in half and then into thin strips. (If you have a food processor, the grating blade is perfect for this step.)

3. Add the beet and lemon strips to the sugar mixture. Cover and let simmer slowly about 1½ hours, stirring occasionally. Do not let them stick.

4. Uncover and add the ginger. Simmer about another 30 minutes, or until you test it with a spoon to see if it is thick. Turn off the heat and let it cool overnight.

5. Next day, toast the almonds and fold them into the cold preserves. Seal in a jam jar.

SHAVUOT

SHAVUOT

Honey and milk are under thy tongue.

Song of Songs 4:11

A mountain of God is the mountain of Bashan;
A mountain of peaks is the mountain of Bashan.
Why look ye askance, ye mountains of peaks,
At the mountain which God hath desired for His abode?
Yes, the Lord will dwell therein for ever.

Psalm 68:16–17

Shavuot, or the Feast of Weeks, comes seven weeks after Passover and was originally the celebration of the completion of the barley harvest with the sacrificial offering of the first fruits at the Temple. Later, it came to commemorate the giving of the Ten Commandments on Mount Sinai.

It is customary to eat dairy food at Shavuot. How do dairy dishes fit into a barley harvest festival? At this time of year, late May or early June, such foods are eaten because of the large amount of cheese produced. Churning and cheese-making are common features of spring harvest festivals the world over, when goats, sheep, and cows begin to graze more and thus produce more milk.

As if a pastoral explanation were not enough, Jewish scholars have discovered additional ones. In the above psalm, for example, Mount Sinai, on which the Ten Commandments were given, is called by six different names—mountain of God, mountain of Bashan, and mountain of peaks (*har gavnunim*) are mentioned in the psalm. *Gavnunim* means "gibbous, many-peaked," but the word has the same root as *gevinah,* Hebrew for cheese. Thus it could also be called Cheese Mountain, a common folk image. Accordingly, the eating of cheese at this season is a reminder of the giving of the Law. In addition, the Torah is likened to milk and honey in the Song of Songs.

Another explanation for cheese eating is that by the time the Israelites had returned to their camp after receiving the Ten Commandments, so much time had elapsed that their milk had turned sour—the first step in making cheese.

According to another rabbinic source, the Israelites fasted while they went to receive the Ten Commandments and returned so hungry that they drank milk immediately rather than go through the long process of preparing a meat meal. To this day, some Jews have first a milk meal at Shavuot, followed by a meat one.

At the celebration of the barley harvest, two loaves of bread were offered in the Temple. They were often shaped in long loaves with four corners to symbolize the four methods of interpreting the scriptural text: the simple, the esoteric, the homiletical, and the allegorical meanings. The Torah is also likened to bread; thus the long Shavuot loaf symbolizes the length and breadth of the Law.

MENUS

HUNGARIAN
Cold Sour Cherry Soup
Rachal (Fish with Sour Cream and Potatoes)
Green Salad
Palacsinta Filled with Cheese or Apricot Preserves

AMERICAN DAIRY
Wolfie's Borscht
Zamosc Gefilte Fish or Pickled Carp Bread
Grossinger's Blintzes Filled with Cheese

DAIRY LUNCH
Palestinian Fruit Soup
Heidi Wortzel's Cheese Knishes
Herring in Sour Cream
Salad
Fresh Strawberries
Cheesecake

MOROCCAN
Sephardic Cold Spicy Fish
Spinach Soufflé
Moroccan Carrot Salad
Yogurt with Sugar

SYRIAN CHEESE *SAMBUSAK*

(Cheese Turnovers)

From Mansoura Middle Eastern Pastries

MAKES ABOUT 60 SAMBUSAK. (D)

A Syrian Jewish home today would not be Syrian without a freezer filled with cheese *sambusak*. "Syrian women make them for breakfast, for a card game, for a brit or a bar mitzvah," said Josiane Mansoura, whose store is always stocked with these filled crescent-shaped pastries. "More are eaten at Shavuot than at any other holiday."

Originally stuffed with the goat cheese of Syria, *sambusak* can be made with Muenster, the Balkan cheese *kashkeval*, or any hard gratable cheese. Semolina adds a crunchy texture to the dough, which in this particular version is baked, a healthier alternative to the traditional fried version. *Sambusak* stuffed with chicken or potatoes are eaten as well by Indian, Iraqi, and Persian Jews.

THE DOUGH:

1½ cups *smead** (semolina, not semolina flour)

3 cups unbleached all-purpose flour

Dash of salt

3 tablespoons vegetable oil

12 tablespoons (1½ sticks) unsalted butter, at room temperature

¾ cup cold water

THE FILLING:†

4 large eggs

2 pounds Muenster cheese, grated, or, for a tangier filling, 3 parts grated Muenster to 1 part crumbled feta cheese

Dash of salt

2 cups sesame seeds

*Available at Middle Eastern markets.
†See also the spinach filling on page 415.

1. Mix the semolina with the all-purpose flour in a large bowl. Add the salt, oil, and butter. With a fork or your fingers, work in the butter until the dough is lumpy; do not overmix. Add the water, a little at a time, bringing the dough together until it is smooth and pliable. (You can also make the dough in a food processor fitted with the steel blade, pulsing as you mix in the butter and then the water a little at a time.) Set the dough aside.

2. To prepare the filling, beat the eggs and combine with the grated cheese and salt. The mixture should be slightly dry.

3. Preheat the oven to 350 degrees and grease 2 cookie sheets.

4. Place the sesame seeds on a large plate. Tear the dough into walnut-size pieces and roll them with your hands into 1-inch balls. Flatten them slightly and dip one side into the sesame seeds. Then flatten to an ⅛-inch thickness with a rolling pin, your hands, or a tortilla press. If using a tortilla press, cover with plastic wrap so the dough doesn't stick to the press.

5. With the sesame-seed side of the dough circle facing down, place 1 table-spoon of the filling in the middle of the circle. Fold one side over the other to form a half moon. Press the edges to close, and crimp them, if desired. Place the *sambusak* on the 2 cookie sheets, leaving ½ inch between them.

6. Bake the *sambusak* for 20–25 minutes on the middle and lower racks of the oven until slightly golden, switching racks after 10 minutes. Do not overcook.

VARIATION: SPINACH FILLING

20 ounces fresh spinach, cleaned and chopped	4 ounces goat cheese, crumbled
	Salt and freshly ground pepper

Fill each *sambusak* with 1 tablespoon spinach and ½ teaspoon goat cheese. Lightly sprinkle with salt and pepper. Fold over, seal, and bake as above.

HUNGARIAN *POGACSA*

(Sweet Biscuits)

From Alex Lichtman

MAKES ABOUT 20 *POGACSA*. (D)

I will never forget the first time I tasted *pogacsa* at the home of Cissie Klavens, Alex Lichtman's daughter (see pages 194–95). She served them with homemade apricot jam. Since then, these round buttery biscuits, a cross between a scone and a brioche, have become my special-occasion breakfast treat. They are also wonderful with tea.

George Lang, the doyen of Hungarian cuisine, serves tiny versions of *pogacsa* as hors d'oeuvres at his Gundel's Restaurant in Budapest. Alex Lichtman used to make his with *griebenes* (rendered goose-fat cracklings) in the old Hungarian Jewish way. Originally a simple wheat bread baked in ashes, coming from the Turkish *bogaca*, *pogacsa* became progressively enriched through the centuries until its present glorious state, translated below.

1 scant tablespoon (1 package) active dry yeast	1 teaspoon salt
3 tablespoons warm milk	¼ teaspoon vanilla extract
½ pound (2 sticks) unsalted butter, at room temperature	¼ cup plus 2 tablespoons sugar
3½ cups unbleached all-purpose flour	½ cup sour cream
	2 large egg yolks
	1 large egg, beaten

1. In a small bowl, mix the yeast with the warm milk.
2. In an electric mixer fitted with the paddle, beat together the butter, 3 cups of the flour, the salt, and the vanilla on low speed for 2 minutes.
3. Add the sugar and continue beating on low speed for 2 more minutes. Add the sour cream, yeast mixture, and egg yolks. Continue beating on low speed for 3 minutes more, then 2 more minutes on medium speed. The dough will form a ball quickly.

4. Place the dough on a work surface covered with the remaining ½ cup flour and roll it out to a rectangle about 9 by 13 inches, ½ inch thick. Working from the shorter side, fold one-third of the dough up; then fold the top third of the dough down and over it, like a business letter. Refrigerate in a lightly floured pan for 15 minutes. Then repeat the procedure: Roll out the dough again, fold again, and refrigerate again for 15 minutes.

5. Roll out the dough to a rectangle ⅓ inch thick and brush with the beaten egg. This time, fold the 2 shorter ends of the rectangle in to meet at the center, then fold in half the other way. Cover and refrigerate the dough overnight.

6. Remove the dough from the refrigerator and let it soften about 10 minutes before rolling. Then roll the dough out on a lightly floured board to a rectangle about 8 by 10 inches, ¾ inch thick. For decoration, use the tip of a knife to gently draw diagonal lines about ¼ inch apart to make a grid or crisscross pattern.

7. Using a floured 2-inch round cookie cutter, cut out circles of dough and place them on 2 greased cookie sheets. Scrape up the dough scraps, roll out again, and cut more biscuits. Brush the biscuits with the beaten egg, then allow them to rise and dry for 35 minutes.

8. Preheat the oven to 350 degrees. Again, lightly brush the biscuits with the beaten egg.

9. Bake the *pogacsa* on the middle rack of the oven for 20–25 minutes, or until lightly golden. Serve with apricot jam.

MEA SHEARIM CHEESE DANISH

From Brizel's Bakery

MAKES 2 LARGE DANISH OR 36 INDIVIDUAL DANISH. (D)

This old-fashioned cheese Danish, made with a buttery yeast dough and filled with farmer cheese, is one of the most popular pastries at this well-known Jerusalem bakery. Mr. Brizel let me watch the process of smearing butter onto the dough and then folding it in. He shared the recipe with me before he ran off to late-morning prayers with his father.

Retired baker Fred Loeb kindly spent a day teaching me how to translate this process into a great cheese Danish.

Unfortunately, Danish making is a dying art. In most bakeries today, the convenient commercial puff pastry and cream cheese have replaced Danish dough and the authentic farmer cheese filling.

THE DOUGH:

¾ cup sugar

¼ pound (1 stick) plus 2 tablespoons unsalted butter, pareve margarine, or vegetable shortening, at room temperature

½ teaspoon salt

½ teaspoon vanilla extract

Grated zest of ½ lemon

3 large eggs

1 large egg yolk

1½ cups cold water

1 scant tablespoon (1 package) active dry yeast

4 cups unbleached all-purpose flour, plus more for sprinkling

¼ cup slivered toasted almonds for garnish (optional)

Confectioners' sugar for garnish (optional)

THE FILLING:

1½ pounds farmer cheese, drained

3 cups sugar

6 tablespoons unsalted butter

3 large eggs

Pinch of salt

⅓ cup unbleached all-purpose flour

1½ teaspoons vanilla extract

THE DOUGH:

1. In the bowl of an electric mixer fitted with the paddle, cream ¼ cup of the sugar with 3 tablespoons of the butter, margarine, or vegetable shortening, the salt, vanilla, and lemon zest. Add 2 of the eggs, the egg yolk, and 1 cup of the water and mix well, about 4 minutes.

2. Attach the dough hook and gradually add the yeast and flour as you continue mixing for about 5 minutes at medium speed. The dough will be very sticky.

3. Sprinkle flour on your hands and on the dough, remove the dough from the bowl, and place it on a floured surface. Gently pat the dough out into a rectangle about 6 by 8 inches and fold it in half over itself. Repeat this process

about 6 times, turning the dough a quarter turn each time. Then, still using your hands, pat the dough into a rectangle about 8 by 10 inches. Cut up the remaining butter into tiny pieces and place on two-thirds of the dough, leaving a shorter side free of butter. Take this unbuttered third and fold over the center third. Then take the remaining one-third and fold it over the center third. You will now have dough folded in thirds, like a business letter.

4. Roll the dough out with a rolling pin to a rectangle about 8 by 14 inches. Fold in thirds from a shorter side, dusting off the excess flour. Let the dough rest for 5 minutes.

5. Roll the dough out again to another rectangle 8 by 14 inches and fold in thirds from a shorter side, as above. Cover the dough with a towel and let it rest for 15 minutes in the refrigerator. Repeat this rolling and folding in thirds process 3 more times and refrigerate. A baker's trick to help remember which roll you are on is to use your thumb to make 1, 2, 3, or 4 indentations in the dough.

6. Refrigerate at least 30 minutes or overnight.

FILLING AND BAKING THE DANISH:

7. Put all the ingredients for the filling in a food processor fitted with the steel blade. Pulse just until smooth. Refrigerate for several hours.

8. Take one half of the dough and roll it out on a lightly floured board to a rectangle 11 by 14 inches, ¼ inch thick. Whisk the remaining egg in a small bowl

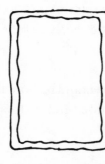

| Brush dough surface with egg wash | Spread with filling, leaving 1-inch border | Fold | Brush egg wash over top of Danish |

to make an egg wash. Brush this wash over the dough surface. Spread with half the cheese filling, leaving a 1-inch border. From a longer side, fold one third over the middle third, and then fold the remaining third over the dough. Brush the top with the egg wash. Repeat this process with the other half of the dough. Let the Danish rise, covered, for another hour on a greased cookie sheet. (In place of this rising, you can freeze the Danish at this point. Defrost 4 hours at room temperature, on a greased cookie sheet, before baking.)

9. Preheat the oven to 400 degrees. Place the sheet with the 2 Danish on the middle rack and bake for 20 minutes, or until golden brown.

TOPPING THE DANISH:

10. While the Danish are baking, place the remaining ½ cup water and ½ cup sugar in a saucepan to make a syrup. Bring to a boil and let boil for 3–4 minutes, uncovered. Turn off the heat.

11. Remove the Danish from the oven and brush the warm syrup over them. Scatter slivered almonds on top or dust with confectioners' sugar. Let the Danish cool before serving them. Better yet, serve them the next day.

VARIATION: INDIVIDUAL DANISH

1. Once you have completed steps 1–6 above, roll out one half of the dough on a lightly floured board to a square about 16 by 16 inches, ⅛ inch thick. Cut into 4-inch squares, brush each with the egg wash, and place a heaping tablespoon of filling in the center of each square. Fold 2 opposite corners in over the filling so they meet at the center, and then the other 2 opposite corners. Brush again with the egg wash. Repeat this process with the other half of the dough. Remove to 2 greased cookie sheets. Let the Danish sit about 1 hour, covered.

2. Preheat the oven to 400 degrees.

3. Place the Danish on the cookie sheets and bake them 15–20 minutes, or until golden brown. Follow the instructions under "Topping the Danish" above.

COLD SOUR CHERRY SOUP

SERVES 6–8. (M)

When my Hungarian-born grandfather, Henry Gluck, was in his nineties, I used to go with him to Tik Tak, a marvelous Hungarian restaurant on Second Avenue in New York. One of my favorite dishes was a cold sour cherry soup. Ava Ehrlich, who emigrated from Budapest to Bethesda, Maryland, shared this recipe with me. The addition of wine makes it a sweet alternative to Bloody Marys for a Sunday brunch.

Two 20-ounce cans or 2 pounds fresh pitted sour cherries

1 cup sugar, or to taste

1 cinnamon stick

1 cup sour cream, plus additional for garnish

1 cup dry red wine (optional)

1. Drain the canned cherries and pour the juice in a saucepan. Set the cherries aside. Add enough water to the juice to make 3 cups. If using fresh cherries, add 3 cups water. Add the sugar and the cinnamon stick. Bring to a boil, stirring to dissolve the sugar, and add the cherries. Partially cover and simmer over low heat for 10–15 minutes.
2. Remove the cinnamon stick. Remove a few cherries (and return them later for texture) and blend the rest in a food processor equipped with a steel blade until smooth.
3. Bring the soup back to a boil. Let it cool a bit and then whisk in the sour cream, letting it dissolve. Add the reserved cherries and chill.
4. Before serving, add the wine, if using. Garnish each bowl with a dollop of sour cream or pass the sour cream at the table.

PALESTINIAN FRUIT SOUP

SERVES 6. (D)

Every synagogue cookbook needs at least one or two prime movers to complete the always-more-tedious-than-expected project. Cleveland's Rebecca Brickner, wife of the late Rabbi Barnett Brickner and mother of Rabbi Balfour Brickner of New York, is just such a person. It was she who was the honorary chairman of the Fairmont Cookbook Committee in 1957. *The Fairmont Cookbook* is, to my mind, still one of the finest of the many synagogue cookbooks.

Mrs. Brickner learned to make the fruit soup recipe featured in the book as a student in Palestine in 1931–32. Fruit soups have become extremely popular in Israel; they originated with German Jews who began making them while summering on the shores of the Baltic.

2 oranges, peeled and diced
2 stalks rhubarb, cut in pieces
About ¼ of a fresh pineapple
1 cup strawberries, hulled
1 cup cherries, pitted
6 cups water

1 cup brown sugar or honey
½ teaspoon salt
½ teaspoon cinnamon
2 tablespoons lemon juice
1 cup sour cream

1. Combine the oranges, rhubarb, pineapple, strawberries, cherries, water, brown sugar or honey, salt, cinnamon, and lemon juice.
2. Simmer, covered, for about 20 minutes, or until the fruit is tender.
3. Purée in a blender or food processor or force through a sieve.
4. Chill thoroughly and add the sour cream before serving.

Note: Other fruits may be substituted, but make sure there is a combination of tart and sweet.

WOLFIE'S BORSCHT

SERVES 10. (D)

The epithet "Borscht Belt" was coined in an article in *Variety* when a journalist described the Jewish hotels in the Catskills as the place where so many vaudeville actors got their start and where Russian borscht was a menu staple. Since then, borscht, originally a Ukrainian dish, has been associated with Jews.

The following cold borscht recipe comes from Wolfie's Restaurant, once the Sardi's and Lindy's of Miami Beach. It is another fresh hot-weather drink.

2½ pounds beets, peeled and diced (or quartered)

1 onion, sliced

1 stalk celery, chopped

2½ quarts water

½–1 cup sugar

1 tablespoon sour salt (citric acid) or lemon juice

Salt

6 large eggs, slightly beaten

Sour cream

Fresh dill, chopped (optional)

1. Simmer the beets, onion, and celery in the water, covered, for about 40 minutes, or until the beets are tender.
2. Add the sugar and sour salt or lemon juice. Strain the soup or place in a blender and purée. Add salt to taste. The strained beet juice will keep for several days in the refrigerator.
3. Return the soup to a simmer. Add 1 cup of soup to the eggs, whisking constantly, then slowly beat the eggs into the rest of the soup. Remove from the heat and let the soup cool. Top each bowl with sour cream and, if you like, sprinkle with chopped fresh dill.

RADISHES IN SOUR CREAM

SERVES 6. (D)

Black radishes were eaten as snacks, sliced with onion on black bread, and turned into *eingemachts* (preserves) in the poor shtetls of Eastern Europe. The wide use of sour cream, too, came from this area. Served generously over vegetables, sour cream makes a popular main dish for a milk meal. It is also poured over cottage cheese, used as a dressing for blintzes, and served on radishes.

Poor Jews would include only one salad in a main milk meal, but for the rich a radish salad might be one of the many fish and vegetable appetizers that began each meal.

1 bunch red radishes	1 teaspoon vinegar
½ teaspoon salt	Sprinkling of black pepper
3 tablespoons sour cream	

1. Rinse and dry the radishes. Slice them thin, but not paper-thin. Place them in a shallow dish and sprinkle with salt. Put a weight such as a heavy plate on top. After 30 minutes, drain off the excess water.
2. Place the radish slices in a bowl, stir in the sour cream and vinegar, and sprinkle with the pepper. Serve chilled.

THOMAS JEFFERSON'S FRIED FISH, JEWISH FASHION

Thomas Jefferson was a remarkable man. Among his many talents, he was this country's first well-known gourmet. It was he who had the foresight to import to the United States macaroni, Parmesan cheese, figs, raisins, almonds, mustard, good vinegar, oil, anchovies, and vanilla.

At Monticello he built a small outdoor fish pond adjacent to the house. Local fish were caught in nets in nearby streams and lakes and then placed in his pool, whereby he could have fresh fish whenever he wished.

It seems that one of his favorite recipes was fried fish, Jewish fashion. This we know from a collection of favorite recipes assembled by his granddaughter, Virginia Randolph, who grew up in her grandfather's home. Without her grandfather's original, she may have found a written recipe for a dish in *A Shilling Cookery Book for the People*, written in 1855 by Alexis Soyer, the noted chef of London's exclusive Reform Club.

To this day, English Jews eat fried fish on Friday night, having the cold leftovers the following day. Brought to England by Dutch Jews originally from Spain and Portugal, the dish was possibly tasted by Jefferson during his sojourn in Europe or later at the home of a Virginia or Georgia Jew.

Here is what Soyer had to say about Fried Fish, Jewish Fashion:

> *Here is another excellent way of frying fish, which is constantly in use by the children of Israel, and I cannot recommend it too highly; so much so, that various kinds of fish which many people despise, are excellent cooked by this process; in eating them many persons are deceived, and would suppose them to be the most expensive of fish. The process is at once simple, effective, and economical; not that I would recommend it for invalids, as the process imbibes some of the fat, which, however palatable, would not do for the dyspeptic or invalid.*
>
> *Proceed thus:—Cut one or two pounds of halibut in one piece, lay it in a dish, cover the top with a little salt, put some water in the dish, but not to cover the fish; let it remain thus for one hour. The water being below, causes the salt to penetrate into the fish. Take it out and dry it; cut out the bone, and the fins off; it is then in two pieces. Lay the pieces on the side, and divide them into slices half an inch thick; put into a frying pan, with a quarter of a pound of fat, lard, or dripping (the Jews use oil); then put two ounces of flour into a soup-plate, or basin, which mix with water, to form a smooth batter, not too thick. Dip the fish in it, that the pieces are well covered, then have the fat, not too hot, put the pieces in it, and fry till a nice colour, turning them over. When done, take it out with a slice, let it drain, dish up, and serve. Any kind of sauce that is liked may be used with it; but plain, with a little salt and lemon, is excellent. This fish is often only threepence to*

fourpence per pound; it containing but little bone renders it very economical. It is excellent cold, and can be eaten with oil, vinegar, and cucumbers, in summer time, and is exceedingly cooling. An egg is an improvement in the batter.

The same fish as before mentioned as fit for frying, may be fried in this manner. Eels are excellent done so; the batter absorbs the oil which is in them.

Flounders may also be done in this way. A little salt should be sprinkled over before serving.

In some Jewish families all this kind of fish is fried in oil, and dipped in batter, as described below. In some families they dip the fish first in flour, and then in egg, and fry in oil. This plan is superior to that fried in fat or dripping, but more expensive.

Many of the above-mentioned families have stated days on which they fry, or stew their fish, which will keep good several days in summer, and I may almost say, weeks in winter; and being generally eaten cold, it saves them a deal of cooking. Still, I must say that there is nothing like a hot dinner.

And here is Thomas Jefferson's recipe made more modern in the late Marie Kimball's compilation of *Thomas Jefferson's Cook Book.*

FRIED FISH, JEWISH FASHION

Take a pound piece of halibut, lay in a dish. Sprinkle salt on the top and put some water in the dish, about half way up the fish. Let stand one hour. Take it out, dry it, cut out the bones. It is then in two pieces. Lay the pieces on their side and cut in slices one-half inch thick. Put ¼ pound of any desired fat in a frying pan. Mix four tablespoonfuls of flour with one egg and a little water to form a smooth batter, not too thick. Dip the fish in this, until well covered, drop in the hot fat and fry to a golden brown. Drain in brown paper, put on platter and serve. Any desired sauce may be used, but plain, with salt and lemon is usual. Other fish may be done in this way.

RACHAL

(Fish with Sour Cream and Potatoes)

SERVES 6. (D)

Rachal is a delicious Hungarian fish dish that Jews prepare on Shavuot, when it coincides with Friday night. The Jews replaced the bacon of the original recipe with butter.

6 medium boiling potatoes
¼–½ pound (1–2 sticks) butter
Salt
Paprika
3 pounds carp, rockfish, or
  haddock (half of a 6-pound
  fish with head removed,

bones intact, and cut in 6
  steaks)
1 tablespoon bread crumbs
1 tablespoon chopped fresh dill
1 cup sour cream

1. Preheat the oven to 350 degrees.
2. Boil the potatoes in their skins. When they are cool enough to handle, peel them and slice them thinly.
3. Liberally butter a baking-serving casserole, such as an oblong gratin dish. Layer the bottom of the casserole with the potato slices. Sprinkle with salt and paprika to taste. Continue layering until all the potatoes are placed in the casserole.
4. Place the fish on top of the potatoes. Sprinkle the fish with about 1 tablespoon paprika, 1 teaspoon salt, the bread crumbs, and dill. Dot with the remaining butter. Cover the fish with the sour cream and bake for 30 minutes, or until the fish flakes easily with a fork. (This dish can also include green pepper and tomato slices.)

GROSSINGER'S BLINTZES

*Golde appeared with the blintzes piled high on a platter, plump and juicy,
and "sweet as the life-giving manna from heaven."*

Sholem Aleichem, "Schprintze"

Blinchiki, the ancestors of blintzes, were brought to other parts of Russia and
Poland, as well as to the United States, by Jews from the Ukraine. Unlike the
Russian blini, they are not yeast risen. Blintzes are filled with blueberries, strawberries, or more usually a combination of farmer cheese and eggs, and then
baked or fried. Spread with cinnamon or sugar or sour cream, they are delicious.

The following recipe comes from that haven of mammoth meals, Grossinger's. Grossinger's opened in 1914 as a boardinghouse in New York's Catskill
mountains for poor sweatshop workers who needed a place in the country. It
advertised three healthy, well-balanced meals and fresh air for congested lungs.
The word spread quickly, and trainloads of people went up to the Catskills.

Until it closed, the menus at Grossinger's included endless choices, although
my husband insists the portions had decreased since his days as a waiter in the
Catskills. A *milchig* lunch included such items as cold borscht with a boiled
potato; their famous pickled herring in cream; marinated carp; heavy sour cream
with bananas, peaches, or fresh strawberries; and, of course, Grossinger's famous
blintzes with blueberries and sour cream.

BATTER:

MAKES ABOUT 18. (P OR D)

3 large eggs
1 cup milk or water
½ teaspoon salt

2 tablespoons vegetable oil
¾ cup sifted all-purpose flour
Butter or oil for frying

1. Beat the eggs, milk, salt, and oil together. Stir in the flour.
2. Heat a little butter or oil in a 6-inch skillet, preferably nonstick. Pour about
   2 tablespoons of the batter into it, tilting the pan to coat the bottom. Use just

enough batter to make a very thin pancake. Let the bottom brown, then carefully turn out onto a plate, browned side up. Make the rest of the pancakes the same way, adding butter and oil to the pan if the pancakes begin to stick.

3. Spread 1 heaping tablespoon of the cheese or blueberry filling, or apple jelly, along one side of the pancake. Turn the opposite sides in and roll the pancake up like a jelly roll.

4. You can then fry the blintzes in butter or oil or bake them in a single layer in a 425-degree oven until brown. Serve dairy blintzes with sour cream.

SOUR CREAM BATTER:

MAKES ABOUT 16. (D)

1 large egg	⅛ teaspoon salt
¼ cup milk	1 cup sifted all-purpose flour
¾ cup sour cream	Butter for frying

1. Preheat the oven to 450 degrees.

2. Beat together the egg, milk, sour cream, and salt. Stir in the flour, mixing until smooth.

3. Heat some butter in a 6-inch skillet. Pour about 2 tablespoons of the batter into it, tilting the pan to spread the batter evenly. Fry until browned and turn to brown the other side.

4. Place a heaping tablespoon of cheese filling on each pancake. Tuck in the opposite sides and roll up like a jelly roll. Arrange the blintzes in a buttered baking dish and bake 10 minutes. This batter makes a rich pancake and is suitable for fruit fillings.

CHEESE FILLING:

(D)

2 cups farmer cheese	2 tablespoons sugar (optional)
1 egg yolk	1 teaspoon fresh lemon juice
½ teaspoon salt	½ teaspoon vanilla extract
1 tablespoon butter	

In a small bowl, mash the farmer cheese. Stir in the egg yolk, salt, butter, sugar, if using, lemon juice, and vanilla.

BLUEBERRY FILLING:

(D)

1½ cups blueberries	1 tablespoon cornstarch
3 tablespoons sugar	⅛ teaspoon ground nutmeg

Toss all the ingredients together in a bowl. For another sweet filling, see page 385.

Note: Blintzes can be filled, then frozen, without losing taste or texture. Do *not* thaw them before frying or baking—just cook longer.

If you use cottage cheese instead of farmer cheese, it must be drained through cheesecloth or a sieve; otherwise the filling will be too loose.

If you don't wish the blintzes to be sweet, leave the sugar out of the filling.

HUNGARIAN CHERRY EVEN-WEIGHT CAKE

(Egyensuly)

SERVES 8. (D)

This "even-weight" cake is literally a pound cake, which often includes a pound or thereabouts of eggs weighed in their shells. Flour, butter, and sugar are then added to equal the weight of the eggs. This recipe calls for about ¾ pound of each ingredient.

¾ pound (3 sticks) unsalted butter	Pinch of salt
¾ pound (1½ cups) sugar	Grated zest of 1 lemon
¾ pound (about 6) large eggs	1 pound sweet or sour pitted cherries or sliced peaches
¾ pound (about 3 cups) sifted all-purpose flour	

1. Preheat the oven to 350 degrees and grease and flour a 9-inch springform, Bundt, or loaf pan.
2. Cream the butter and sugar extremely well with an electric mixer or food processor.
3. Add the eggs, 1 at a time, beating well after each addition.
4. Sift the flour with the pinch of salt 4 times through a sifter held high in the air. This adds more air to the cake, making it lighter.
5. Add the flour gradually and the lemon zest to the batter. Mix well, being sure to scrape the sides of the bowl back into the mixture.
6. Fold in the cherries or peaches.
7. Pour the batter into the greased pan and bake for 1 hour, or until the cake springs back when touched and pulls away from the sides of the pan. Cool on a rack and turn out.

VIENNESE TORTES

"I wasn't educated for anything," stated Alice Broch, the original Viennese baker behind Cambridge's celebrated Window Shop bakery on Brattle Street. "In the Vienna of Franz Liszt, Gustav Mahler, and Johann Strauss, a proper young girl's education included music, languages, and cooking: to play lilting waltzes on the piano, to speak the languages of the countries near Vienna, and to prepare the delicacies for the food-conscious Viennese."

When in the 1930s Mrs. Broch felt the growing horror of Hitler's policies toward the Jews, she realized she would have to prepare for a new life elsewhere. Deciding to bring with her the secrets of Viennese pastry, she sat down each day with her cook, Maria, and copied the recipes for all the marvelous meringues, tortes, and rich creams of her youth. "I knew that my musical talents would not be sufficient to help me get by in the United States, but I did think that there might be a demand for Viennese pastry."

How right Mrs. Broch was! When she arrived in Boston with her husband, two sons, and Maria's cookbook, she was practically penniless. The reception she and other formerly well-to-do, educated Jewish and non-Jewish refugees received from the Cambridge community, however, proved a wonderful surprise. Shortly after arriving, Mrs. Broch met the directors of the already existing Window Shop, which then specialized in handicrafts made by refugees. One board member said to her, "You are Viennese and all Viennese are good cooks." Urging Mrs. Broch to start a bakery, she handed her a check for $300. Before she knew it, Mrs. Broch and two immigrant friends were adapting Maria's Viennese recipes to fit the proportions of American ingredients.

As Mrs. Broch told it, the Window Shop success story was not without its measure of hard work. "My day began at 5:00 a.m." In the early years, she had to experiment with Maria's recipes, adjusting them to the new measurements, flours, sugars, chocolate, etc. First, she had to transfer grams to pounds and ounces and then to convert Viennese flour to our pastry, bread, and cake flour. Whereas in Vienna there was one kind of sugar, we use three—granulated, superfine, and confectioners'. When a recipe in Maria's book called for *vier Tafeln Schokolade*—four tablets of chocolate—Mrs. Broch had to figure out the exact weight of an Austrian tablet.

At first she had to make fondant, an elaborately prepared sugar icing used in Austrian tortes—first boiling sugar and water to the soft-ball stage, cooling to tepid, kneading, and finally mixing with chocolate and butter—until she learned she could buy fifty-pound cans of fondant ready-made.

While we in this country normally use dry yeast, Mrs. Broch was accustomed to wet yeast. Then there was the absence of European baking tins, which after some time she was able to locate in New York. To give one example, Mrs. Broch experimented eleven times with the famous Linzertorte until she reached the correct formula.

Viennese pastry is rarely from Vienna. Vienna was the crossroads of Central Europe, located so close to Italy, France, and Germany that the cooking was always influenced by its neighbors, keeping the best of each. Streusel cakes—sponge cakes topped with fruit and a butter, flour, and sugar crumb mixture—are Czech. Linzertorte is from the Austrian town of Linz, and Dobos torte is a rich chocolate-layered wonder from the Hungarian town of Dobos.

Regardless of the origin of a particular Viennese pastry, one thing is certain: only the best-quality sweet butter, chocolate, almonds, hazelnuts, flour, eggs, and sugar serve as the ingredients, with delicate hand decorations as the finishing touch. Vienna is especially well known for its tortes, round cakes with either ground nuts or flour and sometimes a combination of both.

Following are two recipes adapted from Maria's handwritten book.

BLITZ MERINGUE TORTE

SERVES 8. (D)

CREAM FILLING:

1 large egg

3 tablespoons sugar

1 tablespoon cornstarch

1 cup sour cream

Zest and a few drops of juice from
    1 lemon

TORTE:

4 tablespoons (½ stick) unsalted
    butter, softened

⅓ cup sugar

3 egg yolks

1 cup all-purpose flour

½ tablespoon baking powder

¼ cup light cream

MERINGUE:

3 egg whites

¼ teaspoon cream of tartar

¾ cup sugar

1 teaspoon almond extract

¾ cup slivered almonds

Whipped cream or jam

1. Preheat the oven to 275 degrees and grease and flour two 8-inch round pans.
2. Prepare the filling: Mix together the egg, sugar, cornstarch, and sour cream of the filling and cook in a double boiler, stirring constantly, until thick, about 5 minutes. Remove from the heat and allow the mixture to cool.
3. Add the lemon zest and juice and set aside in the refrigerator.
4. For the torte, cream together the butter, sugar, and egg yolks.
5. Sift the flour with the baking powder. Add the flour to the butter mixture, alternating with the light cream. Blend very well.
6. Divide the batter between the 2 greased pans. Don't be surprised if the batter is heavy and there is very little of it.
7. For the meringue, whip the egg whites with the cream of tartar until soft peaks form. Then gradually add the sugar and the almond extract, all the time whipping the egg whites until stiff.
8. Top the batter in the cake pans with the meringue mixture. Sprinkle some of the almonds on one of the cakes.

9. Bake for 30 minutes, or until the top is firm and slightly golden. Cool in the pans until lukewarm. Turn out the tortes and cool on a cake rack so that the meringue is facing up.

10. When the tortes are cool, spread the sour cream filling over the bottom layer and place the almond-coated one on top.

11. To add a final decorative (and delicious) touch, use a spatula to spread the sides with whipped cream or jam. With your hand, spread the remaining almonds on the cream or jam. Store in a cool place.

BLUEBERRY STREUSEL TORTE

SERVES 8. (D)

STREUSEL:

3 tablespoons unsalted butter
⅓ cup confectioners' sugar
½ cup all-purpose flour

1 teaspoon cinnamon
¼ cup grated almonds or walnuts
   (optional)

TORTE:

5 tablespoons unsalted butter,
   pareve margarine, or vegetable
   shortening
½ cup sugar
Zest and juice of 1 lemon

2 eggs, separated
1⅓ cups all-purpose flour
½ teaspoon baking powder
3 tablespoons milk
2 cups frozen or fresh blueberries

1. Preheat the oven to 350 degrees and grease and flour a 9-inch springform pan.

2. Mix the streusel ingredients with your hands and set aside.

3. For the torte, cream the butter, sugar, and lemon zest and juice until fluffy. Add the egg yolks. Cream well until the mixture is light yellow in color.

4. Sift the flour and baking powder. Add the flour to the egg yolk mixture, alternating with the milk. Beat just until the flour is incorporated. The dough will be very stiff.

5. Whip the egg whites until stiff, then fold into the flour mixture.

6. Spread the torte batter evenly over the bottom of the springform pan. Cover with the blueberries and then top with the streusel.
7. Bake for 50–60 minutes, until the top is light brown. This torte is delicious warm for brunch or served with ice cream.

RASPBERRY MELBA TORTE

SERVES 6–8. (D OR P)

Raspberries can grow like weeds. If you know the right places to find them or have bushes in your yard, you do not have to pay the premium asked in local supermarkets. In Europe, raspberries were available at the time of Shavuot and later in the summer merely by picking the wild berries off bushes.

This exquisite torte recipe has had a long journey. Originating in prewar Warsaw, it traveled through Russia and then Australia before moving, one generation later, to London, to Brookline, Massachusetts, and then to New York where Irene Pletka now lives. Her mother, visiting from Australia, shared it with me. Needless to say, it is prepared only for very special occasions. The original recipe calls for 2–3 pints of fresh raspberries. I have reduced the amount of raspberries and added peaches.

CRUST:

¼ pound (1 stick) unsalted butter or pareve margarine
10 tablespoons sugar
Pinch of salt
Zest of 1 lemon

Juice of ½ lemon
½ teaspoon vanilla extract
1½ cups all-purpose flour
½ teaspoon baking powder

FILLING:

2 tablespoons raspberry jam
2 pints fresh raspberries or 1 pint raspberries and 5 freestone peaches

Confectioners' sugar

1. For the crust, cream the butter or margarine and sugar. Add the salt, lemon zest and juice, and vanilla.
2. Work the flour and baking powder into the above ingredients with a food processor, mixer, or your hands. Wrap in waxed paper and let stand in the refrigerator overnight.
3. When ready to bake, preheat the oven to 375 degrees.
4. Take one third of the dough and press it onto the bottom of a 9-inch spring-form pan. Bake 15 minutes. Remove from the oven.
5. Press one-third of the dough onto the sides of the pan. Brush the bottom with the raspberry jam.
6. Spread all the raspberries over the bottom of the crust. (If using the peach-raspberry combination, peel the peaches and slice in crescent shapes. Arrange in the pan. Cover with the raspberries.)
7. Cover the fruit with a lattice crust and then, with the remaining dough, make a border around the edge, attaching the lattice top to the sides.
8. Return to the oven and bake 45 minutes, or until golden. Remove from the oven and sprinkle with confectioners' sugar. When cool, remove from the pan and serve.

CHEESECAKE

SERVES 8. (D)

It has been rumored that Lindy's restaurant in New York City invented its famous cheesecake. Not so. The chef may have perfected this heavy, velvety, lemony cheesecake of cheesecakes, but the genre has a much longer history. It probably originated with the first ovens, after the early peoples of the Middle East learned to place soured cream in a bag, hang it up, and allow it to drain. To the curd that formed, they added honey, lemon peel, and egg yolks, as well as some more soured cream; they then baked the cakes, which were probably rather lumpy. In any event, Judith brought cheesecake to the court of Holofernes. The Crusaders carried the recipes to Europe; the Mongols brought curd to Russia; and the Jews carried cheesecake recipes to all the places of their wanderings. In Poland, for example, a cheesecake eaten at Shavuot consisted of farmer cheese and sugar. The French have a main-course quiche Lorraine, a Genoise cake base with pastry up the sides and a rich filling of cream cheese and pot cheese, or a simple cream cheese tart. Hungarians serve strudel filled with cottage cheese and raisins.

The most intricate and perhaps the granddaddy of all Western cheesecakes, however, is the Russian Easter *paskha*. Beginning days in advance, cottage cheese is made from raw milk. Using a fine sieve, the whey is removed from the curd. When the cottage cheese reaches the desired consistency after several days of hanging, it is mixed with sugar, eggs, sour cream, butter, and chopped nuts. Then it is cooked briefly. A special wooden mold is filled with this mixture, covered with cheesecloth, and set in a cool place for twenty hours to allow the liquid to drain out. When it is ready, the mold is inverted and the *paskha* can be decorated with spring flowers or candied fruits.

Less difficult than the Russian *paskha,* and creamier, is the following recipe. It came from Gisella Warburg Wyzanski, of the famous Warburg banking family of Hamburg. Gisella came to this country in 1939 and knew how to cook "absolutely nothing," since at the Warburg home cooking was left entirely to the servants. She learned to cook in Cambridge and was one of the prime movers behind the Window Shop bakery.

6 tablespoons unsalted butter	1 cup sugar
1 cup graham cracker crumbs	Juice of ½ lemon
6 eggs, separated	1 teaspoon vanilla extract
1 pound cream cheese	2 tablespoons all-purpose flour
2 cups sour cream	

1. Preheat the oven to 300 degrees. Grease the sides of a 9-inch springform pan.
2. Melt the butter and combine with the graham cracker crumbs. Press the crumbs onto the bottom of the pan. Save some crumbs.
3. Combine the egg yolks, cream cheese, sour cream, sugar, lemon juice, vanilla, and flour. Beat very well until light and fluffy.
4. Beat the egg whites until stiff peaks form. Fold into the cream cheese mixture. Pour the batter into the pan and sprinkle with the remaining graham cracker crumbs.
5. Bake 1 hour. Turn off the oven and leave the cake in the oven 1 additional hour. Then leave the oven door ajar 30 minutes more.

LEMON CHEESECAKE

Adapted from Ann Amernick

MAKES ONE 10-INCH CHEESECAKE. (D)

To make a great cheesecake, there is no substitute for good-quality ingredients—real vanilla extract, the best cream cheese and sour cream. This version has a very smooth and pleasingly tart filling. I love Ann's addition of walnuts to the crust.

THE CRUST:

½ cup walnuts

½ cup sugar

¼ pound (1 stick) unsalted butter, cold

1 cup unbleached all-purpose flour

THE FILLING:

2 pounds cream cheese, at room temperature

¾ cup sugar

4 large eggs

2 large egg yolks

1 cup sour cream

Grated zest and juice of 1 lemon

1 teaspoon vanilla extract

3 tablespoons unbleached all-purpose flour

THE TOPPING:

2 cups sour cream, at room temperature

2 teaspoons vanilla extract

2 tablespoons sugar

1. To make the crust, grind the nuts with 1 tablespoon of the sugar in a food processor fitted with the steel blade. Cut up the butter and add the pieces to the processor with the remaining sugar and the flour. Process, pulsing, until a ball of dough is formed.
2. Cover the dough with plastic wrap and refrigerate for 30 minutes.
3. Preheat the oven to 350 degrees and press the dough onto the bottom of a greased 10-inch springform pan.

4. Bake the crust on the middle rack of the oven for 20–25 minutes, or until golden in color. Remove from the oven and let cool. Leave the oven on.

5. To make the filling, put the cream cheese in the bowl of an electric mixer and beat with the whisk on the lowest speed for about 10 minutes, or until soft and smooth, while gradually adding the sugar and scraping the sides occasionally. This long, slow action will give the filling a silky texture.

6. Add the eggs, egg yolks, sour cream, lemon zest and juice, and vanilla; mix again on the lowest speed for a few minutes, scraping the sides and beaters frequently. Then gradually add the flour.

7. Scoop the cream cheese mixture onto the prepared crust. Place a pan of water in the oven on the lowest rack. Turn the oven down to 325 degrees and bake the cheesecake on the middle rack for 1¼–1½ hours.

8. Remove the cheesecake from the oven and let it cool for 10–15 minutes. Do not turn off the oven.

9. Put the sour cream, vanilla, and sugar in a bowl and mix well. Spoon the mixture evenly over the top of the slightly cooled cheesecake.

10. Return the cheesecake to the oven for 10 minutes. After baking it, let it cool, remove the sides of the springform, and transfer it to a serving plate.

POLISH-PARISIAN CHEESECAKE

Adapted from Finkelsztajn's

MAKES ONE 9-INCH CHEESECAKE. (D)

This is the way Jewish cheesecake must have tasted in Lodz, Poland. Before Jews came to America they used a rich farmer cheese instead of our processed cream cheese. After tasting this cheesecake from Finkelsztajn's Bakery in Paris, I went to a market near the bakery, bought a wheel of farmer cheese, and carried it back to the United States—just so I could test the real recipe. Although our commercial farmer cheese does well as a substitute, nothing really takes the place of cheese fresh from the farm.

THE CRUST:

5⅓ tablespoons unsalted butter, cold

¼ cup sugar

Dash of salt

1⅓ cups unbleached all-purpose flour

¼ cup ice water

THE FILLING:

½ cup raisins (optional)

½ cup milk

Three 7½-ounce packages farmer cheese, at room temperature

½ cup unbleached all-purpose flour

5 large eggs, separated

⅔ cup sugar

Grated zest of 1 lemon

2 tablespoons lemon juice

1 teaspoon vanilla extract

Dash of salt

½ cup slivered almonds

1. To make the crust, use a food processor fitted with the steel blade to combine the butter and sugar, pulsing. Add the salt and flour, pulse, then add the ice water and pulse until a ball is formed, adding more flour if it is too sticky. Remove the dough, cover with plastic wrap, and refrigerate for about 1 hour.

2. To make the filling, drop the raisins into the milk and let them sit for 1 hour.

3. Drain the raisins, reserving the milk. Combine the milk with the cheese, flour, egg yolks, sugar, lemon zest and juice, vanilla, and salt in a food processor; pulse to blend thoroughly. Remove to a bowl and stir in the raisins.

4. Beat the egg whites until stiff peaks form and fold them into the cheese mixture.

5. Preheat the oven to 350 degrees and butter a 9-inch springform pan. Quickly press the crust dough into the bottom and 2 inches up the sides. Pour the filling into the crust and sprinkle with the almonds.

6. Bake the cheesecake on the middle rack of the oven for 40 minutes, or until a toothpick inserted in the center comes out clean. Cool in the pan for 15 minutes before removing the springform sides. Chill and serve garnished with fresh mint and fruit.

THE
MINOR HOLIDAYS

THE MINOR HOLIDAYS

God increase our worldly goods,
And guard us soon and late,
And multiply our bliss like seeds
Of pomegranate.
For our Redeemer do we wait
All the long night through,
To bring a dawn as roseate
As Apple's hue.
Sin, like a stubborn shell and hard,
Is wrapped around our soul;
Lord, break the husk and let the Nut
Come out whole!

God give us many friends, renew
Our old prosperity,
And be our foemen shrivell'd up
Like Carobs dry.

Behold, from hour to hour we wait
The dayspring yet to be
While all our hearts are dark and black
As Mulberry.

Judah Kala'i, *Fruit of the Goodly Tree*

Within the seasonal cycle are major and minor festivals. Two minor ones are of special interest, Tu Bi-Shevat and Lag Ba-Omer.

Tu Bi-Shevat, the New Year of Trees, is one of the four natural new years mentioned in the Mishnah. At about Shevat 15, in early February, the sap begins to rise in the fruit trees of Israel. To celebrate this event, it is customary to eat up to fifteen different kinds of fruits and nuts. Some people stay up the night before, reciting the passages of the Bible referring to fruits or the earth's fertility. Under the influence of the American Arbor Day, Israelis go out and plant saplings. In the United States, Tu Bi-Shevat is the time to focus on the environment and to collect funds for reforestation in Israel.

Sephardim chant the Judah Kala'i poem above and eat traditional fruits and nuts. The apple represents the glowing splendor of God. Hard, medium, and soft nuts depict the three different characters of Jews. The almond stands for the swiftness of divine retribution, since it blooms before any other tree. The pomegranate is a sign of fertility, peace, and prosperity. The carob, the food of the poor, represents humility, a necessary element of penitence.

Today in America my children have attended Tu Bi-Shevat Seders, a custom derived from Spain and Eastern countries. The children drink four cups of "wine" symbolizing the changes that nature undergoes in the four seasons. The lightest, apple juice, symbolizes the slumber that had descended upon nature in the fall. Then, to symbolize the changes, they drink orange, then cranberry, and finally dark grape juice, which symbolizes the awakening and blossoming of nature on the fifteenth of Shevat.

The first category of fruit has a peel or a shell, which cannot be eaten: pistachio nuts, bananas, kiwis, oranges, avocados, almonds, pineapples, melons. The second has a pit inside that cannot be eaten: prunes, dates, apricots, plums, cherries, olives. The third fruit can be eaten entirely: strawberries, grapes, pears, figs, apples, and raisins. The foods are accompanied by a text compiled from Jewish teachings on nature and the environment.

At our own home we try to have a fruit-and-nut meal at Tu Bi-Shevat. You can even add nuts and raisins to your challah if you like.

Thirty-three days in the counting of the *omer,* the period between Passover and Shavuot, comes the festival of Lag Ba-Omer. Since ancient times Jews have refrained from having feasts or special occasions such as weddings (or, for the very religious, haircuts) in this period. This may come from an ancient superstition of observing semimourning to ensure a good wheat harvest for the coming year. On Lag Ba-Omer, however, feasting is permitted. Not a sacred occasion, it is a time for picnicking in the forest and countryside.

MENUS

TU BI-SHEVAT
Baked Whitefish
Persian *Fesenjan* (Pomegranate-Walnut Chicken)
Chelou (Crunchy Persian Rice)
Syrian Stuffed Prunes
Baklava

GERMAN AND PERSIAN
German Sweet-and-Sour Carp
Heidi Wortzel's Cheese Knishes
Persian Cucumber-Yogurt Salad
Carob Brownies
Figs Stuffed with Walnuts

ISRAELI INDEPENDENCE DAY
Israeli Felafel
Jerusalem Hummus
Madeleine Kamman's Jaffa Salad
Israeli Eggplant Salad
Jaffa Oranges

LAG BA-OMER PICNIC
Roast Chicken
Eggplant Salad
German Potato Salad
Moroccan Carrot Salad
Fresh Fruit
Aunt Eva's Cookies

FRUIT AND NUT
Tu Bi-Shevat Salad
Pot Roast
Poached Figs, Prunes, and Pecans with Wine

TU BI-SHEVAT SALAD

SERVES 6. (P)

1 orange, peeled and cut into
   round slices
1 avocado, sliced
1 endive, separated
1 bunch watercress

½ head romaine lettuce
2 pitted dates, diced small
Seeds of ¼ pomegranate or ¼ cup
   cranberries

1. Combine all the ingredients in a salad bowl.
2. Just before serving, mix in the salad dressing. Toss 15 times (in honor of the 15 different kinds of fruits and nuts eaten on the fifteenth of Shevat).

SALAD DRESSING:

2 tablespoons balsamic or red
   wine vinegar
1 clove garlic, crushed
Dash of salt
Dash of sugar

1 egg yolk
1 teaspoon Dijon mustard
Freshly ground pepper to taste
5 tablespoons olive or vegetable
   oil

1. Combine all the ingredients except the oil.
2. Slowly whisk in the oil and pour over the salad.

ISRAELI FELAFEL

(Chickpea Patties)

MAKES ABOUT 2 DOZEN. (P)

For Jews, this Pan–Middle Eastern recipe and the one that follows it have come to symbolize Israeli cuisine. They are appropriate for Israeli Independence Day.

2 cups chickpeas, which have been soaked in water overnight
1 large onion, chopped
2 tablespoons finely chopped fresh flat-leaf parsley
1 large egg
1 teaspoon salt
2 cloves garlic, peeled

1 teaspoon dried chili pepper flakes
1 teaspoon ground cumin
Dash of coriander seed
½ cup fine bulgur, which has been soaked in water for 1 hour
Vegetable oil for frying

1. Combine the drained chickpeas and the onion. Add the parsley, egg, salt, garlic, and spices. Whirl in a blender or food processor. Add the bulgur until the mixture forms a small ball without sticking to your hands. Refrigerate for at least 1 hour. Form the chickpea mixture into small balls about the size of a walnut, or use a felafel measuring gadget.*
2. Heat 2 inches of oil in a large frying pan. Flatten the patties slightly and fry them until golden brown on each side. Drain the felafel on paper towels.

*Available in Middle Eastern markets.

JERUSALEM HUMMUS

MAKES ABOUT 2 CUPS. (P)

1 cup raw chickpeas
1 cup tahini
½ cup fresh lemon juice, or to
    taste
2 cloves garlic, peeled
1 teaspoon salt
Freshly ground pepper

¼ teaspoon ground cumin, or to
    taste
Olive oil
Paprika
2 tablespoons fresh flat-leaf
    parsley
Olives

1. Soak the chickpeas in water overnight. Add additional water to cover by ⅓ and simmer, covered, for about 1 hour, or until the skin separates. Drain.

2. Reserving ½ cup of the chickpeas, place the rest in a food processor or blender with the tahini, lemon juice, garlic, salt, pepper to taste, and cumin. Process or whirl until smooth. To serve, place the hummus on a large, attractive flat plate. Smooth it down with the back of a spoon. Sprinkle with the remaining chickpeas and oil and paprika to taste. Garnish with the parsley and olives.

3. Serve with a large basket filled with hot pita cut into wedges for dipping.

POACHED FIGS, PRUNES, AND PECANS WITH WINE

SERVES 6–8. (P)

An old Jewish man in ancient Israel was planting a fig tree. The Roman Emperor passed by and said to him, "Why do you do that, old man? Surely you will not live long enough to see it bear fruit."

"In that case," replied the aged man, "I will leave it for my son, as my father left the fruit of his labor for me."

The Emperor admired his spirit. "If you do live to see the figs on your tree ripen," he said, "let me know about it."

The old man lived to eat of the fruit, and remembering the Emperor's words, brought him a basket of figs. The Emperor was so pleased that he filled the old man's basket with gold.

A greedy woman who heard of the gift made her husband go to the Emperor too. "He loves figs," she said, "and he will surely fill your basket with gold."

The man listened to his wife, brought the figs to the palace, and said, "These figs are for the Emperor. Empty my basket and fill it with gold!"

When Hadrian heard this, he ordered the guard to have all the people who passed by throw figs at the man. When the man finally escaped, he ran home and told his wife what had happened.

"Well," she said, "you are lucky. Think what would have happened if the figs had been coconuts!"

6 ounces pitted prunes	1 stick cinnamon
6 ounces figs	4 whole cloves
½ cup pecan halves	Grated zest of 1 lemon
1½ cups dry red wine	½ sliced orange
¼ cup sweet red wine or port	1 handful of juniper berries
¼ cup dark brown sugar, or to taste	

1. Place the prunes, figs, and pecan halves in a small saucepan. Add enough wine to come ¾ of the way up the fruits and nuts.
2. Add the remaining ingredients and simmer, uncovered, over low heat for about 20 minutes.
3. Serve with whipped cream. This dessert is very rich, so be frugal with the size of your servings.

THE
LIFE CYCLE

THE LIFE CYCLE

The river of life . . . flows from birth toward death. Day follows day with wearisome monotony. Only the holidays twine themselves together to form the circle of the year. Only through the holidays does life experience the eternity of the river that returns to its source. Then life becomes eternal.

Franz Rosenzweig

This little child, may he become great. Even as he has entered into the Covenant, so may he enter into the Torah, the nuptial canopy, and into good deeds.

Circumcision blessing

Blessed art Thou, O Lord our God, King of the Universe, who hath created joy and gladness, bridegroom and bride, mirth and exultation, pleasure and delight, love and brotherhood, and peace and friendship. O Lord our God, may there be heard in the cities of Judah and in the streets of Jerusalem the voice of joy and the voice of gladness, the voice of the bridegroom and the voice of the bride, the jubilant voice of the bridegrooms from their canopies and of youths from their feasts of song. Blessed art Thou, O Lord, who maketh the bridegroom to rejoice with the bride.

Last of the seven wedding benedictions,
based on Jeremiah 33:10–11

The family gatherings at circumcision, bar mitzvah, marriage, and death differ greatly from those of the seasonal holidays. While the latter events take place for everyone, year after year, the former can happen at any time within the year and affect each individual in a different way. Yet the celebration surrounding each event is more than a family affair. Through these bonds, all Jews show their responsibility for one another. The individual or couple reinforces its position as a member of the Jewish religious community. A festive communal gathering becomes a means of celebrating the wish for health, wealth, happiness, children, wisdom, and good deeds.

People are never left unaccompanied at what we may call life-cycle events. The woman about to give birth is closely watched; the newborn baby is never left alone until after the circumcision or baby naming; the bride and groom are surrounded by family and friends for sometimes as many as seven days prior to the wedding; the mourner has family and friends around him. And if this natural accompaniment were not enough, a *minyan* is needed to perform circumcisions, bar mitzvahs, weddings, and funerals. These are all means of binding the individual to the covenant of Judaism.

Wine, the symbol of joy, is present at all these events.

Bread—made from the seven grains of Israel—has also become a catalyst for symbols at such events. The mother in childbirth was allowed to eat only a piece of *afikomen* or the blossom end of the *etrog,* presumably symbols of good luck. "One more child—one more loaf of bread" came to be a Jewish folk saying. At the bar mitzvah and wedding feasts, the blessing over bread is recited and challah eaten before the meal begins. A loaf of bread is the traditional gift to someone with a new home. A loaf of bread was to be set beside a dying man to straighten his limbs and ease his final moments.

Although we like to think of Jews as rational, it is surprising how many superstitions originating in ancient times have carried over to this day. Foods were often a means of showing magical or symbolic power. On the one hand, people hoped for many children, happiness, peace, and wisdom. But they were also fearful that the evil eye, Lilith, or other demons would harm them or their family. So means were devised to combat these evil forces. Chickens, fish, circles, and the lucky number seven all have magical significance. A woman in childbirth, for example, might have a chicken swung around her head seven times to ward off evil spirits. Seven benedictions were and are still read at the marriage ceremony.

Circular symbolism is carried over to the table. Circular foods, available year-round, were used since the events of our lives have no seasons. Beans, eggs, lentils, and peas were round and abundant; they were used whenever the mystery of life had to be explained.

Rich foods took on a special significance, to show the wealth of the family performing the wedding or the bar mitzvah. They were also used to wish for wealth and fertility, as in the *goldene yoikh*—the golden chicken soup with rich rings of fat—eaten by the bridal couple immediately after the ceremony.

Fish, too, symbolize wealth and fertility. In some countries the bride will jump over a fish presented by the bridegroom before the wedding to symbolize the wish for many children. As far back as Talmudic times, it was customary to strew fish, wine, oil, parched corn, nuts, and meats before the bridal pair. In the Middle Ages, grains of wheat were strewn; today it is rice.

Meals for such events usually take on the tone of the country in which the family resides. But despite the dispersals, the symbolic foods remain pretty much the same.

MENUS

BRIT MILAH (BREAKFAST)
Herring in Sour Cream
Gravlaks
Bagels
Whitefish Salad
Cream Cheese
Lox
Honey Cake or Hungarian *Kugelhopf*
Coffee and Wine

BRIT MILAH (LUNCHTIME)
Cold Cuts
Whitefish Salad
German Potato Salad
Coleslaw
Honey Cake or Anise Cookies
Wine Punch
Coffee

MY WEDDING MENU
Finger Appetizers
Hummus*
Tahina*
Pita Bread
Honey-Orange Chicken

*In Nathan, *The Foods of Israel Today.*

Rice
Eggplant Kugel[†]
Green Salad
Chocolate Wedding Cake with White Icing

BAR MITZVAH
Finger Appetizers
Salad
Honey-Orange Chicken
Green Beans Amandine
Baked *Kishke* with Prunes
Chocolate Mousse Torte

SEPHARDIC BAR MITZVAH OR WEDDING
Syrian *Yaprak* (Stuffed Grape Leaves with Apricots)
Lahmajoun[†]
Kibbes[†]
Sambusak (meat-filled)
*Tahina**
Eggplant Salad
Fruits

BAR MITZVAH
Gravlaks
Mustard Sauce
Whitefish Roulade
Marinated Vegetables
Cold Rice Salad
Bagels
Cream Cheese
Chocolate Fudge Cake

*In Nathan, *The Foods of Israel Today.*
[†]In Nathan and Goldman, *The Flavor of Jerusalem.*

EAST EUROPEAN WEDDING

Schnapps

Zamosc Gefilte Fish

Goldene Yoikh (Chicken Soup)

Roast Chicken

Lokshen Kugel or Potato Kugel

Hot Fruit Compote

Heidi Wortzel's Honey Cake

Mead and Wine

MOURNERS' MEAL

Huevos Haminadav (Hard-boiled Eggs, Sephardic Style)

Mujeddrah (Rice with Lentils, Esau Style)

Bagels

Cream Cheese

Lox

WHITEFISH SALAD

MAKES ABOUT 1 CUP. (D)

Fish, both smoked and pickled, are symbolic foods eaten at a *brit*. This delicious salad was one of the dishes brought to our son David's.

4 stalks celery, peeled and diced fine	3 tablespoons sour cream
2 tablespoons fresh lemon juice	1 smoked whitefish to yield 2 cups fish, bones removed
3 tablespoons mayonnaise	White pepper

1. Combine the celery, lemon juice, mayonnaise, and sour cream. Then combine with the whitefish, handling the fish gently. Add white pepper to taste.
2. Serve as is on bagels or crackers, or stuff back into the skin of the whitefish.

HEIDI WORTZEL'S KNISHES

"Ron's getting married!" Julie screamed at me when I came through the door. "Ron's getting married!! . . . This afternoon he told us. They spoke long distance for forty minutes last night. She's flying here next week, and there's going to be a huge wedding. My parents are flittering all over the place. They've got to arrange everything in about a day or two."

Philip Roth, *Goodbye, Columbus*

MAKES ABOUT 70. (P OR D)

The movie *Goodbye, Columbus* has probably done more than anything else to immortalize the American Jewish wedding. Jewish caterers have also played their part. Not only have they preserved Eastern European culinary customs, but they have also transformed what was once a simple occasion into a considerably more elaborate one. A *brit milah* or a bar mitzvah was celebrated with a little bit of honey cake and some wine or brandy. A wedding meal included gefilte fish, *goldene yoikh*, noodle or potato kugel, brisket or corned beef, compote, and mead and wine. There were no American wedding cakes.

Today a veritable feast is prepared. Knishes, sushi, tiny frankfurters, or stuffed mushrooms—to name only a few of the hors d'oeuvres—are followed by an elaborate seated meal, ending with a huge buffet of rich Viennese pastries.

Pastries such as Russian pirogi or knishes (of Slovakian origin) stuffed with cheese or potatoes for Shavuot, cabbage for Sukkot, kasha for Hanukkah, and chicken liver for Rosh Hashanah were once served with potato or beet soup. That was the whole meal. In this country, their form has become daintier: they are now standard Jewish finger hors d'oeuvres.

This particular recipe for knishes comes from Heidi Wortzel, a former French cooking instructor who studied at Paris's Cordon Bleu Cooking School. At a bar mitzvah, Heidi tasted marvelous knishes filled with potatoes and cracked pepper. At home, she experimented until satisfied she had achieved the original taste. Here it is.

When I taught this recipe at the 92nd Street Y in New York, one student rolled the dough into a circle, filled it, and twisted it as she would have a Chinese dumpling.

PASTRY:

4 cups sifted all-purpose flour
1 teaspoon salt
½ pound (2 sticks) butter or
  pareve margarine, chilled

6 tablespoons vegetable
  shortening
10–13 tablespoons ice water
1 large egg yolk

1. Sift the flour and salt into a large bowl. Cut the butter or margarine into small pieces and add to the flour along with the shortening. Blend with a pastry blender until the mixture resembles coarse flakes of oatmeal. Add the ice water and blend with the cupped palm of your hand until a single mass is formed.
2. Divide the dough in half. Place one portion on a lightly floured surface. Quickly push the dough away from you, taking small amounts at a time, to

blend the flour and shortening. Gather it up in a ball, dust with flour, cover with plastic wrap, and refrigerate overnight. Repeat the process with the second ball of dough.

3. Preheat the oven to 425 degrees.
4. Taking the balls of dough one at a time, roll each out on a lightly floured surface into a rectangle. Cut the rectangle into strips about 8 inches long and 3 inches wide. Place a strip of filling down the center of the strip of pastry and fold over the sides to completely enclose the filling. Cut the pastry into 2-inch lengths and round the ends with your hands.
5. Place the knishes on an ungreased baking sheet and brush them with a mixture of 1 egg yolk and 1 tablespoon water.
6. Bake the knishes for 20 minutes, or until they are golden brown.

Note: These knishes can be baked, cooled, and then frozen. Reheat them on a cookie sheet in a 375-degree oven for 12–15 minutes. The fillings can be made a day ahead and refrigerated.

POTATO FILLING:

(P OR D)

3 large baking potatoes, peeled and quartered
3 tablespoons butter or pareve margarine
3 tablespoons oil

2 large onions, chopped
¼ cup chopped flat-leaf parsley
Salt
Cracked pepper
2 large eggs, slightly beaten

1. Place the potatoes in a 2-quart saucepan. Cover them with cold water, bring to a boil, and cook until the potatoes are very tender, about 25 minutes.
2. While the potatoes are cooking, melt the butter or margarine and oil together in a skillet. Add the chopped onions and fry until golden brown but not quite crisp.
3. Drain the potatoes and mash them with a ricer or masher until smooth. Stir in the sautéed onions, chopped parsley, salt and pepper to taste, and eggs. The filling should have a slightly peppery taste, which can be obtained by using cracked pepper instead of ground.

CHEESE FILLING:

(D)

1 pound farmer cheese	1 large egg, beaten
4 tablespoons butter or pareve margarine	2 tablespoons chopped fresh flat-leaf parsley
1 cup chopped scallions, some green included	2 tablespoons sour cream
	Salt and freshly ground pepper

1. In a mixing bowl, mash the farmer cheese until smooth.
2. In a skillet, melt the butter or margarine. Add the scallions and sauté until they are limp but not brown. Scrape them into the mixing bowl. Add the egg, parsley, sour cream, and salt and pepper to taste. Mix thoroughly.

SAUERKRAUT FILLING:

(P OR D)

One 16-ounce can sauerkraut	1 large onion, chopped
3 tablespoons butter or pareve margarine	Salt and cracked pepper
	Pinch of sugar

1. Rinse the sauerkraut thoroughly under cold water. Drain and pat dry. Chop the drained sauerkraut and set aside.
2. In a skillet, melt the butter or margarine and add the chopped onion. Sauté over low heat for 5 minutes. Add the drained sauerkraut and sauté 3 minutes longer. Add the salt and pepper to taste, and the sugar. Let cool.

SYRIAN *YAPRAK*

(Stuffed Grape Leaves with Apricots)

MAKES ABOUT 36. (D)

Yaprak—stuffed grape leaves with apricots—are, like Hungarian stuffed cabbage, symbols of plenty and usually served at Sukkot. They are easily adaptable as finger food and are traditionally served at Sephardic life-cycle functions. The following recipe is often served in the Brooklyn, New York, and Deal, New Jersey, Syrian communities.

½ pound grape leaves, fresh,
    frozen, or bottled
1 pound ground beef or lamb
½ cup uncooked rice, which has
    been washed in cold water
2 tablespoons water
1 teaspoon salt
¼ teaspoon allspice
Dash of white pepper

Dash of turmeric (optional)
½ tablespoon dried mint
15–30 dried apricot halves
⅓ cup prune juice or ¾ cup
    tamarind syrup
Juice of 1 large lemon
¾ cup hot water
1 tablespoon sugar, or to taste

1. If using frozen grape leaves, thaw them in lukewarm water 1 hour before starting. If using bottled leaves, soak them in cold water for just a few minutes.
2. Mix the beef or lamb with the rice, water, salt, allspice, pepper, turmeric, if using, and mint.
3. Scatter some of the apricot halves on the bottom of a heavy pot.
4. Place a grape leaf, dull side up and stem removed, on a flat surface, with the stem end away from you. Place a tablespoon of filling on the leaf, near the stem end; flatten the filling out to the width of the leaf. Fold the stem end over the filling. Press the filling firmly underneath the leaf. Fold the sides in and roll from the top toward you. Place the stuffed grape leaves and the remaining apricots in alternate layers in the pot.

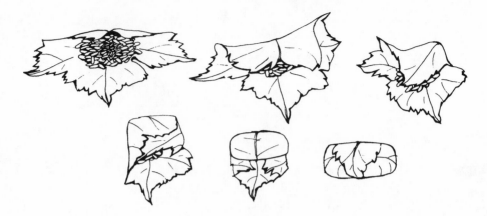

Stuffing the grape leaves (drawing: Debbie Insetta)

5. Cover with a heatproof plate to keep the *yaprak* down and then place a regular cover on the pot. Steam the grape leaves over a very low flame for about 20 minutes.
6. Combine the prune juice or tamarind syrup, lemon juice, hot water, and sugar. Simmer for about 30 minutes and adjust the seasoning to taste.
7. Cover the *yaprak* with the sauce. Bring to a boil and simmer for 1 hour.
8. Allow to cool in the pot and then chill.

MEAT *PASTELS*

MAKES 200 *PASTELS*, ALLOWING ABOUT 3 PER PERSON. (M)

Just as the Ashkenazic caterers have transformed knishes into finger food, Sephardim have learned to make tiny torpedo-shaped *kibbes, burekas* (puff-pastry dough filled with spinach, eggplant, or cheese), *sambusaks,* and *pastels.* Sambusaks are made by Iraqi and Syrian Jews, and *burekas* by Turkish and Balkan Jews. Perhaps the grandmother of them all is the *pastel,* a fancy Friday night pastry supposedly brought from Spain to Turkey. The dough can be made like that for *sambusak* (page 300), or you can fill phyllo or egg-roll wrappers, as in this Moroccan recipe from Casablanca.

100 fine egg-roll wrappers
2 pounds lean ground meat
½ cup chopped fresh flat-leaf
   parsley
1 cup grated onions
1 teaspoon ground mace
1 teaspoon ground nutmeg
½ teaspoon allspice
½ teaspoon salt
2 cups water
Vegetable oil for deep-frying

1. One hour before beginning, remove the egg-roll wrappers from the freezer. Sauté the ground meat over low heat, stirring occasionally. Add the parsley, onions, and seasonings. Blend well and gradually add the water. Cover and simmer, stirring occasionally, until the water evaporates and the meat is very soft, about 1 hour.
2. Grind the meat mixture in a food processor or meat grinder until it is smooth.

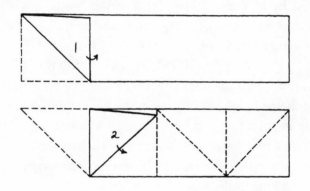

Folding the pastels (drawing: Debbie Insetta)

3. Cut an egg-roll wrapper in half and fold it lengthwise.
4. Take 1 heaping teaspoon of the filling and place it at one corner of the wrapper. Fold the corner over into a triangle and fold it up like a flag. The bottom corner is folded last. Repeat until all the wrappers are filled.
5. Freeze for later use or finish cooking immediately.
6. In a heavy-bottomed pan, heat 4 inches of oil to 375 degrees. Deep-fry a few *pastels* at a time, turning when they are golden. Drain them on paper towels. Cut each *pastel* in half. Before serving, place them in a warm oven to heat through.

BAR MITZVAH GRAVLAKS

(Pickled Salmon)

SERVES APPROXIMATELY 8 PEOPLE PER POUND OF FISH. (P)

One of the most delicious bar mitzvah meals I have ever tasted was that of Joseph Richman, son of Phyllis Richman, former restaurant critic of the *Washington Post*. For this Sunday morning feast (it was Rosh Hodesh), Phyllis decided to have a spring *milchig* brunch-luncheon at the auditorium of their Conservative Tifereth Israel Synagogue in Washington. Potted geraniums bought at a garden show decorated the tables, and the entire menu for over two hundred guests reflected the springtime availability of fresh foods. A cold rice mold with bits of parsley was surrounded by blanched, crisp, fresh string beans and asparagus spears. Whitefish soufflé rolls, marinated vegetables, and mock lox—or gravlaks—were eaten with miniature bagels and cream cheese. Red and white wines were the only drink, and a chocolate praline cake modeled after the *gâteau marjolaine* of Les Pyramides restaurant in Vienne, France, made by Ann Amernick, the only dessert. Friends helped cook everything in the synagogue's kosher kitchen.

Not wanting to spend the prohibitive price for fresh lox, Phyllis decided to make her own. She marinated gravlaks in the kitchen for three days. Although she actually served a plateful at each table, she suggests having an entire fish elegantly carved on a long buffet table.

I have been making this for years, ever since Phyllis told me how to cure the fish. Sometimes I add more sugar. I serve it with mustard-dill sauce on multigrain bread.

¾ cup kosher salt
¼ cup sugar
1 whole salmon or sea bass or
   1 side of salmon cut into

2 equal pieces, cleaned, split,
   with bones removed
Cracked pepper
1 bunch of fresh dill

1. Mix the salt and sugar and rub them over the fish. Place ½ of the fish, skin side down, on a stainless-steel dish or glass platter. Sprinkle the top with cracked pepper to taste and then spread on a layer of dill.

2. Place the other half of the fish, skin side up, on top of the first. Slide the fish into a plastic bag. Then slide it the other way into a second one. Top with a plate weighted down with a couple of bricks for even pressure.

3. Refrigerate for 2–3 days. Every 12 hours, turn the fish and, if you like, baste with the liquid from the fish.

4. After 3 days, scrape away the dill and cracked pepper and then drain the fish. Transfer the fish to a board and with a very sharp knife slice thinly at an angle almost parallel to the board. Serve with horseradish, mustard sauce, or alone. The gravlaks will keep refrigerated after curing for at least 1 week.

BEET AND GEFILTE FISH MOLD

SERVES AT LEAST 12. (M)

This molded gelatin gefilte fish salad epitomized the American Jewish kitchen of the 1950s. It is still popular today, perfect for large gatherings like bar mitzvahs.

One 15½-ounce can whole beets
One 3-ounce package lime-flavored kosher gelatin
2 packages unflavored kosher gelatin
Juice of 1 lemon
Salt
4 tablespoons prepared red horseradish
One 28-ounce jar of oblong-shaped gefilte fish

1. Drain the beets and heat the juice, adding enough water to make 2 cups. Add the gelatins, lemon juice, and salt to taste to the hot beet juice.

2. Meanwhile, grate the beets. When the beet juice mixture starts to jell, add the grated beets with the horseradish. Place in a large round mold. Push the gefilte fish down into the mold, one touching the other (about 6–8) to form a ring. Refrigerate until set.

3. To unmold, wrap the mold in a hot wet towel, run a knife around the mold, and flip onto a plate. When you slice the mold, you'll have a round circle of gefilte fish in each slice.

HUEVOS HAMINADOS
(Hard-boiled Eggs, Sephardic Style)

MAKES 12. (P)

The spirit of God broods over the silent waters of creation like a great bird tending its nest.

Rashi's commentary on Genesis 1:2

As the bride went forth from her father's home, an egg was broken above her head. Preceded by fife and drum, she arrived at her home as though deaf and dumb, as she pretended to be while being decked out, then under the canopy, until she went forth and lay on her bed, a statue of stone.

Traveler's description of a wedding in Tangiers

A legend in the Talmud describes God taking up two halves of an egg, which fertilize each other and then result in the creation of the world. The round, perfect egg has always been associated with the mysteries of life and death, of fertility and immortality. Thus, the egg on the veil of the Moroccan bride ensures the abundance of the *hen,* good luck, and many children.

In Judaism, as in most religions, superstitions abound surrounding the egg. Moroccan girls, for example, step over fish roe to increase their fertility. Barrenness is believed to be cured by eating a double-yolked egg. In circumcision rites, an egg ensures the sexual capacity of the young boy. Two eggs are often brought for luck on the first visit to a newborn boy; one to a girl. It is said that an egg thief brings seven years' bad luck and often death. The body of such a thief rolls around in the grave and is never still.

Mourning eggs are eaten by all Jews. They represent the roundness of the world and the mourning that comes to us all.

For many centuries, Sephardim have been eating *huevos haminados.* These dark brown creamy-tasting eggs are colored with onion peel or coffee grounds and gently simmered or baked for many hours, sometimes overnight. Cooked in the Saturday *dafina,* or long-simmering stew, they are also eaten alone as part of the Saturday morning *desayuno,* or breakfast, with *burekas* and coffee.

12 large eggs	1 teaspoon salt
Outer skin of 6–10 brown onions	1 teaspoon freshly ground pepper
Coffee grounds (optional)	Water
¼ cup olive oil or vegetable oil	

Place the eggs, onion skins, coffee grounds, if using, oil, salt, and pepper in a large casserole. Add enough water to cover the eggs. Bring the water to a boil. Cover and cook over a very low heat for 6 hours or overnight, or bake in a 225-degree oven overnight.

GOLDENE YOIKH

(Chicken Soup)

SERVES 8–10. (M)

And God blessed them, saying: "Be fruitful, and multiply, and fill the waters in the seas, and let fowl multiply in the earth."

Genesis 1:22

Chickens have always been one of the symbols of fertility and prosperity for the Jewish people. For poor people, where meat in general was scarce and poultry a luxury, chickens and particularly hens, with their mystical egg, excited the imagination.

In early Israel, a cock and a hen were carried in front of the bridal pair as they were escorted under the canopy. This Talmudic custom was transmuted in the Middle Ages to flying a pair of fowl over the heads of the bride and groom. In fifteenth-century Mainz, the bride and groom broke their prewedding fast by eating an egg and a hen after the ceremony.

For the New Year and for weddings, it was customary in Eastern Europe to serve *goldene yoikh,* or the fattest chicken soup possible. To poor people, wanting in substantial food, the *goldene yoikh* evoked images of wealth and success. Today, in affluent America, the yellow rings of chicken fat are not necessary.

One 4–5-pound soup chicken	1 onion, quartered
2 large celery stalks with leaves, sliced	3 sprigs of flat-leaf parsley
	Salt
2 large carrots, peeled and sliced in 2-inch diagonals	White pepper to taste

1. Clean and wash the chicken and place it in a large pot. Cover it with cold water. Bring to a boil and skim the broth thoroughly.
2. Add the vegetables and seasoning. Cover and simmer slowly for about 3 hours. When it's done, strain the soup. Serve as broth or with vegetables and chicken.

PASTILLA

(Chicken and Almond Pie)

SERVES 6–8 AS A MAIN DISH AND 12–15 AS AN HORS D'OEUVRE. (M)

This extraordinary crunchy pie can be served as an hors d'oeuvre or main dish for a special occasion. Ordinarily prepared with pigeons in Morocco, it is used there by Jews for a wedding, a bar mitzvah, or a *brit.* Typically Arab, it is usually made with dough similar to that of egg-roll wrappers and cooked brushed with butter (Jews use vegetable oil).

12–15 sheets phyllo dough
Salt and pepper
One 3-pound chicken, cut up
3 onions, finely chopped
1 cup flat-leaf parsley, finely
 chopped
1 cup vegetable oil or 2 sticks
 pareve margarine, melted
1 tablespoon fresh cilantro, finely
 chopped, or 1 teaspoon
 ground coriander
¼ teaspoon turmeric

1¼ teaspoons cinnamon
1 teaspoon ground ginger
Pinch of saffron in ½ cup warm
 water
½ teaspoon ground allspice
2 cups water (or more)
12 ounces blanched almonds
2 tablespoons sugar
8 large eggs, beaten
Confectioners' sugar and
 cinnamon for garnish

1. About 2 hours before starting, remove the phyllo from the freezer, but keep tightly covered.
2. Salt and pepper the chicken. Brown it in its own juices in a heavy skillet. Remove to a plate. Add the onions and parsley to the skillet. Sauté in 2 tablespoons of the oil or margarine until golden, stirring frequently.
3. Return the chicken to the skillet and add the cilantro or coriander, turmeric, 1 teaspoon of the cinnamon, ginger, saffron in water, allspice, and 2 cups water (or more if you think it is needed). Bring to a slow boil. Cover and simmer for about 45 minutes, or until the chicken is done.
4. Meanwhile, sauté the almonds in 4 tablespoons of oil or margarine until brown. Remove them and dry on paper towels. When cool and dry, chop them coarsely and combine with the sugar and the remaining ¼ teaspoon cinnamon.
5. If you are going to cook the *pastilla* immediately, preheat the oven to 375 degrees.
6. When the chicken is done, remove it from the skillet and let it cool.
7. If you wish, skim off some of the fat from the sauce. Leave the sauce over a low flame to reduce it to about 1½ cups.
8. When the chicken is cool, debone it and, using your fingers, break it into small chunks, about ¼ inch each. (Except for very fatty parts, use the entire chicken.)

9. When the sauce has reduced, slowly add the beaten eggs and stir over a low flame for 1–2 minutes until the eggs become custardlike. Do not let the sauce become too dry.

10. You can assemble the pie several ways, using either a round 9-inch quiche pan or a 9- by 13-inch glass baking pan. Brush oil on the bottom of the pan.

11. Rectangular method: Place 1 phyllo sheet in the pan and brush it with oil. Repeat with 5 more sheets. Over them, spread half of the nuts, half of the egg mixture, all the chicken, the remaining egg mixture, and the remaining nuts. Cover with 5–6 sheets of phyllo, again brushing with oil each time. Fold over any loose ends and brush the tops with oil. Taking a last leaf of phyllo, fold its edges down around the filling so that it neatly covers the pie, and brush it with oil. (You can also layer the phyllo between the different foods.)

12. Circular method: Place 1 sheet of phyllo in the middle of the quiche pan. Brush it with oil and then repeat with 5 more phyllo sheets, turning the pan a bit after each sheet of phyllo is added so that the phyllo fans the entire pan. Fold 2 pieces of phyllo and place them side by side in the center. In a circle 9 inches in diameter, leaving a ½-inch border, sprinkle half of the almonds, then half of the egg mixture, all the chicken, the remaining egg mixture, and finally the remaining almonds. Cover with the extended edges of the 6 phyllo sheets, brushing the edges with oil first. Seal down, then place 2 more sheets of phyllo on top; fold them over and seal underneath, so that an enclosed circular crust is formed.

13. Bake the pie 30–45 minutes, until the top is evenly browned. When the pie is ready to serve, sprinkle it with confectioners' sugar and cinnamon, almonds, or both, in crisscross fashion over the entire *pastilla.* Serve hot.

Note: If preparing in advance, do steps 1–12, cover with aluminum foil, and freeze. Remove a few hours before baking and bake as normal (perhaps a bit longer).

MUJEDDRAH

(Rice with Lentils, Esau Style)

And Jacob sod pottage; and Esau came in from the field, and he was faint. And Esau said to Jacob: "Let me swallow, I pray thee, some of this red, red pottage; for I am faint." . . . And Jacob said: "Swear to me first"; and he swore unto him; and he sold his birthright unto Jacob. And Jacob gave Esau bread and pottage of lentils; and he did eat and drink, and rose up, and went his way.

Genesis 25:29–34

SERVES 4–6. (P)

After the death of Abraham, Jacob prepared lentils for his father. A dish of lentils was the prominent food served at the mourners' meal following a funeral during biblical times. Later it was replaced by eggs as the main dish.

Circular legumes symbolize immortality and are a magical means of keeping away evil spirits. Thus, it is natural that these round natural foods should have a place at events when preserving life is important. On the Friday night preceding a *brit milah* and on the Watch Night before the *brit,* cooked beans (fava beans) and peas (chickpeas) are eaten. The Watch Night meal is to help the child's lucky star. The legumes were regarded as a sort of offering to appease the demons. The rounded lentil was also used to combat the evil influence of Lilith, who was feared as a threat to lying-in women and their offspring.

Esau's pottage was probably not lentil soup but more like *mujeddrah,* a delicious combination of lentils, onions, and rice traditionally stewed in olive oil. I have decreased the amount of oil in the following recipe and it is still tasty.

1 cup brown lentils	2 large onions, sliced in rings
2 teaspoons salt	2 tablespoons vegetable oil or
1 cup long-grain rice	olive oil

1. Pick over the lentils; wash and drain. Boil in 2 cups water with 1 teaspoon of the salt for about 30 minutes, or until tender.

2. Slowly sauté the onions in the oil in a frying pan until the onions are golden brown.

3. Meanwhile, drain and rinse the lentils and rice. Combine. Bring about 1½ cups water to a boil. Put in the lentils and rice, cover, and simmer slowly about 20 minutes, or until the rice is cooked. To serve, place the lentils and rice on a platter and sprinkle with the onions.

BAKED *KISHKE* WITH PRUNES

SERVES 8–10. (M)

Kishke (stuffed derma or intestine), *ganef* (stuffed gooseback), or *helzel* (stuffed goose or chicken neck) is eaten by traditional Jews at the Sabbath noon meal. In Eastern Europe, the dish is usually made from flour or bread crumbs, spices, egg, fat, and minced onion stuffed in a casing or the neck skin.

The Sephardim make theirs differently. In Syria, for example, Jews make it from pine nuts, meat, green peppers, and spices. Once the filling is stuffed into the cleaned intestine of a goat or cow, it is sewn up at the open end and either cooked together with the *cholent* (as on pages 77–81) or roasted separately. Today a thin plastic casing is used for the stuffing.

American-Jewish caterers have given *kishke*, known here as stuffed derma, a new gastronomic life. It is now served as a starch at weddings and bar mitzvahs. This is a family recipe of Paul and Debbie Berger of Chevy Chase, Maryland.

    12 ounces pitted prunes
    1 length (about 1 pound) *kishke**

1. Boil the prunes in 1 cup water, simmering until the prunes are soft, about 10 minutes.

2. Mash all except 8–10 prunes with a potato masher. Slice the *kishke* into ¾-inch-thick slices.

*Available at kosher delicatessens.

3. Preheat the oven to 325 degrees.
4. Layer the bottom of a 9-inch pie plate with some mashed prunes. Top with the *kishke* rounds and then another layer of mashed prunes. Add another layer of *kishke* and top with a whole prune in the center of each *kishke* round. Add water up to 1 inch.
5. Bake, uncovered, for about 1 hour.

CHOCOLATE FUDGE CAKE

SERVES 8–10. (D)

The only birthday mentioned in the entire Bible is that of Pharaoh. Which is not to say that Jews do not celebrate birthdays today; they are merely not a written part of Jewish custom. Historically, it is the *Yahrzeit*, the anniversary of someone's death, that is remembered in the cycle of life. Living in Christian cultures where birthdays and often saints' days are celebrated, Jews have adapted the birthday party as their own.

What is more American and more perfect for a birthday than an old-fashioned, homemade, rich chocolate fudge cake? Rosalyn Talisman of Cleveland learned to make the following recipe over forty years ago from her late neighbor, Elinor Lee. Thirty-five years later, Elinor tasted the cake at Rosalyn's and liked it so well she asked for the recipe! This and the following Sacher torte have become the official birthday cakes of the Nathan-Gerson household.

½ cup cocoa powder
1 cup boiling water
¼ pound (1 stick) butter
2 cups sifted all-purpose flour
2 cups sugar

1½ teaspoons baking soda
1 teaspoon salt
2 large eggs
½ cup sour cream
1 teaspoon vanilla extract

FROSTING:

2½ cups confectioners' sugar

4 ounces (½ cup) cream cheese

½ cup cocoa powder (more if you
want a darker frosting)

1 teaspoon vanilla extract

2 tablespoons sour cream (more
for a thinner frosting)

1. Preheat the oven to 350 degrees and grease and flour a 9-inch tube pan.
2. For the cake: Mix the cocoa, boiling water, and butter until the cocoa has dissolved. Allow the mixture to cool.
3. Combine the flour, sugar, baking soda, and salt.
4. Slowly mix the dry ingredients into the cooled cocoa mixture. Add the eggs, 1 at a time, beating well after each addition. Add the sour cream and vanilla.
5. Bake in the tube pan for 1 hour, or until a toothpick inserted in the cake comes out clean.
6. When the cake is cool, remove from pan. Cool cake upside down on a wire rack. Combine the frosting ingredients, blending them very well. Spread the frosting over the cake.

SACHER TORTE

SERVES 8. (D OR P)

Invented in 1832 by Viennese chef Franz Sacher for the renowned statesman Prince Klemens von Metternich, the Sacher torte is a rich chocolate cake covered with apricot jam and a chocolate glaze. My grandmother made her own version, which she served on special occasions in Bavaria. As long as I can remember, the Sacher torte has meant birthdays, since my father always requested one for his. The advent of pareve margarine at the turn of the century enabled German and Austrian Jews who kept kosher homes to eat this chocolate temptation at a meat meal.

¼ pound (1 stick) unsalted butter
or pareve margarine, at room
temperature

½ cup sugar

6 ounces semisweet chocolate

1 teaspoon vanilla extract

2 tablespoons strong brewed coffee

6 large eggs, separated

1 cup unbleached all-purpose
   flour

3 tablespoons potato flour

Pinch of salt

½ cup apricot preserves

1. Preheat the oven to 325 degrees and grease and flour a 9-inch springform pan.
2. Cream the butter or margarine. Add the sugar and cream the mixture until fluffy.
3. Melt the chocolate with the vanilla and coffee in a double boiler, then add it to the butter-sugar mixture. Blend well.
4. Add the egg yolks, 1 at a time, mixing well after each addition.
5. Sift the flour with the potato flour and the salt, and then add it to the chocolate mixture.
6. Beat the egg whites until stiff but not dry, and then fold them gently into the batter, which will be very heavy.
7. Turn the batter into the springform pan and bake for 1 hour, or until a toothpick inserted in the center comes out clean. Cool the torte on a cake rack, right side up. The torte will fall somewhat.
8. When cool, invert the cake to remove from pan. Cover the torte with the apricot preserves and the chocolate glaze.

CHOCOLATE GLAZE:

½ pound semisweet chocolate

½ cup sugar

½ cup water

1. Combine the chocolate with the sugar and the water in a saucepan set over low heat, stirring constantly until the chocolate melts, about 10 minutes.
2. Set the cake rack on a piece of waxed paper. Holding the saucepan about 2 inches above the cake, pour the glaze over it evenly. Smooth the glaze with a metal spatula. Let the cake stand until the glaze stops dripping. Then, using 2 metal spatulas or a cake trowel, transfer it to a plate and refrigerate for 3 hours to harden the glaze. Remove from the refrigerator 30 minutes before serving. Serve alone or with whipped cream (*schlag*).

MRS. GOLDMAN'S CHOCOLATE "EGYPTIAN" CAKE

MAKES 1 CAKE. (D)

The following so-called Egyptian cake has been handed down for at least four generations in the Goldman family of San Francisco. Mr. Goldman's grandmother, Mary Kaufman Wertheim, was born in Woodland, California. Her father had gone there from Germany during the Gold Rush. Since he did not strike gold, the family moved back to Bavaria when Mary was a little girl. She later returned to America and lived in Great Falls, Montana, where her daughter Alice Wertheim Goldman was born. When Alice Goldman married and moved to San Francisco, she brought with her the recipe for this cake, filled with currant preserves and coated with a chocolate cream-cheese frosting, which was served with applesauce for special occasions.

Although I searched everywhere for a recipe for this cake, I could find none. The closest I found was an "Araby Spice Cake" in *Choice Recipes by Moscow Women,* published in Moscow, Idaho, in 1931. *Choice San Francisco,* a cookbook published by the San Francisco section of the Council of Jewish Women in 1908–1909, includes a recipe for a "Reliable Cake" with a jam filling and a boiled icing.

I believe that the Goldman family cake was originally a Sacher-like torte, very much a German-Jewish special-occasion cake. When Mary Kaufman's family went to California from Bavaria, they probably brought a Sacher torte recipe with them. Later, when Mary returned to live in the States, she doubtless learned about baking powder, which makes a lighter cake. Eventually, instead of topping the cake with preserves and then a chocolate glaze, she may have preferred to fill the center with the preserves. Then, when chocolate cream cheese frosting became popular, she could have used it to replace the original chocolate glaze. I still have no idea how it came to be known as an "Egyptian" cake. The Goldman family prefers Ghirardelli cocoa powder, a San Francisco standard.

4 heaping tablespoons Ghirardelli or other unsweetened cocoa powder

5 tablespoons boiling water

½ pound (2 sticks) butter or pareve margarine

1½ cups sugar, sifted

4 large egg yolks

1¾ cups cake flour, sifted

2 rounded teaspoons baking powder

½ cup milk

4 large egg whites, stiffly beaten

1 teaspoon vanilla extract

2 cups currant jelly

1. Preheat the oven to 350 degrees and grease three 8-inch layer cake pans.
2. Dissolve the chocolate in the boiling water. Cream the butter and sugar until very creamy. Add the egg yolks, 1 at a time, beating well after each addition. Combine 2 tablespoons of flour with the baking powder; set aside. Add the milk, melted chocolate, and remaining flour alternately to the butter-sugar mixture; mix well, preferably by hand. Fold in the stiffly beaten egg whites and the vanilla. Finally, add the flour and baking powder mixture.
3. Bake in the prepared 8-inch pans for 30 to 35 minutes. Do not overbake. Cool on a rack completely before removing from pans.
4. Spread the currant jelly on the bottom and middle layers. Frost the top and sides with the chocolate cream cheese frosting (below). Refrigerate until serving.

CHOCOLATE CREAM CHEESE FROSTING:

14 ounces cream cheese, softened

¼ cup milk

4 squares unsweetened chocolate, melted

2 pinches of salt

2½ cups sifted confectioners' sugar

Beat the ingredients well in an electric mixer.

HUNGARIAN *DOBOS* TORTE

From Alex Lichtman

MAKES ONE 9-INCH ROUND TORTE; SERVES 16. (D)

When I was a child, I used to visit my grandparents in New York. My grandmother bought a *dobos* torte from Mrs. Herbst's Bakery for every birthday. To us children it was "seven-layer cake." In Hungarian, *dobos* means "like a drum," not just because the original was shaped like a little drum, but also because when you tap the caramel top crust of a true *dobos* torte, the caramel will resound like a drum. This cake takes care and time to prepare, but it is a wonderful challenge, well worth the effort.

Make sure you read the instructions through entirely before beginning this cake, and follow them exactly. It is very important to put the buttercream on the 6 layers, to refrigerate the layers, and then make the caramel for the seventh layer separately. Alex Lichtman used half butter and half vegetable shortening at Mrs. Herbst's, but in Hungary he would have used all butter. This delicious *dobos* torte is a tribute to Mrs. Herbst's Bakery, its bakers, and the magnificence of Austro-Hungarian pastries.

THE CAKE:

8 large eggs, separated, plus 1 large
    egg white
1 cup sugar
¼ cup milk
Grated zest of ½ lemon
Pinch of salt

1 teaspoon vanilla extract
1½ cups unbleached all-purpose
    flour, sifted
Softened unsalted butter for
    greasing the pans
Flour for dusting

THE CHOCOLATE BUTTERCREAM FILLING:

12 ounces bittersweet chocolate,
    preferably imported, broken
    in pieces

1 pound (4 sticks) plus 4
    tablespoons (½ stick) unsalted
    butter, at room temperature

Pinch of salt

1 tablespoon vanilla extract

4 cups confectioners' sugar, sifted

2 large eggs

THE CARAMEL TOPPING:

½ tablespoon cold vegetable shortening, for greasing the work surface

1 cup sugar

1. Preheat the oven to 400 degrees and cut two 10-inch circles out of cardboard.
2. Prepare the cake: Beat the egg whites, gradually adding the sugar, until soft peaks are formed. Do not beat until stiff.
3. In an electric mixer fitted with the paddle, mix the egg yolks with the milk, lemon zest, salt, and vanilla until well blended.
4. Gently fold the egg whites into the egg yolk mixture, then fold in the flour until smooth.
5. Remove the sides from a 9-inch springform pan and grease the bottom and sides generously with softened butter. Dust with flour, then knock off the excess flour. Replace the sides. Using a spatula, spread 1⅓ cups of the batter evenly over the pan bottom to a thickness of ⅛ inch, keeping an ⅛-inch border all around. Bake on the middle rack of the oven until brown spots appear on the layer, about 5–8 minutes. Using a spatula, remove the cake layer from the pan, dust it lightly with flour right away, and put it on a cookie sheet to cool. Repeat 6 more times, to make 7 layers.
6. Stack the cake layers with waxed paper in between, cover them with a towel, and refrigerate several hours or overnight.
7. To make the chocolate buttercream filling, melt the chocolate in a double boiler over simmering water on low heat. Let it cool while you mix the buttercream.
8. For the buttercream, place the butter, salt, and vanilla in the bowl of an electric mixer fitted with the paddle. Beat on low speed for 3 minutes. Add the confectioners' sugar slowly and continue mixing on low speed for 2–3 more minutes.
9. Increase to medium speed for 4–5 minutes. Add the eggs, 1 at a time; then beat on high 4–5 minutes. Use a rubber scraper for the sides and the bottom of the mixing bowl.

10. Add the cooled, melted chocolate and mix for 3–4 minutes more at low speed.

11. Place a cake layer on one of the cardboard circles and spread the top of it with buttercream to a ⅜-inch thickness all the way to the edge. Cover with another layer and press down lightly—this is important. Spread with another layer of buttercream, and repeat until 5 layers have been used. Top with a sixth layer, but do not cover with the buttercream; reserve the rest of the buttercream for the last layer and the sides of the cake. Smooth any buttercream that has been pressed out from between the layers around the sides of the cake. Place the cake in the refrigerator to set, about 5–6 hours. Refrigerate the remaining buttercream. Cover the seventh layer with plastic wrap and refrigerate.

12. Grease the surface of the second cardboard circle very lightly with vegetable shortening. Unwrap and place the seventh cake layer on top of the greased cardboard.

13. For the topping, pour the sugar into an 8-inch nonstick skillet. Using a wooden spoon, stir the sugar over a high flame until it is halfway melted. Turn down the heat and keep stirring for about 3 minutes. Remove the pan from the heat and continue stirring until the sugar is a light caramel color and the thickness of heavy cream. Pour the caramel onto the middle of the seventh layer and spread swiftly, carefully, and evenly with an oiled knife (caramel hardens very fast). Spread it to the edges of this top layer. Quickly and lightly touch the dull edge of the oiled knife into the caramel on the cake to make 16 pie-shaped wedges, which are decorative and will be used as guidelines for cutting the cake. Oil the knife again and retouch the markings. Remove this top layer from the cardboard and place it on a surface lightly dusted with granulated sugar so that it won't stick while the caramel cools.

14. Remove the torte from the refrigerator and smooth part of the remaining chocolate buttercream on top of the sixth cake layer. Lift the caramel-covered cake layer off the sugar onto the top of the torte. With a spatula, smooth the sides of the cake with the rest of the buttercream.

15. Refrigerate the torte until 15 minutes before serving.

LINZERTORTE

SERVES 8. (D)

The Austrian *Linzertorte* is a single-layer almond crust filled with raspberry preserves and covered with latticework. It is the choice for birthdays of my French-born, German-descended cousin Eveline Moos Weyl.

1 cup unbleached all-purpose flour	½ pound (2 sticks) unsalted butter, softened
Dash of cloves	1 cup thick raspberry or currant jam
Dash of cinnamon	
2 cups finely ground almonds	1 egg white
½ cup sugar	Confectioners' sugar
2 egg yolks	

1. Sift together the flour, cloves, and cinnamon. Add the almonds, sugar, and egg yolks.
2. With a wooden spoon or food processor, work in the butter to make a smooth dough. Refrigerate for at least 30 minutes, or until firm.
3. Preheat the oven to 300 degrees.
4. Roll out about half of the dough to a thickness of ½ inch and press onto the bottom and sides of a shallow 9-inch cake or springform pan.
5. Spread the jam on top. Roll out the remaining dough and, using a pastry cutter or sharp knife, cut into ½-inch-wide strips. Put them on top of the torte in a dainty lattice. Brush with the egg white.
6. Bake for about 1 hour, or until it is lightly browned. Let the cake cool for 5 minutes and then sprinkle with confectioners' sugar.

PALACSINTA

(Hungarian Crêpes)

MAKES 12. (D OR P)

A combination of Hungarian crêpes, apricot preserves, and chocolate would make a stunningly appropriate birthday cake to bake for someone of Hungarian descent!

1½ cups sifted all-purpose flour	Butter or pareve margarine for
2 whole eggs	frying
1½ cups soda water	

1. Combine the flour and the eggs. Add ½ cup of the soda water and mix into a paste. Using a wooden spoon, beat until all the lumps disappear. Stirring constantly, slowly add the remaining soda water.
2. Heat a small frying pan or crêpe pan over a medium flame. Add about ¼ teaspoon butter or margarine and swoosh it around. Pour in the batter with a small soup ladle, moving the pan around until it is thinly and evenly coated. Let it heat awhile, until bubbly and dry. Then slide a knife, dipped into the butter, underneath the edge of the pancake. When ready, turn it over and cook for about 30 seconds. Remove to a plate. Repeat the process, adding butter each time. These crêpes freeze well.

Palacsintas can be used as is for blintzes (see pages 385 and 429–30 for fillings) or served Hungarian style with a filling of apricot preserves and sprinkled with confectioners' sugar. The following layered crêpes are a Hungarian dessert for special occasions.

PALACSINTATORTE

(Chocolate Apricot Crêpe Cake)

SERVES 6–8. (P)

12 pareve crêpes (recipe page 486)   ¼ cup chopped walnuts
1 cup apricot preserves   1 tablespoon raisins
1 tablespoon cocoa powder   2 egg whites
4 teaspoons sugar

1. Preheat the oven to 300 degrees. Grease a round, ovenproof plate.
2. Place 1 crêpe on the plate. Top it with a thin layer of apricot preserves. Cover it with another crêpe and sprinkle with cocoa and sugar. Cover with another crêpe and sprinkle with some nuts and raisins. Continue in alternating layers until all the crêpes are used up. (You may want to use more or less cocoa mixture or apricot preserves, according to your taste.)
3. Mix the egg whites with 1 teaspoon of the apricot preserves and about 1 teaspoon of the sugar. Beat the mixture until shiny and pour it over the top crêpe.
4. Bake until the meringue is brown, about 10–15 minutes. Serve immediately.

GESUNDHEITSKUCHEN

(Southern German "Good Health Cake")

From Lisl Nathan Regensteiner

MAKES 1 LARGE OR 2 SMALL CAKES; SERVES 8–10. (D)

This popular southern German cake, which could be called in English "Don't Sneeze Cake," was my aunt Lisl's signature dish. Baked in a family-heirloom Bundt pan brought with her from Germany, the cake was served during shiva but also for birthdays, for tea, and at celebrations of the birth of children. Easily prepared, it was the kind of cake that could be made quickly for unexpected guests. In the late nineteenth century in this country, baking powder lightened the cake. Soon poppy seeds and even chocolate chips were added. It is a simple, soothing cake, one that gets gobbled up in my house. This is Lisl's version, with some of my American embellishments.

3 large eggs
1 cup sugar
½ pound (2 sticks) unsalted
    butter or pareve margarine,
    melted and cooled
1 teaspoon vanilla extract
Grated zest and juice of 1 lemon
1 cup milk

2½ cups unbleached all-purpose
    flour
1 heaping tablespoon baking
    powder
½ teaspoon salt
⅓ cup poppy seeds (optional)
Confectioners' sugar

1. Preheat the oven to 350 degrees. Grease and lightly flour a Bundt pan or two 9- by 5- by 4-inch loaf pans.
2. In the bowl of an electric mixer fitted with the whisk, beat the eggs well with the sugar. Add the cooled butter (minus any milky residue), the vanilla, lemon zest and juice, and milk.
3. Gradually add the flour, baking powder, and salt as you beat at low speed. When the batter is smooth, turn off the mixer. Add the poppy seeds, if using.
4. Pour the batter into the greased pan or pans and bake on the middle rack of the oven for 45 minutes, or until a toothpick inserted in the center comes out clean. Cool in the pan for 10 minutes, then turn the cake out and cool completely on a rack. Sprinkle the top with confectioners' sugar just before serving.

ANISE COOKIES

MAKES ABOUT 20. (P)

In Germany my grandmother gave this easily digestible cookie to nursing mothers.

4 large eggs
1 cup sugar
2 cups all-purpose flour
½ teaspoon salt

½ teaspoon baking powder
½ teaspoon vanilla extract
Grated zest of ½ lemon
1 teaspoon anise seed

1. Preheat the oven to 325 degrees and grease a large baking pan.
2. Beat the eggs and sugar together.
3. Sift the flour with the salt and baking powder and add to the egg mixture. Blend in the vanilla, lemon zest, and anise seed.
4. Spoon the mixture into the prepared pan. Bake for about 45 minutes, or until light brown.
5. Slice the cake while still warm into ⅓-inch-thick pieces. Place them on a large cookie sheet and toast in the oven until golden, then turn them over and toast the other side.

WEDDING CAKE

On the wedding day, immediately after the marriage ceremony, there was a collation of all kinds of the finest sweetmeats, foreign wines and out-of-season fruits. . . . After the ceremony all the guests were led into a great hall, the walls of which were lined with gilded leather. A long table crowded with regal delicacies stood in the center, and each guest was served in order of rank.

Glückel of Hameln, 1672, description of her
daughter's wedding in Amsterdam

My wedding was at a time of many shortages after a lost war and a revolution. My mother had a most difficult time getting a festival together. In fact, we had two meals, dinner and supper, for between forty and fifty guests. The ceremony took place in our lovely synagogue in Augsburg, but afterward we drove home by horse and buggy where a beautiful table had been set. I don't remember the menu exactly, but usually a wedding meal consisted of many courses, including soup, fish, chicken, a roast, with cakes and ices for dessert. In the evening, cold cuts with various salads were served. As a special treat, we had Vollbeer—beer with full alcohol content, a luxury at this difficult time. I don't think we had a wedding cake; it was not customary. The one good Jewish restaurant in our town catered the meals at my wedding. There was a piano player for entertainment, but the very nice thing was that our friends wrote plays and songs which they performed and which contained episodes of our lives.

Recollections of my aunt Lisl's wedding in Augsburg, Germany, 1920

Probably more than any other event, the wedding meal is influenced by wealth and the food customs of the country in which the bridal couple resides.

The wealthy Dutch of the seventeenth century ate sweetmeats at their weddings. My middle-class aunt in Germany shortly after World War I had a less elaborate meal. Although she does not recall her menu, it may have been similar to that of her parents' wedding in 1897. Theirs included a rich chicken soup; salmon and trout with Hollandaise sauce; potatoes; carrots and peas with warm tongue; young roast goose with salad and various fruit sauces; chocolate pudding, cold sherbets, tortes, and petits fours. The evening meal featured cold cuts with salad.

Wedding cake as we know it does not appear until the end of the nineteenth century. Here is the first American-Jewish recipe for wedding cake, from Esther Levy's *Jewish Cookery Book,* published in 1871.

A FINE COWLEDGE, OR WEDDING CAKE

Wash two and a half pounds of fresh butter in spring water first, then in rose water, beat the butter to a cream; beat twenty eggs, yolks and whites separately, half an hour; have ready two pounds and a half of the finest flour, well dried and kept hot, a pound and a half of sifted sugar, one ounce of spices, in fine powder, three pounds of currants, nicely cleaned and dry, half a pound of blanched almonds, three-quarters of a pound of citron mixed with orange and lemon; let all be kept by the fire; mix all the dry ingredients in by degrees; beat them thoroughly; then add a half pound of stoned raisins, chopped as fine as possible, so that there are no lumps, and a teacupful of orange flower water; beat it all together for one hour; have a good sized cake tin; it should not be more than three parts full, as there must be space allowed for rising. It will take from three to four hours' baking.

THE BAKLAVA STORY

A Christian, a Jew, and a Moslem went to Istanbul to try their luck. Time passed, and they wanted to sleep. It was very cold, and each of them was keen to sleep in the middle, as it was warmer there between the others.

The Jew said, "It is written in the Holy Torah that I must sleep in the middle."

The Christian and Moslem wondered.

"Look," continued the Jew. "You, Suleiman, celebrate your Sabbath on Friday. You, George, celebrate yours on Sunday, but mine is in the middle, on Saturday. As my feast day is in the middle, my place to sleep must also be in the middle."

The other two agreed to this, and the Jew snuggled up to sleep between the two of them.

When they reached Istanbul, they found a golden coin in the street and started to discuss what to do with it. The Jew kept quiet. The Christian and Moslem decided after a long quarrel and much talking that with the money they could buy a baklava, a sweet Turkish cake, and the one who dreamed the most beautiful dream would eat it in the morning.

In the night the Jew woke up and felt very hungry. He tasted the cake. He tried to awaken his friends, but they were sound asleep and did not hear him. The Jew went to sleep for an hour; again he woke up and ate another piece of the cake. He tried again to awaken his friends, but again he was unsuccessful. So he continued to nibble at the cake all night, until not a morsel remained.

In the morning the three friends went to a café in the market. Many people were assembled there; Moslems, Christians, and Jews. Suleiman told them what had happened—how they had found a golden coin in the street and spent it on a baklava. Now they wanted the people to judge who had dreamed the most beautiful dream.

The Christian told his dream first. "I dreamed that Jesus himself came to me and carried me on his wings to the Garden of Eden. When we arrived there, he pointed out to me all the saints sitting around and entertaining each other."

Then it was Suleiman's turn. "I dreamed that Mohammed himself appeared before me and took me to have a look at the Garden of Eden. Is there any dream more beautiful than that?" he asked the people.

When the Jew's turn came, he said, "My dream was different from yours. Unfortunately, I was not lucky enough to visit the Garden of Eden as both of you did. But Moses, our lawgiver, came to me and said, 'Suleiman is with his master, Mohammed, in Mecca; George is with his master, Jesus, in Nazareth. Who knows if either of them will return or not?' And he advised me to eat the baklava."

"Did you eat it?" they asked eagerly.

"Of course," came the answer. "Do you think that I disobey our lawgiver's advice!"

Isaac Al-Bahri, recorded by Elisheva Schoenfeld, *Folktales of Israel*

Baklava, the dream bread in this tale of a Turkish Jew, is a very old sweet, ideal for large functions. Originally a many-layered phyllo Turkish pastry filled with nuts and a syrup of honey or sugar and water, it is made in variations throughout the Middle East.

SYRIAN BAKLAVA

From Mansoura Middle Eastern Pastries

MAKES 24 SERVINGS. (D OR P)

Baklava is to Jews of Syrian and Middle Eastern descent what strudel is to those of Central European origins. However, the technique of making the phyllo dough for baklava is quite different from that of making strudel dough. Unlike strudel dough, made from melted butter or oil, flour, water, and egg, phyllo is made from flour, water, and occasionally an egg. "We mixed the flour and water and let the dough set for two hours," said Alan Mansoura, the last of eight generations to make phyllo. "First we sprinkled cornstarch on a huge table, rolled out a ball of dough on top, then sprinkled the dough again with cornstarch. We repeated this process for about twenty-four layers, rolling each ball of dough on top of the one before, and separating each with the cornstarch. When the dough got wider than the rolling pin we switched to a stick about six feet long— a broom handle is great for this—and an inch and a half in diameter." Alan and his father slowly rolled the dough out paper-thin, until it was five feet in diameter, the entire process taking about an hour. "We would transfer the leaves of dough and cover them with a moist cloth. Then we would use the dough as we needed it."

"Baklava is served at every celebratory function imaginable," said Josiane Mansoura. "It ensures tradition." Since phyllo is now made commercially, however, the family has forgone that arduous part of the tradition.

This recipe, with a sugar-rosewater syrup, is lighter and less sweet than those made with honey. The baklava can be frozen before baking. The Mansouras put bright green pistachios from Afghanistan in their version; you can substitute walnuts. If you are using a food processor to chop the nuts, do not pulverize them—they should be chopped roughly to retain their texture.

1 pound prepared phyllo dough (approximately 20 sheets, 14 by 18 inches)	½ pound (2 sticks) unsalted butter or pareve margarine, melted
3½ cups coarsely chopped walnuts or pistachio nuts	2 cups sugar
	1 cup water
1 teaspoon cinnamon, if using walnuts	1 cinnamon stick
	1 teaspoon rose water (optional)*

1. Carefully remove the phyllo from its plastic container and unroll. You will have about 20 rectangular sheets. Cover the sheets with a damp towel.

*Obtainable at Middle Eastern markets.

2. Preheat the oven to 350 degrees. Cut 2 pieces of phyllo to the exact size of a 9-inch round or a 9- by 12-inch rectangular pan. Set these sheets aside, covered with a damp cloth.

3. If you wish to use walnuts, mix the nuts and cinnamon in a small bowl and set aside.

4. Using a large brush, paint the bottom of the pan with some of the melted butter or margarine. Cut each of the remaining sheets of phyllo in half horizontally. Layer one-fourth of these sheets into the bottom of the pan, brushing melted butter or margarine over the top layer and pressing down any that overlap the pan. Again, layer with another quarter of the sheets, brush again with the melted butter or margarine, and press down any sheets that overlap.

5. Sprinkle all the nut mixture evenly over the phyllo, pressing down gently with your fingers. Layer on the third quarter of the phyllo sheets, brushing generously with the butter or margarine; layer the remaining quarter on top and brush again. Then trim away the overhang with scissors or a sharp knife. Finally, take the reserved 2 phyllo sheets, place them on top of the baklava, and press down gently with the flat side of a large knife. Brush the top phyllo sheets with melted butter or margarine.

6. With a long, sharp knife, cut across the baklava on a diagonal every 1½ inches, placing your thumb and second finger gently on the dough to hold it down; then cut diagonally in the opposite direction to make diamond shapes. Brush the top again with the remaining melted butter or margarine.

7. Bake the baklava on the middle rack of the oven for 45 minutes to 1 hour, or until golden brown.

8. Meanwhile, put the sugar, water, cinnamon stick, and rose water in a small saucepan. Bring to a boil, reduce the heat, and simmer gently for 30 minutes, or until the mixture coats the back of a spoon.

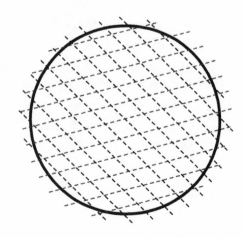

9. Remove the cinnamon stick and pour the warm syrup over the baked baklava. Let it stand for several hours or overnight, covered with plastic wrap.

KADAIF

MAKES 40–50. (P OR D)

This Lebanese version of *kadaif* comes from Annie Totah.

Vegetable shortening

3 cups ground walnuts, or 1 cup ground unsalted pistachio nuts and 2 cups ground walnuts

2 teaspoons cinnamon

3¼ cups sugar

2 tablespoons honey

1 pound (4 sticks) unsalted butter or unsalted pareve margarine

2 pounds shredded *kadaif* dough,* at room temperature

1½ cups water

1 tablespoon fresh lemon juice

1. Preheat the oven to 400 degrees and grease an 18- by 11- by 2-inch pan with vegetable shortening.
2. Mix together the nuts, cinnamon, ¼ cup of the sugar, and 1 tablespoon of the honey. Set aside.
3. Melt and clarify the butter or margarine.
4. Spread the dough on a table or place it in a large bowl. Pour the butter over it and, with your fingers, separate the shredded dough until all is well buttered. Divide the dough into 2 equal halves. Spread half on the bottom of the pan and gently press with your fingers to cover the surface completely. Spread the nut filling evenly over the dough and cover with the remaining dough.
5. Bake for 20–30, minutes or until golden brown. Cool in the pan for about 10 minutes.
6. Boil together the remaining 3 cups sugar, the remaining 1 tablespoon honey, the water, and the lemon juice. Simmer for 15 minutes. Let stand for 10 minutes.
7. Using a tablespoon, ladle the hot syrup over the warm *kadaif*. Let it stand for about 15 minutes, covered, and then cut into squares.

*Kadaif dough can be purchased at Greek or Middle Eastern specialty stores.

WINE

WINE

A NOTE ON WINE

And Noah the husbandman began, and planted a vineyard.
And he drank of the wine, and was drunken.

Genesis 9:20–21

Ever since Noah descended from the ark and planted his vineyard, Jews have had a special attachment to wine. The connection has always been largely religious and sacramental. A benediction is recited over wine before it is drunk. Before a baby is circumcised, his lips are brushed with wine. Among Conservative and Reform Jews, it is customary that a bar or bat mitzvah say his or her first kiddush (blessing over the wine) at the pulpit. At wedding ceremonies, a glass of wine is sipped by the bride and groom. At least four cups are drunk at the Passover Seder. Drinking and even drunkenness are tolerated at Purim and Simhat Torah. A blessing over wine, which symbolizes everything that grows from the vine, precedes the Friday night and Sabbath noon meals. Wine, for Jews, is good medicine. *Lehayyim*—"To life!"—is our standard toast. The Jewish custom of drinking wine before the start of a meal induces the appetite while adding a certain formality to the proceedings that follow.

From earliest times, wine played an important role in the Jewish economy. By the time of the First Temple, taxes were payable in olive oil and wine. Wine was obligatory at public religious functions and for domestic ceremonies. It symbolized the hospitality and prosperity of the city dweller or of the peasant settled on his own land. (In shepherds' tents, only water or milk was drunk.)

Although early wine came from grapes, pomegranates, raisins, figs, and dates, only grape wine was used for sacramental purposes. In fact, throughout the Bible the vineyard is a recurring metaphor for the people of Israel. In Deuteronomy 32:38 it is stated: "Who did eat the fat of their sacrifices, And drank the wine of their drink-offering? Let him rise up and help you, Let him be your protection." From this rabbis deduced that only wines made and handled by Jews under religious supervision could be called kosher. This prohibition dates to the time that ancient Israelites lived among pagan peoples, who used wine as a libation to their gods. Thus, almost from the beginning, Jews have been vintners.

For a wine to be kosher, it must be made from grapes that have been touched only by Jews, from the time they are pressed until the wine is bottled and poured. Such wines bear the *hecksher*—"the rabbi's certificate of approval"—on the label. Other wine-based drinks, like vermouth, Champagne, and brandy, must comply with the same rules to be kosher. Beer, vodka, arak, and gin—and other grain and potato alcohols that have no wine in them—do not have to be made kosher like wine (though at Passover, any alcohol made from grain cannot be served). Blended whiskey that contains no form of wine is permissible to all Jews.

Although the custom of drinking only kosher wine continues, the reasons the rabbis gave changed in the sixteenth century. Although Christians could not be considered pagans, there was a strong fear of social intercourse, leading to intermarriage. Therefore, the halakhic authorities thought it best for Jews to drink wine processed and bottled only by Jews. This prohibition often ran into problems. What to do with Champagne, for example? If a kosher caterer employs non-Jewish waiters to pour Champagne at a wedding, the Orthodox Jew will not touch it. To overcome this problem, wine companies began boiling their wine just before bottling, most often at the juice stage before vinification. If so pasteurized, the wine could be considered kosher even if it afterwards was touched by gentile hands. Strides have been made in the past few years to improve kosher wines. And now, this process takes place at the juice stage prior to fermentation, which may enhance some aromas and the stability of the wine. (An interesting sidelight on kosher wine: Some manufacturers of non-kosher wine cleanse their factory every few years and work with rabbis to produce a certain amount of kosher stock.)

Until the eighth century, Jews produced wine in Palestine. With the Muslim conquest, it was prohibited because of Muslim religious restrictions. It was not until the 1880s, when Edmond de Rothschild established wineries at Rishon-le-Zion and Zichron-Jacob, that production began again in earnest. These wineries produce the bulk of Israel's wine today. Most of the vineyards are planted with common French red and white grapes. Seventy percent of Israel's wine exports go to the United States; most bear the label of Carmel wine, Israel's best-known winery.

As the Jews dispersed throughout the world, they needed to produce their own wine for religious purposes. Thus, wherever they lived in the Diaspora, Jews were found in the wine business. In some Russian and Polish towns in the eighteenth and nineteenth centuries, as much as 85 percent of the Jewish population was somehow involved in wine or liquor production or distribution. With all the limits placed on Jews, alcohol was one of the few trades they could easily enter (although they paid a high tax to do so). They were even tavern keepers in Eastern Europe. This profession has carried over to the United States, where most wine or liquor concerns started as mom-and-pop grocery stores, like Schapiro's on New York's Lower East Side, and spread outward.

During Prohibition, wine—along with all other alcoholic beverages—was illegal. But Catholic and Jewish wines were permitted for religious purposes. Shortly after Prohibition ended in 1933, Leo Star and his Monarch Wine Company began making kosher wines. Star contracted with Manischewitz, now owned by Canandaigua Wine Company, in the mid-1940s, after which the Manischewitz label appeared on the bottle in a licensing agreement. Kedem Winery was founded in 1946 on Manhattan's Lower East Side. They are owned by the Royal Wine Corporation, which also produces Baron Herzog and imports Rothschild's Kosher Bordeaux and Carmel wines. Mogen David has its vineyards in upstate New York. Today, kosher wine is not synonymous with sweet. Some examples are Napa Valley's Ha Gafen and Weinstock wines, Australia's Teal Lake, Sonoma County's Gan Eden, and Israel's Yarden and Gamla. So drink "*Lehayyim,*" "to life," and if you are enterprising, try to make your own wine. Here is an old recipe for Concord grape wine from—where else?—Concord, Massachusetts.

CONCORD GRAPE WINE

18 quarts Concord grapes   15 pounds sugar

1. Either pick or buy the grapes. Wash them thoroughly. After draining all the water from the grapes, put them in a 5-gallon earthenware crock.
2. Add the sugar, shaking the crock gently to distribute evenly. Cover the crock tightly and bind it with cloth over the cover to seal securely.
3. Keep in a warm place for about 3 weeks. After the first 3–4 days, uncover the crock and stir with a large, long-handled spoon to dissolve the sugar. Cover tightly and seal with a cloth as before. Do this every few days. If the fruit ferments too much, move to a slightly cooler place.
4. After 3 weeks in a warm place, remove the crock to a cool place. Let it stand for 2–3 weeks more, until the fruit settles. Strain the liquid through a cloth-lined strainer.
5. Bottle in jugs, jars, or bottles and put away in a cold place. When the wine is ready to use, the sediment will have settled to the bottom, and the wine at the top should be clear and bright.

BOMBAY KIDDUSH WINE

(Currant Wine for Kiddush)

MAKES ABOUT 3 CUPS.

Jewish table customs are often connected with wine. In nineteenth-century Turkey, for example, after saying the kiddush on Friday evening, it was the custom to take a cup of wine and drop some of its contents on the floor of every room in the house, saying: "Elijah the Prophet, Elijah the Prophet, come quickly to us with the Messiah, son of David." Elijah the Prophet was always considered the precursor of the Messiah, and the Messiah is to come on Passover. We all know that Elijah is expected in each Jewish home at the Seder meal, and so a silver cup is placed on the table filled with wine for his arrival.

Whatever the custom, the kiddush opens the meal. Today most Jews merely buy their wine from a store that carries kosher wines. They probably once traded a goose or other commodity raised or produced at home for their kiddush wine. Nevertheless, some Jews did and do make their own.

Pearl Sofaer, born in Bombay and now living in Sausalito, California, was the firstborn daughter in her family. It was her task to make the kiddush wine each Thursday evening from large black currants, for it is permissible to use a common national drink in place of true wine. Any leftover wine was put in large olive casks from Baghdad and eventually turned into vinegar.

1 cup large black currants*

1. On Thursday evening the eldest daughter of the family should wash and pit the currants and place them in a bottle with 2 cups of water.
2. Cover the bottle and keep it in a room with the temperature at about 90 degrees (obviously, this must be made in the summer).
3. On Friday night pour the wine, say the kiddush over it, and drink.

Note: Any leftover wine can be stored in a large cask. In six months you will have delicious vinegar.

CHAMPAGNE

It is a common legend that the monk Dom Pérignon discovered Champagne. What is less well known is the fact that a Portuguese-Jewish wine merchant named Dom Isaac Levy, whose family had fled to France during the Inquisition, inadvertently invented the sparkling wine in a case of wine from Dom Pérignon's cellar. As a vintner, Dom Levy had thought it a good idea to use Portuguese cork in bottling aged wine to prevent the fermentation gases from escaping. He sent some corks with a shipment of wine to the Duke of Bedford at Woburn Abbey, England. Instead of letting the casked wine age before transferring it, the Duke

*Large currants are available at some Greek and Mediterranean specialty-food stores.

had it bottled and corked without the aging process. Six weeks later, corks flew in the wine cellar as the accumulated gas shot out of the bottles with tremendous force. Champagne was born! When the Duke requested more of this same wine, Dom Levy contacted Dom Pérignon and the latter tested different wines to come up with the real Champagne.

Now, all that was needed was for the cork to be kept down. Simon Benvenisti, a Jewish wine merchant from Amsterdam, came up with the thin, strong wire that is looped around the cork and twisted around the neck of the bottle.

The following is my family's Champagne punch recipe, which comes from Bavaria.

DAD'S CHAMPAGNE PUNCH

SERVES 20.

2 bottles Chablis, chilled
Two 20-ounce cans pineapple
    chunks in juice, chilled

2 bottles Champagne, chilled

1. Six hours before serving, marinate the Chablis with the pineapple chunks and pineapple juice.
2. Just before serving, add the Champagne.

ACKNOWLEDGMENTS

The seed for the original *Jewish Holiday Kitchen* was planted during my stay in Jerusalem from 1970 to 1972. It germinated during the academic year of 1975–76, when I was fortunate to be studying at the John F. Kennedy School of Government at Harvard University, on a fellowship from the Smith Fund. I am especially grateful to three professors I met there who encouraged me to study Jewish food within the context of an ethnic society. Wilma Wetterstrom's course on nutrition and sociocultural systems directed my approach to Jewish cuisine. Daniel Patrick Moynihan allowed me to deviate in his course on ethnicity and politics to write a paper on ethnicity and food, which has formed the basis for the introduction to this book. Folklorist Dov Noy, on sabbatical from the Hebrew University, Jerusalem, encouraged my exploration into the folklore surrounding Jewish food and introduced me to the concept of seasonal and life cycles.

A Jewish cookbook that tries to be in some way comprehensive cannot be written without the help of the many Jewish cooks, around the United States and abroad, who have inherited and shared treasured family recipes. Wherever possible, I have gratefully acknowledged their contribution.

Many people helped test recipes and looked over the manuscript for this book. In particular I want to thank Sarah Wattenberg, Marie Marcel Auguste, Leslie Katz, Ellen Gold, and Matt McMillen. Through the years they have helped cook, and they have watched my children so that I could cook, research, and write.

I am appreciative of the time David Altschuler, Molly G. Schuchat, and Mickey and Mordechai Feinberg spent reading the original manuscript. They generously shared with me their religious, historical, and anthropological expertise.

Whenever I needed technical information, I turned to the indefatigable and extraordinarily knowledgeable staff of the Library of Congress's Hebraic Section. Without the assistance of the late Myron Weinstein, Feiga Zylberminc, and later, Peggy Pearlstein, this book could not have been written. And, of course, it was my agent, Susan Lescher, and my editors, Cherie Gillette, Marcy Posner, Seymour Barofsky, Beverly Colman, and Rahel Lerner, who helped me to execute the writing of the various editions of my cookbook.

Many of the recipes in this book come from the people I have interviewed for Jewish holiday articles in the *New York Times*. I am grateful to my editors, Michelline Busico and Sam Sifton, for encouraging me to write the kinds of articles I like writing.

My in-laws, Morton and Paula Gerson, my father, Ernest, and my aunt Lisl Regensteiner shared with me so much more than food before they died. A little of my love for them is in these pages. My cousin Dorothy Regensteiner and my mother, Pearl Nathan, continue to share graciously with me those Jewish roots and recipes that have made up my own culinary heritage.

A very special note of appreciation is due to my husband, Allan Gerson, who—always in good spirits—has played the role of quality controller in tasting all the recipes in this book. Thirty years after I began this work, these recipes are still part of our lives in the many gatherings at holidays and shabbat we have shared with our family and friends. Both the interviews with the elderly and the recipes I collected have provided my husband Allan and me with a priceless culinary heritage to hand down to our three children, Daneila, Merissa, and David, whom I hope will continue using them in their own lives.

GLOSSARY OF JEWISH HOLIDAY
AND FESTIVAL FOOD TERMS

ADAFINA   Moroccan long-simmering stew (*hamim*), similar to *cholent,* made with meat, potatoes, chickpeas, vegetables, rice, etc.

AFIKOMEN   Piece of matzah broken off from the middle of three matzot used at the Passover Seder and set aside—and often hidden—to be eaten at the end of the meal.

APFELBUWELE   Bavarian Jewish apple dessert in a crust, usually baked in a heavy iron pot.

ASHKENAZIM   Central and Eastern European, including Yiddish-speaking, Jews and their descendants.

BAGEL   A roll with a hole.

BAR MITZVAH   Jewish boy who has reached his thirteenth birthday and attained the age of religious duty and responsibilities.

BAS (BAT) MITZVAH   Jewish girl who has reached her twelfth birthday and attained the age of religious duty and responsibilities.

BERCHES   German and Central European challah often made from potatoes, tasting somewhat like sourdough bread.

BLINTZ   A crêpelike pancake with a filling, usually of cheese.

BORSCHT   A soup having fermented or fresh red beet juice as the foundation, often with cabbage or meat or both added.

BRIT MILAH   Ceremony of circumcision performed on a male child on the eighth day after birth.

BUREKAS   A triangular and sometimes round pastry of Turkish origin filled with spinach, spinach and cheese, potato, eggplant, mushroom, or meat.

CHALLAH   Traditional Sabbath and holiday loaf of white bread, often baked in braided or twisted form. Originally, the portion of dough given to the priests in the time of the Temple in Jerusalem. Today, religious Jews still remove and burn a small portion of dough before baking the loaves.

CHELOU   Persian steamed rice.

CHOLENT   Sabbath stew of slow-baked meat, potatoes, and beans.

COCIDO   Spanish stew thought to be akin to *adafina.*

507

DAFINA   See *ADAFINA*.

DESAYUNO   Sephardic Sabbath breakfast.

EINGEMACHTS   Jam or preserves made from beets, radishes, carrots, cherries, or lemons and walnuts, often eaten during Passover with a spoon and served with tea.

ETROG   Fruit of the citron, used with the *lulav* in celebrating Sukkot.

EGYENSULY   Hungarian cherry pound cake.

FARFEL   Noodle dough or matzah in the form of small pellets or granules.

FASSOULIA   A stew of green beans and meat.

FESENJAN   A stew of pomegranates and chicken.

FIDELLOS   Hair-thin pasta.

FIJUELAS   Moroccan deep-fried pastry.

FLEISHIG   Made of, prepared with, or used for meat or meat products.

GEFILTE FISH   Stewed or baked fish, stuffed with a mixture of the fish flesh, bread or matzah crumbs, eggs, and seasonings, or prepared as balls or oval cakes that are boiled in a fish stock.

GOLDENE YOIKH   Rich, golden chicken soup, traditionally served at weddings.

GRIEBEN   Cracklings from goose fat and goose skin, usually salted.

GRIBENES   Fried chicken fat.

HAMANTASHEN   Triangular-shaped Purim cookie, filled with prunes, poppy seeds, preserves, nuts, or even chocolate chips.

HAMETZ   Leavened products.

HAMIM   Long-simmering stew served by Sephardim on the Sabbath.

HANUKKAH   Festival of Lights celebrating the Maccabean victory over the Seleucids in 164 B.C.E.

HAROSET   Pastelike mixture of fruit, nuts, cinnamon, and wine eaten during the Passover Seder and symbolic of the mortar the Israelites used in building during the Egyptian slavery.

HAVDALAH   Ceremony marking the close of Sabbath or of holidays and consisting of a recital by the head of the household of the appropriate benediction over a cup of wine, a spice box, and a newly lighted special candle.

HUEVOS HAMINADOS   Long-cooked eggs served by Sephardic Jews on the Sabbath and other holidays.

KAPPAROT   Symbolic ceremony on the eve of Yom Kippur in which a cock, hen, or coin is swung around the head and offered as ransom in atonement for one's sins.

KARPAS   Piece of parsley, celery, or lettuce placed on the Seder plate as a symbol of spring or hope and dipped in salt water in remembrance of the hyssop and blood of the Passover in Egypt.

KASHA   Coarse, cracked buckwheat, barley, millet, or wheat; or the mush made from it.

KIDDUSH   Ceremony proclaiming the holiness of the incoming Sabbath or festival; it consists of a benediction pronounced customarily before the evening meal over a cup of wine and usually two loaves of challah.

KINDLI   Hungarian cookies for Purim.

KISHKE   Beef or fowl casing (derma) stuffed with a savory filling (such as matzah meal, chicken fat, and onion) and roasted.

KNEYDLAKH   Soup dumplings made from matzah meal, eggs, chicken fat, and sometimes ground almonds; usually boiled but sometimes fried.

KNISH   A round or square of rich baking-powder or strudel dough, folded over a savory meat, cheese, or potato filling and baked or fried.

KOFTA   Sephardic meatball or fried patty, generally.

KOSHER   Sanctioned by Jewish law, ritually fit, clean, or prepared for use according to Jewish law.

KREPLAKH   Triangular pockets of noodle dough filled with chopped or ground meat or cheese, boiled and eaten with soup or fried and eaten as a side dish.

KRIMSEL   Deep-fried fritter made from matzot or matzah meal.

KUGEL   Baked sweet or savory pudding or casserole made of noodles, potatoes, bread, or vegetables, often served on the Sabbath or festivals.

KUGELHOPF   Semisweet cake of Alsatian origin, usually of yeast-leavened dough containing raisins, citron, and nuts, baked in a fluted tube pan.

LAG BA-OMER   Holiday falling on the thirty-third day of the counting of the *omer* between Passover and Shavuot.

LATKE   Pancake usually made from grated raw potatoes and eaten during Hanukkah.

LEKAKH   Honey cake.

LOKSHEN   Egg noodles.

LOX   Smoked and salted salmon.

LULAV   Traditional festive palm branch carried and waved during Sukkot.

MAROR   Bitter herbs of horseradish or romaine eaten at Passover Seders in remembrance of the bitterness of slavery.

MATZAH   Unleavened bread of affliction and freedom eaten during Passover.

MEGILLAH   Scroll of the Book of Esther read at Purim.

MENORAH   Originally the holy Temple candelabra, with seven branches; today, usually the nine-candle *hanukkiah* used at Hanukkah.

MILCHIG   Made of, or derived from, milk or dairy products.

MOHN   Poppy seeds.

MOHRRÜBEN   Carrots.

OMER   Offering of barley, representing the first reaping of the grain harvest and presented to the priest in a Temple ceremony on the second day of Passover.

OZNE HAMAN   Haman's ears; known as *Hamansooren* in the Netherlands, *orecchie de Aman* in Italy, and *hojuelo de Haman* in Ladino. Deep-fried pastry, served with sugar at Purim.

PAN DE ESPAÑA   Lemon sponge cake of Sephardic origin.

PAREVE   Made without milk, meat, or their derivatives.

PASSOVER   Festival of freedom celebrating the Exodus from Egypt.

PASTEL   Turnover filled with meat, vegetables, or cheese.

PHYLLO   Paper-thin dough.

PETCHA   Calves' foot jelly.

PIROGI   Small pastry turnovers stuffed with savory filling.

PRACHES   Stuffed cabbage.

PURIM   Festival celebrating the deliverance of the Jews from the machinations of Haman, described in the Book of Esther.

ROSH HASHANAH   Jewish New Year.

SCHALET   Dessert pudding often made with apples.

SEDER   Home or community service and ceremonial dinner on the first and second nights of Passover, commemorating the Exodus from Egypt.

SEPHARDIM   Jews who settled in Spain and Portugal at an early date and later spread to Greece, the Middle East, England, the Netherlands, and the Americas, and their descendants.

SEUDAT PURIM   Meal eaten on Purim.

SHABBAT   Sabbath.

SHALAH MANOT   Food portions consisting of at least one fruit and one sweet made from flour, given at Purim.

SHAVUOT   Feast of Weeks, commemorating the revelation of the Law on Mount Sinai; a wheat festival in biblical times.

SHOHET   Person officially licensed by rabbinic authority as a slaughterer for food in accordance with Jewish dietary laws.

SHTETL   Yiddish word for a small town in Eastern Europe.

SHULHAN ARUKH   Code of Jewish law.

SUFGANIYOT   Doughnuts served at Hanukkah in Israel.

SUKKOT   Thanksgiving festival, originating as an autumn harvest festival celebrated by eating out of doors in a sukkah.

TEYGLAKH   Small pieces of dough boiled in honey.

TISHA BE-AV   Fast day observed on the ninth day of the month of Av, in commemoration of the destruction of the First and Second Temples in Jerusalem.

TREF   Ritually unfit; unkosher.

TSIMMES   Sweetened, baked combination of vegetables or meat and vegetables, often with dried fruits.

TU BI-SHEVAT   New Year of Trees.

VARNISHKES   Noodles, often square or, in America, shaped like a bow tie.

YAPRAK   Stuffed grape leaves.

YOM KIPPUR   Day of Atonement, a solemn Jewish fast day.

BIBLIOGRAPHY

Many sources were consulted in the writing of this book. The following is a list of those books that were exceptionally helpful. (Works listed at the end of each quotation are not included here.)

Abrahams, Israel. *Jewish Life in the Middle Ages.* London, 1896.

Appel, Gersion. *The Concise Code of Jewish Law.* New York, 1977.

Baron, Salo W., et al. *Economic History of the Jews.* New York, 1976.

Douglas, Mary. *Purity and Danger: An Analysis of Concepts of Pollution and Taboo.* New York, 1966.

Encyclopedia Judaica. Jerusalem, 1971.

Gaster, Theodor H. *Customs and Folkways of Jewish Life.* New York, 1955.

———. *Festivals of the Jewish Year.* New York, 1953.

———. *The Holy and the Profane.* New York, 1955.

Ginzberg, Louis. *Legends of the Jews.* 7 vols. Philadelphia, 1909–38.

Jacob, H. E. *Six Thousand Years of Bread.* New York, 1944.

Schauss, Hayim. *The Jewish Festivals.* Cincinnati, 1938.

———. *The Lifetime of a Jew.* Cincinnati, 1950.

Sperling, Abraham I. *Reasons for Jewish Customs and Traditions.* New York, 1975.

Trachtenberg, Joshua. *Jewish Magic and Superstition.* New York, 1939.

Universal Jewish Encyclopedia. New York, 1939/40–43.

INDEX